CHINESE LEGAL REFORM AND THE GLOBAL LEGAL ORDER

This volume critically evaluates the latest legal reform of China, covering major areas such as trade and securities law, online privacy law, criminal law, human rights and international law. It represents a bold departure from the most recent works on Chinese legal reform by engaging the ideas of experts in contemporary Chinese law with the archival scholarship of Chinese legal historians. This unique interdisciplinary feature affords readers a more nuanced view of the complexities and specificities of how China has problematised legal reforms in various historical contexts when building a progressive yet sustainable legal system. This volume appraises the most current reform in Chinese law by considering China's engagement with globalisation, increasingly complicated domestic situation and historical legal transplantation experiences. It will be of huge interest to students, researchers and practitioners interested in Chinese law and policy, China and Asian studies and Chinese legal history.

YUN ZHAO is Professor and Head of Department of Law at the University of Hong Kong; PhD (Erasmus University Rotterdam); LLM (Leiden University); LLM & LLB (China University of Political Science and Law).

MICHAEL NG is Assistant Professor and Director of Centre for Chinese Law at the Faculty of Law of the University of Hong Kong.

CHINESE LEGAL REFORM AND THE GLOBAL LEGAL ORDER

Adoption and Adaptation

Edited by

YUN ZHAO
The University of Hong Kong

MICHAEL NG
The University of Hong Kong

CAMBRIDGE
UNIVERSITY PRESS

CAMBRIDGE
UNIVERSITY PRESS

University Printing House, Cambridge CB2 8BS, United Kingdom

One Liberty Plaza, 20th Floor, New York, NY 10006, USA

477 Williamstown Road, Port Melbourne, VIC 3207, Australia

4843/24, 2nd Floor, Ansari Road, Daryaganj, Delhi – 110002, India

79 Anson Road, #06–04/06, Singapore 079906

Cambridge University Press is part of the University of Cambridge.

It furthers the University's mission by disseminating knowledge in the pursuit of education, learning and research at the highest international levels of excellence.

www.cambridge.org
Information on this title: www.cambridge.org/9781107182004
DOI: 10.1017/9781316855645

© Cambridge University Press 2018

First published 2018

Printed in the United Kingdom by Clays, St Ives plc

A catalogue record for this publication is available from the British Library.

Library of Congress Cataloging-in-Publication Data
Names: Zhao, Yun, editor. | Ng, Michael H. K., editor.
Title: Chinese legal reform and the global legal order : adoption and adaptation / edited by Yun Zhao, the University of Hong Kong; Michael Ng, the University of Hong Kong.
Description: Cambridge [UK]; New York : Cambridge University Press, 2017. | Includes index.
Identifiers: LCCN 2017023169 | ISBN 9781107182004 (Hardback)
Subjects: LCSH: Law reform–China. | Law–China. | Human rights–China. | Law and socialism.
Classification: LCC KNQ470 .C477 2017 | DDC 340/.30951–dc23
LC record available at https://lccn.loc.gov/2017023169

ISBN 978-1-107-18200-4 Hardback

CONTENTS

FIGURES

TABLES

CONTRIBUTORS

BILLY K. L. SO is a legal and economic historian and Head of the Division of Humanities at The Hong Kong University of Science and Technology. He authored *Prosperity, Region, and Institutions in Maritime China: The South Fukien Pattern, 946–1368* and co-edited *The Treaty Port Economy in Modern China: Empirical Studies of Institutional Change and Economic Performance*. More recently Dr So has been engaged in several research projects that take a comparative perspective including one on comparative constitutional naturalism in modern Japan, China, America and the Nordic countries. He has published articles in journals such as *T'oung Pao, Annales: Histoire, Sciences Sociales, Tsinghua Law Journal* and *Hong Kong Law Journal*, among others.

BJÖRN AHL is Professor and Chair of Chinese Legal Culture at the Institute of East Asian Studies of Cologne University. His main areas of research include Chinese and comparative public law, Chinese practice of public international law, judicial reforms, legal culture and legal transfer. His most recent book is *Justizreformen in China*. Björn Ahl studied law and Chinese language at Heidelberg University and Nanjing University. He held positions at the Max Planck Institute of Comparative Public Law and International Law in Heidelberg, the Sino German Institute of Legal Studies at Nanjing University, the City University of Hong Kong and the China EU School of Law at the China University of Political Science and Law in Beijing.

CASEY WATTERS is an Assistant Professor at the Nottingham University Business School, Ningbo China and an Associate at Singapore Management University Law School's Centre for Cross-Border Commercial Law in Asia (CEBCLA). Dr Watters received his PhD from Shanghai Jiao Tong University and Juris Doctor from the University of California,

Hastings College of the Law. His research is focused on commercial law, with a primary interest in insolvency. His works have appeared in the *Northwestern Journal of International Law & Business*, the *Company Lawyer* and the *China Review*, among others.

CHAO XI is Professor and Vice Chancellor's Outstanding Fellow of the Faculty of Law, The Chinese University of Hong Kong (CUHK), and he concurrently serves as the Director of the Chinese Law Program, CUHK's Hong Kong Institute of Asia-Pacific Studies. He specialises in comparative corporate law, securities regulation and financial regulation and has published extensively in leading peer-reviewed international journals. His research has received significant funding support from the Hong Kong SAR Government Research Grants Council, the PRC Ministry of Education and the Sumitomo Foundation. He is a member of the Chartered Institute of Arbitrators (CIArb), United Kingdom.

LI CHEN is Associate Professor of History and Chair of the Department of Historical and Cultural Studies at the University of Toronto. Since 2014, he has been President of the International Society for Chinese Law and History and a member of the Editorial Board of the *Law and History Review*. He is author of *Chinese Law in Imperial Eyes: Sovereignty, Justice, and Transcultural Politics* and co-editor of *Chinese Law: Knowledge, Practice and Transformation, 1530s–1950s*. His research focuses on the intersections of law, culture and politics in Chinese and global history since the 1500s.

LIANG ZHAO is an assistant professor at the School of Law at City University of Hong Kong and Associate Director of the Hong Kong Centre for Maritime and Transportation Law. He obtained his LLB at Dalian Maritime University, LLM at Southampton University and PhD at The University of Hong Kong. His research interests include maritime law, commercial contract law and Chinese law. He has published academic papers in reputable periodicals, including *Journal of Business Law*, *Lloyd's Maritime and Commercial Law Quarterly*, *Journal of International Maritime Law*, *Arbitration International* and *Hong Kong Law Journal*. He is the author of the chapter 'Ship Finance' for *Maritime Law and Practice in Hong Kong* and co-author of the book *Maritime Law and Practice in China*.

MARIA ADELE CARRAI is Princeton–Harvard China and the World Program Fellow (2017–2018) and a Marie Skłodowska-Curie Fellow at the Leuven Center for Global Governance Studies of KU Leuven working on Chinese legal history in the early twentieth century. Previously she was a Max Weber Fellow in Law at the European University Institute and a Global Hauser Fellow at New York University Law School. She completed her PhD in history of international law in 2016 from The University of Hong Kong with a dissertation on the conceptual genealogy of sovereignty in China from 1840s to the present. Her work on Chinese approaches to international law and on the history of international law in China has appeared in leading refereed journals such as the *Leiden Journal of International Law*, *Storica* and the Chinese journal *Zhengzhi sixiang shi*, among others.

MICHAEL NG is a legal historian and Director of the Centre for Chinese Law at the Faculty of Law of The University of Hong Kong. Author of *Legal Transplantation in Early 20th Century China: Practicing Law in Republican Beijing (1910s–1930s)*, co-editor of *Chinese Legal Reform and the Global Legal Order: Adoption and Adaptation* (Cambridge) and *Civil Unrest and Governance in Hong Kong: Law and Order from Historical and Cultural Perspectives*, Dr Ng specialises in the legal history of China and Hong Kong during the nineteenth and twentieth centuries. His works have appeared in leading international refereed journals such as *Law and History Review*, *Law and Literature*, *International Journal of Asian Studies*, *Business History* and *Journal of Comparative Law*, among others.

SARAH BIDDULPH is an Australian Research Council Future Fellow (2014–2018) and Professor of Law at the Melbourne Law School. Sarah's research focuses on the Chinese legal system with a particular emphasis on legal policy, law-making and enforcement as they affect the administration of justice in China. Her particular areas of research are contemporary Chinese administrative law, criminal procedure, labour, comparative law and the law regulating social and economic rights.

SHUCHENG WANG has been teaching in JD, LLM and LLB programs at City University of Hong Kong since 2012. Meanwhile, he holds the position of Chutian Scholar Professorship at Zhongnan University of Economics and Law in China and is Affiliated Faculty at the Global

Institute for Health and Human Rights, State University of New York at Albany, in the United States. Dr Wang's research interests include public law, Chinese and comparative law, international law and human rights. He has published over fifty journal articles, appearing or forthcoming in leading English and Chinese law journals in the United States, Australia, Hong Kong, the United Kingdom and Mainland China, including *Human Rights Quarterly*, *Public Law Review*, *Hong Kong Law Journal*, *Statute Law Review* and *Chinese Journal of Law* [*Faxue Yanjiu*].

SUFUMI SO, an applied linguist, is an author and co-author of several papers published in such journals as *Journal of Second Language Writing* and *ADFL Bulletin* as well as *Learners' Stories* (edited by P. Benson and D. Nunan, Cambridge), among others. More recently her interest in writing has shifted towards contributing to creating knowledge interweaving the elements of prosperity, justice, space and identity in historical perspective through ongoing historical research projects in comparative perspective. She has co-authored several papers in this area as well, including one published in the *Bulletin of the School of Oriental and African Studies*.

WENWEI GUAN is assistant professor at the School of Law, City University of Hong Kong. Research interests cover intellectual property, international trade, trade and investment in the PRC and legal theory. Publications include the book, *Intellectual Property Theory and Practice*, and peer-reviewed articles in various journals such as *Asian Journal of Comparative Law*, *Leiden Journal of International Law*, *Journal of International Economic Law*, *Journal of World Trade* and *Hong Kong Law Journal*.

XIFEN LIN is a law professor at KoGuan Law School of Shanghai Jiao Tong University. Author of *Wrongful Conviction in Transitional China: An Empirical and Comparative Study*, *Exclusionary Rule in China: Theory and Practice* and *China's Criminal Justice: Toward the Rule of Law*, Dr Lin specialises in criminal procedure, law and society and empirical legal studies. His works have appeared in both international and Chinese refereed journals such as *International Journal of Law, Crime and Justice* and *China Legal Science*, among others.

XUANMING PAN is Associate Research Fellow at the School of Law of Sun Yat-sen University (Guangzhou, China), Visiting Fellow at the Centre for Chinese Law of HKU and Honorary Research Associate at the Hong Kong Institute of Asia-Pacific Studies of CUHK. Apart from academic writing, Dr Pan has committed to a variety of legal services for civil society associations and disadvantaged groups. He received his PhD in law at The Chinese University of Hong Kong, where he completed his doctoral thesis on grassroots legal services in China. He was an R. Randle Edwards Fellow at Columbia Law School (New York) in 2013.

YUN ZHAO, PhD (Erasmus University Rotterdam), LLM (Leiden University), LLM and LLB (China University of Political Science and Law) is Professor and Head of Department of Law at The University of Hong Kong. Prof Zhao was also Chen An Chair Professor in International Law at Xiamen University (2015) and Siyuan Scholar Chair Professor at Shanghai University of Foreign Trade (2012–2014). He is listed as arbitrator in several international arbitration commissions. He is also a founding Council member of Hong Kong Internet Forum (HKIF), a member of the International Institute of Space Law at Paris and a member of the Asia Pacific Law Association and Beijing International Law Society. He sits on the editorial teams of several SSCI journals, including *Hong Kong Law Journal* (as China Law Editor) and *Journal of East Asia and International Law* (as Executive Editor).

ZHAOXIN JIANG is an associate law professor in Shandong University. His academic interests include Chinese legal history, post-1949 Taiwanese judicial history and comparative constitutional law. He earned a PhD from The Chinese University of Hong Kong, an MA from Stanford University and an MA from Beijing University. He worked as a postdoctoral associate at Cornell Law School for two years and worked for a trans-Pacific non-partisan think tank, Meridian 180. In addition to multiple journal articles, he is the author of two books, *The Judicial Nationalism Movements: A View on the Judicial History of ROC* (forthcoming) and *China's Law 'Cannot See China': A Study of Judicial Reforms during 1930s–1940s* (2010), and co-author of a textbook, *Lectures on Chinese Modern Legal History* (2016).

ACKNOWLEDGEMENTS

This volume would not have been made possible without the support from all contributors, financial sponsorship of the Faculty of Law of The University of Hong Kong (HKU) and logistical support of HKU's Centre for Chinese Law for organising a symposium on 2 June 2015. The editors would also like to thank Miss Shelby Chan and Miss Erika Hebblethwaite for their important assistance in the editorial process.

1

The Law, China and the World

An Introduction

YUN ZHAO AND MICHAEL NG

China has undertaken a series of legal reforms of varying scales over the past century, borrowing models from a disparate range of countries. Since the late Qing period, laws and legal concepts from Germany, France, Switzerland, Japan, the United Kingdom and United States, and the former Soviet Union, among other countries, have been transplanted into China at various times. The latest wave of legal reforms originated in the office of Xi Jinping, who set the law as the central theme of the Chinese Communist Party's Eighteenth Central Committee Plenary Session in October 2014. Yet, despite these century-long efforts, as contributor Li Chen puts it, the reformed Chinese legal system often appears 'too foreign to the Chinese and too Chinese to foreigners'.

The aim of this volume is not only to identify such a Chinese-foreign gap in China's latest wave of legal reforms under Xi's leadership, but also to reappraise that gap by taking into account the country's engagement with globalisation, increasingly complicated domestic situation and historical experiences of legal transplantation. With regard to the last factor – history – the volume represents a bold departure from the most recent works on Chinese legal reform by engaging the ideas of international scholars of contemporary Chinese law with the archival scholarship of Chinese legal historians.[1] Archival research into the legal reform experience of Qing and Republican China affords us a more nuanced view of the complexities and specificities of how China has problematised legal reforms in various historical contexts than traditional –

---

[1] Other important works on the recent legal reforms of China include, for example, John Garrick and Yan Chang Bennett, eds., *China's Socialist Rule of Law Reforms under Xi jinping* (New York: Routledge, 2016) and Lisa Toohey, Colin B. Picker and Jonathan Greenacre, eds., *China in the International Economic Order: New Directions and Changing Paradigms* (Cambridge: Cambridge University Press, 2015).

and perhaps overly convenient – narratives attributing the aforementioned gap to an essentialised version of Chinese culture that restricts itself to Confucianism and Legalism. Whilst we agree that historical experiences may not always be predictive of future behaviour, neither can they be ignored in considering the legal ideas, laws and legal systems that make sense for China's governance and development.

Chinese law experts from Canada, Germany, Italy, Mainland China and Hong Kong met at a symposium in the summer of 2015 to consider China's legal reform and its interaction with the world's legal order. They discussed approaches to and the challenges of reforming Chinese law in the areas of criminal justice, human rights, privacy protection, trade and investment law, and international law. This volume is the result of those discussions. Together with the aforementioned historical archival scholarship, the resulting chapters point to the drivers and factors underpinning the Chinese model of learning from, and at the same time shaping, the world's legal order.

Sarah Biddulph's chapter (Chapter 2) examines the gap in China's post-*laojiao* (re-education through labour) punishment system through in-depth comparisons and analysis of several ongoing debates concerning proposed legislative and policy reforms. She applies both domestic and international experience and institutional solutions for reappraising minor crime in terms of its categorisation and definition in law, as well as approaches to dealing with such crime and the related punishment regimes. She also explores the debates surrounding the categories and recognition of security punishment (*bao'an chufen*) in Chinese law. In an attempt to find answers to the question of 'what and who should be punished and how' in China's reformed punishment system, Biddulph analyses a number of post-*laojiao* reform proposals concerning criminal law. She posits that although incremental reforms appear to be responsive to domestic concerns, the experience of common law systems can contribute concrete learning examples in the arena of minor offences. She also argues that current reforms, and the debates surrounding them, lack a normative shift towards finding a way to balance the empowerment of state agencies with the need to protect individual rights in this post-*laojiao* period, although some of the debates have addressed outstanding abuses. In particular, Biddulph believes that the current debates over security measure categories are dangerously vague and lacking in criteria, which risks the introduction of various powers without adequate consideration or justification. Based on the existing evidence, she concludes that the country's reformers appear to prefer a more conservative and incremental approach to reforming the system of punishments in China, even though such an approach renders it more difficult to reform the institutional structures that underpin abusive practices.

Xifen Lin and Casey Watters (Chapter 3) illustrate ways of understanding the presumption of innocence (POI) in China from the institutional and practical perspectives. In a section entitled 'POI in the International Context', they argue that it is insufficient to limit POI to the field of evidence law, which does not accord with the spirit of the rule of law in modern societies. Instead, the meta-principle of the POI standard in China encompasses such principles as 'only the judiciary has the power to determine guilt', 'the prosecutor bears the burden of proof', 'guilty verdicts must be based on evidence', 'defendants should be treated with dignity and respect' and 'in *dubio pro reo*'. In a discussion of POI misunderstandings in China, they analyse the sixty-year development of the POI concept, suggesting that its translation into Chinese may be partly responsible for those misunderstandings because *wuzui tuiding* in Chinese refers to finding the accused innocent through inference, whilst its intended meaning is 'assumption'. They also compare POI enforcement in various countries with that in China, a comparison which suggests that although a nation's inclusion of POI in its written laws is a significant factor in ensuring POI in practice, it is not the most significant factor. Even in countries applying the same approach to guaranteeing POI, the right can be simulated to varying degrees, and policies for protecting POI can also vary significantly over time within a country. Lin and Watters also examine China's progress towards enforcing POI by means of a review of legislation history, in particular the country's first version of the Criminal Procedure Law (CPL) in 1979 and its subsequent amendments in 1996 and 2012. They argue that implementation of the CPL, with its clear stipulation of the burden of proof resting with the prosecutor and adherence to the principle of in *dubio pro reo*, remains unsatisfactory in practice. In the final section of the chapter, they offer suggestions for reform to promote POI in China. For instance, they recommend that judicial review be introduced to restrain the security organs' powers of investigation, that a subtle and reasonable interpretative method be applied to promote defendants' fundamental rights and that courts avoid finding the accused guilty when his or her guilt cannot be confirmed beyond reasonable doubt.

Shucheng Wang's main thesis in the chapter entitled 'Judicial Approach to Human Rights in Transitional China' (Chapter 4) is that the case of China provides the possibility of establishing a judicial system that enforces human rights under authoritarianism. He explains that even illiberal states can enforce their own mechanisms of human rights regardless of their considerable difference from those of liberal democracies. In the case of China, he illustrates two aspects of the country's distinctive mechanism of judicial human rights enforcement. The first is that the Chinese judicial system lacks parallel courts and judicial independence, which is contrary to the situation in liberal democracies, where judicial independence is constitutionally guaranteed. However, Wang also indicates that within the context of developing a free economy since economic reforms were introduced in 1978, the need for individual liberty and economic prosperity have been both emphasised and reflected in Chinese legislation, for example, the judicial review power stipulated in the Administrative Procedure Law (APL) and the 2014 APL amendment aimed at broadening the court's jurisdictional scope over government agency cases. He argues that although the complete fulfilment of constitutional rights may not be guaranteed, a specific legal right legalised through ordinary legislation concurrently enforces the corresponding constitutional right, at least in part. The second aspect is the Supreme People's Court alone having the authority to interpret the legislative nature of a specific issue regarding application of the law in trial work, as well as, owing to the lack of a case law system, a certain degree of interpretative discretion, with the rationale for some judicial decisions binding only with respect to specific cases. Wang concludes that the absence of a constitutional judicial review system leads to limitations on legal rights via legislation, thus restraining civil and political rights protected in the constitution. He deems the China case an example of a dual model of judicial human rights enforcement in an illiberal state in which economic development is paramount.

In 'Public Enforcement of Securities Laws: A Case of Convergence?' Chao Xi and Xuanming Pan (Chapter 5) examine the interaction between a foreign legal framework of securities regulation and its development by the China Securities Regulatory Commission (CSRC), and introduce two 'salient features' of Chinese securities regulation. In the first section of the chapter, they illustrate the impact of foreign experience, the US experience in the main, on the formation and evolution of China's approach to securities regulation. The next section provides an overview of the CSRC enforcement programme, based primarily on statistical analysis of CSRC enforcement actions during the 2006–2014 period, and discusses the institutional framework of that programme in the areas of investigation and adjudication. Chapter 5, Section 3 proceeds to an examination of the relationship between the role of enforcement and that of the CSRC, emphasising the increasing importance of securities regulation enforcement over the past decade. The authors then turn to a discussion of how US-style trial-like procedures have begun to affect CSRC enforcement actions and of how the 2006 CSRC reform promotes the 'judicialisation' of the administrative process through the empowerment of the Administrative Sanction Commission (ASC) with its own secretariat and independent support from the central government budget. Xi and Pan conclude that although US-style securities regulation has inspired China's securities regulation and the CSRC enforcement programme, such prima facie convergence has limitations.

Wenwei Guan's chapter (Chapter 6) examines the evolution of free trade in China and its significance for trade liberalisation and the decentralisation of foreign direct investment (FDI) control. He also compares the Beijing Consensus with the Washington Consensus from a legal perspective. With regard to the evolution of free trade, Guan introduces the history of China's reform and opening-up policy and its impact on the country's trade market, particularly the laws governing FDI and evolution of the FDI guidance system. With regard to the sovereign power to regulate trade and investment, he argues that China's liberalisation and decentralisation of FDI control have implications for self-restraint with respect to compliance with international standards and the country's obligations under the WTO agreement. He also mentions the 2015 draft of the PRC Foreign Investment Law for public consultation, which will supersede the current Equity Joint Venture (EJV), Wholly Foreign-Owned Enterprise (WFOE) and Chinese-Foreign Contractual Joint Venture (CJV) laws if adopted, and significantly change the current FDI approval system in accordance with the 'negative list' system in free trade zones (FTZs). However, a change in the legal nature of FTZs will not affect the country's goal of trade and investment liberalisation. In his comparison of the Beijing Consensus and Washington Consensus, Guan notes that free trade development (from special economic zones [SEZs] to the CEPA framework to FTZs) and the evolution of the FDI regulatory regime (i.e. the flexibility in investment vehicle choices afforded by the EJV, WFOE and CJV models) reflect the Chinese authority's pragmatism and willingness to decentralise FDI control and that its emphasis on self-determination and resisting 'the installation of democracy' clearly distinguish it from the self-legitimisation of the Washington Consensus. He further provides evidence to show that the gradual decentralisation of China's trade and investment regime has not been interrupted by the overall depressed state of the world economy, which has boosted foreign investors' confidence in its trade liberalisation and market predictability in general. Guan concludes the chapter by arguing that the Beijing Consensus attends to local conditions and emphasises self-determination, which not only affords it a certain legitimacy, but also both challenges and enriches the Washington Consensus by means of a process of selective adaptation that relaxes the tension between international convergence and divergence.

In 'Achievements and Challenges of Chinese Maritime Judicial Practice', Liang Zhao (Chapter 7) examines and analyses the history and development of maritime judicial practice in China over a thirty-year period. The formation of the maritime adjudication system, two specific types of maritime cases, varieties of maritime disputes and maritime jurisdiction issues are all introduced in the section headed 'Maritime Courts in the PRC'. Zhao argues that Chinese maritime judicial practice commenced even before any maritime legislation entered into force. Since enactment of the Maritime Code of 1992, some elements of traditional maritime judicial practice still apply and are stipulated in the code (e.g. the three basic functions of a bill of lading). However, the CPL of 1991 was applied as procedural law in maritime adjudication before 1999, when the Special Maritime Procedure Law of 1999 was promulgated, filling the legislative gaps in specialised maritime rules and facilitating the establishment of a maritime legal system. However, the lack of any necessity to follow precedent by Chinese maritime judges has led to inconsistent maritime adjudication in practice, with different or even contradictory judgments made concerning the same maritime dispute. Zhao argues that the doctrine of precedent in common law is the only effective means of resolving these inconsistencies and harmonisation issues, noting that the doctrine would also alleviate the predicament of discretionary power being used by maritime judges without appropriate controls in place. He recommends that China adopt the doctrine of precedent and recognise select leading cases as legally binding case law to resolve the current disharmony in judicial practice.

Björn Ahl (Chapter 8) explores areas of legislative insufficiency in relation to implementation of the Convention against Torture and relevant recent legal reforms of the CPL, as well as the factors that triggered those reforms, with reference to five main points. With respect to 'Chinese law and legal doctrine and the interaction of international treaties and national law', he states that there are 'no statutory reference provisions in the field of criminal procedure that refer directly to the Convention against Torture', suggesting that 'adopting legislative steps that bring criminal procedure law in line with the convention's requirements appears to be the preferred mode of treaty implementation in this case'. His second point is the 'lack of proper legislation to implement the Convention', examples of which include interpretation of articles 247 and 248 of the country's Criminal Law, indicating the Chinese government's failure to incorporate a definition of torture in line with the Convention against Torture into domestic law. In a section headed 'Recent Reforms of Criminal Procedure Law', Ahl discusses the significance of the Notice Regarding the Regulations on the Examination and Evaluation of Evidence in Capital Cases and Regulations on the Exclusion of Illegally Obtained Evidence in Criminal Cases, along with specific analysis of the provisions of the Evidence Exclusion Regulations, Death Penalty Evidence Regulations and revised CPL, as well as their compliance issues concerning the Convention. As to the 'reasons for criminal procedure law reform as reflected discourses', he indicates that the dominant factor leading to the adoption of a mechanism for excluding coerced confessions was the leadership's implementation of sentence reductions in miscarriages of justice, with international organisations and factors exerting a quite limited influence on triggering the recent reforms. Finally, Ahl explains why China took over twenty years to bring the CPL into alignment with its obligations under the Convention against Torture with reference to the concept of 'selective adaptation', which comprises the elements of perception, complementarity and legitimacy. He also notes that the exclusionary rule was long seen as an important factor in the delay to bringing the CPL into line with article 15 of the Convention.

In a chapter entitled 'Online Privacy Protection: A Legal Regime for Personal Data Protection in China', Yun Zhao (Chapter 9) examines China's current legal framework in the area of privacy protection and the latest developments in the laws and regulations concerning personal data protection. Zhao argues that the new initiatives undertaken by the Chinese government suggest a promising future for privacy protection in China. He also provides several possible approaches to the better resolution of legal regime–related problems with respect to personal data protection. More specifically, in a section called 'International Regime for Privacy Protection', he introduces three basic models of such protection at the international level. For instance, the EU has implemented an overall framework for personal data protection within its jurisdiction (i.e. the EU Data Protection Directive), whilst other countries/regions have adopted a sectoral approach or self-regulatory model. Zhao indicates that a national legal regime governing privacy protection that is modelled on the EU approach is becoming prevalent in China. He further examines the history and current status of the Chinese legal regime governing privacy protection, noting that the country already has various related rules (e.g. the Tort Law) in place. However, he also admits that personal data protection lacked any systematic regime before 2011, particularly with regard to the collection, storage and use of such data. He goes on to examine the important progress made since then, including the Ministry of Industry and Information Technology (MIIT) provisions on regulating the market order of Internet information services, namely, Information Security Technology – Guidelines of Personal Information Protection in Public and Commercial Service Information System, proposed amendment to the administrative regulations covering such services, the 2012 NPCSC decision, 2013 MIIT rules and amendments to the Consumer Protection Law. Zhao then offers six suggestions for the future development of the country's data protection legal regime. They include the establishment of 'a comprehensive data protection law', 'differentiating related terms of privacy, personal information and personal data', reconsidering 'the scope of personal data and concept of sensitive data', giving consideration to 'national security, commercial secrets and freedom of speech', oversight by the regulatory authority of 'the enforcement of rules enacted' and 'education and promotional campaigns to raise public awareness of the need for personal data protection'. In his conclusion, Zhao posits that a national personal data protection law would not only be the best option for improving the current legal regime in response to the demand for domestic legislation, but also contribute to China's compliance with its international obligations under the WTO agreement.

Li Chen (Chapter 10) begins this volume's section on historical legal reforms in China by asking a very intriguing question about the country's century-old legal transformation: Why does the reformed Chinese legal system often appear too foreign to the Chinese and too Chinese to foreigners? Drawing on archival materials from the Qing and Republican eras, he answers that question by narrating the epistemic history of how legal modernity and tradition were imagined, defined and politicised in China from the late nineteenth to early twentieth centuries. He argues that 'the history of Chinese legal modernity since the late Qing period should be understood as a constant struggle for balance between anxiety about cultural identity and a yearning for international recognition by the dominant powers'. Chen uses the important reform of the criminal code during the Qing and Republican periods to illustrate his arguments.

Despite military defeats and the rise of a Eurocentric discourse positioning the Chinese legal system as backward, uncivilised and inferior (discourse that Chen dubs 'epistemic violence'), legal reformers and Qing officials from the 1870s onwards made efforts to justify their proposals to reform the legal system by acknowledging the practical advantages of 'Western ideas and practices without forfeiting [China's] claim to be an ancient and potentially modernising civilisation'. Such 'bifurcation' strategies failed to continue as the national crisis and geopolitics worsened after the turn of the century. In the wake of the Boxer Uprising and occupation of Beijing by foreign powers, increasing numbers of educated Chinese began to prefer a more radical break from Chinese legal tradition and to advocate for the wholesale transplantation of a Western legal system, thereby 'self-Orientalising' and traditionalising the Chinese legal culture and reinforcing its incommensurability with legal modernity. However, Chen offers archival evidence revealing that the drafters and advocates of the transplanted Chinese Criminal Code based on a Western model subsequently admitted the mistakes of wholesale transplantation and the erroneous nature of their earlier dismissive attitude towards China's own legal culture under the influence of Western ideas. The story of the reformation of Chinese criminal law reminds us, as Chen concludes, that to 'better understand modern Chinese law, it is important to keep in mind the tensions, ambivalence and intercultural politics that have shaped its trajectory over the past century'.

The Orientalising or traditionalising of Chinese legal culture did not end with the demise of the imperialist world order, as Michael Ng's chapter (Chapter 11) illustrates. The Hong Kong courts have over one hundred years of experience dealing with cases of historical Chinese marriage that took place in Republican China (1912–1949), forming a common-law narrative of the historical changes that the law underwent from the imperial to modern legal systems. Into the twenty-first century, family and succession law cases involving issues relating to historical marriages continue to be brought before the Hong Kong courts, which apply only the transplanted civil code, i.e. the Book of Family, if the matters in question occurred after that code's effective date of 5 May 1931. Imperial Chinese jurisprudence and legal practices are regarded as incompatible with 'modern' law, and thus ignored. This conventional judicial practice of demarcating the Chinese legal past by a binary division between pre-transplant customary Chinese law on the one hand and post-transplant modern Chinese law on the other has gone largely unchallenged for the past hundred years in both common law courts and

legal scholarship in Hong Kong and other former British colonies in
which Chinese law remains relevant to civil lawsuits. Ng, through a
critique of a recent Hong Kong Court of Final Appeal case involving
two women who became concubines in Shanghai in the 1930s, argues
that this century-old approach to narrating how family law changed in
China is flawed and Orientalist and disregards the legal assimilation of
Chinese and foreign legal norms in Chinese legal reform. More importantly, he further posits that such a judicial approach is but one example
of the Orientalist knowledge system governing Chinese legal traditions
and legal culture in general, family law and custom included, within
common law. Such a knowledge system continues to colonise the legal
discourse on the traditional Chinese legal system and cement the cultural
distance in law between the modern West and the traditional Orient even
now that the colonial era has come to an end.

It was not only family law reform in the Republican era that resulted
in a hybrid product of Chinese legal practices and imported ideas.
Commercial law reform in the early twentieth century featured a similar
process of legal assimilation. Billy K. L. So and Sufumi So (Chapter 12)
examine how entrepreneurs in the book publishing and distribution
industry in early twentieth-century Shanghai negotiated the challenges
of adapting to new legal institutions, from the law courts to the alternative dispute resolution (ADR) system modelled on the Western legal
approach to commercial dispute resolution. Drawing on extensive archival sources, including arbitration case reports stored in the Shanghai
Municipal Archive, their chapter elucidates 'how these transplanted
legal institutions evolved in the local environment' and 'the roles that
those who acted as both local agents of change and the consumers of
such institutions played in shaping the process of transplantation'. So
and So examine a number of copyright disputes between major book
publishers in early twentieth-century Shanghai to make their case.
Western-style arbitration was formally introduced into Chinese law in
1904, and detailed regulations were promulgated following the Xinhai
Revolution in 1911. 'When the Western arbitration model was first
transplanted in China, some of its most important features were missing', the authors explain, 'including the contractual requirement that all
parties must agree in advance to abide by the ultimate arbitration
decision'. Therefore, they continue, 'the choice between arbitration
and court proceedings was largely a matter of a rational calculation of
self-interest, but it also rested on the historical and socio-cultural factors
that had shaped Chinese business, which resulted in a preference for

non-confrontational conflict resolution and distaste for the imposition
of decisions reached by third parties'.

Such 'adaptive flexibility', as So and So term it, can also be seen in
China's practice of adopting international law doctrines from the Western powers, as outlined in Maria Adele Carrai's chapter (Chapter 13). In
1926, the Republican Chinese government unilaterally abrogated the
Sino–Belgium Treaty it had signed in 1865. Such abrogation marked an
important milestone in China's demonstration to the world of its understanding of international law and efforts to relinquish the 'unequal
treaties' that had legalised the Western powers' encroachment of Chinese
sovereignty for more than half a century by imposing, among other
measures, extraterritoriality and the loss of tariff autonomy. During the
process of arguing for termination of the aforementioned treaty, Chinese
diplomats on the one hand adopted the foreign legal idea of sovereignty
in international law whilst on the other hand departing from it by
affirming China's existential equality, challenging the main doctrine of
juridical sovereignty that implicitly categorises countries as civilised or
uncivilised. The country's unilateral abrogation of the Sino–Belgian
Treaty shows not only that China has selectively appropriated and
flexibly adapted imported notions of international law, but that such
appropriation and adaptation have also helped to shape the development
of those notions within the international legal world by overcoming the
anti-pluralistic mentality that characterised the Western doctrine and
practice of international law during the days of imperialism. Carrai
attempts to 'depart from the Eurocentric histories of international law
that relegate China to the status of passive receiver of international legal
norms', demonstrating that China's transplantation experience in the
early twentieth century produced new hybrid legal notions that led to a
more pluralistic, inclusive and less hierarchical international legal order
among countries, large and small.

The volume's final chapter offers a theoretical comparative-law exploration of judicial activism in Republican China. Zhaoxin Jiang (Chapter 14)
argues that the participation of Republican judges in politics should
not be assessed merely as a form of non-compliance with the judicial
independence principle, but rather within the analytical framework of
consequential court theory that has been used to explain and compare
Euro–American judicial activism. In the judicial history of modern
China, he argues, the court has become 'an independent partner, not
merely an agent', rendering the court 'itself a consequential participant
in legal change and national governance'. From this perspective,

Jiang suggests a study of judicial leadership in legal and political reforms, an under-researched area in Chinese legal history.

The distinguished group of Chinese law scholars and experts contributing to this book have made tremendous efforts to ensure its success. The book provides valuable research materials and practical methods for analysing the current Chinese legal system and its reform process from both a contemporary and a historical perspective. Although difficulties and challenges are inevitable in the course of future legal reforms, and finding a way to resolve the conflicts between domestic and international legal standards will not be an easy task, bearing in mind the dynamics of and driving forces behind China's interaction with the world in law will help legal reformers to formulate appropriate approaches to building a progressive yet sustainable legal system. This volume will serve as an invaluable guide in helping them to do so.

PART I

Chinese Legal Reform in Xi Jinping's Era

2

Punishments in the Post Re-Education through Labour World

Questions about Minor Crime in China

SARAH BIDDULPH

1 Introduction

Sometimes reform in a particular area can highlight the need for more thorough-going change.* The decision in China to abolish the much-maligned administrative detention power of re-education through labour (*laojiao*) in December 2013 was one of these reforms.[1] *Laojiao* was abolished without putting a clear alternative power or powers in its place. Its abolition thus left open questions about what, if anything, should replace it. But more than that, it highlighted fundamental questions about the scope and structure of China's system of punishments. Announcing its decision to abolish *laojiao*, the Central Committee of the Chinese Communist Party (CCP or Party) also announced the need for work to be done to 'perfect the system of laws for punishment and correction of unlawful and criminal acts'.[2] In this formulation, 'unlawful and criminal' acts (*weifa fanzui*) is an ambiguous term that covers both administrative and criminal punishments. Hence, the Central Committee effectively called for a review of the whole system of punishments. This major policy decision, coupled with the lack of a simple substitute for *laojiao*, has prompted renewed interest in the legal structure of both

* This research was supported by grants from the Australian Research Council (DP0988179 and FT130100412).
[1] Effected with the decision of the Central Committee of the CCP's *Decision on Several Major Issues in Comprehensively Deepening Reform* (*Zhonggong Zhongyang Guanyu Quanmian Shenhua Gaige Ruogan Zhongda Wenti de Jueding*).
[2] Section IX point 34; translation at www.china.org.cn/china/third_plenary_session/2014-01/16/content_31212602.htm

punishments and other measures for the correction of unlawful conduct and criminal offending.[3]

This chapter examines how reforms, both undertaken and proposed, have been shaped by perceptions that the abolition of *laojiao* has left a gap in the system of punishments that needs to be filled. To what extent have these reforms and reform proposals also drawn on foreign models and experiences, or have they been primarily shaped by the existing structure and priorities of the domestic system? It asks to what extent these reforms are purely a technical readjustment, or do they also reflect a change in the values and priorities of the system of punishments? In addressing these questions, the focus of this chapter is on the punishment of minor offending: the space allegedly left by *laojiao*. Its main argument is that whilst responding to the abolition of *laojiao* has had an identifiable influence on specific reforms, more broad-ranging reform proposals have drawn extensively on foreign systems and experience. In terms of normative change, it argues that some of the incremental reforms have sought to ameliorate areas of entrenched abuse, such as extended detention prior to trial, but that the reforms and reform proposals reveal no sustained shift towards greater protection of individuals when they encounter the state's punitive power.

The structure of punishments has commonly been described along a continuum ranging from least to most severe. At the bottom, minor offending is punishable under the provisions of the 2006 Public Security Administrative Punishments Law (PSAPL; *Zhi'an Guanli Chufa Fa*) (amended in 2012). Administrative punishments include a warning, administrative fine or period of administrative detention imposed by the police of up to twenty days (PSAPL article 16).[4] This law empowers the police to question suspects and to take coercive measures to prevent persons from harming themselves or others. Above the PSAPL, in the middle range, is a group of more severe administrative detention powers, of which *laojiao* was the harshest. Under *laojiao*, a person could be detained (administratively) for between one and three years (with a possible one-year extension). The powers in this middle range are used to sanction socially harmful conduct that is considered to be too serious to be punished under the PSAPL but not sufficiently serious to warrant a

---

[3] Dong Wei, 'Reform of the security punishment after China's abolition of re-education through labor' (2015) 1 *Journal of Sichuan University*, 81.

[4] In this chapter, reference to the police is to the public security organs (*gong'an jiguan*) organised under the Ministry of Public Security.

criminal sanction or which by its nature is outside the scope of criminal law. At the top of this conceptual structure is the criminal justice system and criminal punishment.

After the abolition of *laojiao*, an open question about which there is no ready consensus is whether there is now a gap in the system of punishments. If such a gap exists, how is it to be filled? Should it be filled at all? This chapter considers this question. It examines the extent to which there is an overlap between *laojiao* and existing powers, both criminal and administrative. As the abolition of *laojiao* took decades to achieve, a number of reforms were put in place that reduced the scope of *laojiao* and transferred punishment of some types of offending to other administrative and criminal powers.

In terms of proposals for reform after the abolition of *laojiao*, some scholars argue that the system of punishments is already gap-free.[5] There was thus no need for a power such as *laojiao* to occupy an intermediate space for the system of punishments, as administrative punishments under the PSAPL and criminal punishments under the Criminal Law (CL) already cover all conduct that *should* be punished. These scholars advance both a positive and a normative position. As a question of analysis, there is no gap in the system of punishments. At a normative level, the intermediate category of administrative punishments is unnecessary. Others approach the normative question in a more cautious manner, focusing on technical arrangements of power and arguing that the gap, which they posit does exist, can be addressed by disaggregating the conduct targeted under *laojiao*. More serious offending, they argue, can be diverted into the criminal justice system as 'minor crime', with less serious offending handled by the administrative punishments system. In fact, from the mid-1980s this was an influential proposal, effectively to reform *laojiao* out of existence.[6]

---

[5] Benson Li, 'Security punishments should not be the direction for reform of re-education through labour', Chinese Social Science News, 9 September 2013, p. 499.

[6] Renwen Liu, 'Thoughts on bringing public order detention and re-education through labour in the criminal law' ('*Zhi'an juliu he laodong jiaoyang naru xingfa de sikao*') (2010) 8(1) *Journal of the China Procurators College*, 94–100; Chuanwei Zhang, 'From embarrassment and subversion to rebirth: an analysis of the reform of re-education through labour to community corrections' ('*Cong ganga, dianfu zouxiang xinsheng: laodong jiaoyang gaizao wei shequ jiaozheng zhi fenxi*') (2009) 1 *Journal of Beijing Administrative College (Beijing Xingzheng Xueyuan Xuebao)*, 80–85; Qihan Jiang and Kaiyin Yuan, 'Discussion of problems of re-education through labor' ('*Laodong jioyang wenti shulue*') (1990) 4 *Public Security Studies (Gong'an Yanjiu)*, 46–48.

After examining the question of whether there is a gap in the punishments system, this chapter goes on to explore two main areas in which there has been a reappraisal of the system of punishments: minor crime and security punishments. Minor crime is a major focus of this reappraisal, both because of the extent of overlap with the now defunct *laojiao* and because, at a practical level, the abolition of *laojiao* has contributed to a significant increase in the number of minor criminal cases being tried in the Chinese courts.[7] The Fourth Five-Year Court Reform Plan (2014–2018) (*Renmin Fayuan Di Sige Wunian Gaige Gangyao*, 2014–2018) (Supreme People's Court (SPC) Opinion on Comprehensively Deepening Reform in the People's Courts (*Guanyu Quanmian Shenhua Renmin Fayuan Gaige de Yijian*)) has given policy priority to the question of minor crime, identifying the task of 'completing systems for the expedited handling of minor criminal cases' as one of the core areas for judicial reform (point 12). However, the CL does not currently acknowledge the category of minor crime, and it was not created upon the abolition of *laojiao*. Accordingly, the chapter explores some of the basic questions about minor crime. What is minor crime? Should this category be established in law, and if so how should it be defined? How should minor offending be dealt with? Should it be through simplified investigation and adjudication, through the establishment of a specialist minor offences division in the courts, through different punishment regimes or other programmes such as diversion?[8] In searching for answers to these questions, both local and international experience and institutional solutions are drawn upon.

The chapter then turns to an examination of a second concept that has been thrown open to debate by the abolition of *laojiao*: 'security punishment' (*bao'an chufen*) or 'security measures' (*bao'an cuoshi*).[9] Security

---

[7] Na Li, Min Zhang and Yuanyuan Sun, 'A study on the mechanism of expedited justice for minor criminal cases after abolition of the system of re-education through labor' (2014) 1 (1) *Journal of the Beijing Police College*, 14–19.

[8] The term *jianyi chengxu* can also be translated as 'summary procedure'. However, in this chapter, I have chosen the term 'simplified procedure' because it is closer to the actual Chinese term and to distinguish the scope and operation of simplified procedure in the Chinese system from the quite different ways in which summary procedure operates in foreign jurisdictions such as Australia.

[9] I previously translated this term as 'security defence punishment', that is, punishment for defending security (see Sarah Biddulph, *Legal Reform and Administrative Detention Powers in China* [Cambridge: Cambridge University Press, 2007], pp. 345–348) but have now decided that that translation is more convoluted than it need be and could be misunderstood. There is no convenient translation for *bao'an*, which literally means

punishment focuses on the risk that certain conduct and people pose to society. It includes preventative measures and prohibition orders of various types. As with minor crime, the category of security punishment is not enacted in Chinese law. In the same way that minor crime was linked to debates about *laojiao*, debates about security punishments were also originally linked to debates about the reform or abolition of *laojiao* and criminal law reform from the mid-1980s. If a security punishment category were to be recognised, where should it be located conceptually and what powers should be included? The normative desirability or otherwise of introducing such a category into the Chinese legal system has been hotly debated for decades. It is a debate that has drawn heavily on the European experience of the abuse of security punishments in the mid-twentieth century.

Some post-*laojiao* reform proposals suggest that the Criminal Law should be amended to include provisions addressing either minor crime or security punishments or both, a reform that would expand the reach of criminal law and criminalise a number of administrative sanctions.[10] These proposals are by no means uncontroversial. Expansion of the scope of criminal law and the creation of new categories of minor crime and security punishments are fiercely opposed by those who see them as unwarranted and readily productive of injustice. They instead advocate minor, incremental reforms to address any reform issues left after the abolition of *laojiao*. Embedded in each technical question, the gap in the system of punishments and the scope and nature of reforms to establish minor crime and security punishments, lie unresolved normative questions about China's justice system: what and who should be punished and how?

2 Is There a Gap in the System of Punishments?

2.1 Scope of Laojiao

One of the notable features of *laojiao* was its flexibility. As the political and social order environment changed, the scope of *laojiao* was constantly adjusted and readjusted to encompass new and emerging

protecting order/peace. The use of this term in Chinese (both in Republican China and in the PRC) has been drawn from and is an interpretation of European conceptions. In other jurisdictions such as Germany, terms such as preventive detention or preventive measures are used to cover similar types of powers.

[10] Liu, 'Thoughts on bringing public order', 94.

social problems. Beginning from the 1950s, this process of incremental expansion continued throughout the reform period to encompass newly emerging forms of socially disruptive or unlawful conduct. As the problem of drug use and dependency deepened from the 1980s, the proportion of drug-dependent people in *laojiao* increased dramatically. Repeat and nuisance petitioners, people criticising government and Party officials, and those committing petty theft, fraud or other conduct considered to be anti-socialist or anti-Party could conveniently fall within the amorphous bounds of *laojiao*. Chen Xinliang in a 2001 article estimated that approximately one-third of the total *laojiao* population was drug dependent; that about one-third had committed minor crimes such as theft, fraud, fighting and public brawling; and that the other one-third had engaged in other types of conduct (including prostitution, repeat and nuisance petitioning, public advocacy and criticism of government officials).[11] The Regulations on Public Security Organs Handling Re-Education through Labour Cases (*Gong'an Jiguan Banli Laodong Jiaoyang Anjian Guiding*) issued on 1 June 2002 by the Ministry of Public Security was the last regulatory consolidation of *laojiao* targets, although the scope of targets continued to be expanded on an ad hoc basis after that.

Based on that consolidation, Xie Chuanyu has divided the types of conduct punishable by *laojiao* into four categories. The first (category A) includes conduct that could constitute a criminal offence but where a decision has been made not to prosecute because the circumstances are clearly minor.[12] Such conduct, an example of which might be the acceptance of a bribe whose amount falls below the threshold of a criminal offence, is not otherwise punishable by administrative sanction as it falls outside the scope of administrative laws. Category B offences are those where formal procedures to prosecute as a criminal offence have commenced, but because the circumstances are minor a decision has been made not to pursue the matter or to exempt the person from punishment. The procuratorate or court may determine either not to prosecute or not to proceed with the trial.[13] Category C offences encompass those

---

[11] Xingliang Chen, 'Research on China's system of re-education through labour: from the perspective of criminal rule of law' (2001) 13(6) *Peking University Law Journal*, 694.

[12] Chuanyu Xie, *On the Sanction System of Offences* (*Weihai Shehui Xingwei de Zhicai Tixi Yanjiu*) (Beijing: Law Press, 2013).

[13] The procuratorate may decide not to prosecute if it considers that the evidence is not reliable and sufficient (Criminal Procedure Law (CPL) 2012 article 171), where the

where the conduct constitutes a public order offence and so is liable to administrative punishment, or where the circumstances are comparatively serious, but not sufficiently so to constitute a criminal offence. Category D offences are administrative breaches where the person in question has repeatedly failed to reform after having been punished (*lujiao bugai*).[14] This characterisation of the types of conduct punished under *laojiao* helps to shape an evaluation of what, if any, gaps exist in the punishments system as well as the impact and reach of reform proposals.

2.2 Alternative Punishments: Sex Workers and The Drug Dependent

Whilst many of those detained under *laojiao* were punished for having committed criminal offences too minor to warrant criminal punishment, a significant proportion of detainees were people whose conduct was only ever an administrative wrong, i.e. a category D offence in Xie's schema.[15] Two large groups within this category were sex workers and their clients who had been repeatedly sanctioned and drug-dependent individuals who had been repeatedly sent for coercive drug detoxification. Since the abolition of *laojiao*, both types of conduct remain punishable, albeit under different administrative powers.

Engaging in sex work, unless knowingly infected with a sexually transmissible infection (STI), has never been a criminal offence in China. The legal regime proscribing sex work enables a first offence to be punished under the provisions of the PSAPL (article 66). Where the circumstances are minor or solicitation occurs in a public place, the police may impose a fine of up to RMB500 or administrative detention

---

offence is minor and the procuratorate determines that the offender need not be punished (CPL 2012 article 173), or if it considers that the provisions of CPL 2012 article 15 apply: i.e. the acts are obviously minor, caused no serious harm and it is deemed that no crime exists (CPL 2012 article 173). For a discussion of the regime under the 1996 CPL, see Mike McConville, Satnam Choongh, Pinky Choy, Eric Chui, Ian Dobinson and Carol Jones, *Criminal Justice in China: An Empirical Inquiry* (Cheltenham, UK: Edward Elgar, 2011), pp. 106–110. The court may also determine to dismiss a case under CPL 2012 article 15.

[14] The term *lujiao bugai* literally states that the person has been 'educated repeatedly and has not reformed'. In this situation, education means that the person has been punished and has failed to learn from that punishment by reforming and ceasing to engage in unlawful conduct. See Xie, *On the Sanction System*, pp. 110–114.

[15] Xie, *On the Sanction System*.

of up to five days. In other circumstances, the person may be punished by
between ten and fifteen days' administrative detention and a police-
imposed fine of up to RMB5,000. Sex workers and their clients may also
be gathered up for detention for education (*shourong jiaoyu*) for between
six months and two years in accordance with the provisions of the
1991 National People's Congress (NPC) Standing Committee's Decision
on Strictly Prohibiting Prostitution and Using Prostitutes (*Guanyu
Yanjin Maiyin Piaochang de Jueding*) (paragraph 4.2).[16] This form of
detention may be imposed either instead of or subsequent to punishment
under the PSAPL. The law provides no guidelines for enforcement
agencies in determining which punishment to impose or the length of
detention within the legally prescribed range. The abolition of *laojiao*
reduced the number of interlinked administrative powers available to
sanction the parties to a prostitution transaction, but left a similar form
of administrative detention, *shourong jiaoyu*, in place.

One of the major reforms to *laojiao* that arguably cleared the way for
its abolition was the transfer of drug-dependent people out of *laojiao*
and into a specialist form of detention for treatment under the provisions of the 2007 Drug Prohibition Law (DPL). The DPL reorganised
the state's approach to regulating and sanctioning drug use and dependency (amongst other things). It replaced two pre-existing detention
powers, coercive drug rehabilitation for between three and six months
in police-run detention facilities, and *laojiao* for between one and three
years, with another form of administrative detention, i.e. Coercive
Quarantine for Drug Rehabilitation (CQDR; *qiangzhi geli jie du*).[17]
The DPL also created two new community-based compulsory treatment

---

[16] A number of different translations have been used for the term *shourong*, including
'shelter', for example (*shourong shencha*), meaning 'to shelter for investigation'. In other
situations, it has been translated as 'custody', in the case of custody for repatriation
(*shourong qiansong*). In this chapter, I have chosen to translate the term *shourong* as
'detention'. My reasoning is that the term itself means 'to take in or shelter'. However,
shelter is a very inaccurate term to describe what actually happens to people taken in
under these powers. The word 'custody' as well implies a comparatively short period of
deprivation of liberty. The period of confinement under these powers, however, can be for
up to two years, rather more substantial than the word custody implies.

[17] Taiyun Huang (ed.), *Explanatory Reader on the PRC Illicit Drugs Prohibition Law*
(*Zhongua Renmin Gongheguo Jindu Fa Jiedu*) (Beijing: China Legal System Publishing
House, 2008); Hong Yang and Chun Zhang, 'The necessity and feasibility for forced
detoxification replacing detoxification via re-education through labour' ('*Qiangzhi geli
jiedu qudai laodong jiaoyang jiedu de biyao yu kexing*') (2008) 23(6) *Journal of Guangxi
Administrative Cadre Institute of Politics and Law*, 82–86.

orders, giving up drugs in the community (*shequ jiedu*) and recovering health (and giving up drugs) in the community (*shequ kangfu*),[18] each for a maximum of three years. The DPL specifies that CQDR may be imposed for an initial period of two years, which may be either reduced by a maximum of one year if the detainee reforms or extended for one year if the detainee does not (articles 38 and 47). The period of detention under this new power is thus between one and three years, the same as the period of detention originally imposed under *laojiao*. We can thus reasonably see it as a substitute for *laojiao* with respect to the drug dependent.[19]

As a result of this legal reform, those detained in police-run coercive drug rehabilitation and *laojiao* were transferred to specialist drug treatment facilities. This group represented a substantial proportion of the total population of detainees under *laojiao*. By 2005, official estimates suggest that the number of drug dependent individuals in *laojiao* had increased to 580,000, constituting over 50 per cent of the total *laojiao* population, with more than 200 *laojiao* camps designated as specialist camps for the drug dependent.[20] Another estimate suggests that by the time the DPL came into effect, two-thirds of the total *laojiao* population was transferred to this new form of detention.[21] In fact, the *laojiao* camps that were effectively already specialist drug detention facilities simply changed their names.

2.3 Overlap between Administrative and Criminal Laws

Particularly in the area of public order offences, there is a strong overlap between conduct punishable under the PSAPL, *laojiao* and the CL. For example, each authorises punishment for 'picking quarrels and causing trouble': in PSAPL article 26(4), Regulations on Public Security Organs

---

[18] Sarah Biddulph and Chuanyu Xie, 'Regulating drug dependency in China: the 2008 Drugs Prohibition Law' (2011) 51(6) *British Journal of Criminology*, 1–19.

[19] Ibid.

[20] Bixue Wang, 'The basic shape of my country's re-education through labour drug rehabilitation model', People's Daily, 24 June 2005.

[21] 'Prospects for reforming China's re-education through labor system', Congressional Executive Committee Meeting, 9 May 2013. Official statistics show that in 2009 173,000 people were sent to CQDR. See Office of the National Narcotics Control Commission (NNCC), Annual Report on Drug Control in China, Section 4: Deepen Giving up Drugs and Prevention of Drug Use (Beijing: Office of the NNCC, 2010. Available at www.jhak.com/jdzy/zgjdzy/20100327/1674.html

Handling Re-Education through Labour Cases article 9(4) and CL article 293(4). Such public order offences originally punished by *laojiao* would constitute a category C offence in Xie's schema[22] if the circumstances were not seen as sufficiently serious for prosecution as a criminal offence or a category D offence if the person in question were a repeat offender. Where the definition of the offence in criminal law is broadly worded and the criteria vague, the police retain discretion to determine whether to pursue administrative or criminal sanctions. The boundary of the CL is also vague, and, for that reason, public order offences such as those under article 293 of the law have been labelled 'pocket' offences, so-called because the police have enormous flexibility in determining what conduct falls within the scope of the provision.[23]

In fact, there is evidence to suggest the increasing use of that discretion to initiate criminal prosecutions for disrupting public order. Since the abolition of *laojiao*, the offences of 'picking quarrels and causing trouble' (article 293) and 'gathering a crowd to disturb social order' (article 290) have attracted a great deal of critical attention. Human rights NGOs have noted a dramatic upswing in the conviction under these offences of rights lawyers, civil society activists, public intellectuals and anyone engaged in conduct construed as opposing the party-state, who might otherwise have been punished with *laojiao*.[24] The degree of overlap in the legal provisions defining the offence of disrupting public order certainly makes it possible to use existing criminal offences to punish people who might previously have been punished administratively.

2.4   Lowering the Threshold of Some Criminal Offences

Reforms to lower the threshold for filing a case against certain types of criminal offences have also captured certain types of conduct that were previously punished only under *laojiao*.[25] These types of conduct would fall within category C of Xie's schema (serious administrative

---

[22] Xie, *On the Sanction System*.

[23] Qianfan Zhang, 'Extending "picking quarrels and causing trouble" to Internet speech' (*'Yanshen dao wangluo yanlun de "xunxin zishi"'*) FT Chinese Web, 4 February 2015.

[24] Dui Hua, 'Criminal detention as punishment in the post-RTL era', *Dui Hua Human Rights Journal*, 22 January 2014.

[25] Hongxian Mo and Dongli Ma, 'Cohesion and coordination of criminal and administrative punishments – from the perspective of abolition of re-education through labour' (2014) 141(1) *Journal of Henan Finance and Economics Politics and Law University*, 43.

infringements that do not constitute a criminal offence). The eighth amendment to the CL in 2011 and subsequent judicial interpretations[26] lowered the threshold for filing a criminal case in areas such as disturbing social order, traffic and driving offences, theft, forgery, bribery, fraud and corruption-related activities that could be punished by up to three years' imprisonment.[27] The ninth amendment in 2015 also increased the scope of conduct punishable in areas such as disrupting order and spreading false information, which can conveniently be used to punish conduct construed by the state as dissent or anti-state (conduct originally targeted for punishment under *laojiao*). Article 290 now extends punishment to people who have been repeatedly punished for disruptive conduct and have not reformed. Provisions have been added to article 308 to punish lawyers and other participants in litigation for revealing information disclosed in court proceedings that had not been made public. Article 309 makes disruptive behaviour in and around courts an offence, including gathering a crowd to disrupt the courtroom; beating and abusing judicial officers or other participants; insulting, slandering and threatening judicial officers; disobeying an order to stop; damaging court property and litigation documents; and seriously disrupting court order.

These reforms to the CL do not criminalise all types of minor offending that were previously punished under *laojiao*, but they go some way towards it (and may even encompass some category A offences in Xie's schema, offences too minor to punish as criminal offences and not otherwise punishable administratively).

---

[26] These interpretations were incorporated into the ninth amendment to the Criminal Law (CL) in 2015 and include the Supreme People's Court (SPC) and Supreme People's Procuratorate's (SPP) *Interpretation on Several Questions on the Applicable Law for Handling Criminal Cases of Theft* (*Guanyu Banli Daoqie Xingshi Anjian Shiyong Falu Ruogan Wenti de Jieshi*), effective from 2 April 2013 (reproduced at www.spp.gov.cn/zdgz/201304/t20130403_57894.shtml) and SPC and SPP's *Interpretation on Several Questions on the Applicable Law for Handling Criminal Cases of Picking Quarrels and Causing Trouble* (*Guanyu Banli Xunxin Zishi Xingshi Anjian Shiyong Falu Ruogan Wenti de Jieshi*), effective from 22 July 2013 (reproduced at http://news.xinhuanet.com/legal/2013-07/20/c_125038626.htm).

[27] Including article 291 (spreading rumours on the Internet), article 133 (in relation to drunk and dangerous driving), articles 267 and 280 (in relation to theft and forgery) and articles 164, 302, 383 and 390 (in relation to fraud, bribery and corruption related offences). Text available at www.npc.gov.cn/npc/xinwen/2015-08/31/content_1945587.htm.

2.5   Other Areas of Flexibility in the Criminal Justice System

There are circumstances in which the use of criminal coercive powers for the
investigation of suspected criminal offences can be used in ways that are
punitive even if the matter under investigation does not proceed to criminal
prosecution. They include criminal detention, investigative detention (after
arrest) and residential surveillance. The criminal coercive power of detention (*xingshi juliu*) enables the police to detain for interrogation a major
criminal suspect under article 80 of the Criminal Procedure Law (CPL;
Xingshi Susong Fa). The police may ordinarily detain a person for three days
before applying for an arrest warrant, but in some circumstances a person
may be held for a maximum of thirty-seven days before an arrest is
approved by the procuratorate or he/she is released. Following their arrest,
suspects may be detained for long periods prior to trial, either unlawfully or
through the use and misuse of a range of lawfully available extensions and
other devices such as commencing the investigation of a new and different
offence when the period of detention for another has expired.[28]

The criminal coercive power of residential surveillance also enables the
police to exercise close control over a person's life and actions. Particularly
the power to hold individuals in residential surveillance away from their
homes at a location designated by the police (under CPL article 73) has
become a de facto alternative to detention.[29] *Shuanggui*, the power exercised by the CCP's Discipline Inspection Committee to detain for interrogation Party officials suspected of breaching Party discipline (i.e. suspected
of corruption), is also commonly used prior to or instead of arrest. This
power has been used extensively to investigate official corruption, and
these cases are transferred to the criminal justice system once a decision
has been made to prosecute and sufficient evidence has been obtained.[30]

During investigation, there is a strong preference for keeping suspects
in detention rather than using a non-custodial coercive measure such as
bail. As McConville et al. note, the conditions in detention centres 'may
be appalling'.[31] Thus, in practice, the use of these forms of detention

---

[28] McConville et al., *Criminal Justice in China*, pp. 45–46.
[29] Joshua Rosenzweig, 'Residential surveillance: evolution of a Janus-faced measure' (12
October 2013). Available at SSRN: https://ssrn.com/abstract=2641010; Joshua Rosenzweig, Flora Sapio, Jue Jiang, Biao Teng and Eva Pils, 'Comments on the 2012 revision of
the Chinese criminal procedure law', in Mike McConville and Eva Pils, eds., *Comparative
Perspectives on Criminal Justice in China* (Cheltenham: Edward Elgar), pp. 455–503.
[30] Flora Sapio, 'Shuanggui and extralegal detention in China' (2008) 22 *China Information*,
7–37.
[31] McConville et al., *Criminal Justice in China*, p. 45.

when a person may be eligible for a non-custodial measure to be imposed, or when there is no real prospect that a criminal investigation or prosecution will proceed, becomes punitive.

2.6 Mind the Gap

The foregoing discussion shows that, to a certain extent, there is an overlap (and hence no gap) between conduct punishable under both *laojiao* and other administrative punishments, or *laojiao* and criminal punishment. Some of this overlap stems from the vague and expansive descriptions of an offence. In other cases, revisions to the CL have lowered the threshold for filing a criminal offence and the flexibilities in the CPL have enabled coercive powers to be used in ways not apparent from the text of the law. The supposed 'gap' in the system of punishments has also been reduced by the existence of alternative administrative powers to impose extended periods of detention on those whose conduct did not and still does not fall within the purview of criminal law: that is, the drug dependent and sex workers and their clients. The imposition of administrative sanctions in these types of cases remains legally ill defined, and the police retain wide discretionary powers and are subject to limited procedural controls in exercising those powers.

However, the abolition of *laojiao* has in fact changed the punishment landscape. Whilst some forms of conduct punished under *laojiao* may now be subject to criminal punishment, pursuing a criminal prosecution is not as institutionally convenient as imposing *laojiao* because of the involvement of a greater number of agencies – the police, procuratorate and courts – each with its own powers and institutional interests. In the case of administrative detention, the abolition of *laojiao* removed a layer in the overlapping web of administrative punishments for category D offences (repeated infringements).

That abolition has also resulted in certain types of conduct no longer being subject to punishment. In cases where the conduct does not fall within the generally more rigidly defined boundaries of the PSAPL or CL, or where the police are unable to obtain sufficient evidence to file a case and obtain approval from the procuratorate for an arrest (e.g. in the case of category A or B offences in Xie's schema),[32] a person may escape punishment. There are good policy reasons for not expanding the

---

[32] Xie, *On the Sanction System.*

scope of criminal punishments to cover this type of conduct, as the debates concerning minor crime and security punishments examined later attest. For conduct falling within category A or B, both the CL (article 13) and CPL draw a lower limit with respect to very minor offending to prevent such offenders from entering the criminal justice system or to enable them to exit the system before a criminal conviction is recorded. These are important protections for those who have committed very minor offences, as the recording of a criminal conviction has detrimental implications for all aspects of a person's work and life.

3   Minor Crimes

A number of changes have converged to underpin the current interest in minor crime (*qing zui*). One is the adoption of the criminal justice policy of 'balancing leniency and severity' (*kuanyan xiangji*), which acknowledges that criminal law is not merely a tool for harsh punishment. Another important factor is that the proportion of minor offences has increased dramatically both in absolute numerical terms and as a proportion of the overall number of criminal cases. For example, one report states that in 1978, in 39.7 per cent of criminal cases, punishment of five years or longer fixed-term imprisonment was imposed. In 2007, that percentage had declined to 16.22 per cent of all criminal cases (with there being no suggestion that the decrease was attributable to increasing leniency in punishment).[33] In some economically developed areas with a large migrant labour population and a crime rate higher than the national average, the proportion of minor crimes is very high. For example, in Jiangyin city in Jiangsu province, a punishment of less than three years' imprisonment was imposed in 88.9 per cent of the 2,420 criminal cases adjudicated in 2013. Of those cases, over 14 per cent involved drunk or dangerous driving.[34]

Discussions of minor crime include concerns about definition and policy, that is, what constitutes a minor crime, where does it sit in the overall criminal justice system, and how should minor offending be punished? This, in turn, is linked to another set of questions about the procedural issues raised in responding to the increased cost and

---

[33] Xiaodong Zhang, 'How much do you know about speedy criminal determination?' (2014) 15 *Fangyuan Magazine*, 56–59.

[34] Ibid.

institutional workload of the police, procuratorate and courts.[35] What forms of investigation, prosecution and adjudication are appropriate or necessary for dealing efficiently and fairly with minor offences if they are to be handled using expedited procedures? In terms of reform proposals, another question is whether minor crime should be embraced as a category, requiring both formal legal and institutional changes to establish it as such, or whether it should remain descriptive in terms of identifying certain types of offending and the expedited processes and lenient treatment in place to handle them.

A number of incremental changes have been made in criminal law, procedure and practice to deal more efficiently with less serious crime. These reforms have enabled certain types of minor offending originally punished by *laojiao* to be dealt with through the criminal justice system. The reforms began prior to the abolition of *laojiao* and include expanding the scope of matters that fall within the definition of crime, expanding the scope of matters that may be dealt with by simplified procedures and instituting non-custodial sentences for minor crimes. If a decision is ever made to establish the legal category of minor crime, then more far-reaching structural reforms will be required.

3.1   Policy Issues

Instituting systems for the expedited handling of minor criminal offences is identified as a core area for reform in the Fourth Five-Year Court Reform Plan (SPC's Opinion on Comprehensively Deepening Reform in the People's Courts, point 12). On 23 October 2013, SPC Chief Judge Zhou Qiang, in reporting on a meeting convened to discuss SPC work, including its response to the abolition of *laojiao*, urged local-level courts to establish procedures for expedited adjudication to cope with the increase in the number of minor offences anticipated after that abolition, as well as to promote the scope of community corrections to ensure an early return to the community of minor offenders.[36]

---

[35] Li, Zhang and Sun, 'A study on the mechanism'; Zaishang Chen and Xiangqian Cui, 'Three-dimensional defects and remodelling of the system of re-education-through-labour' ('*Laodong jiaoyang zhidu de sanwei quexian yu chongsu*') (2008) 4 *Journal of the Railway Police College* (*Tiedao Jingguan Gaodeng Zhuanke Xuexiao Xuebao*), 32–38.

[36] *Zuigao Fa Tichu Tansuo Wanshan Qingwei Xingan Kuaishen Kuaijie Jizhi*, 24 October 2013, available at http://news.sina.com.cn/c/2013-10-24/023928515178.shtml.

Whilst a degree of momentum has built around defining the scope and institutional mechanisms for handling minor criminal offences, there is by no means unanimity about the desirability of reforms to establish a category of 'minor crime'. Wei Dong, for example, suggests that establishing such a category would do violence to the long-established policy of the scope of criminal law remaining small (*xiao xingfa guannian*). He argues that the threshold for criminal offences should not be lowered to include a wide range of conduct currently punished as administrative infringements, and goes on to argue that the legislative and institutional changes required to establish such a category would be too extensive and disruptive of the established system.[37]

The opposing view recognises the fact that there has been a marked increase in the number of minor offences being tried in the criminal division of the People's Courts and points to the inadequacy of existing procedures for expediting the handling of such cases. Existing procedures, this point of view holds, are currently geared to a criminal justice system that is orientated towards harsh punishment, are too cumbersome and costly and are, in fact, inappropriate for dealing with minor offending. The danger of failing to introduce expedited investigation, prosecution and adjudication measures in respect of minor offences is that many people will be held in pre-trial detention for unnecessarily long periods when their case could have been dealt with quickly. With the increasing use of non-custodial sentencing for minor offences, this view argues that a more comprehensive reform is clearly warranted.

3.2   Definitional Issues

China's CL itself does not categorise crime as minor or serious, unlike the criminal laws of many other jurisdictions. So, at present, the category of minor crime has no legislative definition, and nor does it have any specific institutional structure such as a magistrate's court or minor crime division or any special procedures for expedited prosecution and adjudication. Some suggest that the boundary for minor crime should be offences for which punishment of less than three years' fixed-term imprisonment, criminal detention, control or a fine may be given. They suggest that the definition should also encompass certain categories of offenders who are eligible for lenient treatment under the policy of

---

[37] Wei, 'Reform of the security punishment', 82.

balancing leniency and severity, including juvenile offenders and first time offenders.[38]

The distinction between minor and serious crime, to the extent it exists at present, lies in the circumstances in which the given offence takes place or the circumstances that render the offence serious, very serious or odious. However, such degrees of distinction do not map well onto the categories of minor and serious crime, as some offences such as murder are serious by their very nature. The law at present does not specify a clear boundary between minor and serious crime in the way that Australian jurisdictions, for example, draw a legal distinction between summary and indictable offences.

3.3 Criminal Procedure Reforms

In the absence of a substantive category of minor crime, reforms to criminal procedure to expedite the handling of certain types of cases correspond only partially with minor offending. However, two reforms have been identified as particularly relevant to handling minor offences: the expansion of simplified procedure (*jianyi chengxu*) and criminal reconciliation (*xingshi hejie*).

3.3.1 Simplified Procedure

Simplified procedure was introduced into criminal procedure in the 1996 amendments to the CPL following the first trial conducted in the Haidian district court in Beijing in 1995.[39] The 1996 amendments confine the use of simplified procedure to publicly prosecuted cases for which the possible sentence is less than three years' fixed-term imprisonment, criminal detention, control or a fine; cases filed on complaint; or privately initiated prosecutions where there is evidence of a minor crime (article 174). In simplified procedure the Procuratorate may decide not to attend the court hearing, the proceedings of which must be completed by the court within twenty days of accepting the case (articles 175, 176).

The 2012 reforms to the CPL expand the jurisdiction to try matters with a single judge using simplified procedure to basic level courts and remove the restriction concerning the maximum punishment (article 208). Simplified procedure may be used in cases where the facts are clear

---

[38] Huawei Gong, 'A study of the criminal policy of minor crime' (2006) 89(3) *Journal of Tianjin Administrative College of Politics and Law*, 8.

[39] Zhang, 'How much do you know?'

and the evidence sufficient, and the defendant confesses to the crime, raises no objection to the charges and does not object to simplified procedure being used (article 208). A distinction is still drawn between cases where the maximum punishment is three years' imprisonment and more serious offences in that the former may be tried by a single judge, whilst the latter must be tried by a collegiate bench (of three) (article 201).

Such reforms enable the expeditious processing of criminal trials when the main facts are not in contention, or at least when the defendant does not raise any objections to the evidence and/or charges. However, the extensive fieldwork of McConville et al. indicates that simplified procedure has not been universally welcomed, by judges at least. Many have indicated that they feel simplified procedure places much greater responsibility on the individual judge concerned. It also adds to their workload because of their felt need to adduce and check evidence in addition to their responsibilities for adjudication.[40]

Simplified procedure is thus not confined to, and nor does it perfectly correspond to, the prosecution and trial of minor crime. However, the expansion to basic level courts in the 2012 CPL amendments has made its use attractive in trials of minor offences where the evidence is clear and uncontested. Initial research suggests that the number of offences tried using simplified procedure has expanded dramatically.[41] Such an expedited trial procedure does enable the courts to deal with straightforward matters quickly, and goes some way towards addressing concerns that the diversion of people originally punished by *laojiao* would increase the criminal justice system caseload and overwhelm the courts' capacity to deal with minor crime.

3.3.2 Pilot Sites on Expedited Investigation, Prosecution and Adjudication

Particularly since 2010, trials concerning different aspects of the expedited handling of minor offences have proliferated. These pilots do not correspond exactly to the simplified procedure parameters discussed

[40] McConville et al., *Criminal Justice in China*, pp. 206–207.
[41] Meng Fang, 'Current situation, existing problems, causes and perfection of summary procedure since the implementation of new criminal procedure law – a case study of Q county in Sichuan province' ('Xin xingsufa shishi hou jianyi chengxu kaizhan xianzhuang, cunzai wenti, yuanyin ji wanshan duice') (2014) 4 *Journal of Guizhou Police Officer Vocational College*, 35–40.

previously, as they generally focus on criminal offences for which the maximum punishment is three years' fixed-term imprisonment, whilst simplified procedure can also be used in serious cases. Many of the pilots relate to such offences as dangerous driving, theft, deception, blackmail, damage to property, picking quarrels and causing trouble, crimes related to drug addiction or sex work and criminal cases where a civil compensation agreement has been reached, and some have involved the physical relocation of the court to the detention facility where suspects are awaiting trial (e.g. Yangpu district in Shanghai, Dezhou in Shandong).

Following the inclusion of expedited handling for minor criminal cases in the Fourth Five-Year Court Reform Plan, on 27 June 2014 the NPC Standing Committee authorised the SPC and Supreme People's Procuratorate (SPP) to carry out a range of trials over the two-year period between 2014 and 2016.[42] The scope of criminal offences covered in these pilots includes dangerous driving, traffic offences, theft, deception, robbery, causing injury, and provoking quarrels and causing trouble. Cases must also meet the criteria set out for simplified procedure: that is, the facts are clear, there is (legally) sufficient evidence, the accused acknowledges guilt and there are no disputes about the applicable law. Pilots authorised under this 2014 NPC Standing Committee decision apply only to offences with a maximum of one-year fixed-term imprisonment, in contrast to earlier trials that applied to offences punishable by a maximum of three years' imprisonment.

Whilst much consideration has been given to expediting court adjudication, expediting the investigation and prosecution of minor offences for which the evidence and law are straightforward has also been mooted. A range of reforms in this respect have been undertaken, with more proposed. For example, in December 2006 the SPP mandated the expedited prosecution of minor criminal cases that could be tried using simplified procedure under the 1996 version of the CPL (articles 3 and 4).[43] In expedited matters, the time limits for approving arrest and deciding whether to commence prosecution are truncated. Documentation of arrest and prosecution decisions and evidence lists may be completed in

---

[42] Decision on Authorising the SPC and SPP to Conduct Trials on Expedited Decisions in Criminal Cases in Some Locations (*Guanyu Shouquan Zuigao Renmin Fayuan, Zuigao Renmin Jianchayuan Zai Bufen Diqu Kaizhan Xingshi Anjian Sucai Chengxu Shidian Gongzuo de Jueding*).

[43] Opinion on Expedited Handling of Minor Criminal Cases According to the Law (*Guanyu Yifa Kuaisu Banli Qingwei Xingshi Anjian de Yijian*).

simplified form. In the prosecution recommendation, the Procuratorate should also recommend that the court use simplified procedure to try the matter (article 9).

Some suggest that the expedited handling of minor criminal cases should also include expedited investigation by the police. A trial was launched by the Beijing police in 2011 to establish a system for expedited investigation, and the Henan provincial court, procuratorate and public security organs subsequently set up a trial led by a specialist team to consider systems for expediting the handling of minor criminal cases.[44] A stated objective of the latter was to reduce the number of suspects detained during the investigation period, or at least to reduce the amount of time they spent in detention.[45] Other solutions to issues of pre-trial detention can be found in locations such as Guangzhou, where a second detention facility is being planned to allow people charged with serious offences to be separated from minor offenders.

As is evident from this account, significant incremental reforms to expedite the handling of minor offences have already been undertaken and are being trialled throughout the country. Another pilot reform was authorised by the NPC Standing Committee on 3 September 2016 to run between 2016 and 2018; *Decision on Authorising the SPC and SPP to Conduct Pilots on Plea Agreements for Lenient Punishment in Criminal Cases in Some Locations*. However, these reforms appear to be designed to streamline the existing regulatory framework rather than to devise a model for more systematic reform of the existing system of criminal law and procedure.

3.3.3   Criminal Reconciliation

Whilst not directed explicitly at minor offending, criminal reconciliation has in practice played a role in facilitating the quick resolution of minor offences since its inclusion in the 1996 amendments to the CPL (article 172). It was expanded and included as a special procedure in the 2012 amendments to the law. Under this process, the offender negotiates for forgiveness from the victim in exchange for an expression of regret and payment of an agreed amount in compensation for losses suffered as a result of the criminal conduct (article 277). Criminal reconciliation may be conducted at all stages of investigation, prosecution and trial, and will be led by the agency responsible for the stage in question. If an agreement is reached, that agreement may be taken into account by the police in

---

[44] Li, Zhang and Sun, 'A study on the mechanism', 15.   [45] Ibid.

recommending to the procuratorate that a lenient approach be taken, possibly prosecution for a lesser offence or a decision not to prosecute under CPL article 142(2). If reconciliation is successful at the investigation or trial stage, the procuratorate may recommend that the court take this into account as a mitigating factor in sentencing (article 279). Liebman's study of everyday justice in selected lower level courts in Henan during 2010 indicates the widespread use of criminal reconciliation to resolve ordinary criminal matters. His work suggests that reaching an agreement and paying compensation to the victim or his/her family are the most important factors in a court's determination to impose lenient punishment or even discharge the case.[46]

Criminal reconciliation is not confined to minor offences, but is used primarily in cases involving criminal infringement upon a person or property (CL part 2, chapters 4 and 5) where the sentence that could be imposed is less than three years' imprisonment, control or a fine and in negligent crimes (article 278). Over 70 per cent of mediated cases involve crimes of intentional (minor) injury, stealing and traffic offences. Like the trials on the expedited handling of minor crimes, one aim of criminal reconciliation is to reduce the amount of time those who have committed a minor crime spend in pre-trial detention.[47]

3.4 Sentencing Minor Offending

Courts have a range of sentencing options in punishing minor offenders. They may impose lenient sentences (including successful reconciliation with and payment to the victim), suspended sentences or a sentence served non-custodially as community corrections. Whilst sentences may be suspended for serious crimes for which the death sentence is imposed, suspended sentences are also a particularly common way of imposing a lenient sentence in respect of minor crimes.[48] Community correction may be imposed in a range of circumstances: where the person is sentenced to the criminal punishment of control (CL article 38), given a suspended sentence (CL article 76), granted parole (CL article 85) or ordered to serve the sentence out of custody. The number of people given

---

[46] Benjamin Liebman, 'Leniency in Chinese criminal law? Everyday justice in Henan' (2014) 14–406 *Columbia Law School Public Law & Legal Theory Working Paper Group*, 25, 33.
[47] Ting He, 'The practice and legislation of criminal reconciliation in China' (March 2012) *Melbourne Law School Conference Proceedings*, 6.
[48] Liebman, 'Leniency in Chinese criminal law?', 24–25.

community corrections has increased dramatically in recent years. In November 2014, Deputy Justice Minister Zhang Sujun stated that since the beginning of trials in selected locations from 2003, a total of 2,113,000 people had been punished under the community corrections system.[49] Whilst community correction does not act as a substitute sanction for *laojiao* (as a person must first be convicted of a criminal offence), its inclusion in the 2011 revisions to the CL has expanded its use nationwide and provides a convenient alternative for punishing minor offences that might previously have been punished by *laojiao*.

4   Security Measures and Punishments

The abolition of *laojiao* spurred renewed interest in minor crime as the prospect of transferring the punishment of serious administrative infringements (Xie's category C offences) into the criminal justice system was considered. The discussion of security measures (*bao'an cuoshi*) and security punishments (*bao'an chufen*) has also been entwined in debates about reform or *laojiao* its abolition. In the mid-1990s, one option mooted for reforming *laojiao* was to include it in the broader category of 'security punishments' or 'security measures'. At that time, it was argued that *laojiao* was not so much a punishment as a coercive measure for education and correction (discussions on this point are set out in my own prior work).[50]

After the abolition of *laojiao*, some suggested that the 'gap' should be filled with a range of security punishments.[51] They pointed out that a number of administrative detention powers occupying the middle ground in the structure of punishments similar to *laojiao* still exist, so much so that they are characterised as *laojiao*-type powers (*lei laojiao*) or 'Big Laojiao' (*da laojiao*).[52] These powers include the detention for education of sex workers and their clients (*shourong jiaoyu*), compulsory

---

[49] 'Deputy Minister of Justice: the draft community corrections law for examination has been completed' ('*Sifabu fubuzhang: shequ jiaozheng fa cao'an songshengao zheng wanshan*') Chinanews.com, 5 November 2014.

[50] Biddulph, *Legal Reform*, pp. 260–264, 345–248.

[51] Ying Song, 'An exploration of problems of the nature and convergence with criminal punishment of detention for education after abolition of re-education through labour' ('*Hou laojiao shidai shourong jiaoyu de xingszhi yu xingfa xianjie wenti tanjiu*') (2015) 1 *Western Region Law Review*, 113–114.

[52] See, e.g. Renwen Liu, 'Security punishments and the reform of China's administrative detention system' ('*Bao'an chufen yu zhongguo xingzheng jujin zhidu de gaige*') (2014) 6 *Rule of Law Studies*, 13.

treatment of drug-dependent people (*qiangzhi geli jiedu*), and the administrative detention of juvenile offenders who fall outside the scope of the criminal justice system. Just because *laojiao* was abolished, it does not automatically follow that *laojiao*-type powers were also abolished. However, pressure to provide a coherent and acceptable legal justification for these powers certainly increased after its abolition.[53]

The concept of security punishments has been revived in an attempt to rationalise and provide a more defensible legal basis for the remaining administrative detention powers. The argument for creating a category of security punishments runs; that their rationale is 'education, reform and rescue' (*jiaoyu, ganhua, wanjiu*) and not punishment at all.[54] Their function is to prevent the risk to society caused by habitual offenders (category D in Xie Chuanyu's schema, including administrative offences where a person is punished repeatedly but fails to reform).[55] However, one of the problems confronting those who would create a category of coercive powers defined around the prevention of risk is that there is no consensus that this is a sound or desirable approach. More specific questions concern whether such a category is warranted and, if it is, what types of powers should be included and where they should be located in the overall system of punishments. A number of different approaches have been mooted.

Liu Renwen would distinguish security punishments from criminal punishments and coercive measures by including all types of administrative action involving the deprivation of personal freedom that are not for the purpose of criminal investigation or criminal punishment.[56] He would thus include *laojiao* (before it was abolished), the detention for education (*shourong jiaoyu*) of sex workers and their clients for a period of between six months and two years, compulsory detention for the rehabilitation of drug-dependent people, compulsory community rehabilitation orders under the DPL, detention for re-education (*shourong*

[53] Wei, 'Reform of the security punishment', 82.
[54] Weihong Li, 'The balance between security defence punishments and criminal punishments' (*'Bao'an chufen yu Zuixing junheng'*)(1997) 3 *Journal of Yantai University* (*Yantai Danxue Xuebao*), 30; Weixin Gao and Xin Chen, 'The jurisprudential basis of the system of security defence punishments and their establishment in China' (*'Bao'an chufen zhidu de fali jichu ji qi zai woguo de goujian'*) (2003) 3(1) *Journal of Shihezi University* (*Shihezi Daxue Xuebao*), 57.
[55] Haiying Song and Yan Song, 'The mechanisms for protection of human rights in the system of social defence punishments and the criminal law' (*'Bao'an chufen zhidu yu xing fa zhong de renquan baozhang jizhi'*), in Weiguo Zhu (ed.), *Reflection on the Public Order Regulation* (*Zhi'an Guanli Zhidu Sicun*) (Beijing: Falu Chubanshe, 2003), pp. 232–235.
[56] Liu, 'Security punishments'.

jiaoyang) for between one and three years of juvenile offenders who are ineligible to be punished under the CL, compulsory testing and medical treatment for STIs under the 1991 NPC Standing Committee's Decision on Strictly Prohibiting Prostitution and Using Prostitutes 4(4), and administrative detention (*xingzheng juliu*).[57] These powers would be used as a supplement or alternative to criminal punishment.[58]

Others define the scope of security measures with reference to their purpose, which is to protect the safety of society (and the individual in cases of self-harm). Their targets are people who pose a definite risk to society, such as habitual offenders; people with mental illness who pose a danger to themselves and society; and juveniles who have committed serious offences but because of their youth are ineligible for criminal sanction. With sex workers, for example, the theory is that detention protects society by enabling compulsory medical examination and treatment for STIs, as well as the stated objective of education, reform and rescue to prevent repeat offending.[59] They are thus seen as measures to be taken against specifically defined 'dangerous people' to correct (*jiaozheng*), transform (*ganhua*), give medical treatment (*yiliao*) and/or impose prohibitions (*jinjie*).[60] Such a purposive definition encompasses both criminal and administrative compulsory measures, and would extend to a court order that persons undergoing community correction be subject to 'supervision of their activities' (*xingwei jiandu*) and involuntary committal to a psychiatric facility under the 2012 amendments to the CPL and the 2013 Mental Health Law. In addition to measures for the deprivation of liberty, a range of prohibition orders – from driving for habitually drunk or dangerous drivers to a prohibition order under CL article 38(2) preventing people sentenced to control (*guanzhi*) from engaging in certain designated conduct or entering certain locations – would also fall within this definition of security punishments.

In the lead-up to the 1997 revisions to the CL, a group of influential criminal law academics led by Zhao Bingzhi argued unsuccessfully that a chapter on security measures be included in the revised law. The scope of measures that they would have included was much narrower than the more broadly inclusive approaches described earlier, and was limited to the detention for education of juvenile offenders and compulsory

---

[57] Ibid., 18.
[58] Ibid., 13; Xuewu Qu, 'Security punishments and China's criminal law reform' (1996) 18 (5) *Chinese Journal of Law*, 55–68.
[59] Song, 'An exploration of problems', 115.   [60] Liu, 'Security punishments', 13.

rehabilitation of the drug dependent.[61] Their proposal was reinvigorated after the abolition of *laojiao*.[62] In fact, the 2012 reforms to the CPL to transfer the power to issue an involuntary committal order for mentally ill offenders from the public security organs to the courts has been seen by some as a step in this direction.[63]

Perhaps more critically, there is a great deal of wariness about embracing this category at all. As with minor crime, the category of security punishments does not exist in the Chinese legislative regime. The concept, its necessity, scope and purpose remain highly controversial topics.[64] Proponents argue that whilst the term 'security punishment' does not appear in the text of any legislation, the measure already exists in fact.[65] They argue that the category is justified as it reflects actual powers and actual social needs. Justification for creation of a conceptual category of security punishments also draws heavily on evidence that security measures and punishments are common throughout the world. Proponents point out that every country has in place certain measures to deal with dangerous habitual criminals and people with mental illness who are a danger to society and themselves, even if they are not officially labelled security measures.[66] Establishing a category of security punishments to cover the remaining *laojiao*-type powers is also advocated by those who object to proposals to expand the scope of criminal law through creation of a category of minor crime.[67] Even proponents, however, recognise the real risks of serious abuse if the scope of these powers is allowed to expand beyond a narrow and well-defined range and if appropriate procedural safeguards are not in place. The enthusiastic use and abuse of security measures by the Nazi regime are an ever-present element in Chinese discussions about security measures and security punishments.[68] For those advocating the legalisation of security

---

[61] Bingzhi Zhao, Xingwang He, Maokun Yan and Zhonghua Xiao, 'Research into several questions on the reform of China's criminal law' (1995) 18(5) *CASS Journal of Law*, 10.

[62] Liu, 'Security punishments', 19; Qu, 'Security punishments and China's criminal law reform', 59–60.

[63] Song, 'An exploration of problems', 113; Liu, 'Security punishments', 19.

[64] Li, 'Security punishments should not be the direction'.

[65] Yan Zhou, 'Proposals for reform of my country's re-education through labour system' (*'Woguo laodong jiaoyang zhidu gaige chuyi'*) (1999) 42(6) *China Criminal Science (Zhongghuo Xingshifa Zazhi)*, 23.

[66] An oft-cited example is Title 6 of the German Criminal Code Measures of Rehabilitation and Incapacitation, which sets out custodial orders, including the mental hospital order, the custodial addiction treatment order and detention for the purpose of incapacitation.

[67] Wei, 'Reform of the security punishment', 82.   [68] Liu, 'Security punishments', 14–15.

punishments, the question is how these punishments should be regulated to mitigate the risks. For those opposed, it is precisely the propensity for abuse that constitutes the core problem. For them, the criteria of 'dangerousness' and 'risk' are just too imprecise and malleable to justify their general application.[69] Those opposed to the reform of *laojiao* by transforming it into a security punishment (prior to its abolition) pointed out that, reclassified as such, it would have been very easy for its already broad scope to have been expanded even further to cover habitual drunks, the unemployed, vagrants and beggars.[70]

5   Conclusion

This chapter has documented the ways in which debates about proposed legislative and policy reforms in China's post-*laojiao* punishment landscape have been shaped by perceptions that the abolition of *laojiao* has left a gap in the system of punishments. Most proceed on the basis that there is indeed a gap and that the gap needs to be filled at least in part. Some reforms, such as lowering the threshold for certain criminal offences, have gone some way towards absorbing the more serious end of transgressions originally punished under *laojiao* (Xie's category C offences) within the criminal justice system. The existence of overlapping administrative powers means that in some areas (category D offences) there is no gap at all. The extent to which some conduct originally punished under *laojiao* is no longer punished reflects a tacit acknowledgement that there is no need to punish very minor offending.

To date, reforms have been incremental and appear to be primarily responsive to domestic concerns. However, in formulating these reforms and, more transparently, in the debates over more wide-ranging reforms on subjects such as minor crime and security punishments, the influence of foreign models and experience can be seen. Debates about minor crime and the mechanisms that might be introduced to give it substantive and procedural form draw extensively on the experience of both civil law and common law systems. Particular emphasis has been placed on the systems for conducting a document-based examination of minor offences

---

[69] Li, 'Security punishments should not be the direction'; Zhongdong Zhai, 'The bottleneck on application of security defence punishments and its resolution' (*'Bao'an chufen shiyong de pingjing ji qi jiejue'*) (2002) 17(6) *Legal Forum* (*Faxui Luntan*), 28; Song and Song, 'The mechanisms for protection', 245.

[70] Li, 'Security punishments should not be the direction'.

and issuing a criminal penal order (*chuxing mingling*) in Germany (*Strafbefehl*), Taiwan and Japan.[71] Explorations of the desirability of establishing a specialist minor crime division draw on the Australian magistrates' court and the procedures in place for handling summary offences. Similarly, the experience of the United States and other common law jurisdictions with regard to court-ordered diversion programmes, suspended prosecutions and sentences, community-based orders and plea bargaining have all been considered in Chinese debates about minor crime and its expedited handling. The use of criminal fines and suspended sentences in civil law countries such as Germany has also been influential in shaping proposals for reform. In considering the scope and form of security punishments, too, there has been very close examination of the history, development and legal form of those powers in civil systems, whether as a single-track or dual-track system, which are seen as being their conceptual home.[72] Consideration of German and Swiss regulatory history and the perils of the uncontrolled expansion of the scope of such orders has influenced both the proponents and opponents of security punishments.[73] Even though common law systems have not established a separate category of security punishments, reference is also made to the experiences and systems in place in those jurisdictions for dealing with mentally ill offenders, the extension of sentences for serious habitual offenders and measures taken outside the formal criminal justice system against juveniles committing serious offences. In this area at least, the discussion of foreign systems and experience has been central in formulating concrete proposals for the reform of China's system of punishments for minor offending in the post-*laojiao* world.

It is perhaps not surprising that reforms and reform debates have revealed no clear normative shift towards the protection of individual rights. *Laojiao* was abolished without engagement with the broader

---

[71] Zhang, 'How much do you know?'; Liu, 'Thoughts on bringing public order detention'. In Germany a penal order may be imposed without a trial but the punishment is limited to a fine or a suspended prison sentence of less than one year; see Hans-Jörg Albrecht, 'Sentencing in Germany: explaining long-term stability in the structure of criminal sanctions and sentencing' (2013) 76 *Law and Contemporary Problems*, 216.

[72] Germany is seen as having a dual-track system, with one track being criminal punishment based on findings of guilt and the other being measures for rehabilitation and the protection of security by the imposition of treatment or preventive detention based on dangerousness and the continuing risk posed by the offender to society; see Albrecht, 'Sentencing in Germany', 213.

[73] See, e.g. Liu, 'Security punishments'; Qu, 'Security punishments and China's criminal law reform'; Wei, 'Reform of the security punishment'.

debates about how to balance the empowerment of state agencies with the protection of individual rights. There has been no real incentive, so far, to dive into that contentious area when it has been possible to use incremental reforms to reshape the system of punishments in the post-*laojiao* world. However, throughout the debate, there has been sensitivity to the desirability of shaping reforms in a way that addresses outstanding abuses. One is to minimise the problem of extended periods of detention prior to trial, particularly for minor offenders who may not ultimately be sentenced to a custodial term. Trials of the expedited handling of minor cases and criminal reconciliation, for example, have had this as an explicit objective.

In the broader reform proposals, such as those for the establishment of a category of security punishments, the potential for abuse is clearly recognised. Debates about what types of measures should be included within any category of security measures lack criteria beyond statements that security measures are 'preventative' and that they address 'risks to society' posed by 'dangerous people'. Such a description is dangerously vague and may result in a range of powers being included without adequate consideration or justification. Particularly controversial is the power of detention for the education (*shourong jiaoyu*) of sex workers and their clients. This power is criticised on all the same grounds that *laojiao* was. In particular, it lacks proper legal justification in the terms required by the Legislation Law; the description of targets is excessively vague; it imposes a disproportionately heavy punishment of detention for between six months and two years on people who have not committed a criminal offence; the police have excessively broad discretionary power in determining a sanction; and it lacks procedural safeguards and cannot effectively be supervised. It is also unnecessary.[74] The urgent need for a reappraisal of each existing power discussed under the moniker of 'security punishments' is highlighted by the abolition of a number of them in recent years: *laojiao*, detention for repatriation (*shourong qian-song*), retention for in-camp employment (*liuchang jiuye*) and detention for investigation (*shourong shencha*). There is now evidence that the use of *shourong jiaoyu* is being severely curtailed in the same way that *laojiao* was prior to its abolition. It is now possible that *shourong jiaoyu* will ultimately also be abolished.

[74] Lang Chen, 'Discussing security punishments and the retention or abolition of China's system of detention for education' (2014) 9 *Managers Journal*, 241.

Despite the attraction of broad concepts such as security punishments and minor crime, the evidence so far suggests unwillingness to engage in a radical reorganisation of the system of punishments. A more conservative, incremental approach to reform may remain the preferred option, even though this approach makes it more difficult for reforms to be made to the institutional structures that underpin abusive practices.

3

Understanding the Presumption of Innocence in China

Institution and Practice

XIFEN LIN AND CASEY WATTERS

1 Introduction

China has a time-honoured history and culture, but a young and maturing legal system. To those from the West who are used to laws, judicial decisions and regulations, it may seem very strange indeed that China, such a large country both in population and size, did not promulgate its first modern criminal procedure law until 1979.[1] However, even that law, the Criminal Procedure Law (CPL), does not explicitly address a common presumption in the criminal laws of other nations, that is, the presumption of innocence (POI). As POI is a legal principle originating in the West, its acceptance in the criminal justice context of China is a gradual and longstanding process. The CPL's first revision, in 1996, adopts the clause 'no person shall be found guilty without being judged as such by a People's Court according to law',[2] but the protection guaranteed to criminal defendants under Article 12 of the CPL (2012) is different from the classic concept, which, according to the International Covenant on Civil and Political Rights (ICCPR), requires POI.[3] Article 12 focuses on who has the power to issue a guilty verdict

---

[1] Todd D. Epp, 'The new code of criminal procedure in the People's Republic of China: protections, problems, and prediction' (1984) 8 *International Journal of Comparative and Applied Criminal Justice*, 43–53; Ralph H. Folsom and John H. Minan (eds.), *Law in People's Republic of China: Commentary, Readings, and Materials* (Dordrecht: M. Nijhoff, 1989), p. 313.

[2] Article 12 of Criminal Procedure Law (CPL) (1996) of the People's Republic of China.

[3] Article 14(2) of the International Covenant on Civil and Political Rights (ICCPR), United Nations (UN), 19 December 1966, in force 23 March 1976.

rather than on the presumption of the accused's guilt or innocence during the investigation and trial. However, Article 12 holds the key to understanding POI in the Chinese context. To determine whether and how the Western understanding applies in that context, several questions must be answered first: What are the differences between China's POI institution and international POI standards? Is explicitly detailing POI in the CPL the most important factor in evaluating the development of the POI principle? If not, then what needs to change with regard to both the law on the books and the law in practice to promote POI in China?

Section 2 of this chapter briefly outlines the meta-principles of the standard view of POI in the international context. These include the principle that the judiciary alone has the power to adjudicate a criminal proceeding, that the prosecutor bears the burden of proof, that a guilty verdict must be based on evidence, that the defendant should be treated with dignity and respect and that in *dubio pro reo*.[4] Section 3 looks into the misinterpretation and misunderstanding of POI within the Chinese legal context, which to some extent has hindered the principle's acceptance by reformers. Section 4 investigates the institutional arrangements and judicial reality, demonstrating the highly limited scope of POI's implementation in China. Finally, Section 5 concludes the chapter with suggestions for ways to promote POI in China going forward.

2 POI in the International Context

Whilst there is no authoritative definition of POI, its main purpose is commonly agreed to be ensuring that individual defendants are protected by procedural safeguards before and during a trial.[5] Some scholars believe that in the West, POI primarily constitutes a rule requiring the prosecutor to bear the burden of proof.[6] However, limiting POI to the field of evidence law is insufficient to accord with the spirit of the rule of law in modern societies. POI has been endowed with additional

---

[4] A Latin phrase meaning 'when in doubt, for the accused'.
[5] See Magnus Ulväng, 'Criminal and procedural fairness: some challenges to the presumption of innocence' (2014) 8 *Criminal Law and Philosophy*, 469–484.
[6] See, e.g. Andrew Stumer, *The Presumption of Innocence: Evidential and Human Rights Perspectives* (Oxford: Hart, 2010). Stumer thoroughly analyses the presumption of innocence (POI) at the trial stage.

connotations, which are depicted in their broader scope through the meta-principles discussed in the following.[7]

2.1   Only the Judiciary Has the Power to Determine Guilt

POI means that every defendant has the right to be presumed innocent until proven guilty according to the law.[8] The first issue is to whom the accused shall be proven guilty. It appears obvious that only if the accused is proven guilty to an independent and neutral judge or judicial agency can the criminal justice system be deemed fair. No organ or individual other than the judiciary has the power to convict someone of a crime in such a system that is fair, and if judicial procedures are not followed, then the trial and judgment are void.

There are two justifications for the institutional arrangement by which a court or judge possesses the power of judgment. The first is based on the experience of judicial history. Before the separation of powers that now exists in many countries, the powers to prosecute and adjudicate were combined. The adjudicator possessed nearly unlimited powers in both Western and Eastern countries, including investigative, prosecutorial and adjudicative powers, and appeared as the judge but was actually an investigator. According to natural justice, only if an adjudicator has nothing to do with the investigation or prosecution can he or she make a fair judgment regarding the accused. If the accused is tried by an investigator or prosecutor, the lack of impartiality renders the process inherently unfair.

The second justification is based on the notion of proceduralism or due process of law.[9] In modern criminal procedures, trials are characterised by an open, transparent process that ensures the accuracy of fact-finding and the appropriate application of the law while guaranteeing that the accused is treated equally and fairly. Criminal prosecutions, and the verdicts that arise therefrom, have consequences for the freedom,

---

[7] Ulväng uses a similar method to define POI. See Ulväng, 'Criminal and procedural fairness', 470. A broader view of POI is helpful for understanding the limitations of China's current criminal justice system.

[8] Steve Sheppard, 'The metamorphoses of reasonable doubt: how changes in the burden of proof have weakened the presumption of innocence' (2003) 78 Notre Dame Law Review, 1170–1244.

[9] For a broader discussion of due process, see Francis A. Allen, 'Due process and state criminal procedures: another look' (1953–1954) 48 Northwestern University Law Review, 16–35; Ryan C. Williams, 'The one and only substantive due process clause' (2010) 120 Yale Law Journal, 408–512.

property and even life of the accused. Neither the investigative nor prosecutorial process can meet the strict requirements of transparency, equality and fairness in the same manner as the trial process.[10]

2.2 The Prosecutor Bears the Burden of Proof

Because the accused is treated as innocent until proven guilty, the prosecutor rather than the accused shoulders the burden of proof. The prosecutor must strive to collect incriminating evidence and charge the accused only when that evidence is sufficient according to the law. He or she must then persuade the judge and/or jury of the accused's guilt, and risks a failed prosecution if unable to prove that guilt by convincing the judge/jury based on *corpus delicti*.

At the same time, those accused of a crime should not be required to prove their innocence, and nor should they be compelled to testify against themselves.[11] The trial judge may not enter a verdict against the accused simply because he/she does not confess to the crime or answer the prosecutor's questions.[12] In other words, the accused enjoys the right to silence and privilege against self-incrimination. For example, the Fifth Amendment to the US Constitution provides that 'no person … shall be compelled in any criminal case to be a witness against himself, nor be deprived of life, liberty, or property, without due process of law'.[13]

2.3 Guilty Verdicts Must Be Based on Evidence

POI requires charges and verdicts to be based on reliable evidence. In historical terms, POI constitutes a rejection of such ancient 'fact-finding' methods, or more accurately ordeals, as trial by water, trial by fire and judicial duels.[14] The concept of POI not only necessitates the

---

[10] For more on the traits of the trial process, see Ruihua Chen, 'Procedural fairness: an analysis of criminal trial' (1997) 2 *Peking University Law Journal*, 69–77.

[11] See, e.g. Jeffrey K. Walker, 'A comparative discussion of the privilege against self-incrimination' (1993) 14 *New York Law School Journal of International and Comparative Law*, 1–37; Eileen Skinnider and Frances Gordon, 'The right to silence – international norms and domestic realities', paper presented at the Sino-Canadian International Conference on the Ratification and Implementation of Human Rights Covenants, Beijing, 16–25 October 2001.

[12] Ibid.   [13] Amendment 5 of the US Constitution.

[14] For more on trial by ordeal, see Margaret H. Kerr, Richard D. Forsyth and Michael J. Plyly, 'Cold water and hot iron: trial by ordeal in England' (1992) 22 *Journal of Interdisciplinary History*, 573–595.

abandonment of such irrational methods, but also requires the prosecutor to provide solid, reliable evidence of a defendant's criminal conduct. It also, in theory, prohibits subjective conjectures, emotional cognitions and social pressure in the trial process. In addition, proving guilt requires the proof to reach a minimum threshold, namely, beyond reasonable doubt. As stated in *Wilmington v. Director of Public Prosecutions*, 'the accused should be entitled to the right to demand his or her release if according to the evidence adduced by the prosecution or by the defense reasonable doubts still exist after the trial is ended'.[15]

2.4   Defendants Should Be Treated with Dignity and Respect

Where POI prevails, suspects and defendants are to be treated the same as any other citizen, with their dignity and human rights guaranteed, based on the logic that because innocent persons are to be treated with dignity and respect, so too should those presumed to be innocent. In the investigation phase, criminal justice agencies are forbidden to take such compulsory measures as arrest, detention, search, seizure, electronic monitoring or enticement, which violate citizens' dignity and human rights, until there is sufficient evidence to meet a legal threshold. In the trial process, the judiciary should treat the prosecution and defence equally and determine the facts of the case objectively. The probative value of evidence must also outweigh its prejudicial value to ensure fair treatment and prevent a defendant from being labelled as deviant.[16] For this reason, the US Supreme Court established a rule according to which defendants should not be forced to wear prison uniforms during their trial.[17] It should be noted that even when a defendant is found guilty in his or her first trial, the POI principle still applies to a second before the court has given an effective judgment.[18]

2.5   In Dubio Pro Reo

Finally, POI means that courts should rule in favour of the defendant when rendering a judgment if there is any uncertainty about whether he

[15] *Wilmington v. Director of Public Prosecutions* [1935] AC 462.
[16] See, e.g. Victor J. Gold, 'Federal Rule of Evidence 403: observations on the nature of unfairly prejudicial evidence' (1982–1983) 58 *Washington Law Review*, 497–533.
[17] *Estelle v. Williams*, 425 US 501 (1976).
[18] Chaoyi Huang, *The Presumption of Innocence: On the Operation of Criminal Procedure* (Taipei: Wunan Press 2000), p. 4.

or she committed the crime he or she has been charged with by the prosecutor. For example, consider that Hunter A and Hunter B shot C at nearly the same time, and were not conspirators. The autopsy concludes that either bullet alone would have been fatal. However, it remains unclear which bullet hit C first, and therefore which caused his death. According to substantive law, the degree of criminal responsibility that A and B bear largely depends on whether their behaviour is causally related to C's death. Hence, one committed intentional homicide, and the other attempted homicide. However, according to the principle of *in dubio pro reo*, both defendants should be convicted of attempted homicide. Although this result, that is, neither party bears responsibility for the accomplished homicide, is contrary to common sense because either's action was sufficient by itself to have resulted in C's death, it is in accordance with the spirit of *in dubio pro reo*.[19]

3 Misunderstanding of POI in China

Since 1949, there have been three stages of development and debate in China regarding POI. The first stage took place from 1954 to 1958 when the criminal procedure code of the People's Republic of China (PRC) was in the drafting stage. The main topic in this period was whether POI was an academic or political issue.[20] During the second stage, from 1979 to 1996,[21] the influence of political ideology was less prevalent, allowing theorists to discuss the principle academically. As the CPL (1979) did not mention POI among its opening general principles, the principle's applicability in China became the main topic of debate during the law's revision. The focus in the third stage, which began in 1996 and is ongoing, is on what kind of POI exists in China. As a concept, POI has

---

[19] Yuxiong Lin, *Criminal Procedure Law* (Beijing: Renmin University Press, 2005), pp. 3–5.

[20] The 'anti-rightist' movement that began in 1957 rendered serious legal analysis of this and other criminal law issues difficult, forcing any discussions to serve the political dictates of the day. The draft procedure code that had been prepared was shelved in 1957. Although legal discussion and drafting work revived to some extent in the early 1960s, the political movements preceding the Cultural Revolution and then the Cultural Revolution itself soon pre-empted these efforts. Published discussions of POI resumed, naturally enough, in the late 1970s as the old draft code was being reconsidered and shaped into its final form. See Timothy A. Gelatt, 'The People's Republic of China and the presumption of innocence' (1982) 73 *The Journal of Criminal Law & Criminology*, 261–262.

[21] CPL (1996) was based on a law promulgated in 1980. See Jinwen Xia, 'New developments in Chinese Criminal Procedure Law' (2010) 7 *Annual Survey of International & Comparative Law*, 1–7.

been discussed for more than sixty years in China, and many textbooks and the classical literature on criminal procedure law and evidence law define it as a legal presumption.[22] In other words, legal POI requires legal proof.

However, this conventional understanding of the POI concept is incomplete, as POI is not merely a legal presumption. In the West, where the principle of POI is considered the cornerstone of modern criminal procedure, such presumption means that anyone who is charged with a criminal offence is entitled to the right to be deemed innocent until proven guilty. In this sense, POI is an assumption or legal fiction.[23] It requires agents of the state to treat a suspect or defendant in a criminal process as if he or she were in fact innocent.[24] As the principle of POI is imported from the West, improper translation gives rise to many misunderstandings. For example, translating POI into Chinese as *wuzui tuiding* is a mistranslation. The correct translation is *wuzhui jiading*. In Chinese, the basic meaning of *tuiding* is inference or determination, and it thus refers to finding the accused innocent by means of inference. This meaning is obviously inconsistent with the proper definition of POI. *Jiading*, in contrast, means 'assumption', and thus implies treating the accused as if he or she can be assumed to be innocent.

At the same time, the aim of POI is to establish rules on the burden of proof rather than on legal presumption. Although *tuiding* seems to differ from *jiading* only slightly, they differ greatly in essence. *Tuiding* refers to the method of proof, which can be classified into two categories: proof by direct evidence and proof by indirect evidence. The former applies to circumstances in which the evidence collected supports the assertion being made without the need for any intervening inference, whilst the latter is applicable to situations in which the evidence collected has indirect probative value and requires conventional experience and common sense or inference to determine the truth of the fact being proved.[25] In other words, there is a logical link between the known

---

[22] Daming Shen, *Anglo-American Law of Evidence* (Beijing: CITIC, 1996), p. 69.

[23] H.F.M. Crombag, 'Law as a branch of applied psychology' (1994) 1 *Psychology, Crime & Law*, 1–9.

[24] Thomas Weigend and Douglas Husak, 'Assuming that the defendant is not guilty: the presumption of innocence in the German system of criminal justice' (2014) 8 *Criminal Law and Philosophy*, 285–299.

[25] For a discussion of the burdens of proof and evidence, see Joseph Cocozza and Henry Steadman, 'The failure of psychiatric predictions of dangerousness: clear and convincing evidence' (1975–1976) 29 *Rutgers Law Review*, 1084–1101.

and unknown facts in *tuiding*. *Tuiding* is true in most circumstances, and its conclusions tend to be correct. *Jiading* (assumption), in contrast, has no factual basis and therefore should not be categorised as a method of proof. It merely materialises the legal value of human rights protection.

Taiwanese evidence scholar Xuedeng Li pointed out the essence of POI in the Chinese legal context more than twenty years ago:

> The presumption of innocence is prone to being misinterpreted as rules on *tuiding* or even as evidence because of the use of [the] word *tuiding*. Actually, it is neither evidence nor rules of presumption (including the factual presumption (*tuiding*) and legal presumption (*tuiding*)). The POI is due to the legal policy that much attention should be paid to the protection of [the] defendant's human rights. But the translation of *wuzui tuiding* has led to chaos among scholars and legal practitioners.[26]

Although Li's views are well known to criminal justice experts in Mainland China, the differences between *tuiding* and *jiading* have received little attention.

4   Limited Enforcement of POI in China

4.1   *Comparison of POI Enforcement inside and outside China*

Although POI is widely accepted and strongly rooted in modern legal cultures, different versions of POI exist.[27] Accordingly, it is worth asking the following questions. How does POI implementation vary across countries? Are the aforementioned meta-principles protected at the same level by the criminal procedure laws of various countries?

In China, shortly after the CPL's amendment in 2012, some scholars argued that the amended version failed to accord with UN standards of POI. Because China has agreed to the ICCPR, they argued, it had the duty to ensure that its laws were in accordance with international standards.[28] The POI principle, in particular, must be explicitly included in the CPL. This view seems to be widely accepted in academic circles, but may provoke the mistaken belief that the introduction and

---

[26] Xuedeng Li, *A Comparative Study of Evidence Law* (Taipei: Wunan Press, 1992), pp. 668–669.

[27] Ulväng, 'Criminal and procedural fairness', 472.

[28] China signed the ICCPR on 5 October 1998.

enforcement of POI are based primarily on legal provisions. In reality, countries choose different ways of applying the international standard of POI. Accordingly, whilst a nation's inclusion of POI in its written laws is a significant factor in ensuring POI in practice, it is not the most significant factor.

In general, countries utilise three methods to ensure POI. The first, adopted by such countries as Japan, France and Russia, is to write POI into the constitution. The constitutions of some countries not only clearly establish the principle of POI but also explicitly afford the accused the right to silence. For example, the constitution of South Africa entitles every defendant to the right to be presumed innocent, the right to remain silent and the right not to testify in court.[29] The second method is to stipulate POI by statute, particularly within criminal procedure laws. France and Russia enumerate the principle in both those laws and their constitutions. The third method is to use precedents to establish the POI principle, with countries adopting this method relying on *stare decisis* rather than the constitution or criminal procedure law. For example, the US Constitution is silent with regard to POI, but judges established the principle by interpreting the constitution.[30] In Germany, no explicit POI provisions exist in the country's statutes. However, German scholars have embraced the concept of *in dubio pro reo*, and precedents of the German Constitutional Court, German Federal Supreme Court and European Court of Human Rights have developed procedural safeguards that meet the international standard of POI. These procedural safeguards encompass both POI's role (namely, whether it is a constitutional or statutory principle) and its scope.[31] The US and German examples demonstrate that even if a country does not expressly incorporate POI into its criminal procedure laws or constitution, the principle can still be well established in practice. There is little evidence of the existence of poor POI enforcement in countries whose criminal procedure laws or constitutions explicitly mention POI, but the possibility exists because the law on the books often differs from the law in action. Hence, it is to some extent meaningless for Chinese scholars to overly concentrate on Article 12 of the CPL.

[29] Craig M. Bradley (ed.), *Criminal Procedure: A Worldwide Study*, 2nd edn. (Durham, NC: Carolina Academic Press, 2007), p. 473.
[30] See *Coffin v. United States*, 156 US 432, 453–454 (1895).
[31] Claus Roxin, *Criminal Procedure Law*, 24th edn., Liqi Wu (trans.) (Beijing: Legal Press, 2003), pp. 125–128.

Among countries that use the same method of guaranteeing POI, the right can be simulated to varying degrees. For example, although the POI principle is written into South Korea's criminal procedure law, defendants enjoy only the right to be silent during trials.[32] They are not entitled to that right during interrogations by the police or prosecutor at the pre-trial stage.[33] Most continental European and Anglo-American countries, in contrast, provide the accused with the right to silence at both the pre-trial and trial stages, although they differ in other respects. Historically, the former have not protected the right to silence effectively, having gradually strengthened it only since the end of World War II. Even the United Kingdom, the birthplace of the right to silence, has attempted to narrow it over the years.[34] It began limiting the right in 1971, initially only in criminal cases in Northern Ireland. However, limitations on the right were subsequently applied to the entire United Kingdom after passage of the Law of Criminal Justice and Public Order in November 1994.[35] This law severely limits the accused's right to silence and allows judges and juries to consider as evidence of guilt both a suspect's failure to answer police questions during interrogation and a defendant's refusal to testify during his or her trial.[36]

Even within a single country, policies on protecting POI can vary significantly over time. For example, in 2000 France passed a law that strengthened POI and defendants' rights by requiring the investigation organ to notify criminal suspects of their right to silence at the beginning of their detention. However, the law was subsequently perceived as contributing to an increase in the crime rate and deterioration in social security, leading to an adjustment in 2002. The new law requires the investigation organ to notify a detainee that he or she can choose to make a statement, answer investigators' questions or remain silent.[37]

---

[32] Articles 241, 242, 287 and 289 of Criminal Procedure Act of the Republic of Korea.
[33] Ibid.
[34] See, e.g. Gregory W. O'Reilly, 'England limits the right to silence and moves toward an inquisitorial system of justice' (1994) 85 *Journal of Criminal Law and Criminology*, 402–452.
[35] Criminal Justice and Public Order Act 1994 (available at www.legislation.gov.uk/ukpga/1994/33/contents).
[36] O'Reilly 'England limits the right to silence', 402.
[37] For a discussion of the right against self-incrimination in France, see Jacqueline Hodgson, *French Criminal Justice: A Comparative Account of the Investigation and Prosecution of Crime in France* (Oxford: Hart, 2005).

4.2   Enforcing POI in China: Progress and Limitations

4.2.1   China's CPL (1979 and 1996)

In China's first version of the CPL (1979), the goals of maintaining social order and extending judicial power (the power to investigate and prosecute in particular) were afforded much greater emphasis than those of human rights protection and due process. It contained nothing concerning POI. In practice, the accused were treated as guilty until proven innocent. The initial CPL version suffered three distinct problems. First, at the investigation stage, criminal suspects were not entitled to a right against self-incrimination and were duty-bound to answer investigators' questions. Second, at the prosecution stage, the People's Procuratorates had the power to make a highly unusual non-prosecutorial decision; that is, they could exempt suspects from a charge or trial while still convicting them.[38] Furthermore, defendants had no access to effective relief. If they did not accept a Procuratorate decision, their only option was to present a petition to the procuratorial organ that had made that decision. The Procuratorate in question would then re-examine its own decision and notify the defendant of the result. Such a phenomenon seriously violates the principle of adjudicative power belonging solely to the judiciary. Third, *in dubio pro reo* was not effective at the trial stage, meaning that if the court acquitted the accused owing to a lack of evidence, the prosecutor could recharge him or her based on additional evidence collected after the acquittal.[39]

These deficiencies obviously prevented the 1979 CPL from complying with the international standards stipulated in the ICCPR. Hence, whether to establish the POI principle, and if so how to implement it, became a critical issue for the Chinese government in amending the CPL in 1996. One objective of the amendment was to learn from international legislative and judicial experiences. The CPL (1996) includes two meta-principles: only the judiciary has the power to convict someone of a crime and *in dubio pro reo*. On the one hand, according to the interpretation of the legislators who participated in the CPL's revision, Article 12 does not concern the POI principle.[40] They argued as follows.

---

[38] See, e.g. Daphne Huang, 'The right to a fair trial in China' (1998) 7 *Pacific Rim Law & Policy Journal*, 171–196.

[39] See, e.g. Guangzhong Chen and Weimei Zheng, 'On the reform of China's criminal justice supervision procedure' (2005) 2 *Chinese Legal Science*, 168–178.

[40] Kangsheng Hu and Fucheng Li, *Understanding China's Criminal Procedure Law* (Beijing: Legal Press, 1996), p. 15.

We are against the presumption of guilt but we also do not support the POI which is popular in Western countries. What we advocate is to investigate matter-of-fact, objectively collect various [types of] evidence including inculpatory [and] exculpatory. Before the people's court renders a verdict, we don't call defendants criminals. But we also do not argue that [they are] innocent or presume [them to be] innocent. If we presume[d] [them to be] innocent, then the investigative and compulsory measures taken by criminal justice agencies [would] be baseless.[41]

This judicial philosophy originates from the political idea that nothing should be presumed and that the truth should instead be determined from the facts, and expounds the philosophy supported by Mao Zedong. Timothy Gelatt has pointed out that in the PRC, 'POI does not exist, but neither does the presumption of guilt. Instead, the Chinese legal system "presumes" nothing, preferring to seek "truth from facts" by "taking facts as the basis and the law as the yardstick".'[42]

On the other hand, as crime control and social order maintenance remained the predominant values of CPL (1996), a number of law enforcement institutions were not strongly supportive of Article 12. For example, criminal suspects still bore the responsibility to answer investigators' questions. Whether through law or judicial practice, the revised CPL failed to prohibit forced self-incrimination. These factors weakened the impact of the two newly established meta-principles.

4.2.2   China's CPL (2012)

Like CPL (1996), the 2012 amendment restates the principle that the adjudicative power belongs to the judiciary and reaffirms *in dubio pro reo*. In addition, it for the first time stipulates that the People's Procuratorates or private prosecutor should carry 'the burden of proof',[43] that 'adjudication should be based on evidence'[44] and that 'the prosecutor should prove the crime beyond a reasonable doubt'.[45] Yet, CPL (2012) still enforces POI to a degree that falls short of the international standard, which is reflected in the accused's treatment.

The compulsory measures are still not subject to judicial review at the pre-trial stage, and the investigative agencies retain the power to make

---

[41] Ibid.

[42] See Gelatt 'People's Republic of China and the presumption of innocence', 259–316.

[43] Article 49 of CPL (2012).

[44] Article 61 of the Interpretation of the Supreme People's Court on Several Issues concerning the application of 'the People's Republic of China Criminal Procedure Law' (2012).

[45] Article 53 of CPL (2012).

decisions regarding criminal detention, which can limit or deprive a suspect of personal freedom; or use search, seizure and electronic surveillance, which infringe his or her property or privacy rights. The People's Procuratorates still possess the powers of arrest and contingent detention. Although CPL (2012) refines the rules of arrest and renders the rules for granting bail to suspects more applicable, the power structure of the criminal pre-trial process remains intact. It is thus unsurprising in practice to see up to 80 to 90 per cent of suspects detained during the pre-trial stage being subject to criminal proceedings. In some jurisdictions, the figure even exceeds 90 per cent.[46]

The exclusionary rules regulating illegally obtained evidence have been substantially improved. A judge can exclude illegally obtained evidence, such as evidence obtained through torture or threats and physical evidence obtained by means that severely violate the principle of judicial fairness. However, the exclusionary rules do not apply to certain types of inappropriate conduct, including investigations that violate the defendant's right to a defence and illegal secret investigations. In addition, the methods that investigators can use to collect evidence are quite flexible.

In spite of the prohibition on forced self-incrimination provided in CPL (2012), the relationship between that prohibition (Article 50) and the obligation for a perpetrator to truthfully answer questions (Article 118) is unclear. Under the indeterminacy of these articles, the Procuratorates and public security organs can interpret the CPL as they wish. In fact, although scholars tend to argue that the two articles contradict each other, the Procuratorates and public security authorities disagree. During the 2012 amendment process, these two entities surmised that the forced self-incrimination prohibition merely prohibits investigators from obtaining evidence through such coercive means as extorting confessions by torture rather than endowing suspects with the right to silence. As long as investigators do not obtain confessions in a coercive manner, and interrogate criminal suspects in accordance with legal procedures, those suspects still have the duty to answer questions truthfully. The interpretation of the Procuratorates and public security organs is to some extent justifiable because the meaning of Articles 50 and 118 is unclear, but it is clearly not in accordance with the essence of the anti-self-incrimination privilege. The contradiction between the two articles relates to the complexity of that privilege and the right to silence. In common law

---

[46] Yanyou Yi, 'Arrest as punishment: the abuse of arrest in People's Republic of China' (2008) 10 *Punishment & Society*, 9–24.

countries, if the accused exercises his or her right to silence, the interrogation should end immediately.[47] If the accused gives up that right, he or she has an obligation to tell the truth and bears the liability for giving false testimony. However, in civil law countries, the accused has no obligation to tell the truth after waiving his or her right to silence.

The attitude of the People's Procuratorates and public security organs in China can be summarised as follows. First, the accused is not entitled to the right to silence. Second, he or she must answer questions truthfully during an interrogation. Discussion of whether the accused is entitled to the right to lie after giving up the right to silence is moot because he or she is not entitled to the latter right.

4.2.3 POI in the Context of China's Judicial Reality

Looking beyond the articles in the CPL, it may still be very difficult for China to act in accordance with international standards of POI. There are public agencies other than the judiciary that have been granted the power to take measures limiting personal freedoms for a duration that renders those measures akin to criminal sanctions. Perhaps the most infamous example is re-education through labour (RTL),[48] a type of administrative detention that the PRC used until very recently to detain persons for delinquency or such minor crimes as petty theft, prostitution, street fighting and the possession of illegal drugs.[49] The deprivation of freedom under RTL typically lasted for one to three years, with the possibility of an additional one-year extension. The measure was decided by the public security organs rather than the judiciary and seen as a form of administrative punishment. RTL was used for over sixty years (1950s to 2013). Another example of non-judicial punishment is detention and repatriation.[50] Although detention

---

[47] See, e.g. Rinat Kitai-Sangero, 'Respecting the privilege against self-incrimination: a call for providing Miranda warnings in non-custodial interrogations' (2012) 42 *New Mexico Law Review*, 203–235.

[48] See Hong-shan Huang and Wei-ping Wang, 'From "re-education" to "re-education through labor": the origin of China's system of "Re-education through Labor"' (2010) 3 *Hebei Academic Journal*, 73–80.

[49] Ibid.

[50] See Keith Hand, 'Citizens engage the constitution: the Sun Zhigang incident and constitutional review proposals in the People's Republic of China', in Stephanie Balme and Michael W. Dowdle eds., *Building Constitutionalism in China* (New York: Palgrave Macmillan, 2009), p. 221. Hand discusses detention and repatriation in China with reference to the Sun Zhigang case in which Sun Zhigang was sent to a detention centre by an administrative agency and beaten to death. Hand argues that such administrative

and repatriation and RTL were annulled in 1996 and 2013, respectively,[51] similar forms of administrative detention, including detention for the re-education of prostitutes, coercive drug rehabilitation and detention for investigation (also known as shelter and investigation), remain legal and are put into practice on a daily basis.[52] They are all determined by administrative agencies rather than the judicial organs, and thus risk infringing citizens' rights.[53]

Although defendants are exempt from the burden of proof in the CPL,[54] some articles in China's criminal law impose a duty to disprove certain elements of a crime, thereby threatening POI's applicability in China. For example, if a government official holds a substantial amount of property with an unidentified source, he or she must prove that the property has a legal source or risk being convicted of the crime of illicit enrichment.[55] Also, in practice, if a defendant relies on an alibi for his or her defence, is mentally ill or claims that his or her conduct was based on self-defence or an emergency, he or she is sometimes asked to prove that any of these circumstances indeed exists.[56]

Although the facts of a case should be clear and the verdict based on reliable and sufficient evidence,[57] the reality can be quite different. It is worth noting that less than 1 per cent of witnesses testify orally in court in most Chinese jurisdictions. Instead, witness testimonies are nearly always

---

detention violates China's Constitution, and should thus be abolished through the constitutional review system.

[51] Detention for investigation was annulled in 1996 by the first CPL revision. The decision to annul the re-education through labour system was announced in a document entitled 'The Central Committee of the Communist Party of China on Several Major Issues on How to Comprehensively Deepen Reform', issued by Chinese Communist Party on 15 November 2013, and was finally annulled by the Standing Committee of the National People's Congress on 28 December 2013.

[52] See Sarah Biddulph, *Legal Reform and Administrative Detention Powers in China* (Cambridge: Cambridge University Press, 2012).

[53] See Yanyou Yi, 'Can a government compulsorily make her citizens more free? Revisiting non-judicial detentions under the People's Republic of China's administrative regulations and their justifications' (2012) 2 *Tsinghua China Law Review*, 381–417. Yi argues that administrative detentions are considered as a compulsory measure aimed at making citizens 'more free'.

[54] Article 49 of CPL (2012).

[55] For the tension between POI and the goal of effectively prosecuting corruption, see Margaret K. Lewis, 'Presuming innocence, or corruption, in China' (2012) 50 *Columbia Journal of Transnational Law*, 287–369.

[56] However, many Western countries also require defendants to prove elements of what are referred to as 'affirmative defences'.

[57] Article 53 of CPL (2012).

recorded and presented in written form during criminal proceedings. Accordingly, adjudicators are limited in the information that they can obtain from witnesses, and defendants cannot confront or cross-examine witnesses. Furthermore, a witness's conjectures are sometimes considered evidence or even serve as the basis for a judgment. Some empirical studies cite unreliable witness testimonies as one of the main contributing factors to wrongful convictions in China.[58] In addition, the emphasis on crime control and social order maintenance means that the defendant's prior criminal record and bad character usually sneak into judicial decision-making as evidence against him/her. Even worse, as judicial independence is severely restricted in China,[59] there are high-profile cases in which the court has been explicitly or implicitly influenced by such forces as other criminal justice agencies, including such public security organs as the People's Procuratorates, government officials, victims and even the mass media. Hence, when a court makes a judgment under pressure unrelated to the facts of the case or law, the principle of adjudication based on evidence is in essence revoked.

In practice, China's treatment of the accused in neither the pre-trial nor trial stages is in accordance with international standards. The country maintains a policy of limited and cautious detention. The virtues of this abstract policy are counteracted by the arrest and detention-based performance system that prevails among the public security organs. As a result, most suspects remain in custody throughout the criminal proceedings against them, including during the pre-trial phases. Furthermore, the prohibition against forced self-incrimination in the CPL is virtually meaningless. Police officers have been known to take turns questioning suspects until they confess. Interrogations lasting for days have been shown in several high-profile cases of wrongful conviction.[60] Until February 2015, a defendant could choose whether to appear in court wearing a prison uniform according to the Notice on the Dress Code for Criminal Defendants or Appellants Who Appear in Court for Trial, issued by the Supreme People's Court and Public Security Organ. Regardless, however, the spatial structure of the courtroom suggests that

[58] Jiahong He and Ran He, 'Empirical studies of wrongful convictions in mainland China' (2012) 80 *University of Cincinnati Law Review*, 1277–1292; Jiang Na, 'Death penalty reforms in China: lessons from wrongful convictions?' (2013) 5 *Tsinghua China Law Review*, 126–150.

[59] Xin He, 'Ideology or reality?: limited judicial independence in contemporary rural China' (2004) 6 *Australian Journal of Asian Law*, 213–230.

[60] Examples include the Li Jiuming and Du Peiwu cases.

defendants are to be treated as criminals, as they are asked to sit opposite the judge, effectively placing them on display. The prosecutor and defence attorney sit on either side, arguing about the defendant's conviction and sentencing. There is effectively no communication between the defendant and his or her lawyer during the trial.

Although the CPL clearly places the burden of proof on the prosecutor and adheres to the concept of *in dubio pro reo*, implementation in practice is unsatisfactory. At approximately 0.1 per cent, China has one of the lowest rates of acquittal in the world. One reason for the very high conviction rate is that the public security organs and People's Procuratorates screen out most cases lacking sufficient evidence prior to trial. Another important reason is that the courts are reluctant to acquit even when the 'proof' does not meet the standard of beyond reasonable doubt. For example, in the case if Zhao Zuohai, one of the most infamous cases of wrongful conviction in China, even though the evidence against Zhao was insufficiently incriminating, he was charged with murder and subsequently convicted. As a compromise, he was sentenced to death with a reprieve rather than death. There are other cases of insufficient evidence leading to a guilty verdict and discounted sentence, including those of She Xianglin and Du Peiwu.

5   Conclusions Regarding POI Promotion in China

5.1   Applying a Broader POI Definition

Although the simple definition of POI as the prosecutor's duty to prove the defendant's guilt is often cited, POI is in fact more substantial and involves more than the simple restatement of the burden of proof in a criminal trial.[61] It is inspired by a desire to protect human dignity, and is better considered as a procedural safeguard of the defendant with a moral preference for allowing the guilty to go free over punishing the innocent.[62] In this respect, the concepts of only the judiciary having the power to issue a verdict, defendants being treated with dignity and respect, adjudication being based on evidence and *in dubio pro reo* are all related to protecting the basic rights of those accused, and constitute the meta-principles of POI. They prevent criminal justice agencies from treating those merely accused as criminals.

[61] Liz Campbell, James Chalmers and Antony Duff, 'The presumption of innocence' (2014) 8 *Criminal Law and Philosophy*, 283–284.
[62] In some circumstances, it may also be necessary to extend POI into substantive criminal law issues, as some scholars have argued. See, e.g. Patrick Tomlin, 'Could the presumption of innocence protect the guilty?' (2014) 8 *Criminal Law and Philosophy*, 431–447.

Hence, it is far from satisfactory to simply establish the principle that adjudicative power belongs to the judiciary, as does China's 1996 CPL, or to include an article prohibiting forced self-incrimination, as does the 2012 version. China still has a long way to go to reach international standards of POI, particularly with regard to safeguarding a defendant's dignity and protecting his or her fundamental rights.

5.2   Promoting and Safeguarding Defendants' Human Dignity and Fundamental Rights

Whilst well intentioned, CPL (2012) fails to change the system of compulsory measures in any substantial way. Judicial review was not introduced to restrain the security organs' powers of investigation or their ability to implement such measures as search, seizure, arrest, detention and residential surveillance. Hence, China's criminal justice system lacks effective checks and balances, leading to unsatisfactory treatment of those accused of crimes. As the amended CPL has been in existence only three years, it is premature to discuss new amendments. Nevertheless, judicial review mechanisms remain key to reforming the country's compulsory measure system. Only by creating judicial oversight can investigative misconduct be effectively prohibited.

In addition to legislative reform, a subtle and reasonable interpretative approach is needed to promote defendants' fundamental rights. The obligation to provide truthful answers should be interpreted as an obligation to tell the truth if a suspect voluntarily waives his or her right to silence instead of as an obligation to endure interrogation and confess to the crimes of which he or she is accused, the interpretation that the People's Procuratorates and public security organs prefer. At the same time, judges should not issue judgments against defendants simply because they fail to make a statement or answer questions. In other words, the law should be interpreted to ensure that the effect of the recently introduced article protecting a defendant's privilege against self-incrimination is not undermined by the original CPL's provision concerning his or her obligation to tell the truth.

If accepted in practice, that interpretation could provide the basis for potential modification of the CPL and the introduction of a right to avoid self-incrimination. Considering that the public security organs and Procuratorates are highly unlikely to accept the interpretation in practice, it might be better for China to take gradual steps towards enforcing the right to silence. In this regard, the experience of the United Kingdom might prove valuable in devising a modest solution. In principle, a criminal suspect has the right to choose to speak or remain silent. Once he or she chooses to speak, however, then he or she must tell the truth.

CPL (2012) sets the conditions for granting bail and residential surveillance that render these two alternative non-custodial compulsory measures practical. However, these institutional changes are insufficient to lower the rates of pre-trial detention. Individual police officers and prosecutors strive to achieve high rates of detention largely because the performance system on which they are assessed requires them to do so. Clearly, not all suspects need to be detained at the pre-trial stage. Hence, that performance system needs to be abandoned.

Altering the spatial structure of the courtroom to allow defendants to sit with their lawyers would also support defendants' right to a defence. Doing so would also render lawyer–client communication more convenient, as well as make the status between prosecutor and defendant appear more equal and the trial judge appear more neutral. Furthermore, it is essential that defendants no longer be forced to wear prison uniforms in court.

5.3   Reforming the Mechanisms of Criminal Proof and Promoting in Dubio Pro Reo

China should avoid the practice of finding the accused guilty but providing a lighter sentence when the judge cannot confirm his or her guilt beyond reasonable doubt. Whilst the goal of such avoidance is clear, it cannot be achieved without improving investigators' evidence-collecting capacity. In other words, the reason China's criminal justice system emphasises crime control over justice may be that the investigative techniques at the disposal of the police are underdeveloped and unsatisfactory in practice. A solution is to provide the country's investigate agencies with more resources.

Finally, the discrepancy between two types of judgments, that is, finding the accused innocent according to the law and finding him or her innocent owing to a lack of evidence, needs to be abandoned. In the current CPL, even if an individual is found not guilty because of a lack of evidence and released by the court, the police can still continue their investigation and the prosecutor can still recharge him or her based on newfound evidence. Such a situation is not only inconsistent with *in dubio pro reo*, but also renders acquittals inconclusive. Implementation of the reforms proposed herein is consistent with the current statutory regime and would bring POI in China in line with international standards.

4

Judicial Approach to Human Rights in Transitional China*

SHUCHENG WANG

1 Introduction

There is no doubt that the courts, as state actors, play an indispensable role in providing effective judicial remedies to human rights violations. However, current scholarship on the role of the judicial remedies for the violation of international human rights is based primarily on liberal democracies. Little attention has been paid to the effectiveness of judicial enforcement in illiberal states because the assumption is that such states are generally hostile towards genuine human rights. In liberal democracies, it is generally assumed that the courts will provide effective judicial remedies to injured parties through coercive orders, which is largely compatible with the legal maxim that 'where there is no remedy, there is no right'. Nevertheless, current scholarship on models of judicial remedies of human rights violations, whether strong or weak, is grounded primarily in democratic theories of the majority prevailing when, acting through their representatives, they enact statutes that are consistent with reasonable interpretations of the constitution even if those interpretations differ from those of the courts.[1] It is doubtful whether such theories are applicable to illiberal regimes. For instance, authoritarian systems are perceived to rely on the courts to confer legitimacy on decisions that may not be fair or equitable.[2] Moreover, it

---

* This chapter is partly based on my dissertation research in International Human Rights Law (MSt) at the University of Oxford.
[1] Mark Tushnet, *Weak Courts, Strong Rights: Judicial Review and Social Welfare Rights in Comparative Constitutional Law* (Princeton, NJ: Princeton University Press, 2008), p. 264.
[2] Pierre Landry, 'The institutional diffusion of courts in China: evidence from survey data', in Tom Ginsburg and Tamir Moustafa (eds.), *Rule by Law: The Politics of Courts in Authoritarian Regimes* (Cambridge: Cambridge University Press, 2008), p. 207.

is also generally assumed that illiberal regimes use the courts as pawns to uphold the interests of governing elites and frustrate the efforts of their opponents.[3] Thus, the prevailing impression of illiberal or authoritarian states in the context of human rights is that political parties are non-existent, judicial independence is impaired, freedom of the press is suppressed and citizens are stripped of access to institutions that can effectively protect their interests.[4]

However, it cannot be denied that the courts in illiberal states have their own mechanisms of human rights enforcement, no matter how they may differ from those of liberal democracies. On this point, Shapiro explains: 'An authoritarian regime may choose to establish or maintain an inherited, relatively independent, effective judiciary. It may allow that judiciary some human rights leeway. The judges may define the judicial role to include some judicial review of government actions'.[5] In the case of China, although it is an illiberal state under the leadership of the Chinese Communist Party (CCP), it has formally embraced the concept of 'human rights'. Of the thirteen core international human rights treaties highlighted by the Office of the United Nations High Commissioner for Human Rights, China is now a party to six and a signatory to two. Moreover, Chinese domestic law has developed and expanded dramatically since the 1980s. Historically, the expansion of the Chinese legal system, centred on the country's constitution, points in the direction of tremendous progress in the rule of law with regard to human rights, with numerous Chinese laws now containing explicit human rights applications.[6] This observation also ties in with the observation that embracing and strengthening the rule of law automatically bolster the protection of rights, as there is a core of human rights inherent in the law itself.[7]

---

[3] Tamir Moustafa, 'Law and resistance in authoritarian states: the judicialization of politics in Egypt', in Ginsburg and Moustafa, *Rule by Law*, p. 132.

[4] Ibid., p. 143.

[5] Martin Shapiro, 'Courts in authoritarian regimes', in Ginsburg and Moustafa, *Rule by Law*, p. 332.

[6] As noted, by comparison, the United States is a party to five and signatory to three, and Japan is a party to eight. Both Japan and the United States have signed or ratified the same eight treaties as China. See Ming Wan, 'Human rights lawmaking in China: domestic politics, international law, and international politics' (2007) 29 *Human Rights Quarterly*, 727.

[7] Shapiro, 'Courts in authoritarian regimes', pp. 329–330. Shapiro seems to ignore the fact that authoritarian states may embrace human rights formally, although in a different sense from liberal democracies, as he says that authoritarian regimes have no real allegiance to rights.

Admittedly, the vast majority of scholarship exploring the judicial implementation of international human rights has been carried out in the context of liberal democracies with judicial independence,[8] with little attention paid to the issue in illiberal states, where the courts have a distinct status. However, the rapid development of the legal systems in some illiberal states is prompting scholars to shift their attention away from liberal democracies to the court systems and judicial remedies in authoritarian regimes.[9] An important but largely overlooked issue is how and to what extent the courts in illiberal states can enforce human rights domestically. Authoritarian regimes have become increasingly diverse since the end of the Cold War. For example, the human rights regime in China has already deviated from the track of other former communist states, particularly since it adopted an open door policy and began to implement free market mechanisms domestically. However, that deviation is difficult to explain with reference to traditional theories of authoritarianism or liberal democracies.

Against this backdrop, this chapter illustrates the distinctive mechanism of the judicial enforcement of human rights in China. More specifically, it examines (1) the way in which the Chinese courts are weak in remedying human rights abuses, and how they differ from the courts in liberal democracies, and (2) the extent to which the Chinese courts are able to enforce human rights domestically by adjudicating cases lodged by aggrieved parties within their own jurisdictions.

2 Justiciability of Human Rights in China's Weak Courts

In terms of the judicial enforcement of human rights, it is necessary to distinguish between two types of human rights: fundamental human rights and human rights that have been constitutionalised or legalised. According to the orthodox view of positivists, the former lack the legal status that the latter clearly enjoy. As Bentham states, 'Right, the substantive right, is the child of law; from real laws come real rights; but from imaginary laws, from "law of nature" [can only come] "imaginary

---

[8] See, e.g. Rodney Harrison, 'Domestic enforcement of international human rights in courts of law: some recent developments' (1995) 21 *Commonwealth Law Bulletin*, 1290–1305; Edward D. Re, 'Judicial enforcement of international human rights' (1994) 27 *Akron Law Review*, 281–300; M. Shah Alam, 'Enforcement of international human rights law by domestic courts: a theoretical and practical study' (2006) 53 *Netherlands International Law Review*, 339–438.

[9] See, e.g. Ginsburg and Moustafa, *Rule by Law*.

rights".[10] Thus, if the courts are to enforce human rights, those rights must first and foremost be constitutionalised or legalised. Only then can they be judicially enforceable and act as a restraint on a popular government.[11] It is obvious that China lacks parallel courts with judicial independence like those in liberal democracies, where judicial independence is constitutionally guaranteed. In fact, China's court do play a weak role in enforcing human rights, albeit within an illiberal regime.

2.1   Status of the Courts under the People's Congress System in a Single-Party State

Since China launched economic reforms in 1978, it has been gradually embracing the rule-of-law principle and endeavouring to establish an independent judiciary. It has been noted that reliance on familial, tribal, clan and personal solidarities is a tremendously inefficient way of running a modern state with complex bureaucracies. More institutionalised methods of monitoring are necessary for authoritarian states with expansive bureaucracies.[12] In general, such states also have constitutions with entrenched human rights that can be taken as the basis for the ruling regime's legitimacy. Unsurprisingly, authoritarian systems often rely on the courts to confer legitimacy on political decisions that may be neither fair nor equitable. For example, the victims of the Soviet show trials of the 1930s; political opponents in fascist Italy, Argentina and Brazil; and the infamous Gang of Four in China were all tried in formal courts.[13] However, it cannot be denied that, in China at least, an attempt has been made to establish an inherited, relatively independent and effective judiciary, and also to afford the judiciary some leeway where human rights are concerned. One understandable criticism concerning judicial independence in China is that almost all judges are members of the CCP. Therefore, in practice the party can control them through party discipline. Furthermore, information flows are heavily controlled, and social activists and lawyers who take on judicial institutions may be harassed.[14] After all, China's judicial system operates under the People's Congress

---

[10] Jeremy Bentham, *The Works of Jeremy Bentham (Judicial Procedure, Anarchical Fallacies, Works on Taxation)*, (London: Simpkin Marshall & Co, 1843), vol. II, p. 523.

[11] Tushnet, *Weak Courts, Strong Rights*, pp. 230–231; Michael J. Perry, *The Political Morality of Liberal Democracy* (Cambridge: Cambridge University Press, 2010), pp. 159–161.

[12] Moustafa, 'Law and resistance', 141.

[13] Landry, 'The institutional diffusion of courts', 207.   [14] Ibid., 209.

system, within which the National People's Congress (NPC) is the highest organ of state power, with its permanent body being the Standing Committee of the NPC (NPCSC).[15] Accordingly, the local People's Congresses at various levels are local organs of state power.[16] Therefore, although the Chinese Constitution stipulates that the People's Courts should exercise judicial power independently in accordance with the provisions of law and are not subject to interference by any administrative organ, public organisation or individual,[17] they are responsible to the NPC, which created them.[18] The courts are thus weak in the sense that they are under the control of the People's Congress, which has not yet been democratised and can be manipulated by the CCP.[19] In practice, it is principally the CCP that chooses and recommends nominees to the People's Congress for appointment, and single-candidate elections are the primary rule.[20]

Comparatively speaking then, the courts in China are weak in terms of human rights enforcement because they do not enjoy the same degree of judicial independence as those in liberal democracies. However, to say that they are weak with a low degree of judicial independence is not to say that they play no role at all in the human rights arena. By the end of the Cultural Revolution, future Chinese leader Deng Xiaoping had realised that insufficient access to the law was one of the causes of the many abuses during that period, which led him to expand access to state courts and law schools.[21] Those in the legal profession were rehabilitated, and, under the guidelines for developing a free market economy, an independent judiciary was considered a necessary condition for both individual liberty and economic prosperity.[22] Accordingly, the Administrative Procedure Law (APL) afforded the courts a certain degree of judicial review power. Therefore, although China remains an illiberal state, citizens can challenge the government simply by initiating litigation, a process that

---

[15] Constitution of the People's Republic of China (PRC), 1982, art. 57.   [16] Ibid., art. 96.
[17] Ibid., art. 126.   [18] Ibid, art. 128.
[19] See, e.g. Zhe Sun, 'Party and parliament in a reforming socialist state: the remaking of the National People's Congress in China (1979–1999)', PhD thesis, Columbia University (2000).
[20] For more details on the features of communist legislatures, see, e.g. Daniel Nelson and Stephen White, eds., *Communist Legislatures in Comparative Perspective* (London: MacMillan Press, 1982), pp. 1–13.
[21] For more details, see Simon Leys, 'China: from Mao to Deng' (1997) 1 *International Socialist Review*.
[22] World Bank, *World Development Report 2002: Building Institutions for Markets*, available from https://openknowledge.worldbank.org/handle/10986/5984, accessed 2 January 2015.

requires few financial resources and allows activists to circumvent the highly restrictive, corporatist political framework.[23] Furthermore, in 2014, China amended the APL to broaden the scope of court jurisdiction over cases involving government agencies. The amendment stipulates that a citizen, a legal person or an organisation has the right to file a lawsuit in the People's Courts in accordance with the law when they consider that an administrative action by administrative organs or personnel has infringed their lawful rights and interests.[24] In this respect, Shapiro notes that even an authoritarian regime may purport to establish an independent judiciary, and, given the global appeal of 'human rights', the courts are likely to enjoy a certain degree of independence and associate themselves with rights.[25]

Nonetheless, the courts remain weak in that the scope of court jurisdiction over cases is limited by the exclusion of administrative acts of a legislative nature made by government agencies from the scope of judicial review. In addition, China does not yet have an effective system of constitutional judicial review; that is, the courts cannot perform a constitutional review in practice. Interestingly, however, even though taking local officials to court is often akin to throwing an egg against a stone, many victims of administrative malfeasance continue to do so anyway, with the number of administrative lawsuits ballooning from 5,240 in 1987 to 129,133 in 2010.[26] Hence, despite the major shortcomings of the Chinese legal system, and the relatively low status of the judiciary within the political hierarchy, a progressive trend is unmistakable. As noted, the CCP itself is publicly committed to modernising the country's legal system and human rights legislation and to building more autonomous judicial and legal institutions than are typically the case in Leninist regimes.[27]

2.2 Justiciability of Legalised Human Rights

Human rights are not concerned simply with ideals and lofty goals; their focus is on the possibility and feasibility of giving legal effect to ideals and moral norms.[28] General Comment 9 of the UN Committee on Economic,

---

[23] Moustafa, 'Law and resistance', 151.   [24] APL, art. 2.
[25] Shapiro, 'Courts in authoritarian regimes', 334.
[26] Ji Li, 'Suing the leviathan: an empirical analysis of the changing rate of administrative lawsuits in China' (2013) 10 *Journal of Empirical Legal Studies*, 818–819.
[27] Landry, 'The institutional diffusion of courts', 209.   [28] Re, 'Judicial enforcement', 282.

Social and Cultural Rights with respect to the human rights covenant's domestic application makes it clear that legally binding international human rights standards apply to the domestic legal systems of member states, thereby enabling individuals to seek rights enforcement before national courts and tribunals. The rule requiring the exhaustion of domestic remedies reinforces the primacy of national remedies in this respect. The existence and further development of international procedures for the pursuit of individual claims are important, but such procedures are ultimately supplementary to national remedies. Although states adopt a variety of approaches, many constitutional provisions afford the provisions of international human rights treaties priority over inconsistent domestic laws.[29] In other words, legally speaking, the first and most important way for a state to enforce human rights is to constitutionalise or legalise them in a way that allows rights in a moral sense to be transferred into legally enforceable norms, which is a precondition for courts to implement them thereafter.

In fact, chapter 2 of the PRC Constitution enumerates many fundamental rights. Owing to the constitution's high status, it is understandable that certain constitutional rights are further specified and implemented through the enactment of ordinary legislation. For example, the specifics of the right to work, which is enshrined in an abstract sense in the constitution (Article 42), are largely covered by ordinary legislation, including the Labour Law and Employment Promotion Law. Enforcing a specific legal right through ordinary legislation concurrently enforces the corresponding constitutional right in part even though the complete fulfilment of the constitutional right may not be guaranteed.

In the context of China's civil law tradition, the main function of the courts is to apply the laws made by the legislature, thereby remedying violations of legal rights. Given that China has created a comprehensive litigation system, covering civil, criminal and administrative proceedings, any citizen can bring a lawsuit to remedy the violation of his or her human rights on the condition that the rights concerned have been legalised in ordinary legislation. The extent to which the courts can rely on such legislation was specified by the Supreme People's Court (SPC) in

---

[29] See Committee on Economic, Social and Cultural Rights, General Comment 9, The Domestic Application of the Covenant (Nineteenth session, 1998), UN Doc E/C. 12/1998/24 (1998).

2009 in *Provisions on the Citation of Legal Documents as Laws and Regulations in the Judgments* (*Provisions* hereafter), which stipulate that:

1 A criminal judgment shall cite laws, legal interpretations or judicial interpretations. Article 4 of these Provisions shall apply to the citation of normative legal documents in judgments of civil suits collateral to criminal proceedings (Article 3).
2 A civil judgment shall cite laws, legal interpretations or judicial interpretations, and may directly cite the administrative regulations, local regulations, or regulations on the exercise of autonomy and separate regulations that should be applied (Article 4).
3 An administrative judgment shall cite laws, legal interpretations, administrative regulations or judicial interpretations, and may directly cite the local regulations, regulations on the exercise of autonomy and separate regulations, and interpretations of administrative regulations or administrative rules promulgated by the State Council or the departments authorized by the State Council, which should be applied (Article 5).

It is clear that, in the Chinese legal system, the courts can remedy a violation of legislated rights by relying on the following types of ordinary legislation: (1) laws,[30] (2) legal interpretations (*favl jieshi*),[31] (3) judicial interpretations, (4) administrative regulations (*xingzheng fagui*),[32] (5) local regulations (*defang xing fagui*),[33] (6) autonomous regulations

---

[30] Art. 7 of the Legislation Law of the PRC states: 'The National People's Congress enacts and amends basic laws governing criminal offences, civil affairs, the State organs and other matters. The Standing Committee of the National People's Congress enacts and amends laws other than the ones to be enacted by the National People's Congress.'

[31] Art. 42 of the Legislation Law of the PRC states: 'The power of legal interpretation belongs to the Standing Committee of the National People's Congress. A law shall be interpreted by the Standing Committee of the National People's Congress if: (1) the specific meaning of a provision needs to be further defined; or (2) after its enactment, new developments make it necessary to define the basis on which to apply the law.'

[32] Art. 56 of the Legislation Law of the PRC states: 'The State Council shall, in accordance with the Constitution and laws, formulate administrative regulations.'

[33] Art. 63 of the Legislation Law of the PRC states: 'The people's congresses or their standing committees of the provinces, autonomous regions and municipalities directly under the Central Government may, in light of the specific conditions and actual needs of their respective administrative areas, formulate local regulations, provided that such regulations do not contradict the Constitution, the laws and the administrative regulations. The people's congresses or their standing committees of the comparatively larger cities may, in light of the specific local conditions and actual needs, formulate local regulations, provided that they do not contradict the Constitution, the laws, the

(*zizhi tiaolie*), (7) separate regulations (*danxing tiaolie*),[34] (8) interpretations of administrative regulations and (9) administrative rules.

An important point to make is that the *Provisions* deliberately exclude the constitution from this list, and thus it can be logically inferred that constitutional issues are not justiciable in the Chinese courts. In other words, constitutionally entrenched rights are not enforceable judicially. Evidence for this can be taken from the record of *Qi Yuling v. Chen Xiaoqi et al.* and the SPC's response to it.[35] The plaintiff, Qi Yuling, passed the entrance exam for a technical school in China in 1990, but the letter of admission was intercepted by the defendant, Chen Xiaoqi. Chen subsequently registered and studied at the school under Qi's name, and then went on to work in a state-owned bank after finishing her studies. Qi did not discover the deception until 1999, at which point she filed a lawsuit against Chen and others for violating her right to her name and right to receive an education.[36] Because the trial court was unable to deal with Qi's argument that the right to receive an education is a constitutional right rather than a civil right written into civil law, it referred the issue to the SPC for clarification. Almost two years later, in 2001, the SPC issued its official reply concerning whether civil liabilities should be borne for the infringement of a citizen's basic right to education under the constitution:

> The request on the case of Qi Yuling v. Chen Xiaoqi et al (No. 258 [1999] of Final Civil Judgment of Shandong) of your court has been received. Through investigation of the facts in this case, we are of the opinion that Chen Xiaoqi and the others have, by means of infringing upon the right of personal name, infringed upon Qi Yuling's basic right to education, which

administrative regulations and the local regulations of their respective provinces or autonomous regions, and they shall submit the regulations to the standing committees of the people's congresses of the provinces or autonomous regions for approval before implementation.'

[34] Art. 66 of the Legislation Law of the PRC states: 'The people's congresses of the national autonomous areas have the power to formulate autonomous regulations and separate regulations on the basis of the political, economic and cultural characteristics of the local nationality (nationalities). The autonomous regulations and separate regulations of the autonomous prefectures or counties shall be submitted to the standing committees of the people's congresses of the relevant provinces, autonomous regions or municipalities directly under the Central Government for approval and shall go into effect upon approval.'

[35] *Qi Yuling v. Chen Xiaoqi et al.* [2001] 5 Zhonghua Renmin Gongheguo Zui Gao Renmin Fayuan Gongbao [Supreme People's Court Gazette] 158.

[36] Ibid.

she enjoys in accordance with the Constitution. Such infringement has
caused specific losses. Therefore, they shall bear the corresponding civil
liabilities.[37]

This judicial interpretation makes it clear that the SPC was not confining
itself to solving the specific issue involved in this case, but was making an
attempt to expand judicial power in a way that would allow the court to
exercise the power of constitutional judicial review.[38] However, such a
practice is criticised in China because it is argued that empowering the
courts to perform constitutional judicial review would subvert the
People's Congress system, under which state power is distributed in
accordance with democratic centralism; that is, the judicial branch is
created by and responsible to the People's Congress. Undoubtedly, the
constitutional position of the courts is much lower than that of the NPC
and NPCSC, which means that the courts are unable to supervise, but
must instead be supervised by, these two bodies.

Because China does not follow the common law system, the *Qi Yuling*
case did not act as a precedent.[39] The SPC revoked its reply in 2008 without giving a reason, which demonstrates that the courts' ability to enforce
constitutionally entrenched rights is not yet accepted in China. However,
legal rights conferred by ordinary legislation, such as the Civil Law and
Criminal Law, can be enforced by the courts in applying them in
particular cases. In fact, in the *Qi Yuling* case, the plaintiff would have
been better served by referring to the Education Law in seeking legal
remedy for the violation of her right to receive an education.[40]

3   Interpretability of Legalised Human Rights

Given that the Chinese courts are able to play a weak role in enforcing
legal rights contained in ordinary legislation, the next issue is the extent
to which they are able to apply and interpret those rights, particularly
when they are obscure and/or insufficiently specific for the court to apply.
Admittedly, the courts in liberal democracies play an indispensable role

---

[37] *The Official Reply of the Supreme People's Court on Whether the Civil Liabilities Shall Be
Borne for the Infringement upon a Citizen's Basic Right to Education Which Is under the
Protection of the Constitution by Means of Infringing upon the Right of Personal Name*
(Adopted at the 1183rd meeting of the Judicial Committee of the SPC on 28 June 2001)
(2001) 25 *Interpretations of the Supreme People's Court.*
[38] Zhiwei Tong, 'A comment on the rise and fall of the Supreme People's Court's reply to Qi
Yuling's case' (2010) 43 *Suffolk University Law Review*, 671.
[39] Ibid., 673–674.   [40] Ibid., 675.

in developing human rights law through the case law system. For example, 'the New Zealand law relating to enforcement of basic human rights through the Courts has burgeoned from a state of judicial recognition of them at a most rudimentary level, to a significant, exciting and continuously developing body of principles'.[41] Moreover, different from elected or appointed officials, 'judges are granted a special independence which, as a practical matter, guarantees a life tenure subject only to removal by impeachment under extraordinary circumstances'.[42] Therefore, 'in a case where there is no contrary legislative expression, and where the interpretation of the statute is in doubt, courts have the opportunity to interpret and apply the statute'.[43] Such judicial power of interpretation is of enormous importance, and, in the process, relevant human rights norms may inform the court of the specific meaning to be afforded the applicable statutory provision in question.[44]

By analogy, in China, although the courts are incapable of enforcing constitutionally recognised rights, they do have a duty to enforce legalised rights. Owing to the significant increase in the decisional independence of China's courts overall, notwithstanding the problems that remain in politically sensitive and/or socioeconomic cases and a number of institutional weaknesses, particularly in lower level courts,[45] they now enjoy a certain degree of interpretation discretion, which is often necessary when a case involves ambiguities within a statute. For example, as

---

[41] For instance, the first major progression by the New Zealand courts from the recognition and protection of traditional civil rights to a broader range of human rights, as recognised under international law, can perhaps be said to have occurred with two important cases in 1986 and 1987: *Te Weehi v. Regional Fisheries Officer* [1986] 1 NZLR 680 and *New Zealand Maori Council v. Attorney-General* [1987] 1 NZLR 641 (CA). See also Harrison, 'Domestic enforcement', 1291.

[42] Re, 'Judicial enforcement', 288.   [43] Ibid., 286–287.   [44] Ibid.

[45] See, e.g. Randall Peerenboom, 'Judicial independence in China: common myths and unfounded assumptions', in Randall Peerenboom (ed.), *Judicial Independence in China: Lessons for Global Rule of Law Promotion* (Cambridge: Cambridge University Press, 2009). Peerenboom points out that although there is no shortage of off-the-shelf guidelines for promoting judicial independence, there is a danger of description passing as prescription, that is, of taking institutions in the United States or Europe as necessary and sufficient for other countries. Conversely, any deviations from this standard 'model' are condemned. Thus, China's regulatory innovations – including individual case supervision, adjudicative committees, the extensive incentive structure for judges and, most of all, the role of party organs in the court system – have all been widely criticised. However, the wide variation in legal systems calls into question what is actually needed, as do the poor results when developing countries try to mimic institutions and practices that have evolved over centuries in certain developed countries.

noted previously, although the courts cannot rely on constitutional provisions as a legal basis for adjudication, they can use them as reasoning to support claims for legalised rights. In *Guo Guosong v. Fang Shimin*, the court reasoned that the constitution protects the personal dignity of citizens, which is inviolable, and further interpreted 'personal dignity' as including the inherent 'right of reputation', which was legalised by the General Principles of Civil Law (GPCL; *minfa tongze*) and is enforceable judicially.[46] In addition, in *Zhu Guoxia et al. v. Ping An Insurance Company of China*, the court reasoned that 'the citizens, though retired, [still have] the right to work and get [a] corresponding reward, according to the Constitution and relevant labor laws. Therefore, the claim for lost income shall be supported if it involves downtime and the personal income is lost, no matter [whether] the person is retired or not.'[47] These cases, although decided by the lower courts, demonstrate that constitutional provisions can be used in reasoning by the courts in practice. Legally speaking, only the SPC, which is authorised by the NPCSC, is able to engage in judicial interpretation of a legislative nature on specific issues concerning the application of law in trial work. At the same time, owing to the absence of a case law system, the rationale for the aforementioned judicial decision is not binding but applies only to specific cases.

4   Legal Effect of International Human Rights

In terms of international human rights norms, the experience of various jurisdictions shows that courts may play a crucial role in enforcing these internationally accepted moral norms even though not all treaty provisions are self-executing and the implementation of legislation may be required to give certain treaty provisions legal effect as domestic law.[48] Interestingly, the courts, on the one hand, may be criticised for being too conservative in their approach to human rights and for not making sufficiently strong orders against their respective governments to meet

---

[46] *Guo Guosong v. Fang Shimin (Guo Guosong Yu Fang Shimin Minyu Quan Jiufeng Shangsu An)* (2014) 4258 Civil Judgments of Guangzhou Intermediate People's Court [Hui Zhong Fa Min Yi Zhong Zi Di 4258 Hao].

[47] *Zhu Guoxia et al. v. Ping An Insurance Company of China (Zhongguo Pingan Caichan Baoxian Gufeng Youxian Gongsi Liaoning Feng Gongsi Yu Zhu Guoxia Deng Jidong Che Jiaotong Shigu Zeren Jiufeng Shangsu An)* (2014) 2395 Civil Judgments of Shenyang Intermediate People's Court [Shen Zhong Min Yi Zhong Zi Di 02395 Hao]

[48] Re, 'Judicial enforcement', 286.

their obligations. On the other hand, judges face difficulties in handling such claims, particularly in navigating between the traditional domains of distinct organs under the principle of the separation of powers.[49] Despite this situation, however, owing to the universal acknowledgement and acceptance of human rights for individuals, today's courts cannot isolate themselves from the great moral issues of the day and must think of the consequences of their decisions, particularly their effect on human rights.[50] In the era of globalisation, with a truly global morality of human rights,[51] the courts, by exercising judicial power, bring the interpretation of law into closer alignment with the morality of human rights.[52] In this regard, Judge Edward D. Re has noted that

> unless a contrary intention is clearly expressed, [statutes] may be construed in accordance with international legal norms. In an ABA Committee Report on Judicial Education on International Law, it is noted that the applicability of international legal norms in particular cases may be limited by considerations of jurisdiction, equity, and due process that apply in all proceedings before the U.S. courts. It is hoped, however, that those considerations not be invoked merely to disguise an unwillingness to accord international legal norms their rightful place in our legal system.[53]

Therefore, the morality embodied in international human rights instruments may permeate domestic law through the judicial application of laws, which is compatible with the following international principle: 'In

---

[49] Varun Gauri and Daniel M. Brinks, eds., *Courting Social Justice: Judicial Enforcement of Social and Economic Rights in the Developing World* (Cambridge: Cambridge University Press, 2010), p. 13.

[50] Re, 'Judicial enforcement', 581, 591–592.

[51] See Michael J. Perry, 'The morality of human rights' (2013) 50 *San Diego Law Review*, 775. As Perry explains, 'the morality of human rights' consists not only of various rights recognised by the great majority of the countries of the world as human rights but also of a fundamental imperative that directs 'all human beings' to 'act towards one another in a spirit of brotherhood'. The imperative – articulated in the very first article of the foundational human rights document of our time, the Universal Declaration of Human Rights – is fundamental in the sense that it serves, in the morality of human rights, as the normative ground for human rights.

[52] See Michael J. Perry, 'Adjudicating rights-based constitutional claims: the morality of human rights and the power of judicial review' (2014) Emory Legal Studies Research Paper No. 14-271, available from http://ssrn.com/abstract=2383424, accessed 25 December 2014. Perry further elaborates that, in the context of the United States, the courts reduce – but do not eliminate – the extent to which US constitutional law is morally deficient, as evaluated from the perspective of the morality of human rights, from the perspective, in particular, of the human right to democratic governance, a core aspect of which is the presumptive right of the majority to prevail.

[53] Re, 'Judicial enforcement', 592.

general, legally binding international human rights standards should operate directly and immediately within the domestic legal system of each State party, thereby enabling individuals to seek enforcement of their rights before national courts and tribunals.'[54]

In China, it is a fact that in most cases it is sufficient for the courts to rely on domestic laws to make decisions because, by 2010, the country had established a comprehensive legal system that covers all areas of society.[55] In terms of international treaties, China has partly incorporated them into the domestic legal system. For example, according to Article 142 of the GPCL, the general principle in the field of civil and commercial law is the following.

> If any international treaty concluded or acceded to by the People's Republic of China contains provisions differing from those in the civil laws of the People's Republic of China, the provisions of the international treaty shall apply, unless the provisions are ones on which the People's Republic of China has announced reservations. International practice may be applied on matters for which neither the law of the People's Republic of China nor any international treaty concluded or acceded to by the People's Republic of China has any provisions.

In addition, Article 260 of the Civil Procedure Law stipulates that 'where there is any discrepancy between an international treaty concluded or acceded to by the People's Republic of China and this Law, the provisions of the international treaty shall prevail, except clauses to which the People's Republic of China has declared reservations'.[56] At the same time, certain other statutes, such as the APL, have a similar provision concerning the legal effect of treaties. Hence, in the area of civil and commercial law, the courts are able to use international treaties as a legal basis for decision-making, particularly when there is a discrepancy between an international treaty and a domestic law. For example, in the case of *Cyprus Kang Da Shipping Co.'s Application for the Enforcement of Arbitral Award*, the Guangzhou Maritime Court based its decision on Article 5 of the Convention on Recognition and Enforcement of Foreign Arbitral Awards.[57]

---

[54] Committee on Economic, Social and Cultural Rights, General Comment 9.
[55] *China's Comprehensive Legal System*, http://english.cntv.cn/program/china24/20110310/104677.shtml, accessed 26 December 2014.
[56] Civil Procedure Law of the PRC, art. 260.
[57] *Cyprus Kang Da Shipping Co.'s Application for the Enforcement of Arbitral Award Case (Sai Pu Lu Si Kang Te Da Hangyun Youxiao Gongsi Shengqing Chengren He Zhixing*

However, China has not yet drafted any specific law concerning the legal effect of international human rights treaties, although it has ratified six of the nine core international human rights instruments, including (1) the International Convention on the Elimination of All Forms of Racial Discrimination, ratified on 29 December 1981; (2) the International Covenant on Economic, Social and Cultural Rights, ratified on 27 March 2001; (3) the Convention on the Elimination of All Forms of Discrimination against Women, ratified on 4 November 1980; (4) the Convention against Torture and Other Cruel, Inhuman or Degrading Treatment or Punishment, ratified on 4 October 1988; (5) the Convention on the Rights of the Child (CRC), ratified on 2 March 1992 and (6) the Convention on the Rights of Persons with Disabilities, ratified on 1 August 2008.

Although it is generally argued that international human rights instruments differ from other international treaties, and the method of 'transformation' is to be adopted for the implementation of international human rights instruments in China,[58] that argument does not rule out the possibility that judges may use the provisions of international human rights treaties to support certain rights claims in domestic laws, or even to make a judicial decision directly, in connection with Article 142 of the GPCL. For example, in *Dong and Fulan's Divorce Case*, the court stated that because the CRC has been ratified by the NPCSC, it applies domestically in accordance with the GPCL. It further ruled that separating the two children involved in the case from their parents would be compatible with 'the best interests of the child', which is the primary consideration according to the following provisions of the CRC.[59]

> Article 2 (1): States Parties shall respect and ensure the rights set forth in the present Convention to each child within their jurisdiction without

Lundon Zhongcai Caijue An) (1997) 5 Judgments of Guangzhou Maritime Court [Guang Hai Fa Zhan Zi Di 05 Hao].

[58] 'Implementation of international human rights instruments in China: an interview with Professor Mo Jihong' (2008) 37, available from www.humanrights.cn/cn/zt/qita/rqzz/2008/01/t20080417_336844.htm, accessed 11 November 2015.

[59] *Dong and Fulan's Divorce Case (Dong Moumou Yu Fu Lan Moumou Lihun Jiufeng An)* (2013) 1661 Civil Judgment of Shanghai 2nd Intermediate People's Court [Hu Er Zhong Min Yi (Min) Zhong Zi Di 1661 Hao]. For other cases, judges may refer to certain provisions of human rights treaties for the purpose of interpreting domestic laws or to justify their decisions. See *Chen Moumou Robbery Case (Chen Moumou Qiangjie An)*, (2012) 25 Criminal Judgement of Shanghai High People's Court [Hu Gao Xing Fu Zi Di 25 Hao].

discrimination of any kind, irrespective of the child's or his or her parent's or legal guardian's race, colour, sex, language, religion, political or other opinion, national, ethnic or social origin, property, disability, birth or other status.

Article 3 (1): In all actions concerning children, whether undertaken by public or private social welfare institutions, courts of law, administrative authorities or legislative bodies, the best interests of the child shall be a primary consideration.

Article 9 (1): States Parties shall ensure that a child shall not be separated from his or her parents against their will, except when competent authorities subject to judicial review determine, in accordance with applicable law and procedures, that such separation is necessary for the best interests of the child. Such determination may be necessary in a particular case such as one involving abuse or neglect of the child by the parents, or one where the parents are living separately and a decision must be made as to the child's place of residence.

Of course, such a ruling is still rare in trial practice, but is to some extent compatible with China's ongoing ambition to integrate with and gain further influence over the world, as reflected in the country's more active role within the UN Human Rights Council in recent years.

When it comes to civil and political rights, in contrast, as an authoritarian state, China generally adopts an oppositional stance. As Randall Peerenboom points out:

Government leaders have reached out to the foreign community for assistance on many rights issues. However, there has been greater reluctance to accept the advice of foreign parties when it comes to civil and political rights. Government leaders might be more willing to revisit sensitive issues regarding free speech, religious freedoms and the rights of minorities if they felt their concerns were taken more seriously, and the difficulties that many countries face on these issues were acknowledged.[60]

Against this background, the Chinese courts have, in general, proved incapable of adjudicating civil and political rights issues based on international instruments or even the country's own constitution owing to a lack of specific legal instruments, although the possibility remains for citizens to seek civil and political rights remedies on the basis of ordinary domestic legislation if available. Ironically, specific ordinary legislation crafted by the People's Congress under the leadership of the single-party

---

[60] Randall Peerenboom, 'Assessing human rights in China: why the double standard?' (2005) 38 *Cornell International Law Journal*, 163.

state in some instances imposes restraints on civil and political rights. Consider the following necessary conditions on limiting human rights.

> First, any interference with a right should be prescribed by law (condition of legality). Second, it must be justified by the pursuance of a legitimate aim (condition of legitimacy). Third, the interference must be limited to what is necessary for the fulfilment of that aim, which means that it must be appropriate to pursuing the objective, and that it may not go beyond what is required in order to effectively achieve that aim – or, at a minimum, that all the interests involved should be carefully balanced against one another (condition of proportionality).[61]

With regard to the first condition, the perhaps excessive limitation imposed by ordinary legislation on civil and political rights technically meets the condition of legality. However, with regard to the second and third conditions, owing to the absence of a constitutional judicial review system in China, possibly excessive limitations imposed by the law cannot be challenged judicially on a constitutional basis. For example, although freedom of religion is constitutionalised, in practice it is the CCP that dictates the policy on the regulation of religion and enforces that policy in part through laws and administrative regulations, whilst the Politburo acts as a hub responsible for formulating all important CCP policies.[62] Unregistered religious groups such as house churches can be penalised by the government on the grounds of legislation or policy, and even labelled 'evil organisations'. Hence, civil and political rights can be curtailed by ordinary legislation or CCP policies, and the courts are incapable of providing effective remedies. This is of course not to say that Chinese citizens enjoy no civil and political rights at all, but rather that those rights are of a very limited scope or, perhaps rhetorically, are rights with so-called 'Chinese characteristics'.

5 Conclusion

In the judicial approach to human rights, it is generally accepted that such rights must first be constitutionalised or legalised domestically, although international treaties may play a role in the process of statutory

---

[61] Olivier De Schutter, *International Human Rights Law: Cases, Materials, Commentary* (Cambridge: Cambridge University Press, 2010), p. 288.

[62] For further details, see Darin Carlson, 'Understanding Chinese-US conflict over freedom of religion: the Wolf-Spector Freedom from Religious Persecution Acts of 1997 and 1998' (2013) 3 *BYU Law Review*, 563, 578–579.

interpretation, as illustrated in this chapter. In liberal democracies with judicial independence, the courts generally provide effective judicial remedies for violations of legalised rights through the award of damages, mandatory injunctions and the like.[63] However, in China, the courts are weak in the sense that they enjoy a low degree of judicial independence in practice. Although China has embraced the rule-of-law principle whereby all, including the CCP, are subject to the law, in practice judges are members of the CCP and thus subject to party discipline. Also, the courts have been created by and are responsible to the People's Congress system, which has yet to be democratised and can, to a certain extent, be manipulated by the CCP. However, the historical lesson of the Cultural Revolution taught China the importance of judicial independence to economic development because it provides governance with legitimacy and guarantees the interests of investors. Hence, economic rights are largely enforceable by the Chinese courts. In addition, in the process of establishing a comprehensive legal system, China has adopted a form of administrative judicial review through which citizens are able to challenge the government for the violation of human rights. However, as noted, the courts remain weak in the sense that constitutional judicial review is not permitted, and general legislation and regulations are generally not subject to judicial scrutiny. Therefore, the Chinese courts can enforce only those human rights that have been legalised by ordinary legislation, thereby excluding those in the constitution. Owing to the absence of a constitutional judicial review system, limitations on legal rights via legislation, even though perhaps excessive, cannot be challenged with reference to the constitution in the Chinese legal system. In this regard, civil and political rights guaranteed by the constitution can be restrained by legislation. Hence, the Chinese case is an example of a dual model of judicial enforcement of human rights in an illiberal state where economic development is paramount.

---

[63] See Tushnet, *Weak Courts, Strong Rights*.

5

Public Enforcement of Securities Laws

A Case of Convergence?*

CHAO XI AND XUANMING PAN

1 Introduction

This chapter examines the process of adoption and adaption in which foreign norms and local conditions have interacted to shape the evolutionary trajectory of the China Securities Regulatory Commission's (CSRC's) enforcement programme.[1] It argues that two salient features of Chinese securities regulation – the increasing emphasis on enforcement and the increasing reliance on trial-like procedures in enforcement – are likely to have been inspired by exogenous sources, more specifically, the United States (US) approach to securities regulation, and also caused by endogenous conditionalities.

Prima facie, the CSRC has derived some of its philosophies, doctrines, institutions, rules and practices from the United States and, perhaps to a lesser extent, the United Kingdom.[2] The influence of the US experience appears to have been both ideological and institutional. The ideological appeal of US securities regulation has been firm and long-standing amongst Chinese securities regulators, who seem to have perceived a causal link between the US-style securities regulation and its robust securities markets. For example, CSRC founding Chairman Zhou Zhengqing viewed the post–Great Depression development of the US

---

* This research has been supported by a General Research Fund grant from the Research Grants Council of the Hong Kong SAR (CUHK-452913).
[1] For the discourse on divergence/convergence in the context of Chinese corporate governance, see, e.g. Chao Xi, *Corporate Governance and Legal Reform in China* (London: Wildy, Simmons and Hill, 2009).
[2] For a discussion of how the UK and US approaches to takeover regulation have competed to determine the shape of Chinese takeover regulation, see Chao Xi, 'The political economy of takeover regulation: what does the mandatory bid rule in China tell us?' (2015) 2 *Journal of Business Law*, 142–164.

securities markets as a direct consequence of the creation of the US Securities and Exchange Commission (SEC).[3] It thus follows that the future of the Chinese securities markets would hinge upon whether a similarly sophisticated framework of securities regulation can be put in place and take root. This line of reasoning is so deeply entrenched that even the recent global financial crisis – which otherwise casts a long shadow over the legitimacy and appeal of US dominance and Western capitalism as a whole – does not seem to have dissuaded Chinese securities regulators from looking to the US for inspiration. A recent manifestation of this inclination is the widely read 2013 policy piece by former CSRC Chairman Xiao Gang (from 2013 to 2016), published in *Qiushi*, a mouthpiece of the Communist Party of China (CPC), justifying his proposal to re-position the CSRC towards an enforcement-led regulatory agency with reference to the SEC.[4]

The impact of US securities regulation has also been institutionalised and channelled through the roles that influential individuals have played, particularly in the formative years of the CSRC. For example, Gao Xiqing, a vice-chairman of the CSRC between 1999 and 2003, and Laura Cha, the CSRC's vice-chairwoman from 2001 to 2004, both received their legal education and practised law in the United States.[5] Their appointment to senior leadership roles in the CSRC supposedly served as a conduit through which knowledge of the principles and practices of US securities regulation came to influence the fledgling CSRC. The CSRC's International Advisory Council (the Council) was presumably an additional source of foreign input into the body's initial setup and its enforcement programme. The Council's first plenary meeting in 2004 featured the strong presence of members with a US background, including Stanley Fisher (then with Citigroup), John Thornton (formerly with Goldman Sachs), John S. Wadsworth Jr. (then with Morgan Stanley) and, most notably for the purposes of our discussion, Gary G. Lynch,

---

[3] See Zhengqing Zhou, *A Reader on Knowledge of Securities* (Beijing: China Financial Publishing House, 1998), p. 429.

[4] Gang Xiao, 'Regulatory enforcement: the cornerstone of capital market development' (2013) 15 *Qiushi*, 29–31.

[5] Chao Xi, 'In search of an effective monitoring board model: board reforms and the political economy of corporate law in China' (2006) 22(1) *Connecticut Journal of International Law*, 1–46; see also Stephen Green, *China's Stockmarket: A Guide to Its Progress, Players and Prospects* (New York: Bloomberg Press, 2003), p. 237; Svenja Schlichting, *Internationalising China's Financial Markets* (Basingstoke: Palgrave Macmillan, 2008), pp. 153–156.

former Chief of the SEC Division of Enforcement (1985–1989).[6] To the extent that familiarity with a foreign legal system amongst local rule makers and their advisors plays a role in the adoption of that system,[7] the intensive involvement of these senior individuals with extensive professional experience with US securities laws presumably affords the US approach to securities regulation particularly heavy weight.

Having illustrated the relevance of the US experience to the formation and evolution of China's approach to securities regulation, this chapter proceeds to discuss how this foreign origin of Chinese securities regulation might have interacted with domestic conditions to bear on the CSRC enforcement programme. Drawing on a dataset of CSRC enforcement actions taken against securities violations, Section 2 of the chapter demonstrates the intensity of the CSRC securities enforcement and provides an overview of the institutional setup of the CSRC enforcement programme. Section 3 examines the evolving role of enforcement relative to the developmental role of the CSRC, and argues that the role of enforcement is gaining increasing significance. Section 4 then discusses the CSRC's growing reliance on the use of trial-like procedures in the Administrative Sanction Commission (ASC) proceedings. Section 5 concludes the chapter.

2 CSRC Enforcement Programme: An Overview

The CSRC is China's primary securities regulator. It is conferred with the power, amongst other things, to take enforcement actions against securities violations and to engage in agency rule-making on the basis of relevant statutory provisions. The 2005 Securities Law empowers the CSRC with a wide range of authority and discretion to impose administrative sanctions and penalties on regulated entities and individuals. More specifically, the CSRC can, by way of an 'administrative sanction' (or *xingzheng chufa*), impose monetary penalties (i.e. fines), or order for disgorgement of ill-gotten profits, or issue administrative orders to cease

---

[6] See CSRC, www.csrc.gov.cn/pub/newsite/gjb/gzdt/200410/t20041019_79370.html. To be sure, the Council was well balanced, with senior representatives from a number of jurisdictions, including Australia, Germany, Hong Kong, Italy, Taiwan and the United Kingdom.

[7] Curtis Milhaupt, 'In the shadow of Delaware? The rise of hostile takeovers in Japan' (2005) 105 *Columbia Law Review*, 2171–2216.

or correct misconduct.[8] The CSRC can also, by way of an 'industry bar' (or *shichang jinru*), ban an individual from associating with a broker-dealer, or bar a professional from practising before the CSRC.[9] So, the administrative sanction and the industry bar are the two primary forms of enforcement actions that the CSRC can bring against securities misconduct.

2.1   Enforcement Programme: Statistics

Official statistics can provide a window into the scope and scale of CSRC enforcement actions against securities violations in recent years. During the 2006–2014 period, for example, the CSRC issued 496 administrative sanctions and 135 industry bars.[10] In the same period, it collected in excess of RMB2 billion in administrative fines and ordered 2,117 individual culprits to disgorge ill-gotten gains.[11] In addition to these administrative actions, 241 cases were referred to the Ministry of Public Security for further criminal investigation.[12]

Whilst these official figures provide a useful broad-brush view of the CSRC enforcement programme, a closer look is warranted to understand better the nature of that programme. For that purpose, we draw on a unique, hand-collected dataset (Dataset) of all formal enforcement actions taken by the CSRC between 2006 and 2012.

As noted, administrative sanctions and industry bars are the two primary forms of enforcement action taken by the CSRC. During the period between 2006 and 2012, the Dataset records 351 instances of the former and 113 of the latter. The two forms of enforcement action are treated in turn in the following.

As Figure 5.1 shows, the annual number of administrative sanctions exhibits a generally upward trend over the period under investigation. There were fewer than 40 in 2006 and 2007, but since 2008 the number has consistently stood above the 50 mark, peaking in 2009, which saw 58 administrative sanctions. Such sanctions can be taken against both firms and individuals, and we begin our discussion with the former. As

---

[8] Chapter 11 of the 2005 Securities Law.   [9] Article 233 of the 2005 Securities Law.
[10] Jingyu Ma, 'A 13-year review of the separation of investigation and adjudication: the continual improvement of both quality and efficiency in securities regulatory enforcement', *Shanghai Zhengquan Bao*, 25 August 2015, www.csrc.gov.cn/pub/shenzhen/xxfw/mtzs/201508/t20150825_283206.htm.
[11] Ibid.   [12] Ibid.

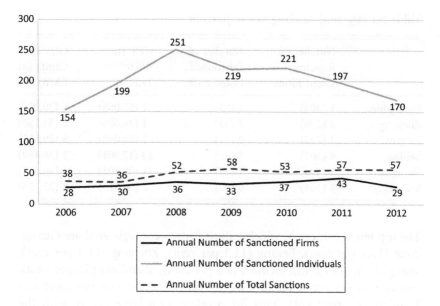

Figure 5.1 Annual load of CSRC administrative sanctions (2006–2012)

Figure 5.1 shows, between 2006 and 2012, 236 firms were sanctioned, with the annual number ranging from 28 to 43, and the average was just shy of 34.

The largest cohort of sanctioned firms during the period of investigation are listed firms (47 per cent) and the firms and individuals that control them (4 per cent). The CSRC also targeted various types of professional service providers, including investment advisors (14 per cent), accounting firms (10 per cent), futures firms (6 per cent) and securities houses (1 per cent). The sanctioned companies include both A-share and B-share firms, although the former (97 per cent) far exceed the latter (3 per cent). Of the A-share firms sanctioned during the period, 53 per cent were listed on the Shenzhen Stock Exchange (SZSE) and 44 per cent on the Shanghai Stock Exchange (SSE).[13]

The places of incorporation of the sanctioned firms indicate some degree of correlation with the strength of various regional economies.

---

[13] To contextualise the SSE versus SZSE divide, as of the end of 2012, there were 2,494 listed companies in the two stock exchanges, of which 954 (38.25 per cent) were listed on the SSE and 1,540 (61.75 per cent) on the SZSE. See CSRC, *2012 Annual Report*, www.csrc.gov.cn/pub/newsite/zjhjs/zjhnb/.

Table 5.1 *Regional ranking in comparison*

	Number of Registered Listed Firms	Number of Sanctioned Listed Firms	GDP (in RMB Trillion)	GDP per Capita (in RMB)
Guangdong	1 (309)	1 (53)	1 (57,068)	4 (30,226)
Zhejiang	2 (226)	3 (35)	4 (34,606)	3 (34,550)
Jiangsu	3 (223)	9 (11)	2 (54,058)	5 (29,677)
Beijing	4 (205)	2 (39)	13 (17,801)	2 (36,469)
Shanghai	5 (194)	4 (27)	11 (20,101)	1 (40,188)
Shandong	6 (144)	6 (17)	3 (50,013)	8 (25,755)

The top ten provinces in which culprit firms were registered are Guangdong (18.1 per cent), Beijing (13.3 per cent), Zhejiang (11.9 per cent), Shanghai (9.2 per cent), Sichuan (7.2 per cent), Shandong (5.8 per cent), Hunan (4.4 per cent), Fujian (4.4 per cent), Jiangsu (3.8 per cent) and Tianjing (2.4 per cent). This list overlaps to a large degree with the ranking of the provinces in which listed firms are registered (see Table 5.1). [14] It also demonstrates some correlation with the ranking of the size and strength of provincial economies, as measured by province-level GDP and per capita GDP, respectively.

We now turn to the individual culprits disciplined by the CSRC by way of administrative sanctions. During the 2006–2012 period, a total of 1,411 individuals were sanctioned. The Dataset reveals some useful information on their attributes. One interesting factual finding is their places of residence, which seem to correlate with the aforementioned places of incorporation of sanctioned firms. The top ten provinces in which the individual culprits resided during the period are Guangdong (16.2 per cent), Beijing (11.3 per cent), Shandong (7.9 per cent), Shanghai (7.7 per cent), Hunan (5.3 per cent), Zhejiang (5.2 per cent), Sichuan (5.2 per cent), Jiangsu (4.8 per cent), Fujian (4.8 per cent) and Hubei (4.8 per cent).

The Dataset also sheds light on the types of sanctions to which individuals are likely to find themselves subjected. In order of severity, these types are warnings, the disgorgement of illegal gains, fines and disqualification orders. They can be used singly and jointly by the CSRC.

[14] Statistics on the places of incorporation were collected from CSMAR. Data on per capita GDP refer to 2012 official statistics on urban and suburban regions; available at http://finance.people.com.cn/GB/8215/356561/359047/.

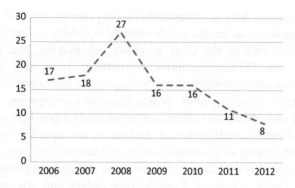

Figure 5.2   CSRC industry bars (2006–2012)

Our findings show warnings and fines to be the two most commonly used disciplinary actions against individual violators. As many as 93 per cent of the individuals involved received either a warning (23 per cent), an order to pay a fine (7 per cent) or a combination of the two (63 per cent). Disqualification orders, which can be very consequential for the individual culprits concerned, were rather uncommon (4 per cent), as were disgorgement orders (3 per cent).

We now turn to the second category of enforcement action, that is, industry bars. As Figure 5.2 shows, the annual number of industry bars fluctuated significantly over the period from 2006 to 2012, increasing from nineteen in 2006 to a peak of twenty-seven in 2008 before dropping considerably to just eight in 2012. In duration, the bars ranged from a two-year bar to a lifetime bar. Three-year, five-year, ten-year and lifetime bars were the most commonly levied in the period under study, with each representing around one-quarter of all bars.

2.2   Institutional Framework of CSRC Enforcement Programme

A defining feature of the CSRC's enforcement programme is formal and organisational separation between the 'investigative' and 'adjudicative' roles. The institutional setup of the two roles, as they currently stand, is discussed in the immediately following, whereas the underlying notion of separation is treated in greater detail in Section 4.

2.2.1   Investigation

The programme's investigative role has three institutional pillars: the Enforcement Bureau (or *jicha ju*), the Enforcement Contingent (or *jicha zongdui*) and the enforcement forces in the CSRC's local offices.

The Enforcement Bureau serves as the nexus point for the CSRC investigation apparatus, and enjoys a wide range of mandates. It first of all plays an important role in the CSRC's agency rule-making, and drafts on behalf of the CSRC substantive regulations, rules and guidelines governing securities enforcement. Perhaps more important is the Bureau's intensive involvement at various stages of investigation. It follows up on tips, complaints and referrals that can lead to investigations; it can initiate informal investigations; it decides on the opening and, where appropriate, closing of investigations; it coordinates (but does not actually undertake) investigations in major cases and cross-regional cases; it can issue temporary travel bans, seizure orders and freezing orders during the course of an investigation; it reviews the investigation reports prepared by the Enforcement Contingent; and it is responsible for the enforcement of any administrative sanctions that the ASC hands out.[15] The Bureau is also concurrently the Office of the Chief Enforcement Officer, which highlights its joint role as overseer and coordinator within the CSRC's investigative functionality.

Despite the Enforcement Bureau's wide-ranging responsibilities, it does not actually carry out any formal investigations, with much of that task relegated to the Enforcement Contingent. The Contingent's jurisdiction focuses on a broad category of so-called 'major, urgent, sensitive or cross-regional' cases, which include potentially violative activities that involve insider trading, market manipulation, misrepresentation and fraudulent share issuance.[16] These types of securities violations are perceived to be of such a serious nature that their investigation is of particular importance and thus needs to be prioritised. These cases presumably require the allocation of considerable resources and the pooling of legal, accounting, auditing and technological expertise. In recognition of this, the Contingent has been allocated a quota of 170 staff members,[17] reportedly making it the most heavily staffed of all CSRC divisions.

In addition to the Enforcement Bureau and Enforcement Contingent, there is a third component of the CSRC investigation apparatus, that is, the investigation forces within the CSRC's local offices. The CSRC's local structure has two limbs. The first comprises the local bureaus in each of the country's twenty-two provinces, four municipalities directly

---

[15] www.csrc.gov.cn/pub/newsite/jcj/.   [16] www.csrc.gov.cn/pub/newsite/jczd/.

[17] CSRC, 'Important reform on the securities enforcement system of our country', 16 November 2007, www.csrc.gov.cn/pub/newsite/zjhxwfb/xwdd/200711/t20071116_68535.html.

under the central government and five autonomous regions, for a total of thirty-one, as well as in each of the five major municipalities (or *jihua danlie shi*). Most of these provincial-level bureaus have at least one internal division (some have two), called the Inspection Division (or *jicha chu*), which is tasked with investigating securities violations. Division personnel typically represent between 11 and 20 per cent of a local bureau's headcount.[18] The second limb of the CSRC's local enforcement structure is the two Commissioner's Offices (or *zhuanyuan ban*) stationed in Shanghai and Shenzhen. These offices are organisationally and operationally separate from the local CSRC bureaus in the two cities. Historically, the Commissioner's Offices have been assigned specific missions on a somewhat ad hoc basis, such as the supervision of distressed securities firms. Starting in 2013, however, when they took over the regional offices of the Enforcement Contingent, their primary mandate has been securities enforcement.[19]

More recently, the CSRC and its local offices have devolved investigative authority to the SSE and SZSE. Under a pilot scheme launched in late 2015, the two exchanges have been delegated the authority to investigate certain designated types of misconduct or specific misconduct on an ad hoc basis. To the extent that the SSE and SZSE are authorised to exercise the investigative power of the CSRC, they act in the name of and on behalf of the CSRC.

2.2.2 Adjudication

The adjudicative role of the CSRC enforcement programme has been in the hands of the ASC since 2002. The ASC operates independently of the CSRC's investigative apparatus, and takes full charge of the adjudicative process by setting up a collegiate bench to hear and decide the individual cases that come before it.[20] It is also tasked with the

---

[18] With the exception of the Shanghai Bureau, where 25 per cent of the staff are with the Inspection Division. See Fenmian Zhou, 'The CSRC reforms its enforcement system', *Fazhi Ribao*, 16 February 2016, www.legaldaily.com.cn/index_article/content/2016-02/15/content_6483432.htm?node=5955

[19] The Enforcement Contingent's own regional offices in Shanghai and Shenzhen were established only in 2012, each with a staffing quota of fifty, presumably with the aim of rendering its forces more proximate to the locations of China's two official stock exchanges. See Xiaohui Zhao and Junjie Tao, 'The CSRC's Enforcement Contingent has appointed two additional forces to expand the enforcement regime', *Xinhua Net*, 30 December 2012, http://news.xinhuanet.com/2012-12/30/c_114206996.htm

[20] Article 4, Rules on the Organisation of the ASC, issued by the CSRC on 29 February 2008.

formulation of the substantive and procedural rules that govern its hearing and decision-making procedures.[21] The ASC comprises both full- and part-time member commissioners, who are typically drawn from the CSRC's own rank-and-file officials, experienced professionals, and senior academics, as well as former members of the judiciary. In an ordinary proceeding, three commissioners sit on a collegiate bench and make an adjudicative decision.[22] The appointment of the bench takes effect with the endorsement of the ASC chairperson, who is also empowered to decide on the recusal of a judge commissioner with respect to given reasons.[23]

The ASC is supported by a dedicated secretariat, which is in turn staffed by professionals with training in the fields of law, accounting and economics who work in the ASC on a full-time basis. They support the ASC with regard to a wide range of routine matters, such as daily clerical administration, policy research and communication with the investigative departments.[24] Furthermore, they may also play a supportive role in drafting, filing, service of process and other procedural matters in the course of adjudication.[25]

The local offices of the CSRC have also recently emerged as important adjudicators in addition to the ASC as a result of the CSRC's devolution of adjudicative power to those offices under a pilot scheme that kicked off in 2010 and has been nationally rolled out since 2013.[26] The local CSRC offices are responsible for the adjudication of administrative sanction cases within their respective jurisdictions.[27]

3   Towards An Enforcement-Led Regulatory Authority

As argued at the outset of this chapter, the SEC has long been a source of inspiration for the CSRC. The SEC is known to be an enforcement-led regulatory agency with a reputation for taking enforcement seriously. The extant discourse defines its regulatory approach as one that assigns a broad range of powers to market participants while maintaining strong

---

[21] Ibid., article 9.   [22] Ibid., article 4.   [23] Ibid., articles 5 and 10.
[24] Ibid., articles 13 and 14.   [25] Ibid.
[26] CSRC, 'The CSRC's local agencies have well accomplished the task of administrative sanction', 25 March 2016, www.csrc.gov.cn/pub/newsite/zjhxwfb/xwdd/201603/t20160325_294745.html.
[27] Rules on the Scope of Official Duty of the CSRC Regional Institutions, issued by the CSRC on 29 October 2015.

oversight of market activities within a robust enforcement tradition.[28] This approach stands in sharp contrast to the United Kingdom's 'light-touch' approach, which emphasises self-regulation to a greater extent. The SEC's enforcement programme serves a critical function in policing compliance with US securities laws.[29]

The ideological appeal of SEC-style, enforcement-led securities regulation is evident in the CSRC's gradual shift from an overall 'developmental' role to one that emphasises enforcement and regulatory discipline. The CSRC's developmental role, which continues to play an important part in China's securities regulation, needs to be understood in the broader context of the country's securities markets. The Chinese stock market was initially created to serve one primary objective: to salvage the ailing state-owned enterprise (SOE) sector by tapping into China's massive pool of household savings.[30] Accordingly, the overriding concern of the CSRC, which was charged with the responsibility for overseeing the stock market, was to ensure the development of a securities market that served precisely that purpose. In light of this, a heavy-handed approach to securities law enforcement was considered to be inconsistent with that goal. Hence, little attention was directed towards the disciplining of market misconduct. The inevitable result was a wave of scandals that undermined market confidence and threatened to derail China's fledgling stock market.

This development coincided with the flourishing academic and policy discourse that emerged, inter alia, in the United States on investor protection and its role in the development of robust domestic securities markets. Amongst the best-known examples of this discourse are the seminal papers of La Porta and his associates, who famously claimed that the greater the legal protection a country affords investors, the stronger

---

[28] Howell E. Jackson and Mark J. Roe, 'Public and private enforcement of securities laws: resource-based evidence' (2009) 93(2) *Journal of Financial Economics*, 207–238 at 214–215; John Armour, Bernard Black, Brian Cheffins and Richard Nolan, 'Private enforcement of corporate law: an empirical comparison of the United Kingdom and the United States' (2009) 6(4) *Journal of Empirical Legal Studies*, 687–722 at 718–720; Kathryn Cearns and Eilis Ferran, 'Non-enforcement-led public oversight of financial and corporate governance disclosures and of auditors' (2008) 8(2) *Journal of Corporate Law Studies*, 191–224.

[29] Paul S. Atkins and Bradley J. Bondi, 'Evaluating the mission: a critical review of the history and evolution of the SEC enforcement program' (2008) 13 *Fordham Journal of Corporate & Financial Law*, 367.

[30] Edward S. Steinfeld, *Forging Reform in China: The Fate of State-Owned Industry* (Cambridge: Cambridge University Press, 1998); Jinglian Wu, *Understanding and Interpreting Chinese Economic Reform* (Mason, OH: Thomson-South-Western, 2005); Barry Naughton, *The Chinese Economy: Transitions and Growth* (Cambridge, MA: MIT Press, 2007).

and more robust its securities market is likely to be.[31] The discourse culminated in Hansmann and Kraakman's bold assertion that the US-style, shareholder-oriented approach to corporate law would constitute the end of history.[32]

The conflation of China's securities market fiasco and the impact of the US discourse seems to have helped the CSRC to shake off its preoccupation with its developmental role. In the years since, it has thus directed greater attention to enforcing the country's securities laws and disciplining violations thereof with a view to boosting investor confidence. As illustrated later, the past decade has witnessed a shifting approach to securities regulation, with increasing emphasis on enforcement.

3.1   Shifting Approach to Regulation

As noted previously, the Chinese securities sector was created with one primary goal in mind: channelling private savings into the securities markets to finance the ailing SOE sector.[33] Thus, in its earlier years, the CSRC's primary role was characteristically a developmental one,[34] that is, developing the securities markets by cherry-picking firms to be granted access to those markets. In order to fulfil that role, the CSRC relied heavily on merit-review and approval[35] in the form of, first, a quota system and, subsequently, a 'review and approval system' from 1993 to 2003.[36] Both regimes were characteristically ex ante in the sense that they emphasised control over access to the stock market rather than ongoing oversight of the conduct of market actors.[37]

---

[31] LaPorta, Rafael, Florencio Lopez-de-Silanes, Andrei Shleifer and Robert Vishny, 'Investor protection and corporate governance' (2000) 58(1) *Journal of Financial Economics*, 3–27; 'Investor protection and corporate valuation' (2002) 57(3) *Journal of Finance*, 1147–1170; Rafael La Porta, Florencio Lopez-de-Silanes and Andrei Shleifer, 'What works in securities laws?' (2006) 61(1) *Journal of Finance*, 1–32.

[32] Henry Hansmann and Reinier Kraakman, 'The end of history for corporate law' (2001) 89 *Georgetown Law Journal*, 439.

[33] OECD, *China in the World Economy: The Domestic Policy Challenges* (Paris: OECD, 2002), p. 497.

[34] Jiangyu Wang, 'The political logic of securities regulation in China', in Guanghua Yu (ed.), *The Development of the Chinese Legal System: Change and Challenges* (Abingdon: Routledge, 2010), p. 242.

[35] Donald Clarke, 'Corporate governance in China: an overview' (2003) 14 *China Economic Review*, 494–507 at 494, 504.

[36] Katharina Pistor and Chenggang Xu, 'Governing stockmarkets in transition economies: lessons from China' (2005) 7(1) *American Law and Economics Review*, 184–210 at 196.

[37] Jiangyu Wang, 'Regulation of initial public offering of shares in China' (2009) 76 *China Law*, 54–65 at 61.

The CSRC's preoccupation with ex ante regulation was compounded by the belief that securities markets should be regulated with a light touch.[38] A heavy-handed approach would, according to that belief, disincentivise market actors to engage in trade and investment in the stock market. Enforcement was regarded as only a secondary, if not adjunct, role of the CSRC. As a result, securities law enforcement was so weak – and violations consequently so rampant – that the Chinese securities markets gained a notorious reputation for being 'worse than a casino'.[39] A string of instances of corporate fraud ensued, and the Chinese stock market entered a long bear period around the turn of the twenty-first century. There was also an outpouring of public anger at the CSRC, with the fact that it had hand-picked listed firms in the first place seen as constituting official endorsement of those firms' credit-worthiness and credibility. The CSRC faced a legitimacy crisis[40] that pushed it to move its enforcement role up the agenda.[41]

With Zhou Xiaochuan at its helm, the CSRC attempted to steer through the crisis by rebuilding its reputation as a law enforcement regulator.[42] With the support of then-Premier Zhu Rongji, Zhou fast-tracked a number of senior and foreign-trained professionals into the CSRC's leadership line-up.[43] Amongst the most important were the two aforementioned vice-chairpersons, Laura Cha and Gao Xiqing, both of whom had received their legal education and practised law in the United States.[44] Their contribution was two-fold. First, under their leadership the administrative approval system was scaled back, relieving the CSRC of its overwhelming ex ante control workload.[45] Second, and perhaps

---

[38] Ibid.

[39] Wu Jinglian, quoted in Stephen Green, *The Development of China's Stockmarket, 1984–2002: Equity Politics and Market Institutions* (London: Routledge, 2004).

[40] Lijia Cao, *A Comparative Study of Securities Enforcement Systems* (Beijing: Beijing University Press, 2008), pp. 220–221; Chen Gongmeng Chen, Michael Firth, Daniel N. Gao and Oliver Rui, 'Is China's securities regulatory agency a toothless tiger? Evidence from enforcement actions' (2005) 224(6) *Journal of Accounting and Public Policy*, 451–488.

[41] Jiangyu Wang, 'Dancing with wolves: regulation and deregulation of foreign investment in China's stock market' (2004) 5 *Asian-Pacific Law & Policy Journal*, 1–61 at 236, 243.

[42] Wang, 'The political logic of securities regulation', 243.

[43] 'Behind the scenes of the shifting leadership in China's financial system', Xinhua Net, 11 February 2003, http://news.xinhuanet.com/newscenter/2003-02/11/content_724409.htm.

[44] See Xi, 'In search of'.

[45] 'The securities regulator should administer according to the law: the training workshop held by the CSRC', *Shanghai Zhengquan Bao*, 29 April 2002, www.china.com.cn/chinese/FI-c/140034.htm.

more significantly, the regulatory reform led by Cha directed the CSRC's attention towards its long-ignored regulatory role and, in the meantime, to a shifting focus on regulatory enforcement. After Cha assumed office in 2001, the CSRC navigated its way through market turbulence with an increasing emphasis on regulatory sanctions and more intensive campaigns to enforce disclosure and anti-fraud rules.[46] Playing hardball with mighty SOEs and powerful businesspeople, Cha earned the nickname 'Iron Lady' and became the subject of blame by both politicians and public investors who suffered market losses.[47] Despite the prevalent criticism and Cha's resignation in 2004, the regulatory reforms launched on her watch successfully laid the foundation for the rise of an increasingly robust enforcement regime. In 2006, under long-term Chairman Shang Fulin, the CSRC ushered in a structural overhaul of its enforcement programme, inter alia, by establishing the Enforcement Contingent and an independent ASC.[48]

The fundamental shift towards an enforcement-led CSRC started under Guo Shuqing's administration. By famously questioning the wisdom of the merit-based review regime that had dominated the CSRC's work since its inception, Guo indicated his personal preference for a shift away from the ex ante approach in favour of ex post regulation.[49] Between the competing objectives of development versus law enforcement, the balance started to tip, at least rhetorically, towards the latter.[50]

The CSRC's strategic re-positioning towards an enforcement-led regulatory agency gathered further momentum with, and arguably culminated in, Xiao Gang's reign at the helm. Xiao publicly advocated the transformation of the CSRC's role and called for the enhancement of its enforcement programme.[51] His 2013 piece published in CPC mouthpiece

---

[46] Wang, 'The political logic of securities regulation', 243.

[47] Beibei Shi and Na Shi, 'The iron lady Laura Cha who brought a new atmoshpere for regulation', *Shanghai Zhengquan Bao*, 30 November 2010, www.cs.com.cn/xwzx/xwzt/101201/02/201011/t20101130_2690835.html.

[48] See Section 4.2 of this chapter.

[49] Liming Huang, Xu Chen and Rongpin Hu, 'CSRC Chairman Guo Shuqing raised a question: can we not retain the approval procedure for IPOs?', *Jingji Guangcha Bao*, 13 February 2002, http://finance.people.com.cn/stock/GB/17091558.html.

[50] Ibid.

[51] See, e.g. Gang Xiao, Speech at 2013 Securities and Futures Enforcement Conference, 19 August 2013; 'To promote regulatory transformation vigourously', speech given at 2014 National Securities and Futures Regulation Conference, 21 January 2014.

Qiushi suggested that the regulatory change was inspired by the US experience.[52] Enforcement is the 'cornerstone' of the development of global capital markets, particularly in the United States, Xiao asserted. Thus, the CSRC should also 're-position itself' and take enforcement to its heart.[53] Using the SEC as a benchmark, Xiao complained that the CSRC had long run short of enforcement staff and expertise and that its enforcement level remained inadequate.[54] The *Qiushi* paper has symbolic significance, arguably constituting the first time the CSRC had made public its will to establish itself as an enforcement-led regulatory authority. In August 2013, it cemented its resolution by translating the rhetorical emphasis on enforcement into a policy paper on future reform.[55]

3.2   Enhanced Enforcement Capacity

The CSRC's rhetoric on transforming itself from a developmental body into an enforcement-led regulatory agency has been matched by a gradually enhanced capacity enabling it to do so in practice. Such capacity was first of all manifested in beefed-up enforcement funding and staffing, with the CSRC's total budget increasing from RMB910 million in 2007 to RMB1.41 billion in 2015.[56] Although the precise budget breakdown with regard to enforcement is not publicly available, a rising tide is likely to have lifted all boats. The change in staffing is also telling. In 1998, when the CSRC set up the Enforcement Bureau, the Bureau's staff comprised a mere thirty-three enforcement officers.[57] By 2000, its enforcement staff had expanded nationwide to 210.[58] In November 2007, the creation of the Enforcement Contingent brought with it the additional support of 170 investigators who strengthened the CSRC's enforcement capacity in the day-to-day surveillance of insider trading and market manipulation.[59] The total number of enforcement officers rose to 560 over time.

---

[52] Xiao, 'Regulatory enforcement'.   [53] Ibid., 29.   [54] Ibid.
[55] See CSRC Opinions on Further Strengthening Enforcement, issued on 19 August 2013.
[56] The 2007 and 2015 budgets implemented by the CSRC are available at www.csrc.gov.cn/pub/zjhpublic/G00306213/201608/t20160808_301837.htm and www.csrc.gov.cn/pub/zjhpublic/G00306213/201608/t20160808_301845.htm, respectively.
[57] Section 3(8) of the Circular on the Rules of the Functions, Organizations and Nomenklatura of the CSRC, issued by the State Council on 28 September 1998.
[58] Cao, *A Comparative Study of Securities Enforcement Systems*, p. 220.
[59] CSRC, *Important Reform*.

In 2013, then-CSRC Chairman Xiao Gang announced the organisation's ambition to double that number to 1,200.[60]

At the local level, all CSRC regional offices have since 2004 established their own in-house enforcement departments under a general requirement that enforcement staff should account for no less than 30 per cent of the total headcounts of the respective offices.[61] The aim of this institutional setup is, inter alia, to enhance the CSRC's ability to react 'promptly' to local-level market misconduct or non-compliance.[62]

4   Trial-Like Procedure in Enforcement Regime

The notion of a trial-like procedure and the use of administrative law judges (ALJs) in securities regulation is a defining feature of US securities regulation. The SEC began holding administrative hearings shortly after its creation in 1934. Experimentation with the notion of trial-like hearings was the epitome of 'judicialisation' reform within the US federal administrative establishment.[63] Since the passage of the federal Administrative Procedure Act (APA) in 1946, the concept of ALJs – as independent presiding officers in trial-like hearings – has become an established administrative law tradition in the United States in general and the SEC in particular.[64] Since the passage of the Securities Enforcement Remedies and Penny Stock Reform Act in 1990 and, more recently, the Dodd-Frank Act in 2010, the SEC enforcement programme features an increasingly expansive use of ALJs, a practice that has recently attracted controversy.[65]

The notion of ALJs was completely alien to the Chinese administrative law regime until the CSRC embraced it in the form of the ASC in the early 2000s. In the years since, the CSRC has increased its reliance on trial-like procedures in the administration of its enforcement programme.

---

[60] Xu Chen, 'Xiao Gang's new deal: the CSRC takes a heavy-hand measure to double the scale of its enforcement forces', *Jingji Guangcha Bao*, 23 August 2013, http://money.163.com/13/0823/23/970G0I4F00251LIE.html.

[61] CSRC, *Twenty Years of China's Capital Market* (Beijing: Zhongxin Press, 2012), p. 340.

[62] CSRC, *Important Reform*.

[63] Before the 1930s, some US federal agencies explored the practice of having regulatory matters heard and processed by an internal 'presiding officer'. See Frederick Davis, 'Judicialization of administrative law: the trial-type hearing and the changing status of the hearing officer' (1977) 2 *Duke Law Journal*, 389–408.

[64] Examiners or presiding officers appointed pursuant to the APA requirements were renamed ALJs in 1972. See Davis, 'Judicialization of administrative law', 383.

[65] See, e.g. David T. Zaring, 'Enforcement discretion at the SEC' (2016) 94(6) *Texas Law Review*, 1155.

Anyone who doubts the CSRC's source of inspiration for this move should look no further than an official publication that provides a strong indication that the increased reliance on trial-like procedures has its roots in US practice.[66] Indeed, the CSRC remains the only central government agency in China to use ALJs in administrative proceedings.

4.1 Emergence of the Trial-Like Procedure Notion

In the CSRC's formative years, its enforcement action decisions were made in old-school fashion, with the CSRC chairman responsible for making a final determination on administrative sanctions based on an investigation report produced by the Enforcement Bureau.[67] There was no involvement by the relatively independent ALJs, and nor were the regulated entities entitled to any notable procedural rights. Hence, whilst the CSRC enjoyed wide discretion in enforcement action decisions, its decision-making process remained opaque.

Although this traditional method of administrative decision-making was not unlike those used in other central government agencies, the CSRC was one of the few regulatory agencies to see its procedural practices face challenges in the courts. Of particular note in this regard is 2000's *Sun Wei v the CSRC*, in which the First Intermediate People's Court of Beijing ruled against the CSRC for its failure to comply with the statutory procedures – pursuant to the 1996 Administrative Sanction Law – for duly serving a notice to the regulated individual against whom the CSRC administrative sanction was issued.[68] The media attention that the case attracted nationwide reportedly put the CSRC under considerable pressure,[69] creating a compelling reason for it to reform the way in which it took decisions concerning administrative sanctions.[70]

---

[66] CSRC, *Twenty Years of China's Capital Market*, p. 343.

[67] Article 38 of the 1996 Administrative Sanction Law; see also Rules on the Functions, Organisation and Nomenklatura of the CSRC, issued by the State Council on 30 September 1998.

[68] Article 31 of the 1996 Administrative Sanction Law; for further details, see Zhongguo Fayuan Wang, 'The lawyer sued the CSRC and the Ministry of Justice has withdrawn the case', 7 January 2003, www.chinacourt.org/article/detail/2003/01/id/30739.shtml.

[69] Yan Si, 'Two defeats in one week: the failure of the CSRC in administrative litigation' (2001) 3 *Dazhong Shangwu*, 3.

[70] Then Vice-Chairman Gao Xiqing related the changing role of the CSRC to these spotlighted cases, see Xiqing Gao, 'Securities regulatory power: the law-abided implementation of securities regulatory power and its mechanical checks in China' (2002) 5 *Zhongguo Faxue*, 12. For further details, see Tao Huang, 'Does the court truly promote

As part of the overhaul of its enforcement programme, the CSRC in 2002 officially adopted a US-style trial-like procedure by way of an initiative called 'separation between the investigative and adjudicative roles' (Separation).[71] More specifically, the notion of Separation emphasises organisational and functional separation, at least on paper, between the CSRC's investigation into alleged securities law violations, on the one hand, and its determination of whether a violation has been established as a result of an investigation, on the other. The former role is taken up by the CSRC's Enforcement Bureau, whereas the latter is to be assigned to the ASC staffed with a collegiate panel of 'judge' members (or commissioners). The creation of the ASC constituted a signature reform, and marked a paradigm shift towards the use of US-style ALJs. It was the first time the CSRC had set up an official committee to take over the adjudicative function that had previously been performed by the Bureau[72] and, more importantly, set down rules for Separation, thereby giving judge-like officers a formal role in the hearing process.[73]

The notion of Separation did not, however, gain much traction in the early years of its implementation, and an independently functioning ASC did not initially materialise. The ASC's supposed responsibilities, such as reviewing investigations, presiding over hearing procedures and overseeing the enforcement of administrative sanctions, were all conferred upon the Legal Department.[74] Organisationally, the ASC was in essence just a sub-committee under the CSRC's Legal Department, and its members did not serve on a full-time basis. Both the hearing and decision-making processes remained administrative-oriented, governed by only relatively primitive rules.[75] It is arguably no exaggeration to say that, in the early 2000s, the ASC's adjudicative role was more nominal than real.

---

the rule of law? Institutional reflection on the financial and administrative cases adjudicated by the Chinese courts' (2011) 2 *Xinzheng Faxue Yanjiu*, 82.

[71] Circular on Further Improvement of the CSRC's Administrative Sanction System (2002 Circular on Administrative Sanctions hereafter) issued by the CSRC on 25 April 2002.

[72] Also of relevance was the dissolution of the Adjudication Division (or *shenli chu*) of the Enforcement Bureau. See Part 2(2) of the 2002 Circular on Administrative Sanctions.

[73] For instance, the CSRC can appoint a member of the ASC as the 'presiding officer (or *zhuchiren*)' to oversee the hearing of an enforcement case. See Part 2(1) of the 2002 Circular on Administrative Sanctions.

[74] See, e.g. Circular on the Adjustment of Major Functional Departments and Nomenklatura of the CSRC issued by the Central Nomenklatura Committee in 2004, DOC No. 7.

[75] These processes were supervised by the Division of Adjudication and Implementation, a sub-division of the CSRC's Legal Department. See Part 2(1) of the 2002 Circular on Administrative Sanctions.

4.2   The 2006 Reform: Judicialisation of Administrative
Process Entrenched

A fuller 'judicialisation' of CSRC enforcement decision-making came
about as part of the CSRC reform of 2006. In October of that year, the
ASC established its own secretariat and started to function independently
of the CSRC Legal Department.[76] In November 2007, the State Council
formally endorsed a new CSRC organisational structure featuring the
empowerment of the ASC with the independent support of a central
government budget and personnel.[77] The notion of Separation has since
been crystallised in a number of important ways, both organisationally
and procedurally.

First and foremost, the ASC has gained a greater level of organisational
independence, now being completely separate organisationally from the
Legal Department, with which it used to be affiliated. Perhaps more
importantly, the ASC has been put on an equal footing with the Legal
Department and other CSRC internal departments and units within the
CSRC's bureaucratic hierarchy. This elevation in status has afforded the
ASC a stronger voice and greater influence in CSRC decision-making in
general and in the enforcement programme in particular. Also of relevance is the ASC's membership and staffing. Notably, the ASC recently
put in place a joint scheme with the Supreme People's Court to appoint
to the ASC senior serving members of the Chinese judiciary on a full-
time basis.[78] This arrangement enables the pooling of expertise and
development of an independent professional identity at the ASC. Profes-
sionalisation of the ASC is said to have helped to streamline its hearing
procedures and improve the consistency and efficiency of its decision-
making.[79]

ASC decisions are the outcome of a trial-like procedure, to be discussed in greater detail in succeeding paragraphs, and are taken by a
court-like decision-making process. By way of comparison, in a typical
court proceeding in China, a civil or administrative case is decided by a

---

[76] CSRC, *Twenty Years of China's Capital Market*, p. 343; 'The CSRC has established a new
administrative sanction commission' (2006) 10 *CSRC Official Bulletin*, 46.

[77] CSRC, *Twenty Years of China's Capital Market*, pp. 339, 346–347.

[78] See, e.g. Xin Li, 'The CSRC has invited two judges to join its administrative sanction
commission', *Caijing Wang*, 28 December 2010, www.caijing.com.cn/2010-12-28/
110604596.html; Baochen Zhu, 'The half year of two judges serving in the CSRC', 15 June
2011, *Zhengquan Ribao*, C03.

[79] CSRC, *Twenty Years of China's Capital Market*, p. 344.

'collegiate panel'[80] generally comprising three judges, one of whom is the 'presiding judge'[81] appointed by the court to oversee the trial procedure and regulate the course of the court hearing. Only in exceptional cases will a single-judge trial be allowed pursuant to statutory provisions.[82] Like Chinese court cases, cases that come before the ASC are heard by a collegiate bench of, typically, three ASC commissioners, one of whom presides over and oversees the proceeding. Through its collegiate bench of commissioners, the ASC adjudicates and decides administrative sanction cases by way of relatively independent trial-like hearings.

Both ASC practices and the hearing procedure are governed by a set of detailed rules.[83] First, by examining the facts and legal foundations of the enforcement case, the presiding commissioner submits a Preliminary Review Report (or *chubu shenli baogao*) to the collegiate bench for further deliberation.[84] Second, the collegiate bench issues a conclusive report determining whether to proceed with or close the enforcement action.[85] Should the bench opt to proceed, the regulated entities are entitled to an official pre-hearing notice (or *xingzheng chufa shixian gaozhishu*)[86] and, subsequently, to a formal hearing by the ASC collegiate bench.[87] After the hearing, the collegiate bench makes a final determination by majority vote, and all bench votes and comments are recorded.[88] Last but not least, the party concerned (i.e. the regulated entity and/or individual) can appeal against the ASC's decision through an administrative review (or *xingzheng fuyi*) procedure within the CSRC itself,

---

[80] See, generally, Albert H. Chen, *An Introduction to the Legal System of the People's Republic of China*, 4th edn. (Hong Kong: LexisNexis, 2011); Randall Peerenboom, *China's Long March toward Rule of Law* (Cambridge: Cambridge University Press, 2002), p. 281.

[81] See, generally, Chen, *An Introduction to the Legal System*; Peerenboom, *China's Long March*, pp. 286–287.

[82] Ibid.

[83] The CSRC has introduced a series of normative documents in this regard. Amongst the most important are the Practice Directions on the Administrative Sanction Commission of the CSRC (2007 ASC Practice Directions hereafter) issued on 18 April 2007 and Rules on the Administrative Sanction Hearings of the CSRC (2007 Hearing Rules) issued on 18 April 2007. Although the 2007 Hearing Rules were amended in 2015, the rules related in this section refer to the 2007 version, unless otherwise specified, to illustrate post-2006 developments.

[84] Articles 9–12 of the 2007 ASC Practice Directions.

[85] Ibid., Articles 13–15 of the 2007 ASC Practice Directions.

[86] Article 7 of the 2007 Hearing Rules.

[87] Article 16 of the 2007 ASC Practice Directions.

[88] Article 19 of the 2007 ASC Practice Directions; Article 16 of the 2007 Hearing Rules.

which can in turn affirm, amend or reverse that decision.[89] Alternatively, the party concerned can initiate an administrative litigation (or *xingzheng susong*) procedure against the CSRC's final decision, thereby applying for a de novo trial by an intermediate court in Beijing, where the CSRC is headquartered.[90]

From the viewpoint of the regulated entities, perhaps the most important element of the new regime is the right to a formal hearing before the ASC. As noted earlier, the trial-like nature of that hearing is an analogy frequently made by civil courts. The ASC-appointed collegiate bench makes decisions on both substantive rights and procedural matters. In a general provision, the hearing should enable the regulated entities to present their positions and statements before the issuance of a formal enforcement action. During the hearing process, for example, they are entitled to the 'presentation of claims and defence' (or *chenshu he shenbian*), 'examination of evidence' (or *zhizheng*)[91] and right of legal representation, as in the case of judicial proceedings.[92] The regulated entities may also, as a matter of due process, apply for the recusal of an ASC judge.[93] Furthermore, such legal documents as the pre-hearing notice and ASC decision shall be served on those entities duly pursuant to the statutory provisions stipulated in China's Civil Procedure Law.[94]

Recent years have seen proliferation of the use of trial-like procedures within the CSRC enforcement programme. As part of its campaign to decentralise securities law enforcement, the CSRC has delegated such procedures to its local offices nationwide, which have since 2010 been authorised to take enforcement actions in given circumstances.[95] The local offices have also established their own hearing rules to guide their enforcement actions.

---

[89] Article 235 of the 2005 Securities Law; Article 9 of the 1999 Administrative Review Law; Article 17 of the 2007 Hearing Rules.

[90] After the first-instance trial, either party concerned is entitled to appeal to the Beijing Higher-Level Court. For the court of jurisdiction, see Article 5 of the 2013 Beijing Higher-Level Court Provisional Rules on the Adjustment in Jurisdiction of the Intermediate Courts issued on 2 August 2013.

[91] See, e.g. Article 11(2) of the 2007 Hearing Rules (which states that the party concerned is entitled to an examination of the evidence collected by the investigating officers).

[92] Articles 10–11 of the 2007 Hearing Rules; Article 17 of the 2007 ASC Practice Directions.

[93] Article 6 of the 2007 Hearing Rules; Article 8 of the 2007 ASC Practice Directions.

[94] Article 24 of the 2007 ASC Practice Directions.

[95] Article 4 of the Practice Directions for the Pilot Schemes of Administrative Sanctions by the Dispatched Institutions of the CSRC, issued by the CSRC on 26 October 2010.

It is clear from the foregoing discussion that the CSRC's reliance on trial-like procedures is now formalised and institutionalised, if not fully entrenched. The judicialisation of the CSRC administrative process and use of ALJs (in the form of ASC commissioners) give the CSRC enforcement programme a distinctive flavour that is reminiscent of the US approach to securities regulation. This has supposedly afforded CSRC-regulated entities greater procedural safeguards in the administrative process that can lead to the imposition of consequential administrative sanctions and industry bans. An institutional benefit for the CSRC itself, in the meantime, is the ability to develop an 'in-house' knowledge base and to play a role in shaping the formulation of judicial rules and standards that affect its own enforcement programme in, for instance, the areas of market manipulation and insider dealing.[96]

5   Concluding Remarks

As with other jurisdictions, the evolution of securities regulation in China has, on occasion, been driven by moments of crisis that have challenged the securities regulator's very legitimacy. In overcoming that challenge, China has taken steps that have prima facie been inspired by the US approach to securities regulation – both ideologically and institutionally. The evolutionary trajectory of the CSRC's enforcement programme seems to have been shaped by this dynamic. Orientationally, the CSRC has adopted rhetoric suggesting that it is willing, if not determined, to move away from its conventional developmental role in favour of an SEC-style, enforcement-led regulatory regime. Institution-wise, the CSRC has put in place and increasingly relies upon a trial-like procedure in the administration of enforcement decision-making, providing regulated entities and individuals with procedural rights that are otherwise not generally available in administrative proceedings under Chinese law.

Such prima facie convergence is not without limitations. For example, the newly developed role of enforcement, which has in recent years gained significance, is expected to coexist and compete with the CSRC's more traditional developmental role. The balance between

---

[96] See, e.g. Provisional Practice Directions on Deciding Insider Trading and Provisional Practice Directions on Deciding Market Manipulation, both issued by the CSRC on 27 March 2007. See also Judicial Conference Summary on the Evidence Rules in Administrative Sanction Cases, issued by the Supreme People's Court on 13 July 2011.

the two will not necessarily be tipped in favour of the former. The effectiveness of the trial-like procedure also hinges critically on the level of independence, professionalism, expertise and authority that the ASC commands and on the resources made available to it. It remains to be seen how far China's enforcement programme will continue to evolve in the direction of the SEC-style enforcement regime that has been a source of inspiration.

6

China's Free Trade from SEZs to CEPA to FTZs

The Beijing Consensus in Global Convergence and Divergence

WENWEI GUAN

1 Introduction

China's legendary economic growth in recent decades is unprecedented in the annals of regional and international development. Since its take-off following the inception of the country's reform and opening-up policy in the late 1970s, China's economy has maintained double-digit growth in most years. In the three decades from 1979 to 2009, Chinese exports grew by 16 per cent each year.[1] In 1983, the country accounted for just 1.1 per cent of merchandise imports and 1.2 per cent of merchandise exports in world trade, significantly behind the United States, the then-number-one merchandise importer and exporter, which accounted for 14.3 and 11.2 per cent of global imports and exports, respectively, in that year.[2] In 2011, however, China accounted for 9.7 per cent of world merchandise imports, ranking a close second to the United States, which accounted for 12.5 per cent. In terms of global exports, it beat the United States into second place, accounting for 10.7 per cent, relative to 8.3 per cent.[3] China is also now the top destination for foreign direct investment (FDI) inflows. It ranked second behind the United States in 2012 and 2013,[4] and then overtook

---

[1] Justin Yifu Lin, 'General discussion: China and the global economy', in Reuven Glick and Mark M. Spiegel (eds.), *Asia's Role in the Post-Crisis Global Economy*, Asia Economic Policy Conference, San Francisco, CA, 29–30 November 2011 (San Francisco: Federal Reserve Bank), p. 231.
[2] WTO Secretariat, *International Trade Statistics 2012* (Geneva: WTO).　　[3] Ibid.
[4] United National Conference on Trade and Development (UNCTAD), Global Investment Trends Monitor, No. 15, 28 January 2014 (UNCTAD/WEB/DIAE/IA/2014/1).

the United States in 2014.[5] Following the outbreak of the global financial crisis in 2008, China continued its legendary growth against the backdrop of a global economic downtown, leading its economic reforms to a new stage through the launch of free trade zones (FTZs) in Shanghai in 2013 and in Guangdong, Fujian and Tianjin in 2015.[6] China's moves have certainly attracted global attention, and it is generally believed that the new FTZs will accelerate its economic reform.[7]

The country's extraordinary economic growth in the past few decades has sparked vigorous debate concerning its development model that goes beyond simple economic issues. Findings on the causes of that growth vary depending on the perspective adopted, and theoretical constructions of the development model thus also vary widely. To date, the economic perspective has largely dominated discussion in this area. Hu and Khan, for example, show that capital accumulation and productivity improvements have contributed significantly to China's economic growth.[8] In particular, its market-orientated reform, which 'brought about an expansion in foreign trade and foreign direct investment', continues to have 'an important effect on the [country's] rapid productivity growth'.[9] Justin Lin argues that there are two 'reasons for China to have [achieved] such a remarkable growth performance over the past thirty years', namely, its adoption of the 'dual-track approach' and the benefits of latecomer advantage.[10] First, the dual-track approach has allowed China to achieve both 'stability and dynamic transformation simultaneously'.[11] Second, as a latecomer, China has developed itself 'according to its comparative advantage' by tapping into the 'potential of the advantage of backwardness'.[12] These arguments raise the issue of China's development model,

[5] UNCTAD, Global Investment Trends Monitor, No. 18, 29 January 2015 (UNCTAD/WEB/DIAE/IA/2015/1).

[6] The China (Shanghai) Pilot Free Trade Zone (SPFTZ) came into operation in September 2013, and the Guangdong, Fujian and Tianjin FTZs in March 2015. For further details, see the discussion in Section 2.3 of this chapter.

[7] Helen Wong, 'China's free trade zones will accelerate reform', Business Spectator, available at www.businessspectator.com.au/article/2015/4/2/china/chinas-free-trade-zones-will-accelerate-reform.

[8] Zuliu F. Hu and Mohsin S. Khan, 'Why is China growing so fast?' (1997) 44 IMF Staff Papers, 127.

[9] Ibid., 128.   [10] Lin, 'China and the global economy'.

[11] Ibid. For further details of Lin's views on the 'latecomer advantage', see Justin Yifu Lin, Demystifying the Chinese Economy (Cambridge: Cambridge University Press, 2012), pp. 129–131.

[12] Lin, 'China and the global economy'; Demystifying the Chinese Economy, 154.

which is heavily dependent on market-orientated reform and yet differs significantly from the liberal market mechanism model constituted by the Washington Consensus,[13] giving rise to the phrase the 'Beijing Consensus', first coined in 2004 by Joshua Ramo.[14]

The debate surrounding the Beijing versus Washington Consensus has travelled beyond the realm of economics to the domain of political legitimacy, and has global implications. As Ramo suggests, both the Beijing Consensus and Washington Consensus concern more than ideas about economics, encompassing such issues as politics, equality and the global balance of power.[15] Halper puts it more straightforwardly, stating that the Beijing Consensus' 'market-authoritarian' model poses a significant challenge to the cornerstone of 'the market-democratic' model, that is, that 'economic freedom needs political freedom and a minimal role for the state',[16] which brings us to the issue of political legitimacy. China's fast-paced economic growth has occurred during the country's gradual integration into the international trading framework – i.e. the World Trade Organization (WTO) system – which is a process of both convergence and divergence. Whilst China's integration into that framework has to some extent brought the country into conformity with and endorsed the legitimacy of the international system, its successful formulation of its own model also challenges the rigidity and legitimacy of that system.[17] The discussion of China's development model therefore has legal significance and global implications, particularly with respect to the issue of legitimacy in the process of global convergence and/or divergence.

With reference to the ongoing debate surrounding the Beijing versus Washington Consensus, this chapter offers a critical examination of China's free trade development from special economic zones (SEZs) in

---

[13] John Williamson, 'The Washington consensus revisited', in Louis Emmerij (ed.), *Economic and Social Development into the XXI Century* (Washington DC: Inter-American Development Bank, 1997), pp. 48–59. According to Lin, however, China's development differentiates it from the Washington Consensus model. See Lin, *Demystifying the Chinese Economy*, pp. 271–277.

[14] Joshua C. Ramo, *The Beijing Consensus* (London: Foreign Policy Centre, 2004).

[15] Ibid., 5.

[16] Stefan Halper, *The Beijing Consensus: How China's Authoritarian Model Will Dominate the Twenty-First Century* (New York: Basic Books, 2010), p. 134.

[17] For China's WTO accession as both conformity with and a challenge to the legitimacy of the international trading system, see Wenwei Guan, *Intellectual Property Theory and Practice: A Critical Examination of China's TRIPS Compliance and Beyond* (Heidelberg: Springer, 2014), pp. 146–149.

the early reform years to the more recent FTZs and the implications of that development. To address the political legitimacy issue, the examination focuses on the government's role in FDI management. The next section offers a brief account of the trajectory from SEZs to the Closer Economic Partnership Arrangement (CEPA) framework in the Pearl River Delta (PRD) and to the aforementioned FTZs in Shanghai, Guangdong, Fujian and Tianjin. This chapter argues that the evolution of free trade and FDI control in China in the past several decades has been a gradual process of ongoing trade liberalisation and decentralisation, during which emphasis has consistently been placed on innovation, sustainability and self-determination. The resulting so-called 'Beijing Consensus' presents a sharp contrast to the neo-liberalist Washington Consensus, which focuses on liberalisation, privatisation and marketisation. With reference to law and development critiques, the chapter moves on in Section 3 to discuss the issue of legitimacy and the contrast between the Beijing and Washington Consensuses in the context of the dynamics of global divergence and convergence, as well as the jurisprudential implications. Section 4 concludes the chapter with a general comment on the latest developments in China's free trade arrangements and the implications for regional and international free trade and cooperation.

2 China's Free Trade from SEZs to FTZs

2.1 Reform and Opening Up to Unlock the Power of the Market

Since China launched its reform and opening-up process in 1979, its economy has undergone unprecedented growth, achieving annual growth of about 9 per cent between 1979 and 1990 and 10.4 per cent in the 1990–2010 period.[18] Research has shown that, in addition to the rise of the rural sector and private business, the opening up to foreign trade and investment brought competitive forces into the Chinese economy, contributing significantly to productivity performance.[19] According to Hu and Khan, two primary factors in productivity growth in the market-orientated reform period were the huge amounts of FDI attracted by China's open-door policy and SEZs and the country's emergence

---

[18] Lin, 'China and the global economy'.
[19] Hu and Khan, 'Why is China growing so fast?' 115–116.

as an 'export powerhouse' through international trade engagement.[20] Productivity growth has been a significant source of economic growth, and accounted for 42 per cent of the output growth seen in the reform period of 1979–1994.[21]

Undoubtedly, China's market-orientated reforms, which attracted significant FDI inflows and facilitated the country's engagement in international trade, unlocked the powerful potential of its gigantic market. The relationship between unlocking the power of the market and economic development has long been recognised, with one of the founding fathers of the United States writing the following more than two hundred years ago.

> If we continue united, we may counteract a policy so unfriendly to our prosperity in a variety of ways. By prohibitory regulations ... we may oblige foreign countries to bid against each other, for the privileges of our markets. This assertion will not appear chimerical to those who are able to appreciate the importance of the markets of three millions of people ... to any manufacturing nation.[22]

The initiatives launched in China in 1979 to some extent share that wisdom about the power of the markets. That year saw the promulgation of the country's first foreign investment law, the Equity Joint Venture (EJV) Law.[23] The 1979–1980 period then saw the strategic establishment of four SEZs, i.e. Shenzhen, Zhuhai, Shantou and Xiamen, to attract FDI from Hong Kong, Macao, the Southeast Asian Chaozhou ethnic group and Taiwan, respectively.[24] Following Deng Xiaoping's successful visit to the Shenzhen SEZ in 1984, a second wave of liberalisation resulted in fourteen new 'Coastal Open Cities', each setting up Economic and Technological Development Zones (ETDZs) to further attract FDI.[25] Subsequent years saw the dramatic proliferation of economic zones, with

---

[20] Ibid., 117–119. According to Hu and Khan, the two other direct factors are the 'reallocation of labor from agriculture to the industry and service sectors' and the rise of the non-state sector.

[21] Ibid., 116–117.

[22] Alexander Hamilton, 'The utility of the union in respect to commercial relations and a navy', in Alexander Hamilton, James Madison and John Jay, *The Federalist Papers*, No. 11 (1787).

[23] The PRC Law on Chinese-Foreign Joint Ventures (EJV Law hereafter) was first promulgated in 1979 and subsequently amended in 1990 and 2001.

[24] Barry Naughton, *The Chinese Economy: Transitions and Growth* (London: MIT Press, 2007), pp. 27–28.

[25] Ibid., p. 409.

China's largest SEZ, the Hainan Island SEZ, established in 1988, followed by a third wave of economic opening marked by the establishment of the Pudong SEZ in Shanghai and the approval of eighteen new ETDZs between 1992 and 1993.[26] By 2003, China had more than one hundred central government-recognised investment zones, six SEZs, fifty-four national-level ETDZs, fifty-three nationally recognised high-tech industrial zones and fifteen bonded zones.[27] The liberalisation of investment policy and proliferation of these zones attracted significant FDI inflows.

In the process of liberalising investment policy, China promulgated another two sets of laws offering a greater choice of FDI vehicles. Following promulgation of the EJV Law in 1979 came the Wholly Foreign-Owned Enterprise (WFOE) Law of 1986[28] and Chinese-Foreign Contractual Joint Venture (CJV) Law of 1988.[29] Different from an EJV-structured investment in which the investment return and risk depend on the parties' equity contributions,[30] a CJV-structured investment is more flexible, with the investment return and risk allocation fully subject to agreement between the parties.[31] The WFOE Law went further, allowing foreign investors to establish WFOEs over which they have full control.[32] All three investment laws encourage the introduction of foreign technology into China.[33] As Hu and Khan have rightly pointed out, 'significant spillover in technology and managerial know-how was likely through the numerous joint ventures and wholly owned foreign enterprises that have sprung up along China's coastal provinces in the last decade'.[34] The liberalisation of investment policy that came with the decentralisation of government control over foreign investments gained foreign investors' trust over time. Whilst EJVs were the primary FDI vehicle between 1987 and 1999, WFOEs became the most popular mode after 1999, accounting for about 70 per cent of all FDI into China in 2005.[35] As we will see in the next section, during the process of

---

[26] Ibid. [27] Ibid., p. 410.
[28] The PRC Law on Wholly Foreign-Owned Enterprises (WFOE Law hereafter) was first promulgated in April 1988 and subsequently amended in October 2000.
[29] The PRC Law on Chinese-Foreign Contractual Joint Ventures-Owned Enterprises (CJV Law hereafter) was promulgated in April 1986 and subsequently amended in October 2000.
[30] Articles 1, 4(1) and 4(3) of EJV Law. [31] Articles 1 and 2 of CJV Law.
[32] Articles 1 and 2 of WFOE Law.
[33] Article 5(1) of EJV Law; Article 3(1) of WFOE Law; Article 4 of CJV Law.
[34] Hu and Khan, 'Why is China growing so fast?' 118–119.
[35] Naughton, The Chinese Economy, p. 412.

decentralising foreign investment control, China continued to improve the FDI management regime.

2.2 Evolution of China's FDI Guidance System

The EJV Law of 1979, WFOE Law of 1986 and CJV Law of 1988 together established a comprehensive foreign investment regime. Although the greater investment vehicle choice that resulted is certainly indicative of the decentralisation of control, China's investment regime never lost sight of its mission to attract foreign capital and technology to facilitate national development. In 1995, several ministerial departments jointly promulgated the Provisional Rules on Guiding Foreign Investment Orientation and the Guiding Catalogue of Industries for Foreign Investment.[36] The 1995 Provisional Rules were then formally repealed and superseded by the State Council's Rules on Guiding Foreign Investment Orientation in 2002,[37] and the 1995 Guiding Catalogue has been amended several times over the years.[38] According to the 2002 Rules, the Guiding Catalogue regulates the approval of foreign investment projects.[39]

According to the 2002 Rules, foreign investment projects are divided into four categories: encouraged, permitted, restricted and prohibited. Those in the restricted category are subject to more requirements and a stricter approval procedure.[40] Under the FDI guidance system, foreign investment projects that introduce new agricultural technology, improve production capacity through high or new technology, meet market needs for competitive capacity, are resource- or environmentally friendly and/ or enhance manpower or resource advantages are categorised as encouraged projects.[41] The system restricts foreign investment in projects that use outdated technologies, exert adverse effects on resources and/or the

---

[36] Provisional Rules on Guiding Foreign Investment Orientation (1995 Provisional Rules hereafter), approved by the State Council and promulgated jointly by the State Planning Commission, State Economy and Trade Commission, and Ministry of Foreign Trade and Economic Cooperation on 20 June 1995.

[37] Rules on Guiding Foreign Investment Orientation (the 2002 Rules hereafter), promulgated by the State Council (Decree No. 346 [2002]) on 11 February 2002, which came into force and replaced the 1995 Provisional Rules on 1 April 2002.

[38] The 1995 Guiding Catalogue was subsequently amended seven times, in 1997, 2000, 2002, 2004, 2007, 2011 and 2015.

[39] Articles 2 and 3 of 2002 Rules.   [40] Articles 4 and 12 of 2002 Rules.

[41] Article 4 of 2002 Rules.

environment, or exploit protected natural resources, as well as those in state-supported infant industries.[42] In addition to enjoying preferential treatment in accordance with the provisions of the relevant laws and administrative regulations, encouraged foreign-funded projects that engage in energy construction and operation, transport and municipal infrastructure, which require large amounts of investment and have a long-term investment return, are permitted to expand their relevant business scope upon approval.[43]

The evolution of the FDI guidance system has been a process of gradual decentralisation of government authority and control. The 1995 Guiding Catalogue was amended seven times between 1995 and 2015. Each amendment saw a substantial reduction in the number of prohibited and restricted areas for foreign investment to facilitate trade and investment liberalisation. In the 2007 Guiding Catalogue, for example, the percentage of encouraged projects amongst the entire project list increased to 73 per cent – compared with 69 per cent in the 2004 Catalogue.[44] The 2007 Guiding Catalogue also encourages FDI in high and clean technology to promote innovation and industrial structure optimisation. The 2011 Guiding Catalogue further opens market access by loosening the FDI equity ratio restrictions in eleven restricted and encouraged categories, increasing three encouraged items, and reducing eight restricted and prohibited items.[45] That edition also emphasises the modernisation of the service industry and encourages foreign investment in 'emerging strategic industries' in high-tech, new energy, new materials, environmental sustainability and value-added manufacturing. The latest version of the catalogue, amended in 2015, reflects the substantial liberalisation of FDI control.[46] The number of FDI projects in the restricted category has been significantly reduced, from seventy-nine to thirty-eight. FDI flexibility has also been enhanced, with the number of

---

[42] Article 6 of 2002 Rules.   [43] Article 9 of 2002 Rules.

[44] The Guiding Catalogue of Industries for Foreign Investment 2007 (2007 Guiding Catalogue hereafter), promulgated by the National Development and Reform commission (NDRC) and Ministry of Commerce (MOFCOM) on 31 October 2007, came into effect and replaced the 2004 Guiding Catalogue on 1 December 2007.

[45] The Guiding Catalogue of Industries for Foreign Investment 2011 (2011 Guiding Catalogue hereafter), promulgated by the NDRC and MOFCOM on 24 December 2011, came into effect and replaced the 2007 Guiding Catalogue on 30 January 2012.

[46] The Guiding Catalogue of Industries for Foreign Investment 2015 (2015 Guiding Catalogue hereafter), promulgated by the NDRC and MOFCOM on 10 March 2015, came into effect and replaced the 2011 Guiding Catalogue on 10 April 2015.

FDI projects designated as either EJV or CJV structures reduced from forty-three to fifteen and the number in which the majority equity share holding is limited to Chinese parties reduced from forty-four to thirty-five. The 2015 Guiding Catalogue also loosens the restrictions on investments in the manufacturing and service industries, including logistics, e-commerce and finance, and foreign-invested enterprise (FIE) commercial distribution rights in the retail and wholesale sectors. The key consideration in this significant liberalisation of FDI control is paving the way for the ongoing FDI regulatory reform from the 'positive list' to the 'negative list' and for a future Foreign Investment Law that will consolidate and eventually supersede the EJV, WFOE and CJV Laws.[47]

China's right to regulate trade and investment is an inherent sovereign power. In the case of *China – Publications and Audiovisual Products*, the WTO Appellate Body's treatment of the tension between China's trade regulations and trading rights commitments[48] touches upon the nature of any government's right to regulate trade and investment. It suggests that China's commitment to trade liberalisation is 'qualified' by the condition 'without prejudice to China's right to regulate trade in a manner consistent with the WTO Agreement'.[49] The Body further points out that

> the 'right to regulate', in the abstract, as an inherent power enjoyed by a Member's government, rather than a right bestowed by international treaties such as the *WTO Agreement*. With respect to trade, the *WTO Agreement* and its Annexes instead operate to, among other things, discipline the exercise of each Member's inherent power to regulate by requiring WTO Members to comply with the obligations that they have assumed thereunder.[50]

Therefore, China's liberalisation of trade and decentralisation of foreign investment control have implications for self-restraint in the sovereign power to regulate.

---

[47] MOFCOM issued the Foreign Investment Law (draft) for public consultation on 19 January 2015. For further details, see the discussion in Section 2.3 of this chapter.
[48] Upon its WTO accession in 2001, China committed to the following (Para. 5.1, China's WTO Accession Protocol): 'Without prejudice to China's right to regulate trade in a manner consistent with the WTO Agreement, China shall progressively liberalize the availability and scope of the right to trade, so that, within three years after accession, all enterprises in China shall have the right to trade in all goods throughout the customs territory of China, except for those goods listed in Annex 2A [subject to state trading].'
[49] *China – Measures Affecting Trading Rights and Distribution Services for Certain Publications and Audiovisual Entertainment Products* (*China – Publications and Audiovisual Products*), WTO Appellate Body Report (WT/DS363/AB/R, 21 December 2009), para. 218.
[50] Ibid., para. 222.

2.3 PRD Free Trade: From CEPA Framework to FTZs

As a result of China's efforts to integrate into the international trading framework, it joined and became a member of the WTO on 11 December 2001.[51] China's WTO accession is both a milestone of international integration and the starting point of a new stage of domestic reform and liberalisation. A key development during the WTO grace period was a regional free trade agreement within the PRD.[52] Mainland China and Hong Kong agreed to the main text of CEPA on 29 June 2003 and to its six annexes on 29 September 2003. CEPA's objectives are to strengthen trade and investment cooperation between and promote the joint development of the mainland and Hong Kong through measures in three areas: liberalisation of trade in goods, liberalisation of trade in services and the promotion of trade and investment facilitation.[53] Pursuant to Article 3 of CEPA, the two sides broadened and enriched its content and signed ten supplements between 2004 and 2013, further expanding market liberalisation, trade and investment, and economic cooperation in the PRD. On 18 December 2014, the two sides signed the Agreement between the Mainland and Hong Kong on Achieving Basic Liberalization of Trade in Services in Guangdong. A similar CEPA framework was concluded between the mainland and Macao on 17 October 2003.[54]

The CEPA framework goes beyond national development in that it creates new business opportunities not only for Mainland China, but also for Hong Kong, Macao and foreign investors. As a form of regional economic integration via the establishment of customs unions or free-trade areas, CEPA is permitted under the WTO framework, as the WTO recognises 'the desirability of increasing freedom of trade by the development, through voluntary agreements, of closer integration between the economies of the countries part[y] to such agreements' for the purpose of trade facilitation between constituent territories.[55]

---

[51] For the terms of China's WTO entry, see 'Protocol on the accession of the People's Republic of China', WTO document, WT/L/432 (Geneva: WTO, 23 November 2001).

[52] It is generally considered that China was granted a three-year grace period to ensure full conformity with the WTO requirements. For China's commitment to the liberalisation of the right to trade, see, e.g. 'Protocol on the accession of the People's Republic of China', para. 5.1.

[53] Article 1 of main text of Mainland and Hong Kong Closer Economic Partnership Arrangement (CEPA hereafter), as concluded in June 2003, available at www.tid.gov.hk/english/cepa/index.html.

[54] 2014 Guangdong Agreement, available at www.cepa.gov.mo/cepaweb/front/eng/itemI_2.htm.

[55] Article XXIV(4), GATT 1994.

Considering that Hong Kong accounts for fifty per cent of FDI inflows into China, the importance of trade and investment liberalisation in the PRD should not be underestimated. On 27 November 2015, on the basis of the 2014 Guangdong Agreement, the mainland and Hong Kong signed a new Agreement on Trade in Service that extends the geographical coverage to the entire mainland for the basic liberalisation of trade in services.[56] The 2015 Agreement sets out restrictive measures under 134 service trade sectors reserved by the mainland on the Hong Kong side that are inconsistent with the national treatment requirement.[57]

Around the time of the CEPA framework's tenth anniversary, China pushed forward the trade liberalisation process through the development of FTZs. The first was the Shanghai FTZ, which came into operation in September 2013.[58] According to the FTZ Framework Plan, the purpose of FTZs is to 'boost China's reform and opening up' and 'expedite the functional transformation of the government, explore administrative innovation, stimulate trading and investment facilitation, and accumulate experience on achieving a more open China economy'.[59] Moreover, the FTZ government 'shall explore the administration approach of "National Treatment" on investment permission and [the] "Negative List" [and] deepen the reform [of the] administrative approval system'.[60] Legally, the reform of the FDI approval regime is based on the authorisation of the Standing Committee of the National People's Congress (NPCSC).[61] The same authorisation was granted by the NPCSC to the State Council to adjust the relevant FIE laws to be applied to the Guangdong, Tianjin and Fujian FTZs as of 1 March 2015. The framework proposals for these three new FTZs were subsequently approved by the State Council on 24 March 2015.[62]

---

[56] The 2015 Agreement is available at www.tid.gov.hk/english/cepa/legaltext/cepa13.html.
[57] Annex 1 to the 2015 Agreement.
[58] State Council, Circular on the Framework Plan for the China (Shanghai) Pilot Free Trade Zone, announced on 18 September 2013, GuoFa [2013] 38.
[59] Ibid., para. 1.   [60] Ibid., para. 2.
[61] NPCSC, The Decision on Authorizing the State Council to Temporarily Adjust the Administrative Examination and Approval of Relevant Laws in China (Shanghai) Pilot Free Trade Zone, issued on 30 August 2013. Under the terms of the decision, the Shanghai FTZ is authorised to suspend implementation of the administrative approval procedure-related provisions contained in the EJV, WFOE and CJV Laws for three years.
[62] NPCSC, The Decision on Authorizing the State Council to Temporarily Adjust the Administrative Examination and Approval of Relevant Laws in China (Guangdong), China (Tianjin), China (Fujian) Pilot Free Trade Zones and China (Shanghai) Pilot Free Trade Zone Extended Areas, issued on 28 December 2014 and took effect on 1 March 2015.

The establishment of FTZs was a significant milestone in the reform of China's FDI approval regime and in the liberalisation and decentralisation of trade and investment control. Such reform was pushed further in 2015. On 19 January 2015, the Ministry of Commerce of the People's Republic of China (MOFCOM) released a draft of the PRC Foreign Investment Law for public consultation.[63] If adopted, the new Foreign Investment Law will supersede the EJV, WFOE and CJV Laws.[64] According to MOFCOM, one of the key purposes of the proposed law is to reform China's FDI approval regime.[65] According to the draft, FDI market access management in accordance with the 'negative list' system would replace the current FDI approval system,[66] with foreign investments entitled to national treatment, subject only to the market access restrictions set forth in a Negative List Special Administrative Measure Catalogue to be announced by the relevant authority.[67] Any foreign investment that falls outside the exhaustive 'negative list' of prohibitions and restrictions would no longer require MOFCOM approval.[68]

Although the legal nature of the free-trade cooperation amongst Guangdong, Hong Kong and Macao under the CEPA framework differs from that of the FTZs, the two share the common goal of trade and investment liberalisation.

3 The Beijing Consensus and 'Selective Adaptation'

3.1 Beijing versus Washington Consensus Debate

When China first embarked on economic reform in the late 1970s, other developing countries implementing reforms were 'guided by the then-prevalent Washington Consensus'.[69] Based on the neo-liberal ideology of privatisation, marketisation and liberalisation, the Washington Consensus calls for fiscal discipline, social expenditure, tax reform, banking supervision, exchange rate mechanisms, trade liberalisation, privatisation

---

[63] The PRC Foreign Investment Law (draft for public consultation) and Explanatory Note, released on 19 January 2015, available at http://tfs.mofcom.gov.cn/article/as/201501/20150100871010.shtml.

[64] Article 170, PRC Foreign Investment Law (draft).

[65] Other purposes are to stream the institutional structure of FDI and incorporate the national security review system into the FDI administration regime. See MOFCOM, Explanatory Note of the PRC Foreign Investment Law (draft), 1–2.

[66] Articles 20–47, Market Access Administration, PRC Foreign Investment Law (draft).

[67] Articles 20–23, PRC Foreign Investment Law (draft).

[68] Articles 24–26, PRC Foreign Investment Law (draft).

[69] Lin, Demystifying the Chinese Economy, pp. xv–xvi.

and deregulation, property rights, independent institutions and educational spending.[70] So-called 'shock therapy' based on the Washington Consensus was a common component of post–Cold War reforms in Eastern Europe, contributing to what many consider a lost decade in that region. As 'a hallmark of end-of-history arrogance', the Washington Consensus unfortunately 'left a trail of destroyed economies and bad feelings around the globe'.[71] According to Williamson, the alternative Beijing Consensus consists of five key elements: 1) incremental reform, 2) innovation and experimentation, 3) export-led growth, 4) state capitalism and 5) authoritarianism.[72] Ramo suggests that the success of the Beijing Consensus lies in its commitment to 'the value of innovation', prioritising of 'sustainability and equality' as first considerations and emphasis on 'self-determination'.[73]

The evolution of China's FDI regulatory regime is a very good example of the Beijing Consensus in action. That regime and the country's free trade development from SEZs to the CEPA framework to FTZs have been part of an ongoing process of trade liberalisation and government control decentralisation. The flexibility in investment vehicle choice afforded by the EJV, WFOE and CJV Laws at the beginning of the reform and opening-up period illustrates the Chinese authority's pragmatism and willingness to decentralise FDI control. The loosening of control over free trade rights and construction of the CEPA framework upon China's WTO entry around the turn of the millennium continued the liberalisation and decentralisation trend. The establishment of the FDI guidance regime in 1995, and its ongoing amendment over the years, attempted a balance between the government's policy priorities of innovation and sustainability – through the encouragement of high, new and environmental technologies – and liberalisation and decentralisation through a reduction in the number of items included in the FDI restricted and prohibited categories. It is worth mentioning here that the FDI guidance regime is a dual-list system that incorporates both a positive list (as seen in the encouraged and permitted categories) and negative list (as seen in the restricted and prohibited categories). The 2014 Guangdong Agreement and

[70] Williamson, 'The Washington consensus revisited', 58.
[71] Ramo, The Beijing Consensus, p. 4.
[72] John Williamson, 'Is the "Beijing consensus" now dominant?' (2012) 13 Asian Policy, 6–7.
[73] Ramo, The Beijing Consensus, pp. 11–12.

2015 Agreement under the CEPA framework further pushed the comprehensive liberalisation of trade in services first to Guangdong and then to the whole of Mainland China with the partial adoption of the negative list system.[74] The comprehensive relaxation of FDI control in the 2015 FDI Guiding Catalogue and full adoption of the negative list in the new wave of FTZ reforms in Shanghai, Guangdong, Tianjin and Fujian also effected significant trade liberalisation and decentralisation. During the whole process of evolution from SEZs to CEPA framework to FTZs, the emphasis on self-determination has been the key factor determining the path, pace, extent and schedule of that liberalisation/ decentralisation.

Interestingly, the Beijing Consensus has also taken root in the so-called 'Third World', specifically in Africa. The African Union's (AU) Agenda 2063 is a case in point,[75] being 'an approach to how the continent should effectively learn from the lessons of the past, build on the progress now underway and strategically exploit all possible opportunities available in the immediate and medium term, so as to ensure positive socioeconomic transformation within the next 50 years'.[76] Under Agenda 2063, in addition to these aspirations lies a commitment to 'inclusive growth and sustainable development'.[77] Together with Agenda 2063, the 2015 AU Summit also approved the first Ten-Year Implementation Plan,[78] which outlines priority areas and institutional arrangements, as well as potential sources of funding.[79] In a visit to Africa in December 2015

---

[74] For further details, see the discussion in Section 2.3 of this chapter.

[75] Agenda 2063, the vision and ideas of which were laid down in the African Union's (AU) 50th Anniversary Solemn Declaration at the 21st ordinary session of the African Summit on 26 May 2013, was adopted at the 24th AU Summit, 30–31 January 2015.

[76] *Vision of the Agenda 2063*, available at http://agenda2063.au.int/en//vision.

[77] Amongst the seven aspirations in Agenda 2063 are (1) an integrated continent, politically united and based on the ideals of Pan-Africanism and the vision of Africa's Renaissance; (2) an Africa of good governance, democracy, respect for human rights, justice and the rule of law; (3) a peaceful and secure Africa; (4) an Africa with a strong cultural identity, common heritage, shared values and ethics; (5) an Africa whose development is people-driven, relying on the potential of African people, especially its women and youth, and caring for children and (6) Africa as a strong, united and influential global player and partner.

[78] Adopted at the 24th AU Summit, 30–31 January 2015.

[79] AU, *Report of the Commission on the African Union Agenda 2063: the Africa We Want in 2063* (Assembly/AU/5(XXIV)A), 12. Accordingly, the Ten-Year Plan seeks to 'identify priority areas, their associated targets/expected outcomes and indicative strategies to stakeholders; highlight the fast track programmes/ projects that will bring quick wins and generate and sustain the interest of the African Citizenry in the African

to attend the Forum on China–Africa Cooperation, Chinese President Xi Jinping announced a US$60 million–backed cooperation framework to improve the strategic partnership between the continent and China.[80] Under the framework's terms, 'the two sides also agreed to carry out 10 major cooperation plans in the next three years in the areas of industrialization, agricultural modernization, infrastructure construction, financial services, green development, trade and investment facilitation, poverty reduction and public welfare, public health, people-to-people exchanges, and peace and security'.[81] The aforementioned US$60 billion in funding support is also aimed at ensuring the smooth implementation of the Ten-Year Implementation Plan.[82] To some extent, Agenda 2063 shares with Chinese developments an emphasis on the importance of self-determination in trade development and a commitment to innovation and sustainability. It should not be surprising that the Beijing Consensus has taken root on the African continent. Of course, Agenda 2016 and the AU's first Ten-Year Implementation Plan in themselves are insufficient to indicate the success of the Beijing Consensus or failure of the Washington Consensus. The AU's moves, however, lead us to the issue of the former's implications and the significant contrast between these two major development models.

The Beijing Consensus's emphasis on self-determination clearly distinguishes it from and challenges the path prescribed by the Washington Consensus. The contrast between the two goes beyond economics to the issue of political legitimacy. According to Ramo, the Beijing Consensus 'is as much about social change as economic change' and 'about using economics and governance to improve society'.[83] Indeed, both the

---

Agenda; assign responsibilities and accountabilities to all stakeholders in the implementation, monitoring and evaluation of the plan and outline the strategies required to ensure resource and capacity availability and sustained citizen's engagement for plan execution'. See AU, First Ten-year Implementation Plan 2014–2023, 14. Available at http://agenda2063.au.int/en/documents/agenda-2063-first-ten-year-implementation-plan-2014–2023-september-2015.

[80] Xinhua News Agency, 'China, Africa map out strategic vision for win-win cooperation with practical action plan', 7 December 2015, available at: http://en.people.cn/n/2015/1207/c90000-8986455.html.

[81] Ibid.

[82] Ibid. Under this framework, China's support 'comprises 5 billion dollars of grant and interest-free loans, 35 billion dollars of preferential loans and export credit, 5 billion dollars of additional capital for the China-Africa Development Fund and the Special Loan for the Development of African SMEs each, and a China-Africa production capacity cooperation fund with the initial capital of 10 billion dollars'.

[83] Ramo, The Beijing Consensus, pp. 4–5.

Beijing and Washington Consensuses extend beyond the realm of economics to touch upon the issue of the global balance of power, equality and political legitimacy.[84] According to Halper, one of the central critiques of the former as a 'market-authoritarian' model centres on its deviation from the 'market-democratic' model's endorsement of economic and political freedom and limited government.[85] Williamson, too, categorises China's pursuit of authoritarianism in resisting 'the installation of democracy' as one of the key features of the Beijing Consensus.[86] If the major contrast between the Beijing and Washington Consensuses is the former's deviation from democracy, then we are left with serious doubts about its political legitimacy.

3.2   Beijing Consensus, Selective Adaptation and Legitimacy

However, each of the two models has its own position with respect to legitimacy. Whilst the Washington Consensus inclines towards self-legitimisation, its Beijing counterpart seeks legitimacy in self-determination and adaptation to local conditions. The Washington Consensus, in Ramo's critical view, is 'an economic theory made famous in the 1990s for its prescriptive, Washington-knows-best approach to telling other nations how to run themselves'.[87] That consensus is thus intended to have universal application, and hence popular legitimacy. The fundamental significance of the emergence of the Beijing Consensus, in contrast, is that it marks China's 'shift from a reform process that was young and susceptible to externalities to one that is now self-fulfilling, cranking like a chain reaction and more determined by its internal dynamics than by the external pushes and pokes of things like WTO accession'.[88] China's attention to its distinct local conditions makes all the difference. This contrasting perspective concerning the legitimacy of the Washington Consensus and Beijing Consensus brings us to the broader issue of the legitimacy of development models, an issue that was once dominated by law and development critiques.

The contemporary development paradigm emerged during the reconstruction of the international order after the Second World War. Development itself as a concept of social programming can be traced back to Truman's reference to a 'fair deal' in his 1949 State of the Union

---

[84] Ibid., p. 5.   [85] Halper, *The Beijing Consensus*, p. 134.
[86] Williamson, 'Is the "Beijing consensus" now dominant?', 7
[87] Ramo, *The Beijing Consensus*, p. 4.   [88] Ibid., 5.

address, in which he proposed 'a program of development based on the concepts of democratic fair dealing' to benefit the lives of those people in the 'underdeveloped areas' of the world.[89] Since the birth of the economic growth–orientated development paradigm, the world has seen the gradual transformation of the development paradigm from an economy-orientated, single-dimensional paradigm to a multi-dimensional paradigm.[90] In its first several decades of life, the focus of the development paradigm shifted from modernisation in the 1950s to poverty alleviation in the 1960s and to social development in the 1970s. After the 'lost decade' of development in the 1980s, featuring the Third World Debt Crisis, the Washington Consensus doctrine emphasising economic liberalisation, privatisation and marketisation returned to prominence in the late 1980s and 1990s.

However, economic collapse in Chile and the Asian financial crisis shook that doctrine and triggered intensive research on development theory.[91] Development critiques have revealed how development projects aimed at providing help turned into destructive forces for the peoples and cultures of the Third World.[92] By problematising the Third World, the development model burnishes the legitimacy of the developed world, thereby further problematising the Third World.[93] Under the contemporary development paradigm, by setting the past of the developed world as the future of the developing world, the Washington Consensus has

[89] Arturo Escobar, *Encountering Development: The Making and Unmaking of the Third World* (Princeton, NJ: Princeton University Press, 1995), p. 3; Ruth E. Gordon and Jon H. Sylvester, 'Deconstructing development', (2004) 22 *Wisconsin International Law Journal*, 9–10.

[90] Escobar, *Encountering Development*, pp. 29–49. See also Deepak Nayyar, 'Globalization and development strategies', in J. Toye (ed.), *Trade and Development: Directions for the 21st Century* (Cheltenham, UK: Edward Elgar, 2003), pp. 36–38.

[91] Wenwai Guan, 'Development deficit and modern law's myth of origin', (2008) 8 *Global Jurist Advances*, 4–5.

[92] Ibid., 8–9.

[93] Some development critiques goes even further to argue that development is 'not a natural process' but rather a 'central myth of Western society' that has been developed from the notion of the perfection of progress since the Enlightenment in which the progression notion was used to 'legitimize slavery, genocide, colonialism and all forms of human exploitation'. Moreover, the concept of 'traditional society' is also an 'invention of the European mind', and the 'modernization of "traditional" societies has involved the colonization of the imagination of other societies'. See Vincent Tucker, 'The myth of development: a critique of a Eurocentric discourse', in Ronaldo Munck and Denis O'Hearn (eds.), *Critical Development Theory: Contributions to a New Paradigm* (London: Zed Books, 1999), pp. 8–11, 21.

functioned to eliminate any other possible model of development, thereby undermining its own legitimacy.[94] The Beijing Consensus's attention to local conditions and emphasis on self-determination in the path and pace of development therefore has some degree of justification.

However, China's unprecedented economic growth in the past three decades has never overshadowed doubts about the China model. Rather, it has left China law scholars contemplating the role that legal reform has played in the country's development.[95] Opinions differ on the effectiveness of China's policy framework and the legitimacy of the China model, or Beijing Consensus. Some China scholars are quite critical and/or pessimistic about its future prospects. According to Stanley Lubman, for example, owing to 'the absence of a unifying concept of law and a considerable fragmentation of authority', as well as weak differentiation of the judicial system from the administrative bureaucracy, China does not have an effective legal system.[96] An intuitive conclusion would be that China's legal regime has not played a positive role in China's rapid economic growth or national development, leading to a legitimacy deficit. As to China's integration with the international trading framework, Donald C. Clarke similarly suggests that China is using the WTO to facilitate its own domestic economic reforms rather than to boost international market access,[97] meaning that China's integration with the world is domestically rather than internationally orientated. Clarke further suggests that 'reforms simply imposed from outside are unlikely to go beyond surface compliance', noting that 'the main driver of change in the Chinese legal system will be internal developments in China, not foreign legal assistance programs'.[98] Deviation from 'the international' undermines the legitimacy of the Beijing Consensus.

However, Randall Peerenboom's examination of the role and rule of law in China suggests that 'despite numerous obstacles', China's legal

---

[94] Guan, 'Development deficit', 9–12.
[95] Jerome A. Cohen, 'China's legal reform at the crossroads' (2006, March) *Far Eastern Economic Review*, 23–27; Stanley B. Lubman, *Bird in a Cage: Legal Reform in China after Mao* (Palo Alto, CA: Stanford University Press, 1999); Randall Peerenboom, *China's Long March toward Rule of Law* (Cambridge: Cambridge University Press, 2002); Pitman B. Potter, *The Chinese Legal System: Globalization and Local Legal Culture* (New York: Routledge, 2001).
[96] Lubman, *Bird in a Cage*, pp. 317–318.
[97] Donald C. Clarke, 'China's legal system and the WTO: prospects for compliance', (2003) 2 *Washington University Global Studies Law Review*, 97.
[98] Ibid., 97–98, 118.

reform indicates 'a shift from a legal regime best characterized as rule by law toward a system that complies with the basic elements of a thin rule of law', a rule of law with Chinese characteristics that is different from and an alternative to a liberal democratic rule of law.[99] Peerenboom's perspective allows recognition of the positive role of legal reform in China's economic development. Another eminent China legal scholar, Pitman Potter, argues that the two decades of legal system development in China before its WTO accession constituted a process of 'selective adaptation' by which 'conditions of [the] local legal culture' constantly mediated the application of foreign norms.[100] According to Potter then, China's economic growth and legal reform are involved in the same process of mutual adaptation and mutual growth. The foregoing review also suggests that PRC legislation in particular and legal reform in general have played an important role in, and constitute an indispensable part of, China's unprecedented growth in the past three decades. In the process of growth, legal reform and economic development have been mutual facilitators.[101]

From both the pessimistic and optimistic perspectives, the differences in evaluations of China's conformity towards international norms presuppose a normative standard of international practice. Lubman's perspective questions China's legitimacy because the country fails to meet international standards of the rule of law. As for Peerenboom's perspective, although he predicts the future triumph of the rule of law in China, his characterisation of the rule of law with Chinese characteristics as a 'thin' rule of law still expresses real doubts about China's conformity. In both of these perspectives, legitimacy is something that is either given or presupposed. The theory of selective adaptation, in contrast, addresses the issue of legitimacy with reference to the dynamic mediation of foreign norms and local imperatives, thereby offering a different perspective on the legitimacy of China's development model. The selective adaptation perspective indeed provides us with a better explanation of the legitimacy issues surrounding the Beijing Consensus. That consensus, whilst holding true to its own local conditions and cultural imperatives, enriches international practice with respect to social development, and thus gains its legitimacy from the perspective of law and development critiques.

[99] Peerenboom, *China's Long March*, p. 558.
[100] Potter, *The Chinese Legal System*, pp. 2–3.
[101] Potter's 'selective adaptation' theory is consistent with this finding.

Furthermore, PRC legal reform and economic development have both undergone a gradual, well-structured 'planned-liberalisation' process. Even in the current depressed state of the world's financial markets, this ongoing liberalisation process has not been interrupted, as seen in the gradual decentralisation of China's trade and investment regime discussed herein. This not only constitutes evidence of the burgeoning confidence of the PRC legal regime over time, but also gives foreign investors confidence in PRC trade liberalisation and market predictability in general.

4   Conclusion: Role of the Beijing Consensus in Global Convergence and Divergence

China's economic growth in the past several decades is unprecedented both regionally and internationally. Looking at China's economic growth from the perspective of the evolution of its trade and investment regime, as this chapter does, presents a quite different picture from that painted in economic-orientated studies. The evolution of that regime from SEZs to the CEPA framework to FTZs has been a constant process of liberalisation and decentralisation, as evidenced by the development of the FDI regulatory regime from a dual positive- and negative-list system from the 1995 FDI guidance regime onwards to the full adoption of the negative list system in the FTZs of Shanghai, Guangdong, Tianjin and Fujian. Throughout the liberalisation/decentralisation process, however, the Chinese authorities have never lost sight of their mission to achieve innovation, sustainability and quality growth. The evolution of China's trade and investment regime is an example of well-planned liberalisation.

The so-called 'Beijing Consensus', with its focus on self-determination, presents a significant contrast to the Washington Consensus, which grounds economic growth in the ideologies of liberalisation, privatisation and democratisation ideology. The contrast between the two presents us with a vivid example of the dynamics between convergence and divergence in both the economic and political arenas. The Beijing Consensus presents an alternative path towards development and diverse economic growth that contrasts sharply with the Washington Consensus.

Moreover, further examination of the contrast between these divergent frameworks brings us to the issue of the political legitimacy of development models more widely. According to law and development critiques, by setting the developed world's past as the developing world's future, the Washington Consensus has eliminated any development alternatives for the latter, thereby undermining its own legitimacy. The Beijing Consensus, in contrast, by attending to local conditions and emphasising self-determination, bears a certain legitimacy. It therefore both challenges and enriches the Washington Consensus through a process of selective adaptation that relaxes the tension between international convergence and divergence. Moreover, the roots that the Beijing Consensus has planted on the African continent, as evidenced in Agenda 2063, show its future potential as a model for the developing world.

7

Achievements and Challenges of Chinese Maritime Judicial Practice

LIANG ZHAO

1 Introduction

Maritime judicial practice in the People's Republic of China (PRC) dates back to 1984. After a thirty-year period of development, a comprehensive maritime adjudicatory mechanism is now in place. The experience of maritime adjudication over that thirty-year period constitutes an important basis for maritime legislation in China, particularly the Maritime Code of 1992 (MC 1992 hereafter) and Special Maritime Procedure Law of 1999 (SMPL 1999 hereafter). In addition, the Supreme People's Court (the SPC) has contributed to both legislation and judicial practice by releasing numerous judicial interpretations. China is now considered by many to operate as a maritime judicial centre for the Asia–Pacific region. However, the disharmony of judicial practice in the maritime courts remains an obstacle to further development of Chinese maritime adjudication. I argue in this chapter that the doctrine of precedent may be an appropriate solution to overcoming that obstacle.

2 Maritime Courts in the PRC

The first six maritime courts in China were established in 1984 based on the water transport courts in Shanghai, Tianjin, Qingdao, Dalian, Guangzhou and Wuhan. The establishment of maritime courts was just the beginning of Chinese maritime adjudication, which initially lacked independence. The six initial courts were operated as administrative rather than judicial entities by the port authorities, maritime transport authorities and other navigational authorities under the Ministry of Communications. In June 1999, the six courts were then transferred organisationally to the joint administration of local Communist Party committees and superior People's Courts as *locus in quo*, thereby becoming completely detached from the Ministry of Communications or its affiliates. China established additional maritime courts in Haikou and Xiamen in 1990, in Ningbo in 1992 and in Beihai in 1999.[1] After the 1999 transfer, all ten maritime courts were officially incorporated into the national judicial system for maritime adjudication.

To date, the PRC's maritime courts have established thirty-nine tribunals in the major port cities within their jurisdictional territories, located in fifteen provinces, municipalities or autonomous regions, to conduct on-site hearings, which has created a specialised maritime adjudication infrastructure covering every port in China and the country's entire body of territorial waters. Over thirty years (1984–2013), the ten maritime courts together dealt with 225,283 cases of all types (131,604 first instance cases, 45,646 special maritime cases and 48,033 maritime enforcement cases), and concluded or enforced 215,826 cases (128,776 at courts of first instance, 40,417 at special maritime proceedings and 46,633 at the enforcement stage), involving about seventy countries and regions in Asia, Europe, Africa, and North and South America.[2]

The formation of the Chinese maritime adjudication system is based on the scheme of second instance finality with three levels of courts, including the maritime courts, Superior People's Courts and SPC. The courts at each level have jurisdiction as courts of first instance, the maritime courts over maritime cases, the Superior People's Courts over maritime cases with major implications within their respective jurisdictions[3] and the SPC over two specific types of maritime cases: (1) cases likely to have a major impact nationally and (2) cases that the SPC has deemed that it shall try.[4] If a given party refuses to accept the judgment of a maritime court as the first instance, he or she may appeal to the Superior People's Court in the province, municipality or autonomous region in which the maritime court is located. However, the appellant is not allowed to appeal to the SPC because of the rule of second instance finality. Similarly, the SPC handles appeals from the first instance trials of

---

[1] All four cities are coastal cities.

[2] *White Book on China's Maritime Adjudication (1984–2014)*, The Supreme People's Court of the PRC, Beijing, pp. 13–14.

[3] Not all Chinese Superior People's Courts have jurisdiction over maritime cases as the court of first instance, only those of the provinces, municipalities or autonomous regions in which the maritime courts are located.

[4] Article 21 of the 1991 Civil Procedure Law of the PRC (CPL 1991), as amended in 2007 and 2012.

the Superior People's Courts. If the SPC hears maritime cases as the court of first instance, the judgments therefrom are final.[5]

The maritime courts deal with actions brought by various parties in respect to maritime tort, disputes over maritime contracts and other maritime disputes as provided for by law.[6] Other maritime disputes include but are not limited to disputes over marine insurance contracts and protection and indemnity contracts; the service contracts of the crew of sea-going ships; maritime security; the ownership, possession, employment and maritime liens of a sea-going ship; the operation of coastal ports; pollution damage to sea areas; disputes over offshore exploration and exploitation contracts performed within the territory of the PRC or in the sea area under the jurisdiction of the PRC;[7] and administrative maritime cases related to maritime enforcement.[8] Both the Superior People's Courts and SPC have the same jurisdiction over maritime cases if they are the courts of first instance.

3 Maritime Law and Maritime Procedure Law

Chinese maritime judicial practice commenced before the existence of maritime law legislation. In the early years of the maritime courts, there were no special maritime laws to apply in adjudicating maritime cases. Accordingly, Chinese maritime judges had to learn from and apply the judicial experiences of other jurisdictions and foreign laws.[9] For example, before the enactment of MC 1992,[10] it was recognised in maritime adjudication that a bill of lading (including a straight bill of lading) had three basic functions: as a receipt of goods, evidence of contract of carriage and a document of title. This judicial practice was later embodied in MC 1992.[11] However, not all judicial practices remained unchanged. For example, for disputes relating to charter parties, Chinese maritime judges applied the six-year time bar under English law before

---

[5] In fact, no maritime case has been accepted or tried by the Superior People's Courts or SPC as the court of first instance.

[6] Article 4 of the Special Maritime Procedure Law of 1999 (SMPL 1999).

[7] Ibid., articles 6 and 7.

[8] Certain Provisions of the SPC on the Acceptance Scope of Maritime Courts (2001) specify four categories and sixty-three types of maritime cases as the scope of acceptance for maritime courts.

[9] Primarily the English law and practice of maritime law.

[10] The Maritime Code of 1992 (MC 1992) entered into force on 1 July 1993.

[11] Article 71 of MC 1992.

1993. However, there is now a two-year time bar for charter party disputes in PRC judicial practice.[12]

Maritime adjudication provided a practical basis and was the direct reason for the establishment of a maritime law system. The enactment of MC 1992 was a landmark in China's maritime legislative history, indicating the beginning of a substantive body of law for maritime adjudication. MC 1992 provides for such substantive systems as the carriage of goods by sea and passengers, ships and crews, salvage, collision, general average, limitation of liabilities for maritime claims and marine insurance.

With regard to procedure law, prior to 1999, the maritime courts applied the PRC's Civil Procedure Law of 1991 (CPL 1991 hereafter) to maritime adjudication. However, CPL 1991 provides no rules for property or evidence preservation or any injunctions before the commencement of litigation.[13] The lack of these special rules hindered the development of maritime adjudication in China until Chinese maritime judges broke through the barriers and established new rules for such adjudication. The SPC began drafting the SMPL in 1994, and it was approved by the Standing Committee of the National People's Congress five years later.[14] SMPL 1999 constitutes a milestone in Chinese maritime legislation, as it signifies the establishment of a maritime legal system in China.

4   Disharmony of Judicial Practice

China is not a common law jurisdiction, and thus Chinese maritime judges do not consider or follow precedents, even those set by higher-level courts such as the SPC. Even when judges have studied and considered precedents collected and released by the SPC, they do not cite them as authorities in their judgments. Unless the judges of inferior courts require clarification or an answer to certain legal problems from higher-level courts, they have discretionary powers to make judgments without the interference of other judges or courts.[15] This situation has resulted in inconsistencies in maritime adjudication. In judicial practice, judges may make different or even contradictory judgments concerning the same maritime dispute. Naturally, this situation is not particular to maritime adjudication, but applies to all civil and commercial

---

[12] Ibid., articles 257 and 259.   [13] CPL 1991 was amended in 2007 and 2012.
[14] SMPL 1999 entered into force on 1 July 2000.
[15] In practice, judicial independence may be affected by other real-world matters in China.

adjudication in China.[16] Although inconsistencies do not arise every day, when they do, they serve to undermine confidence in Chinese maritime adjudication. For example, a typical inconsistency is whether a Chinese free-on-board (FOB) seller can be considered a shipper. Different judges in different maritime courts have expressed different opinions on the matter. Such inconsistencies also affect the harmony of law and practice between China and common law jurisdictions.

Let us consider the matter in closer detail. There are two shippers under Chinese law. Under MC 1992, a 'shipper' is '(a) [t]he person by whom or in whose name or on whose behalf a contract of carriage of goods by sea has been concluded with a carrier [or] (b) the person by whom or in whose name or on whose behalf the goods have been delivered to the carrier in relation to the contract of carriage by sea'.[17] This definition comes from the United Nations Convention on the Carriage of Goods by Sea 1978 (the Hamburg Rules), in which the shipper 'means any person by whom or in whose name or on whose behalf a contract of carriage of goods by sea has been concluded with a carrier, or any person by whom or in whose name or on whose behalf the goods are actually delivered to the carrier in relation to the contract of carriage by sea'.[18] The original purpose of having two shippers was to protect the interests of FOB sellers. In an FOB sale of goods contract, the buyer is the shipper, as the contracting party to the carrier. Thus, the FOB seller is not the contractual shipper. In shipping practice, the carrier issues a bill of lading to the shipper, namely, the FOB buyer. However, the bill of lading is an important security document in international sales of goods. To entitle the FOB seller to obtain a bill of lading, the Hamburg Rules provide for a second shipper, who is usually called the actual shipper in practice. Chinese maritime law follows this approach to protect the large number of Chinese exporters.

It is a common understanding in Chinese maritime adjudication that Chinese FOB sellers are not entitled to see bills of lading in accordance with privity of contract.[19] However, some maritime courts insist that they are entitled to do so even though they are not the contractual shippers. In

---

[16] The SPC conducted research on the harmonisation of judicial practice many years ago, but no substantive outcome has been achieved to date.
[17] Article 42(3) of MC 1992.   [18] Article 1(3) of the Hamburg Rules.
[19] See, e.g. *Wenyang Company v. Shanghai Ocean Shipping Company*, collected in the SPC's *Selected Cases of People's Courts* (Beijing: People's Court Press, 2001), vol. 34, pp. 277–282.

Yekalon v. Maersk (China) Shipping Co Ltd,[20] for example, the carrier, i.e.
Maersk, was forced to issue and deliver bills of lading to Yekalon, the
Chinese FOB seller. The dispute arose from a sale of goods contract
between a Chinese seller and a buyer in Benin. The delivery of goods was
to be FOB in accordance with Incoterms 2000.[21] Maersk issued the bill of
lading for which the buyer was the consignee. However, the bill was not
transferred to the buyer as usual, but taken away by the Chinese seller by
means of Chinese legal proceedings. In the Guangzhou Maritime Court,
the Chinese seller applied for an injunction against Maersk. The court
granted the application, and Maersk was forced to deliver the bill to it.
The legal ground cited was the concept of the shipper under the
MC 1992.

As noted, the aim of the shipper concept under Chinese law is to
protect the interests of Chinese exporters. However, it is inconsistent
with the principle of privity of contract recognised in common law
jurisdictions. The discrepancy sometimes causes problems for carriers,
who may be held liable to third parties owing to the manner in which bills
of lading are delivered to Chinese FOB sellers. The judgment in *Yekalon v.
Maersk (China) Shipping Co Ltd* did not end the dispute for the carrier.
Because the buyer did not pay under the contract of sale, the Chinese
seller did not deliver the bill of lading to the buyer but requested that
Maersk deliver the goods to a new buyer by issuing a new bill of lading to
replace the original one. Maersk ultimately delivered the goods to a new
buyer according to the new bill, but in further legal proceedings brought
against Maersk by the original buyer in Benin it was ruled that the
delivery had not discharged Maersk of liability. The Benin proceedings
relied on a photocopy of the original bill of lading, and the Benin court
awarded the judgment to the original buyer. Faced with the enforcement
of that judgment, Maersk brought proceedings in the English Commercial Court seeking a declaration that the original buyer in Benin court had
no right to sue under the original bill of lading. Although the original
buyer's claim in the Benin court was not due to any fault of the Chinese
FOB seller, the change in the original transaction was the result of the

---

[20] Guangzhou Maritime Court Injunction Nos. 18–23 (2008).
[21] FOB (Free on Board) means that the seller delivers the goods on board the vessel
nominated by the buyer at the named port of shipment. The risk of loss of or damage
to the goods passes when the goods are on board the vessel, and the buyer bears all costs
from that moment onwards. See Jan Ramberg, *ICC guide to incoterms 2010: understanding and practical use* (Paris: ICC Publishing S.A., 2011), p. 171. There is no difference of
FOB under Incoterms 2000 and Incoterms 2010.

previous Chinese court order recognising the Chinese FOB seller as the (actual) shipper. Had the Chinese maritime adjudication been consistent with the globally recognised practice in English maritime law to recognise only the contractual party as the shipper, the dilemma the carrier faced in this case would not have occurred.

The SPC recognises the problem of inconsistency, and has attempted to resolve it by several means. First, the SPC releases its judicial interpretations so as to establish unified rules for maritime adjudication in the inferior courts, including the ten maritime courts. Nevertheless, the legal effect of those interpretations has been criticised, as discussed earlier. Second, the SPC requires the maritime courts and the Superior People's Courts to submit five to ten cases every year, from which a batch of typical model cases is selected for exemplification.[22] In the past five years, over fifty leading maritime cases have been selected and published.[23] The purpose of guiding cases is to avoid inconsistencies in the maritime judgments of different maritime courts. However, in maritime adjudication those cases are for reference purposes alone. In practice, a maritime judge may ignore guiding cases, particularly those from other maritime courts.[24] Since 2006, the SPC has organised the re-evaluation of case quality in four maritime courts or the Superior People's Courts every year. Some of the latter courts have also conducted such work, providing timely feedback on any problems discovered to allow corrections. This re-evaluation mechanism emphasises the quality control of maritime judgments, but may not be helpful in resolving the problem of judgment inconsistency. Third, and more importantly, the SPC has strengthened internal information exchange on such areas as adjudicatory work via information feedback in individual cases, the regular circulation of case quality analysis and an annual summary of maritime trials. At the same time, the ten maritime courts take turns hosting an annual forum, adjudication symposium or enforcement symposium to exchange trial experiences with the aim of harmonising adjudicatory standards and judicial activities. Finally, the SPC organises two to three training sessions or research seminars every year to analyse thorny legal issues in maritime

[22] These cases are available from the *Gazette of the Supreme People's Court, Selected Cases of the People's Courts* and *Guide on Foreign-Related Commercial and Maritime Trials*, available from www.ccmt.org.cn.

[23] These cases have been published in *Selected Cases of Maritime Trial in China* (Beijing: Court Press, 2014).

[24] The extent to which guiding cases are considered or followed in Chinese maritime adjudication is unclear because guiding cases have never been cited in judgments.

trials so as to improve maritime adjudication. The SPC's efforts have reduced inconsistency in such adjudication to some extent, but it has thus far been unable to resolve the problem of a lack of harmonisation. Judgment harmonisation may not be wholly dependent on the personalities or educational qualifications of individual judges.[25] However, the doctrine of precedent in common law is the only effective technique of resolving the inconsistency and harmonisation issues. In common law jurisdictions, precedents must be followed, not merely considered as references, thereby preventing contrary judgments in the same maritime disputes.

5 Judicial Interpretation

Although MC 1992 and SMPL 1999 provide substantive law and procedure law, respectively, for Chinese maritime adjudication, Chinese maritime judges are continually beset by legal difficulties that cannot be resolved or clarified by these laws, with the SPC's judicial interpretations filling the gap. In supervising maritime adjudication, the SPC has formulated a 'three-step' judicial interpretation mechanism: from a research report to directive opinions and, finally, to judicial interpretations. Before MC 1992 and SMPL 1999 came into effect, the interpretational rules promulgated by the SPC provided legal guidance for maritime adjudication in China.[26] Subsequently, they have played an increasingly active role in such adjudication because neither MC 1992 nor SPML 1999 has been amended with solutions and clarifications to the aforementioned legal difficulties.[27]

---

[25] According to the *White Book on China's Maritime Adjudication (1984–2014)*, there were 570 judges working on maritime adjudication in China by the end of 2013, of whom 90 per cent had master's or doctoral degrees. However, that high level of education has not resolved the problem of a lack of harmonisation.

[26] These include Detailed Provisions of the Supreme People's Court on Jurisdiction over Foreign-Related Maritime Cases 1986 (repealed), Detailed Provisions of the Supreme People's Court on Pretrial Arrest of Ship 1986 (repealed), Detailed Provisions of the Supreme People's Court on Mandatorily Selling the Ship Arrested by Auction to Satisfy Debts 1987 (repealed), Provisions of the Supreme People's Court on the Scope of Cases to Be Entertained by Maritime Courts 1989 (repealed), Detailed Provisions (tentative) of the Supreme People's Court on the Trial of Claims for Personal Injury and Loss of Life at Sea 1992 (repealed), Provisions of the Supreme People's Court on Pretrial Arrest of Ships by the Maritime Courts 1994 (repealed) and Provisions of the Supreme People's Court on Maritime Court Selling the Ship Arrested by Auction to Satisfy Debts.

[27] These include Provisions of the Supreme People's Court on the Trial of Claim for Property Damages Arising out of Ship Collision and Touch 1995, Reply of the Supreme People's Court on Limitation Period for Claims by Carrier with Regard to Carriage of

There are three types of judicial interpretations. The first are the interpretational rules adopted by the judicial committee of the SPC and promulgated by the SPC. They constitute a formal kind of interpretation that is generally followed by the maritime courts in China. In fact, some of these rules are actually an interpretation of law, e.g. MC 1992, although others are not. For example, under MC 1992, the limitation period for claims against a carrier with regard to the carriage of goods by sea is one year.[28] However, the law does not give a time bar for claims raised by the carrier against cargo interests. The SPC nevertheless 'interpreted' the limitation period for claims from a carrier against a shipper, consignee and/or bill of lading holder also to be one year.[29] Obviously, the SPC creates law through the adoption of interpretational rules despite having no powers of legislation.[30] This kind of judicial interpretation has been criticised for its quasi-legislative role. The second type are particular replies made by the SPC to inferior courts, i.e. the Superior People's Courts and maritime courts, when those courts request clarification or an answer to specific difficult or controversial questions of law. Those replies are, in principle, binding for the courts that raised the questions, but they may not be followed by other courts. The final type are guiding opinions, notices and general understandings of law from the SPC.[31] Because they serve as general guidance for the implementation of law, they have a less binding effect on maritime adjudication in China.

Goods by Sea against Consignor, Consignee or Holder of Bills of Lading 1997, Reply of the Supreme People's Court on Limitation Period for Claims with Regard to Carriage Goods in Coastal Waters and Inland River 2001, Several Provisions of the Supreme People's Court on Scope of Cases to Be Entertained by Maritime Courts 2001, Interpretations of the Supreme People's Court on the Several Issues Concerning Application of the Maritime Procedure Law of the People's Republic of China 2003, Provisions of the Supreme People's Court on Several Issues Concerning Adjudicating Marine Insurance Disputes 2006, Provisions of the Supreme People's Court on Several Issues Concerning Adjudicating Ship Collision Disputes 2008, Provisions of the Supreme People's Court on Several Issues Concerning Law Application in Adjudicating Disputes Arising out of Delivery of Goods without Production of Original Bills of Lading 2009, Provisions of the Supreme People's Court on Adjudicating Disputes Concerning Limitation of Liability for Maritime Claims 2010, Provisions of the Supreme People's Court on Several Issues Concerning Adjudicating Disputes of Compensation for Ship Oil Pollution Damage 2011 and Provisions of the Supreme People's Court on Several Issues Concerning Adjudicating Disputes of Maritime Freight Forwarding 2012.

[28] Article 257(1) of MC 1992.   [29] SPC Judicial Interpretation (1997), No 3.
[30] Only the National People's Congress and its Standing Committee can exercise legislative power in China. See article 7 of the 2000 Legislation Law of the PRC, as amended in 2015.
[31] These understandings may be provided by individual SPC judges, although they are believed to represent the understandings of the SPC as a whole.

6   Doctrine of Precedent

The doctrine of precedent is an important principle in the court systems
of common law jurisdictions. Common law is created by custom and the
judiciary through the doctrine of precedent, namely, judge-made law.
Under this doctrine, lower courts are bound by the decisions of higher
courts. In the English court system, for example, the inferior courts are
not bound by their own decisions but by the decisions of all relevant
superior courts. The High Court, when hearing actions of first instance, is
not bound by other first instance decisions but by the decisions of the
Court of Appeal and Supreme Court, whilst the Court of Appeal is bound
by the decisions of the Supreme Court and its own decisions. Decisions
of the Supreme Court are binding on all other courts in the United
Kingdom.[32] Based on the hierarchy of the courts and the inter-
relationship amongst them, the binding effect of precedent limits the
discretionary power of judges and keeps judgments consistent with
precedent. In other words, the doctrine of precedent guides the development of English common law in a particular way, without inconsistencies
in adjudication. The existence of precedents and their binding effect also
make the law transparent.

   In China, the SPC began selecting and publishing typical cases in 1985.
However, the selected cases are considered only as a reference in judicial
practice, and thus have no legally binding effect. Even if Chinese judges
did consider or follow those cases, they would not disclose or discuss
them in their judgments. More recently, some local courts have conducted experimental trials adopting the doctrine of precedent. However,
those trials have yet to lead to any substantial reform. Although the SPC
has tried to harmonise adjudication through the release of judicial
interpretations, its power of interpretation is limited by a 2015 amendment to the 2000 Legislation Law of the PRC. According to the Decision
of the National People's Congress on Revising the Legislation Law in
2015,[33] a new clause has been added, as Article 104 of the amended
Legislation Law, which reads: 'The interpretations issued by the Supreme
People's Court and the Supreme People's Procuratorate on the specific
application of the law during adjudication and procuratorial work

---

[32] In addition, the decisions of the EU Court of Justice are binding on all English courts,
including the Supreme Court. The decisions of the Judicial Committee of the Privy
Council are not directly binding on English courts but are of persuasive authority.

[33] Article 46 of the Decision of the National People's Congress on Revising the
Legislation Law.

shall mainly focus on specific legal provisions, and be consistent with legislative purposes, principles and intent.'[34] Therefore, even when MC 1992 and SMPL 1999 cannot provide legal answers to a maritime dispute, the SPC is unable to harmonise judicial practice through the release of judicial interpretations.

Although the SPC's powers of interpretation are limited, Chinese judges are not deprived of their discretionary powers. The Judges Law of the PRC provides that judges must take facts as the basis and laws as the criterion when trying cases.[35] In fact, MC 1992 and SMPL 1999 cannot cover every kind of dispute possible in the real world. Therefore, maritime judges' discretionary power is necessary in Chinese maritime adjudication. However, the way in which the exercise of such power can be controlled remains unresolved in judicial practice. One of the results of that lack of resolution is the inconsistency of maritime adjudication. Adoption of the doctrine of precedent would be a good way to resolve the problem because the exercise of discretionary power is limited by precedent, not determined by the personal characters or educational qualifications of individual judges.

7 Conclusion

Over the past thirty years of maritime adjudication in China, the country's maritime courts have faced difficulties, experimented in practice and marched forward towards reform. To ensure future development, Chinese maritime adjudicatory work must resolve the problem of disharmony in judicial practice. If China adopted the doctrine of precedent and recognised select leading cases as legally binding case law, the problem of inconsistency would be resolved and Chinese maritime adjudication would become more transparent. The ultimate result would be greater certainty in Chinese maritime adjudication, encouraging more shipping parties to resolve their maritime disputes in China.

---

[34] It is now article 104(1) of the 2000 Legislation Law, as amended in 2015.
[35] Article 7(2) of the 1995 Judges Law, as amended in 2001.

8

Interaction of National Law-Making and International Treaties

Implementation of the Convention against Torture in China*

BJÖRN AHL

Legislation that was enacted during the reform and opening period of the People's Republic of China (PRC) often related to the country's obligations under international treaties. Various areas of Chinese legislation such as intellectual property law or foreign trade law were inspired by regulatory models found in international treaties or directly followed treaty obligations.[1] International models were often readily taken over, particularly when economic development required a suitable legal framework and national law provided only rudimentary legislation in the area concerned. In this respect, the Chinese legal system followed the tendency towards global convergence based on international law.

However, the interaction between national legislation and international treaties has differed in the area of human rights, where local variations and deviation from international standards are common. Particularly within the scope of the application of the Convention against Torture, legislation and practice have not been in line with the relevant treaty obligations. The prohibition of torture is not only an ordinary treaty obligation but belongs to the category of fundamental human rights, which is binding on all states as *jus cogens*.[2]

* Thanks Pilar Czoske and Marco Otten for their valuable research assistance.

[1] Julia Ya Qin, 'Trade, investment and beyond: the impact of WTO accession on China's legal system' (2007) 191 *China Quarterly*, 720–741; Rohan Kariyawasam, *Chinese Intellectual Property and Technology Laws* (Cheltenham, UK: Edward Elgar, 2011), p. 7.

[2] Malcolm N. Shaw, *International Law* (Cambridge: Cambridge University Press, 2014), p. 88.

Although the Chinese government has acknowledged the pervasiveness of torture in the PRC criminal justice system and has undertaken efforts to reduce torture practices, the United Nations Special Rapporteur on torture found in his mission to China in 2005 that torture and ill treatment remained widespread.[3] A significant improvement in the legislation that implements the PRC's obligations under the Convention against Torture was achieved with the adoption of the 2010 Evidence Rules by the Supreme People's Court (SPC) and other state organs[4] and the amendment of the Criminal Procedure Law (CPL) in 2012.[5]

This chapter investigates the link between the obligations of the PRC under the Convention against Torture and the recent amendment of the CPL, as well as the enactment of judicial interpretations in relation to criminal procedure by the SPC and other state organs in 2010. As the implementation of an international treaty through national legislation is only one among many policy objectives that law-makers in the Chinese party-state take into account when drafting legislation, the aim of this investigation is to evaluate the impact of the Convention against Torture on the legislative process in relation to other factors that have triggered legislative change. An explanation is sought as to why it took the PRC more than twenty years to introduce an exclusionary rule as an effective instrument to reduce the practice of torture. The chapter is based on analysis of legal documents and relevant legal academic discourses that allow conclusions to be drawn as to the extent to which reference to the Convention against Torture played a role in the process leading to the CPL amendment.

After introducing the law and legal doctrine of the interaction of international treaties and national law in China, the obligations of the PRC government under the Convention against Torture are outlined. Against this backdrop, the chapter describes the areas of legislation insufficient to implement the convention and the relevant recent reforms of the CLP. It then turns to analysis of the legal reform discourses in order to reveal the

---

[3] Commission on Human Rights, 'Report of the Special Rapporteur on Torture and Other Cruel, Inhuman or Degrading Treatment or Punishment, Manfred Nowak – Mission to China', E/CN.4/2006/6/Add.6), 10 March 2006, para. 72.

[4] Rules Concerning Questions on the Exclusion of Illegal Evidence in Handling Criminal Cases (*Zuigao Renmin Fayuan, Zuigao Renmin Jianchayuan, Gonganbu, Guojia Anquanbu, Sifabu guanyu Banli Xingshi Anjian Paichu Feifa Zhengju Ruogan Wenti de Guiding*) 13 June 2010.

[5] Criminal Procedure Law (CPL) of the People's Republic of China (PRC) (*Zhonghua Renmin Gongheguo Xingshi Susongfa*) 1 July 1979, amended 17 March 1996 and 12 March 2012.

factors that played a role in triggering the recent reforms. Finally, the chapter concludes with an explanation of the development of national law in relation to obligations under the Convention against Torture.

1 Chinese Law and Legal Doctrine and the Interaction of International Treaties and National Law

The Chinese legislature and relevant judicial and administrative practices have established a mechanism for the reception of international law in China that allows a maximum degree of flexibility.[6] Chinese doctrine does not understand the interrelation of public international law and municipal law in terms of monism or dualism. Instead, commentators follow the Soviet dialectical model, which stipulates that international law and municipal law are separate systems that infiltrate and supplement rather than conflict with each other.[7]

The Chinese Constitution is silent on the legal effects and status of public international law within the national legal system. Article 67(14) of the Constitution provides that the National People's Congress Standing Committee (NPCSC) decides on the ratification of international treaties. The committee's competence to decide on ratification implies that treaties have the same rank in domestic law as statutes adopted by the NPCSC. However, given the current practice of internal treaty application in the PRC, the NPCSC's decision and subsequent publication of the treaty text in the *Official Gazette* do not have the capacity to allow the administration and courts to apply the treaty provisions directly. To apply a treaty provision directly, the courts or administration would require either a statutory reference norm or a judicial interpretation by the SPC referring to the relevant international treaty.[8] Reference norms are statutory provisions that provide for the application of specific international treaties within municipal law if certain conditions are fulfilled, such as that national law contravenes an international treaty obligation.[9] Neither the effective CPL nor Criminal Law, however,

---

[6] Björn Ahl, 'Chinese law and international treaties' (2009) 39 *Hong Kong Law Journal*, 735–750 at 737; Keyuan Zou, 'International law in the Chinese domestic context' (2009–2010) 44 *Valparaiso University Law Review*, 935–956.

[7] Wang Tieya, *Introduction to International Law (Guojifa Yinlun)* (Beijing: Bei Daxue Chubanshe, 1998), p. 191.

[8] Ahl, 'Chinese law and international treaties', 747–748.

[9] Article 142(2) of General Principles of Civil Law (*Minfa Tongze*) 4 December 1986, amended 27 August 2009: 'If any international treaty concluded or acceded to by the

contains a statutory reference norm that provides for the prior application of an international treaty in the case that national criminal procedure law deviates from the obligations of the PRC under international treaties.[10]

Judicial interpretations of the SPC that provide for the application of international treaty provisions have the purpose of either substituting for or supplementing statutory reference norms. The SPC's Interpretation of Certain Issues Relating to the Implementation of the PRC Criminal Procedure Law of 1998, provided in article 317, states that specific provisions on criminal procedure in international treaties that are binding on China should be applied in criminal litigation.[11] However, the SPC's interpretation of the amended CPL in 2012 no longer contains a provision referring to international treaties.[12] Although some scholars hold that the Chinese courts are obliged to directly apply the Convention against Torture in criminal proceedings whenever there is a Chinese legal provision that contradicts the international treaty,[13] in practice the courts do not do so.[14]

According to Chinese treaty implementation practice, a treaty provision is made part of the municipal legal system by the relevant NPCSC

People's Republic of China contains provisions differing from those in the civil laws of the People's Republic of China, the provisions of the international treaty shall apply, unless the provisions are ones on which the People's Republic of China has announced reservations.'

[10] The only reference to international treaties in the current CPL is contained in article 17, which provides for the conduct of international judicial assistance in criminal matters under relevant international treaties and the principle of reciprocity.

[11] Interpretation of the SPC on Certain Issues Relating to the Implementation of the PRC CPL (*Zuigao Renmin Fayuan Guanyu Zhixing Zhonghua Renmin Gongheguo Xingshi Susongfa Ruogan Wenti de Jieshi*) 2 September 1998; Wan Yi has argued that article 317 of the Interpretation implies the direct application of relevant international treaties by the court. See Wan Yi, 'Discussion of the interpretation of criminal procedure law' (*'Xingshi susongfa jieshilun'*) (2007) *China Law* (*Zhongguo Faxue*), 80–95 at 84–85.

[12] Interpretation of the SPC on the Application of the PRC CPL (*Zuigao Renmin Fayuan Guanyu Shiyong Zhonghua Renmin Gongheguo Xingshi Susongfa de Jieshi*) 5 November 2012.

[13] Wan Yi, 'Discussion of the interpretation and determination of confession by torture' (*'Lun 'Xingxu Bigong' de Jieshi yu Rending'*) (2011) 33 *Modern Law Science* (*Xiandai Faxue*), 174–183 at 176.

[14] Chinese Human Rights Defenders Information Submission to the UN Committee against Torture for Consideration in List of Issues – February 2015, 9 February 2014, para. 1. The Information Submission states that the Chinese Human Rights Defenders 'have not been able to document any cases of direct application of the Convention by any courts in China'.

decision and subsequent publication in the *Official Gazette*. Whether a treaty provision can be directly applied by an administrative organ or court depends on the existence of a provision in municipal law that explicitly refers to the international treaty in question. This rather complex mechanism controlling the application of international treaties in China can be used to limit the effectiveness of domestic treaty implementation because it leaves judicial and administrative organs enough latitude to ignore international obligations. The flexibility inherent in this approach puts the party-state into an advantageous position on the international and national levels. In the case that the PRC government faces criticism for the improper implementation of an international human rights treaty, it can argue either that the treaty has already automatically become part of the domestic legal system or point to the published treaty text in the *Official Gazette* or to a reference norm. At the same time, if a claim before a domestic Chinese court is based on an international human rights treaty, the court can argue either that the preconditions for the application of a reference norm are not fulfilled or that the treaty had already been transformed into domestic law and thus that only the relevant provisions of domestic law should apply.[15]

Apart from allowing for the direct application of international treaties via reference provisions, the domestic legal system can also be harmonised with international treaties by amending existing laws and regulations or by adopting new legislation.[16] As there are no statutory reference provisions in the field of criminal procedure that refer directly to the Convention against Torture, adopting legislative steps that bring criminal procedure law in line with the convention's requirements appears to be the preferred mode of treaty implementation in this case. Further, the convention itself requires states to adopt effective legislative measures to prevent any acts of torture.[17]

---

[15] Björn Ahl, 'Statements of the Chinese government before human rights treaty bodies: doctrine and practice of treaty implementation' (2010) 12 *Australian Journal of Asian Law*, 82–105.

[16] Ming Wan, 'Human rights law-making in China' (2007) 29 *Human Rights Quarterly*, 727–753.

[17] Article 4(1) of Convention against Torture and Other Cruel, Inhuman or Degrading Treatment or Punishment, General Assembly resolution 39/46, 10 December 1984, entry into force 26 June 1987.

2 China's Obligations under the Convention against Torture and Lack of Proper Legislation to Implement It

The 1984 Convention against Torture was signed by the PRC on 12 December 1986 and ratified on 4 October 1988.[18] Although the PRC government was not involved in the drafting of the Convention against Torture, it ratified it at an early date. The convention provides for a definition of torture in article 1(1), according to which

> the term 'torture' means any act by which severe pain or suffering, whether physical or mental, is intentionally inflicted on a person for such purposes as obtaining from him or a third person information or a confession, punishing him for an act he or a third person has committed or is suspected of having committed, or intimidating or coercing him or a third person, or for any reason based on discrimination of any kind, when such pain or suffering is inflicted by or at the instigation of or with the consent or acquiescence of a public official or other person acting in an official capacity.[19]

According to article 4, China has to 'ensure that all acts of torture are offences under its criminal law'.

The Criminal Law of 1997 prohibits law enforcement officials from extorting confessions from criminal suspects by torture, from using force to extract testimony from witnesses and from physically abusing those in custody.[20] However, the stipulations on banning torture in the Chinese Criminal Law fall short of some of the requirements set forth in the

---

[18] Decision of the Standing Committee of the National People's Congress (NPCSC) on the Approval of the Convention against Torture and Other Cruel, Inhuman or Degrading Treatment or Punishment (*Quanguo Renmin Changweihuui Guanyu Pizhun 'Jinzhi Kuxing he Qita Canren, Bu Rendao huo You Ru Renge de Daiyu huo Chufa Gongyue' de Jueding*) 5 September 1988. The PRC expressed reservations concerning articles 20 and 30(1) of the Convention against Torture.

[19] Most definitions of torture in human rights treaties share the first two elements of the severity of the pain or suffering inflicted on the victim and the intentional infliction of pain or suffering. The third element of the definition under the Convention against Torture requires the intentional causing of pain to be for a specific purpose and mentions four typical purposes, such as obtaining information or a confession, punishment, intimidation and discrimination. The fourth element requires that the acts be committed in an official capacity, which means that non-state actors are covered only if the act is committed at the instigation of or with the consent or acquiescence of a public official or other person acting in an official capacity. See David Kretzmer, 'Torture, prohibition of', in Rüdiger Wolfrum (ed.), *Max Planck Encyclopedia of Public International Law* (Oxford: Oxford University Press, 2010).

[20] Articles 247 and 248 of the PRC CPL, 1 July 1979, 14 March 1997.

Convention against Torture.[21] For example, the former includes no reference to the infliction of severe mental pain or suffering, and nor does it address the use of torture for purposes other than to extract confessions.[22] Further, attempts to commit torture and acts of complicity or participation in torture are not criminalised, as required by article 4 of the Convention against Torture. Different from the convention, the Criminal Law extends only to such perpetrators as judicial officers, police officers or other officers in detention facilities.[23] The victims of torture are specified as criminal suspects or defendants. Hence, the ill treatment of persons who have not yet been formally arrested or who are being held in administrative detention would not amount to torture in the sense of article 247 or 248 of the Chinese Criminal Law. The Committee against Torture has frequently criticised the Chinese government for not incorporating into domestic law a definition of torture that fully complies with the definition contained in the Convention against Torture.[24]

With regard to criminal procedure, the convention provides that states have to 'ensure that any statement which is established to have been made as a result of torture shall not be invoked as evidence in any proceedings, except against a person accused of torture as evidence that the statement was made'.[25] Further, it requires measures that are aimed at the prevention of torture and address cases of torture such as the education and training of law enforcement personnel and other officials with regard to the prohibition of torture,[26] systematic review of interrogation rules and instructions and arrangements for detention,[27]

---

[21] Elisa Nesossi, *China's Pre-Trial Justice. Criminal Justice, Human Rights and Legal Reforms in Contemporary China* (London: Wildy, Simmonds & Hill, 2012), pp. 176–177.

[22] Commission on Human Rights, Report of the Special Rapporteur on Torture and Other Cruel, Inhuman or Degrading Treatment or Punishment, para. 17.

[23] Ibid.

[24] The Committee against Torture made the following recommendation: 'The State party should include in its legislation a definition of torture that covers all the elements contained in article 1 of the Convention, including discrimination of any kind. The State party should ensure that persons who are not judicial officers and officers of an institution of confinement, but who act in an official capacity or with the consent or acquiescence of a public official can be prosecuted for torture. The State party should also ensure that its legislation prohibits the use of torture for all intents and purposes.' Concluding Observations of the Committee against Torture – China, Forty-first session, 3–21 November 2008, CAT/C/CHN/CO/4, 12 December 2008, para. 32–33.

[25] Article 15 of Convention against Torture.

[26] Article 10(1) of Convention against Torture.

[27] Article 11 of Convention against Torture.

procedures for complaints and the investigation of cases of alleged torture,[28] and compensation for victims of torture.[29]

Although even before the 2012 revision the PRC CPL contained in article 43 a prohibition against the extortion of confessions by torture, this was regarded as a provision with only declaratory meaning as it did not stipulate the specific legal consequences of its violation.[30] Article 61 of the 1998 CPL interpretation stipulated that evidence obtained by threat, enticement, deceit or other unlawful means may not be used in deciding a case.[31] However, the courts lacked specific guidance on how to determine whether a confession had been obtained through illegal means or how to rule on the exclusion of evidence.[32] Hence, the courts continued to rely on confessions as a basis for determining guilt, and the reforms did not significantly change the widespread practice of coerced confessions.

According to the Special Rapporteur's report, the aforementioned deficiencies in the PRC CPL have contributed to the continuing practice of torture in China. The rules of evidence in force before 2010 were even regarded as creating incentives for interrogators to obtain confessions through torture. Keeping criminal suspects in police custody for long periods of time, the absence of the presumption of innocence or an effective right to remain silent, and restricted rights and access to defence counsel were seen as the main legal factors facilitating the practice of torture.[33] According to the report, the lack of a free and investigatory press and human rights organisations, as well as the institutional weakness of the judiciary, further aggravated the situation.[34]

3   Recent Reforms of Criminal Procedure Law

Before the revision of the CPL in 2012, the SPC, Supreme People's Procuratorate (SPP), Ministry of Public Security, Ministry of State Security and Ministry of Justice, on 13 June 2010, jointly issued a Notice Regarding the Regulations on the Examination and Evaluation of Evidence in Capital Cases and Regulations on the Exclusion of Illegally

---

[28] Articles 12 and 13 of Convention against Torture.
[29] Article 14 of Convention against Torture.
[30] Wan, 'Discussion of the interpretation and determination', 174.
[31] Article 61 of Interpretation of the SPC on Certain Issues Relating to the Implementation of the PRC CPL, 2 September 1998.
[32] Nesossi, *China's Pre-Trial Justice*, p. 179.
[33] Report of the Special Rapporteur, para. 73.   [34] Ibid., para. 74–75.

Obtained Evidence in Criminal Cases.[35] The importance of the Notice
was evidenced not only by the participation in its adoption of the two
powerful ministries responsible for public and state security but also by
its reference to the Communist Party Central Political–Legal Committee
and its then-secretary and Politburo member Zhou Yongkang.

The significance for the party-state of issuing the Notice and the two
evidence-related Regulations lay in the attempt to exercise tighter control
over police conduct at the local level and 'as a mechanism to distance
central policy from local misconduct'.[36] As reports on miscarriages of
justice in the national media undermine the legitimacy of the party-state,
the regulations aimed to restore trust in the state and the judicial system.
The negative impact of reports of coerced confessions leading to wrongful convictions appeared to weigh so heavily on the leadership that it was
prepared to accept far-reaching constraints on the police on which it was
heavily reliant to maintain the system of the one-party state.

The Notice stated that two sets of regulations should be stringently and
thoroughly implemented: first, the equal importance of punishing crime
and protecting human rights and, second, the equal importance of
substantive and procedural law.[37] It thus expressed a fundamental shift
away from the sole focus on crime control. The Regulations on Evidence
in Death Penalty Cases are far more detailed and comprehensive than the
Regulations on the Exclusion of Evidence. The former build on recent
comprehensive policy changes and legal reforms in the handling of death
penalty cases.[38] They specify the standard of proof in capital cases and
require that each item of evidence that is used as a basis for conviction
undergo a legal procedure by which it is examined and verified.[39] The
Regulations on Evidence in Death Penalty Cases further list seven categories of evidence and provide specific factors for each category, which

[35] Notice of the Publication of the 'Regulations on the Examination and Evaluation of
Evidence in Capital Cases' and 'Regulations on the Exclusion of Illegally Obtained
Evidence in Criminal Cases' (*Zuigao Renmin Fayuan, Zuigao Renmin Jianchayuan,
Gonganbu, Guojia Anquanbu, Sifabu Guanyu 'Guanyu Banli Sixing Anjian Shencha
Panduan Zhengju Ruogan Wenti de Guiding' he 'Guanyu Banli Xingshi Anjian Paichu
Feifa Zhengju Ruogan Wenti de Guiding' de Tongzhi*) 13 June 2010.
[36] Margaret K. Lewis, 'Controlling abuse to maintain control: the exclusionary rule in
China' (2011) 43 *New York University Journal of International Law and Politics*,
629–697 at 675.
[37] Article 1 of Notice, 13 June 2010.
[38] Susan Trevaskes, *The Death Penalty in Contemporary China* (New York: Palgrave
Macmillan, 2012).
[39] Article 5 of Death Penalty Evidence Regulations.

judges must take into account when evaluating evidence in death penalty cases.[40] Although the Evidence Exclusion Regulations are less elaborate and detailed, they apply to all categories of criminal cases. They distinguish between oral evidence on the one hand and physical and documentary evidence on the other. Pursuant to the Evidence Exclusion Regulations, 'the category of illegal oral evidence includes statements by criminal suspects or defendants obtained through illegal means such as coerced confession as well as witness testimony or victim statements obtained through illegal means such as use of violence or threats'.[41] Such 'oral evidence that has been determined to be illegal in accordance with the law shall be excluded and may not serve as the basis for conviction'.[42] With regard to the exclusion of physical and documentary evidence, the Regulations do not follow an approach as strict as that concerning oral evidence, stipulating that 'if material or documentary evidence is obtained in a manner that clearly violates the law and may have an impact on the fairness of adjudication, redress or some reasonable explanation should be made, otherwise that material or documentary evidence may not serve as a basis for conviction'.[43] This provision contains both a 'discretionary exclusion' and a 'curable exclusion'. The exclusion is discretionary because trial judges have broad discretion to determine whether a 'clear violation' of the law has occurred and whether the 'fairness of adjudication' is affected. The provision also contains a curable exclusion in that the court may order rectification or explanation of the violation. A procedural violation can be cured by obtaining evidence a second time through legal means or, if that is impossible, by providing a reasonable explanation of why the procedural violation occurred in the first place.[44]

In addition to excluding confessions of criminal suspects or defendants that were extorted by torture or other illegal means, the Regulations also provide for a procedure for determining whether torture has occurred. Before or during the trial, the defendant can challenge a pre-trial confession and initiate a court investigation.[45] He or she has to provide leads or

---

[40] Articles 6–28 of Death Penalty Evidence Regulations.
[41] Article 1 of Evidence Exclusion Regulations.
[42] Article 2 of Evidence Exclusion Regulations.
[43] Article 14 of Evidence Exclusion Regulations.
[44] Chen Ruihua, 'China's new exclusionary rule: an introduction' (2011) 24 *Columbia Journal of Asian Law*, 229–246 at 235.
[45] Articles 4 and 5 of Evidence Exclusion Regulations.

evidence for the alleged illegal obtaining of evidence.[46] If the court has doubts about the legality of the way in which the pre-trial confession was obtained, then the Procuratorate has to provide evidence that the interrogation of the defendant was conducted lawfully. The applicable standard of proof is 'clear facts and reliable, sufficient evidence'.[47] The Procuratorate has to submit interrogation transcripts and audio or video recordings of the interrogation. Further, the court can request that the interrogators provide testimony before the court and confirm that the confession was obtained legally.[48] Under the Evidence Exclusion Regulations, the evidence can be cross-examined by the defence and prosecution.[49] If the Procuratorate does not provide sufficient evidence to confirm the legality of the pre-trial confession, then that confession may not constitute the basis for conviction.[50] Previously, it was very difficult to prove that torture had occurred. The only evidence that the courts would accept was physical evidence on the victim's body or medical reports. If they had only the victim's allegation of torture, the courts were generally satisfied with written police statements, which of course denied that torture had occurred.[51] The Regulations indicate a far-reaching change, as they provide for police officers to appear before the court in person and to both explain and justify their actions. However, they do not provide for a broad rule of exclusion that covers all evidence obtained on the basis of coerced confessions. In particular, the Regulations do not exclude further evidence that is obtained with the aid of illegally obtained evidence (fruit of the poisonous tree).[52]

According to article 54 of the revised CPL, a confession of a criminal suspect or defendant that has been extorted by torture or obtained by

---

[46] Article 14 of Evidence Exclusion Regulations.
[47] Article 11 of Evidence Exclusion Regulations.
[48] Article 7(1) of Evidence Exclusion Regulations.
[49] Article 7(4) of Evidence Exclusion Regulations.
[50] Article 11 of Evidence Exclusion Regulations.
[51] Nesossi, *China's Pre-Trial Justice*, p. 191.
[52] Chen, 'China's new exclusionary rule', 231; Wang Ge, 'On the limited exclusion of illegal evidence – interpretation of five big theoretical problems of the "Regulations on Exclusion of Illegal Evidence"'(*'Feifa Zhengju de Youxian Paichu Zhuyi Zhi Huo – Dui 'Feifa Zhengju Paichu Guiding' Wu Da Lilun Wenti Zhi Jiedu'*) (2010) *Journal of Shandong Police College* (*Shandong Jiancha Xueyuan Xuebao*), 15–20 at 16; Zuo Ning, 'Discussion of the scope of exclusion in China's illegal evidence rules – based on thoughts about the new art. 54 "Criminal Procedure Law" and relevant judicial interpretations' (*'Lun Wo Guo Feifa Zhengju Paichu Guize de Paichu Weifan yu Paichu Jieguo – Jiyu Woguo Xin 'Xingshi Susongfa' Die 54 Tiao yu Sifa Jieshi Xiangguan Guiding de Xingsi'*) (2014) *Law Journal* (*Faxue Zazhi*), 116–123, at 118.

other illegal means, or witness testimony or a victim statement that has been obtained by violence, threats or other illegal means, shall be excluded. With regard to physical or documentary evidence that has not been obtained in accordance with legal procedures and might seriously influence judicial fairness, a correction or reasonable explanation shall be provided; otherwise, such evidence shall be excluded. Article 54 reiterates and codifies into law what was already stated in more detail in the Evidence Exclusion Regulations. Hence, the revision of the CPL did not change the scope or procedure of the SPC's exclusion rule of 2010. Chinese commentators have criticised article 54 of the CPL for not being in line with international standards because only certain specified categories of evidence rather than all kinds of illegally obtained evidence are excluded.[53]

4 Reasons for Criminal Procedure Law Reform as Reflected in Legal Discourses

Official documents on the revision of criminal procedure do not recognise the Convention against Torture as a rationale for legal reform or even as a standard against which the success of criminal procedure reform can be measured. The CPL amendment has primarily been perceived and presented as a measure that deepens the judicial and working mechanism reforms of the Central Party Committee. The relevance of international factors in the development of Chinese laws is expressly limited, with researchers highlighting that the legislature has continued to take national conditions as a starting point for reform and avoided blindly copying foreign judicial or procedural systems.[54] With regard to the formal legislative procedure, the Explanation of the Draft Amendment of the CPL does not refer to implementation of international human rights treaties as an aim of the proposed amendments.[55]

---

[53] Fan Chongyi, *The Road of Fairness and Justice – Commentary of Articles and Explanation of Specific Issues of the Decision on Amending the Criminal Procedure Law* (*Gongping Zhengyi zhi Lu – Xingshi Susongfa Xiugai Guiding Tiaowen Shiyi yu Zhuanti Jiedu*) (Beijing: Zhongguo Renmin Gongan Daxue Chubanshe, 2012), p. 24.

[54] Huang Taiyun, 'Explanation of the amended criminal procedure law' (*'Xingshi Susong Fa Xiugai Shiyi'*) (2012) *People's Procuratorate* (*Renmin Jiancha*), 10–73 at 10.

[55] Explanation of the Draft Amendment of the PRC CPL (*Guanyu Zhonghua Renmin Gongheguo Xingshi Susong Fa Xiuzheng An (Cao An) de Shuoming*) 8 March 2012.

4.1 Arguments Relating to National Exigencies

The criminal procedure law reforms aimed at rooting out coerced confessions were primarily connected to the conviction of innocent persons. The adoption of the judicial interpretation of 2010 that introduced the exclusion of illegal evidence rule was triggered by the nationally reported *Zhao Zuohai* case, which concerned a farmer who had been wrongly convicted of murder and was released from prison only after the alleged murder victim, who was alive and well, returned to his village after a decade away. Zhao had been subjected to physical and mental abuse in police custody and confessed to murder under torture.[56] The *Zhao Zuohai* case was not the only factor leading to the adoption of the exclusion of illegal evidence rule and the procedural safeguards for its implementation, but it functioned as a catalyst for the relevant reforms, as the reasons for and causal links between police torture and confessions and miscarriages of justice had been analysed by Chinese legal scholars for many years.[57]

Miscarriages of justice have contributed to a loss of public trust in both the court system and party-state.[58] After the power shift of 2012–2013, the rehabilitation of miscarriage of justice cases became a focal point in the speeches of political leaders and in reform plans.[59] In September 2013, for example, the SPP issued an Opinion on Preventing and Correcting Miscarriage of Justice Cases.[60] Then, in October 2013 the SPC followed suit with a similar opinion stressing the protection of human rights, independent exercise of trial powers according to the law and

[56] Nesossi, *China's Pre-Trial Justice*, p. 185.

[57] Fang Peng, 'Rational analysis of wrongful convictions in death penalty cases – empirical analysis of 33 wrongful death cases reported by the media' (*'Sixing Cuo'an de Lixing Fenxi – Dui Meiti Baodao de 33 Qi Sixing Cuo'an de Shizheng Kaocha'*) (2006) *Criminal Law Comments* (*Xingfa Pinglun*), 26–91; He Jiahong and He Ran, 'Empirical study and economic analysis of wrongful convictions and evidence problems' (*'Xingshi Cuo'an zhong de Zhengju Wenti – Shizheng Yanjiu yu Jingji Fenxi'*) (2008) *Political Science and Law Tribune* (*Zhengfa Luntan*), 3–19; Lewis, 'Controlling abuse to maintain control', 634.

[58] Ira Belkin, 'China's tortuous path toward ending torture in criminal investigations' (2011) 24 *Columbia Journal of Asian Law*, 273–301 at 277.

[59] Fourth Five-Year Plan on Judicial Reform 2014–2018 (*Renmin Fayuan di Si ge Wu Nian Gaige Gangyao 2014–2018*) 9 July 2014; article 1 of the plan refers to the 'aim of tightly focusing on letting people feel fairness and justice in every single judicial case'.

[60] SPP's Certain Opinions on Properly Performing Prosecutorial Functions to Prevent and Correct Miscarriage of Justice Cases (*Zuigao Renmin Jianchayuan Guanyu Qieshi lüxing Jiancha Zhineng Fangzhi he Jiuzheng Yuan Jia Cuo An de Ruogan Yijian*) 9 September 2013.

adjudication on the basis of evidence.[61] A number of cases that have raised serious doubts are under review, are being retried or have been overturned, and many victims of gross injustice have been compensated.[62] In addition to cases of wrongful conviction, there have been cases of police brutality and the maltreatment of suspects in police detention, as well as widespread public dissatisfaction with how the state administers justice, all of which contributed to the introduction of the 2012 Evidence Exclusion Regulations.[63] Hence, the dominant factor leading to the adoption of a mechanism for excluding coerced confessions was the priority the leadership afforded reductions in miscarriages of justice. Criticisms from international human rights organisations, in particular the concluding observations of the treaty body of the Convention against Torture, and other international factors that may have had a measurable impact on the legislative process played no decisive role in triggering the recent reforms.

4.2 Arguments Relating to the Convention against Torture

A substantial number of academic discussions have attempted to link China's CPL reform with international human rights treaties.[64] Many articles refer in detail to the procedural rights enshrined in the International Covenant on Civil and Political Rights (ICCPR) as a benchmark of criminal procedure reform, although the PRC has signed but not yet

---

[61] SPC's Opinion on Establishing Working Mechanisms to Prevent Miscarriage of Justice in Criminal Cases (*Zuigao Renmin Fayuan Guanyu Jianli Jianquan Fangfan Xingshi Yuan Jia Yuan An Gongzuo Zhidu de Yijian*) 9 October 2010.

[62] Article 2 of 2015 Working Report of the SPC (*2015 Nian Zuigao Renmin Fayuan Gongzuo Baogao*) 3 March 2015.

[63] Lewis, 'Controlling abuse to maintain control', 672–675.

[64] Sun Hongkun, 'Human rights protection and the new revision of the criminal procedure law' ('*Renquan Baozhang yu Xingshi Susongfa de Zai Xiugai*') (2006) 30 *Journal of Anhui University (Philosophy and Social Sciences Edition)* (*Anhui Daxue Xuebao [Zhexue shehui Kexueban]*), 53–58; Cui Kai and Feng Na, 'The influence of the anti-torture convention on the Chinese procedure of criminal prosecution' ('*Jinzhi Kuxing Gongyue' dui Woguo Fanzui Zhuijiu Chengxu de Yingxiang*') (2009) 31 *Journal of Wuhan Technical University* (*Wuhan Gongcheng Daxue Xuebao*), 26–29; Zhao Shanshan, 'From punishment to prevention' ('*Cong Zhengfa Zouxiang Yufang*') (2012) 30 *Tribune of Political Science and Law* (*Zhengfa Luntan*), 107–119; Sun Changyong, 'On the revision of the criminal procedure law' ('*E lun 'Xingshi Susongfa' de Zai Xiugai*') (2004) 26 *Modern Law Science* (*Xiandai Faxue*), 26–31; Ye Qing and Tan Zhepeng, 'Functional analysis of the draft of the revision of the criminal procedure law' ('Xingshi Susongfa Xiuzheng'an (Cao'an)' de Gongnengxing Fenxi') (2012) *Law Journal* (*Faxue Zazhi*), 105–112.

ratified the covenant.[65] As article 7 of the ICCPR prohibits torture and cruel, inhuman or degrading treatment or punishment, the introduction of the exclusionary rule in the CPL brings China's legal system into conformity with the requirements of the ICCPR and paves the way for its future ratification. Some academic articles advocate the view that the CPL reform took the requirements of international treaties into account.[66] Such commentators generally relate the introduction of the exclusionary rule in article 54 of the CPL to the corresponding article 15 of the Convention against Torture.[67] The previous lack of an exclusionary rule is regarded as one of the most striking examples of Chinese domestic law's failure to implement the content of the Convention against Torture.[68] Some authors are more cautious, however, arguing that the convention may have served as an important reference for the CPL reforms, but noting that implementation had to take into account the specific conditions in China and be supported by personnel and institutional reforms.[69]

There has been much discussion of whether the wording of the definition of torture contained in the Convention against Torture, particularly the reference to mental pain and suffering, should have been

[65] Chen Guangzhong and Zhang Jianwei, 'The United Nations ICCPR and Chinese criminal procedure' ('Lianheguo 'Gongmin Quanli he Zhengzhi Quanli Guoji Gongyue' yu Woguo Xingshi Susong') (1998) Chinese Law (Zhongguo Faxue), 98–108; Su Caixia, 'The reform of the retrial procedure in Chinese criminal law from the perspective of the ICCPR' ('Cong 'Gongmin Quanli he Zhengzhi Quanli Guoji Gongyue' Kan Woguo Xingshi Zaishen Chengxu Gaige') (2004) International Law Review (Huanqiu Falü Pinglun), 60–65; Sun Shiyan, 'The Supreme People's Court's first instance jurisdiction in criminal matters viewed from the perspective of art. 14(5) of the ICCPR' ('Cong 'Gongmin Quanli he Zhengzhi Quanli Guoji Gongyue' di 14 Tiao di 5 Kuan Kan Zuigao Renmin Fayuan dui Xingshi Anjian de Yishen Guanxia Quan') (2014) Modern Law (Dangdai Faxue), 142–150; Xie Yanhua, 'The revision of China's criminal procedural law and the strengthening of human rights protection' ('Woguo Xingshi Susongfa de Xiugai yu Renquan Baozhang de Qianghua') (2012) 29 Journal of Hebei University of Engineering (Social Science edn.) (Hebei Gongcheng Daxue Xuebao [Shehui Kexueban]), 74–77.
[66] Ye and Tan, 'Functional analysis of the draft', 107.
[67] Wang Pei, 'Concept of combating torture in the 2012 criminal procedure law' ('Xingshi Susongfa' Zhong de Fan Kuxing Linian') (2013) Journal of Law Application (Falü Shiyong), 50–53 at 50.
[68] Xie Youping and Ren Rong, 'From brutality to civilization: the mechanism and requirements of the CAT' ('Cong Yeman Dao Wenming: Fandui Kuxing Gongyue de Jili yu Yaoqiu') (2006) Fudan Journal (Social Sciences edn.) (Fudan Xuebao [Shehui Kexueban]), 105–110 at 109.
[69] Chen Lin, 'Analysis of torture in China' ('Shixi Zhongguo Kuxing Xianxiang') (2013) China (Shenzhou), 173.

included in the exclusionary rule in article 54 of the revised CPL. However, one commentator reports that during preparation for the amendment the majority of departments and experts found that definition 'too complicated'. They argued that the law does not need to refer explicitly to mental pain and suffering, as it was already encompassed by the broad notion of 'torture' in article 54.[70] Another author recommends using the definition of torture spelt out in the convention as a normative basis for interpretation of the term 'coerced confession' in Chinese judicial practice.[71]

Further, a number of scholars have examined the general issue of whether the definition of torture in article 1 of the Convention against Torture should guide the interpretation of domestic law on the prohibition of coerced confessions.[72] The opposing view holds that owing to 'certain unclear elements' contained in that definition, it cannot be used as a definition of torture in the strict sense under domestic criminal law. It is further argued that the purpose of the definition is to describe the meaning of torture within the context of the international treaty, and thus it cannot be directly applied to Chinese criminal law or criminal procedure law.[73] In contrast, the internationalist view holds that the Convention against Torture is directly applicable to domestic law and constitutes a formal source of law that provides an authoritative legal basis for application of the convention's definition of torture.[74]

The Convention against Torture is also used as an argument in favour of a restrictive interpretation of the new exclusionary rule in article 54 of the CPL to exclude indirect material evidence from the scope of the rule's application. It is argued that contrary to personal testimony the way in which material evidence is gathered does not normally affect the value of that evidence. According to this view, it suffices for the prevention of torture to exclude forced confessions. In order to further strengthen this argument, it is said that it would not be acceptable to the public if persons against whom there was true material evidence were released. However, true evidence is excluded if it discovered to have come from a forced confession. Finally, it is held that article 15 of the Convention against

---

[70] Huang, 'Explanation of the amended criminal procedure', 12.

[71] Fan, *The Road of Fairness and Justice*, p. 25.

[72] Wan, 'Discussion of the interpretation and determination', 176.

[73] Wang Guangxian, 'Analysis of the definition of torture' (*'Kuxing Dingyi Jiexi'*) (2002) *Journal of the National Procurators Academy (Guojia Jianchaguan Xueyuan Xuebao)*, 13–18 at 17.

[74] Wan, 'Discussion of the interpretation and determination', 176.

Torture requires states to exclude only personal testimony acquired through torture, not indirect material evidence.[75] However, international commentators have opined that article 15 stipulates that the poisoned fruits of torture-induced evidence must also be excluded.[76]

The majority of commentators use the standards of the Convention against Torture as an argument for strengthening the prohibition against torture in domestic law, to broaden the definition of coerced confessions or to give the exclusionary rule a wider scope of application. A smaller group, however, argues that Chinese law should not be interpreted as being in conformity with the convention, as the concept of torture used in international law is different from that used in Chinese domestic law. Further, the Convention against Torture is also used as an argument against a broad interpretation of the exclusionary rule, which is not in line with the convention's aims.

5 Selective Adaptation of the Convention against Torture

The predominant policy objective of the criminal procedure reform in the PRC was to prevent future wrongful convictions in order to restore public trust in the justice system and maintain the legitimacy of the political system. Given the strong emphasis of the party-state on preventing wrongful convictions, the primary objective of the reform appears to have been obtaining true evidence in criminal procedures. Better protection of the rights of suspects and defendants was rather a corollary of the introduction of the exclusionary rule, as was the fulfilment of any obligations under international law. The legal transfer of the exclusionary rule mechanism served rather as an instrument to facilitate the implementation of the aforementioned policy objective. Academic discourse that grounds the CPL reform proposals in the Convention against Torture can be regarded as a transfer channel that facilitates the transfer of international legal norms into the domestic legal system. It was indeed reform-minded law professors and legal practitioners who attempted to use international norms in their argumentation in favour of curtailing police power and who introduced, discussed and adopted principles such as the exclusionary rule, which were then later

---

[75] Huang, 'Explanation of the amended criminal procedure', 12.

[76] Manfred Nowak and Elizabeth McArthur, *The United Nations Convention against Torture: A Commentary* (Oxford: Oxford University Press, 2008), p. 88.

taken up by the SPC in its judicial interpretation and by the NPC in drafting the amendments to the CPL.

At the same time, the introduction of the exclusionary rule was also an obligation under article 15 of the Convention against Torture, which became binding on the PRC as early as 1988. However, in the years before 2010, the negative effects of torture were not regarded as sufficiently severe to justify the alignment of criminal procedure law with the country's obligation under international law. The 'selective adaptation' model provides a conclusive explanation for why it took the PRC more than twenty years to bring its criminal procedure law into line with its obligation under the Convention against Torture. According to this model, 'interpretive communities selectively adapt non-local standards for local application in light of their own normative perspectives'.[77] Selective adaptation comprises the elements of perception, complementarity and legitimacy. The perception of international law determines how local communities interpret and apply that law in the domestic context.[78] The perception of international human rights norms by China is shaped by such factors as the country's historical experience, legal culture and domestic political system, as well as by the concepts of international law and international power politics in general.[79] The official human rights concept of the PRC government has had a significant impact on how international human rights are perceived within the domestic legal system. In particular, the subordination of civil and political rights to socioeconomic development, the contingency of rights on local conditions and the primacy of economic growth can explain the government's reluctance to implement proper safeguards against torture, as the realisation of other policy aims is considered more important.[80] Complementarity relates to a situation in which contradictory phenomena are combined in ways 'that preserve essential characteristics of each

---

[77] Pitman Potter, 'China and the international legal system: challenges of participation' (2007) 191 *China Quarterly*, 699–715 at 701.

[78] Pitman Potter, 'Introduction: selective adaptation, institutional capacity, and the reception of international law under conditions of globalization', in Pitman Potter and Ljiljana Biukovic (eds.), *Globalization and Local Adaptation in International Trade Law* (Vancouver: University of British Columbia Press, 2012), pp. 3–20, 11.

[79] Pitman Potter, *Law, Policy, and Practice on China's Periphery: Selective Adaptation and Institutional Capacity* (London: Routledge, 2012), pp. 57–58.

[80] For an account of the official human rights concept, see Dingding Chen, 'Explaining China's changing discourse on human rights, 1978–2004' (2005) 29 *Asian Perspective*, 155–182 at 169, 172.

component and yet allow for them to operate together in a mutually reinforcing and effective manner'.[81] Complementarity relates to the way that a state handles the discrepancy between international standards and local rules with regard to its structural organisation and institutional capacity.[82] The structure of an authoritarian state imposes significant limits on certain civil and political rights. With regard to personal integrity rights such as the right not to be tortured, the party-state has a general interest in safeguarding such rights. However, torture can also be used intentionally to deter dissidents or human rights lawyers and to effectively silence any political dissent regarded as a threat to the political system.[83] From the perspective of complementarity, the delay in reforming criminal procedure law can be explained in terms of capacity constraints. Coerced confessions were accepted in practice as a fast and efficient instrument for closing criminal cases and saving the personnel resources of the public security organs. Further, the party-state was hesitant to exclude the use of illegally obtained evidence in court, as the procedure for establishing whether evidence had been obtained illegally would impose far-reaching constraints on the public security organs. As the party-state is heavily reliant on those organs to maintain the current political system, perceptions of the negative impact of coerced confessions leading to wrongful convictions must have reached a critical level, prompting the party leadership to decide to introduce a court-based procedure for restraining the police. Legitimacy relates to both the acceptance of international legal standards by local communities and the acceptance of China within the international community. Ratification of the Convention against Torture, as well as the presentation of the domestic legal system and legal practice as being in conformity with its obligations under the convention, are aimed at gaining the PRC's acceptance within the international community. One of the main reasons that it took the party-state so long to adopt the exclusionary rule was the 'legitimacy dilemma' that that rule implies. With its procedural safeguards, the exclusionary rule has had the positive effects of minimising wrongful convictions, restoring public trust in the judicial system and tightening control over police conduct at the local levels, all of which are

---

[81] Potter, 'Introduction: selective adaptation', p. 11.
[82] Ljiljana Biukovic, 'International law interrupted: a case of selective adaptation' (2010) 60 *University of New Brunswick Law Journal*, 161–176 at 167.
[83] Amnesty International, *Against the Law: Crackdown on China's Human Rights Lawyers Deepens* (London: Amnesty International, 2011).

likely to be welcomed by Chinese citizens. However, the introduction of the exclusionary rule also comes with the possible negative consequence of failing to convict a 'guilty' person owing to 'procedural technicalities'. Allowing those who are 'guilty' to go free has been long regarded as unacceptable to Chinese citizens, who expect the state to be tough on crime. Hence, an exclusionary rule was long seen as holding the potential to undermine the public's trust in the judiciary and party-state, which constituted an important factor in causing the delay in bringing Chinese criminal procedure law into line with article 15 of the Convention against Torture.

9

Online Privacy Protection

A Legal Regime for Personal Data Protection in China

YUN ZHAO

1 Introduction

Privacy is an important right in modern society, but we lack a clear and universal definition of the concept of 'privacy'. Generally speaking, privacy belongs to the set of human rights that protects individuals' private information from unlawful interference, use and disclosure. Private information can include personal life, personal information and private communication. The Electronic Privacy Information Center (EPIC) and Privacy International (PI) divide privacy into four categories: information privacy, bodily privacy, privacy of communications and territorial privacy.[1]

The cyberspace created by the Internet has brought the world closer than ever before; geographical boundaries are no longer important, as information can transcend national borders easily. Technological developments have rendered the easy collection, storage, analysis, instantaneous disclosure and wide dissemination of private information possible at low cost.[2] Such tools as cookies and web bugs are widely used for online information collection, which is often carried out without users' knowledge.[3] The online sharing culture and active netizen participation pose

---

[1] EPIC – Privacy and Human Rights Report, accessed 3 May 2016, www.worldlii.org/int/journals/EPICPrivHR/2006/PHR2006-Defining.html.

[2] Fuping Gao, 'The e-commerce legal environment in China: status quo and issues' (2004) 18 *Temple International and Comparative Law Journal*, 51, 76; Guosong Shao, *Internet Law in China* (Amsterdam: Elsevier, 2012), p. 141.

[3] Kuang-Wen Wu, Shaio Yan Huang, David C. Yen and Irina Popova, 'The effect of online privacy policy on consumer privacy concern and trust' (2012) 28 *Computers in Human Behavior*, 889.

serious challenges to privacy protection online.[4] First, the scope of online privacy and information is expanding rapidly. In addition to such traditional data as land line and mobile telephone numbers, the privacy of such online personal data as email addresses, user names and instant messaging information (e.g. QQ numbers) is receiving increasing attention from the public. Second, online data are increasingly important to merchants. Hence, online privacy and information should be understood in both personal and economic terms. For example, personal data have become a valuable asset in transactions carried out online. Information collected by online merchants is used to create personal profiles indicating consumer preferences, which subsequently helps merchants to devise tailored marketing strategies. Privacy protection online is thus receiving unprecedented attention. As far as the Internet is concerned, of the four categories identified by EPIC and PI, information privacy is the primary concern. Discussions in this arena concern how best to ensure the legal and reasonable use of online information. Accordingly, this chapter examines the protection of online information, or personal data protection, rather than other aspects of privacy in the context of China.

China does not have a strong tradition of privacy protection.[5] As one scholar has correctly observed, 'the general population of China does not know what the concept of privacy is'.[6] Chinese history presents a picture of non-respect for privacy protection, particularly during the country's successive dynasties and, more recently, the Cultural Revolution period. The online censorship created by the Great Firewall of China is another example of the downplaying of privacy protection in China. However, the situation is changing. The Chinese government has realised the importance of online privacy protection and taken initiatives to improve the legal regime governing it. Chinese citizens' awareness of the need for privacy is also rising along with serious threats to personal data.[7] Furthermore, an increasingly globalised marketplace requires the existence of a data protection regime on par with the standards of other jurisdictions for the promotion of economic activities.

---

[4] Miriam J Metzger and Sharon Docter, 'Public opinion and policy initiatives for online privacy protection' (2010) 47 *Journal of Broadcasting & Electronic Media*, 350.

[5] Cao Jingchun, 'Protecting the right to privacy in China' (2005) 36 *Victoria University Wellington Law Review*, 645, 646.

[6] Bo Zhao, 'Posthumous reputation and posthumous privacy in China: the dead, the law, and the social transition' (2014) 39 *Brooklyn Journal of International Law*, 269.

[7] Yong Jin Park, Scott W. Campbell and Nojin Kwak, 'Affect, cognition and reward: predictors of privacy protection online' (2012) 28 *Computers in Human Behavior*, 1019.

This chapter starts the discussion against this backdrop. Section 2 briefly examines the current situation of privacy protection at the international level, followed by a closer examination of the current legal regime for privacy protection in China in Section 3. The discussion of the relevant laws and regulations in China is by no means exhaustive. In recent years, the Chinese government has taken a number of important steps to protect personal data. Section 4 discusses these new initiatives and confirms that we should be optimistic about future developments in the field in China. Section 5 continues with analysis of the problems with the current legal regime in China and shows the possible ways ahead for personal data protection in the country in future. The chapter concludes in the final section that China is moving steadily, though slowly, towards the construction of a fair legal regime for personal data protection.

2   International Regime for Privacy Protection

As noted, the scope of personal data is becoming broader. Generally speaking, personal data include information that the data subject may be unwilling to share or disclose to the public, such as his or her name, age, gender, height, weight, health condition, medical records, bodily features, residence, race, religion, political affiliation, income and savings, educational background, occupation, marital status, sex life and orientation, family background, and social networks. Several international documents already include relevant privacy protection provisions. The 1948 Universal Declaration of Human Rights, for example, provides that 'no one shall be subjected to arbitrary interference with his privacy, family, home or correspondence, nor to attacks upon his honor and reputation. Everyone has the right to the protection of the law against such interference or attacks'.[8] Similarly, the International Covenant on Civil and Political Rights also provides obligations for governments to protect privacy.[9] As early as 1980, the Organisation for Economic Co-Operation and Development (OECD) released Guidelines on the Protection of Privacy and Transborder Flows of Personal Data (OECD Guidelines hereafter)

---

[8] The Universal Declaration of Human Rights, Article 12. See also Yutian Ling, 'Upholding free speech and privacy online: a legal-based and market-based approach for internet companies in China' (2010) 27 *Santa Clara Computer & High Technology Law Journal*, 175, 188.

[9] Anthony Sebok, 'The invisible borderlines of tort on the internet', in Toshiyuki Kono, Christoph G. Paulus and Harry Rajak (eds.), *Selected Legal Issues of E-Commerce* (The Hague: Kluwer Law International, 2002), p. 49.

governing data privacy protection, which require the transborder flow of personal data to be uninterrupted and secure.[10] The following year, the Council of Europe adopted a convention mandating that personal data be obtained fairly and lawfully, used only for the originally specified purpose and destroyed after that purpose has been completed.[11]

At the moment, there are three basic models for personal data protection worldwide. First, some countries adopt a comprehensive approach, enacting a general law providing clear rules on the collection, use and distribution of personal data, with a supervisory authority created to monitor compliance in the activities of both the private and public sectors. The European Union (EU) is a typical example in this regard. As early as 1995, the EU implemented the Data Protection Directive, which provides an overall framework for the protection of personal data within its jurisdiction.[12] Second, some regions prefer a sectoral approach, that is, to enact rules pertaining to specific industries believed to pose a major threat to data protection.[13] Third, some consider the self-regulatory model to be the best approach to dealing with data protection.[14] According to self-regulation theory, companies and industries are in the best position to establish governance through codes and self-policing.[15]

The wide adoption of electronic commerce is posing serious challenges to personal data protection online. The valuable personal data collected online are particularly vulnerable to misuse. In view of the vulnerability of online personal data, many countries have enacted or modified their personal data protection laws to cope with the collection, storage and use of online data.[16] In this regard, the EU was again the first to act, and has developed rules that are far ahead of many other jurisdictions. Scholars

---

[10] Part 3(16) of OECD Guidelines on the Protection of Privacy and Transborder Flows of Personal Data, accessed 4 May 2016, www.oecd.org/sti/ieconomy/oecd guidelinesontheprotectionofprivacyandtransborderflowsofpersonaldata.htm.

[11] Article 5 of Convention for the Protection of Individuals with Regard to Automatic Processing of Personal Data, Council of Europe, 28 January 1981.

[12] 'Should the U.S. adopt European-style data-privacy protections?', The Wall Street Journal, 10 March 2013, accessed 4 May 2016, www.wsj.com/articles/ SB10001424127887324338604578328393797127094.

[13] Chan-Mo Chung and Ilsoon Shin, 'On-line data protection and cyberlaws in Korea' (1999) 27 Korean Journal of International & Comparative Law, 21.

[14] Jared Strauss and Kenneth S Rogerson, 'Policies for online privacy in the United States and the European Union' (2002) 19 Telematics and Informatics, 173.

[15] Svetlana Milina, 'Let the market do its job: advocating an integrated laissez-faire approach to online profiling regulation' (2003) 21 Cardozo Arts & Entertainment Law Journal, 257.

[16] Eliza Brink and Alana Causey, 'A global debate: online privacy protection versus the expansion of information technology' (2002) 35 Law Technology, 1.

are increasingly concerned about the inadequacy of the self-regulatory model, criticising it in particular for 'insufficient participation, lax enforcement and spotty compliance'.[17] Against this backdrop, a desire to develop a national legal regime consistent with the EU model is becoming prevalent in China.

3   The Chinese Legal Regime for Privacy Protection

As mentioned in the chapter's Introduction, no universally accepted definition for the term 'privacy' exists at the international level. In China, there is no official document offering any definition of privacy. However, the Beijing District Court had the chance to elaborate the national understanding of the concept in *Wang Fei v. Zhang Leyi, Daqi.com and Tianya.cn*.[18] As one scholar summarised,

> according to the court, privacy means private life, information, space, and peace of private life related to a person's interests and personality that he does not intend to share with others. Therefore, the right to privacy is infringed by the disclosure or publication of private information that a person does not want to disclose to others concerning his private life, private areas, or domestic tranquility and connected with his interests or his body.[19]

At the highest level, China has a constitution. Although the Chinese Constitution does not specifically address the protection of personal data, it touches upon the concept of privacy, acknowledging that the personal dignity of citizens is protected by law and that insult, libel, false charges or frame-ups are prohibited.[20] It also protects residences from trespass,[21] and further provides that 'no organizations or individuals may, for whatever reason, infringe upon citizens' freedom and privacy of correspondence, except in cases where to meet the needs of state security or of criminal investigation, public security or procuratorial entities are permitted to censor correspondence in accordance with the procedures prescribed by law'.[22] These provisions are viewed by some scholars as

---

[17] Dennis D Hirsch, 'The law and policy of online privacy: regulation, self-regulation, or co-regulation' (2011) 34 *Seattle University Law Review*, 439.

[18] Beijing Chaoyang District Court, No. 10930 of 2008.

[19] Rebecca Ong, 'Recognition of the right to privacy on the internet in China' (2011) 1 *International Data Privacy Law*, 172, 175.

[20] Constitution of the People's Republic of China, article 38.   [21] Ibid., article 39.

[22] Ibid., article 40.

collectively representing a legal framework for a 'minimum level of protection for the privacy of the citizen for the purpose of social stability'.[23]

Because the constitution cannot be cited in court cases, however, we must turn to more useful rules in laws and regulations below the constitutional level. For example, the National People's Congress Standing Committee (NPCSC) issued a Decision on Safeguarding Internet Security in 2000, defining it as a crime to intercept, tamper with or delete other people's email or other data and/or to violate citizens' freedom and privacy of correspondence illegally.[24] China's Criminal Law also contains several provisions regarding the criminal liability for infringement of the right of communications or for intrusion of residence.[25] For the purposes of the current discussion, we will focus primarily on the civil (rather than criminal) side. The General Principles of Civil Law enacted in 1986 serve as the legal basis for civil rights protection. In this law, privacy is not defined as an independent right, but belongs to the general right of reputation. Three articles are relevant to the protection of privacy: (a) the right to one's name, which prohibits the false representation of personal names;[26] (b) the right to one's portrait, which prohibits the use of a citizen's portrait for commercial purposes without prior consent;[27] and (c) the right to reputation, which protects one's personality and prohibits libel, slander or other means of damaging an individual's reputation.[28] The law further provides for damages, in the form of compensation, an injunction and rehabilitation of reputation, and an apology.[29]

The Supreme People's Court (SPC) has issued several judicial interpretations to elaborate on the application of the preceding provisions. These interpretations show the development of and change in judicial attitudes towards privacy protection. The 1988 SPC judicial interpretation provides that

> any act, written or oral, that exposes another person's private secrets to the public, that fabricates facts in order to defame publicly a person's

---

[23] Arthur Cockfield, 'Legal constraints on transferring personal information across borders: a comparative analysis of PIPEDA and foreign privacy laws', in Elia Zureik et al. (eds.), *Surveillance, Privacy, and the Globalization of Personal Information: International Comparisons* (Montreal: McGill-Queen's University Press, 2010), p. 64.

[24] NPCSC Decision on Safeguarding Internet Security, article 4(2), 28 December 2000.

[25] Criminal Law, articles 245, 252–253.   [26] General Principles of Civil Law, article 99.

[27] Ibid., article 100.   [28] Ibid., article 101.   [29] Ibid., article 120.

dignity, or that employs insult or defamation which clearly damages
another person's reputation, must be deemed an infringement of a citizen's right to his reputation. Any act, written or oral, that damages or
defames the reputation of a legal person, and that causes loss to the legal
person, must be deemed an infringement of the right of a legal person to
its reputation.[30]

This document shows that the right to privacy is intertwined with the
right to reputation and that damage to reputation is a pre-condition for
privacy protection.

Five years after the foregoing interpretation, the SPC issued another
judicial interpretation, which basically repeats the provisions of the
1988 interpretation and again emphasises that the right to reputation is
the cause of action in cases concerning an invasion of privacy. The
1993 interpretation states that 'anyone who discloses the privacy materials of others without their prior consent in writing or orally, which
causes damages to the reputation of others, should be punished for
infringing the reputation right of others'.[31]

A major breakthrough was achieved in the SPC's 2001 judicial interpretation, which for the first time recognises privacy as an independent
personal right; that is, it is no longer affiliated with the right to reputation. According to this interpretation, 'the people's court shall accept, in
accordance with law, cases arising from the violation of societal public
interests or societal morality by infringing upon a person's privacy or
other interests of personality, and brought to the court by the victim as a
civil tort for claiming emotional damages'.[32] It further identifies 'the
unlawful disclosure or use of a deceased's privacy, or the infringement
of the deceased's privacy by means that [violate] societal or public
interests or other societal morality' as torts that entitle the deceased's
family to seek compensatory damages.[33] Accordingly, the perpetrator
shall be liable for compensation for distress or emotional damage caused
by the violation of privacy and the harm to reputation.

---

[30] Opinions of the Supreme People's Court on Several Issues Concerning the Implementation of General Principles of Civil Law (for Trial Implementation), article 140,
2 April 1988.

[31] Reply to Certain Issues Concerning Trials of Cases Involving the Right to Reputation, 15
June 1993.

[32] Interpretation of the Supreme People's Court on Problems Regarding the Ascertainment
of Compensation Liability of Emotional Damages in Civil Torts, article 1, 8 March 2001.

[33] Ibid., article 3(2).

This important breakthrough was not officially adopted into national law until 2009, when the NPCSC adopted Tort Law, giving China for the first time a national law that defines tort liability in areas such as medical negligence, work-related injuries, product liabilities and the liabilities of Internet users and Internet Service Providers (ISPs). In addition, China's Tort Law, again for the first time, also broadly defines civil rights and interests to include the right to privacy as an independent right.[34] Similar to the 2001 SPC judicial interpretation, under Tort Law a victim can claim compensation for mental distress and emotional damage for the infringement of civil rights and interests.[35] One provision in the Tort Law deals specifically with the tort liability of Internet users and ISPs and adopts a 'notice and take-down system'. According to this provision, an Internet user or ISP assumes tort liability for infringing upon the civil rights or interests of another person through an online network.[36] The Tort Law can be seen as an important step towards the establishment of a legal regime governing privacy protection. However, it must be noted that the law provides only for remedies for the intrusion of privacy. It does not address how personal data should be handled at various stages to ensure their proper collection, retrieval and use.

In addition to the Tort Law and General Principles of Civil Law, other national laws also touch upon the issue of privacy protection tangentially. For example, the Consumer Protection Law provides that 'consumers, in purchasing and using commodities and receiving services, enjoy the right to demand respect of their personal dignity and national customs and habits'.[37] The newly amended version of this law further provides that 'business operators should expressly inform ... consumers about the purposes, means and range of ... information collection and use, and get consent from ... consumers'.[38] In addition, the Electronic Signature Law also requires certification service providers to handle all information related to certification properly.[39] At the lower level, there are also various administrative regulations and rules that deal with different aspects of privacy and personal data protection. For example, the Measures for the Administration of Internet Information Services enacted by the State Council in 2000 broadly prohibit information that insults or slanders others or infringes upon their legitimate rights and interests.[40]

---

[34] Tort Law, article 2.   [35] Ibid., article 22.   [36] Ibid., article 36.
[37] Consumer Protection Law, article 14.   [38] Ibid., article 29.
[39] Electronic Signature Law, article 24.
[40] Measures for the Administration of Internet Information Services, article 15(8).

At the ministerial level, the Ministry of Public Security (MPS) and Ministry of Industry and Information Technology (MIIT) are the two major entities regulating online privacy. As early as 1997, the MPS released Measures for the Administration of Protecting the Security of International Connections to the Computer Information Network. This document acknowledges the importance of protecting the freedom and privacy of network users.[41] Almost ten years later, in late 2005 the MPS issued another document, entitled Provisions on the Technical Measures for the Protection of the Security of the Internet, once again emphasising the importance of technical measures in procuring Internet security and preventing the unlawful disclosure of online information. This document provides that 'ISPs and entity users of the Internet shall be responsible for carrying into effect the technical measure for the protection of . . . Internet security and they should guarantee the normal functioning of the technical measure[s] for the protection of . . . Internet security'.[42]

The MIIT is the major governmental organ in charge of Internet regulations. The Administrative Measures for Internet Electronic Messaging Services Provisions it promulgated in 2000 require Internet electronic messaging service providers to keep the personal data of their users confidential and to make no disclosures without users' consent.[43] The Administrative Measures for Internet E-Mail Services take a similar position with regard to keeping users' personal information and email addresses confidential.[44] The measures further reiterate the protection of citizens' privacy of correspondence in using Internet email services, subject only to the exception that 'the public security or procuratorial organ makes an inspection o[f] the contents of the correspondence when required by national security or [the] investigation of crimes'.[45]

In addition to the rules issued by the MPS and MIIT, several other ministerial entities have also enacted rules within their jurisdictions.

---

[41] Measures for the Administration of Protecting the Security of International Connections to the Computer Information Networks, Ministry of Public Security (MPS), 16 December 1997. Article 7 provides: 'the freedom and privacy of network users is protected by law. No unit or individual may, in violation of these regulations, use the Internet to violate the freedom and privacy of network users.'

[42] Provisions on the Technical Measures for the Protection of the Security of the Internet, MPS, article 3, 13 December 2005.

[43] Administrative Measures for Internet Electronic Messaging Services Provisions, Ministry of Industry and Information Technology (MIIT), article 12, 6 November 2000. This document was repealed on 23 September 2014.

[44] Administrative Measures for Internet E-mail Services, MIIT, article 9, 20 February 2006.

[45] Ibid., article 3.

For example, the Ministry of Culture enacted Interim Measures for the Administration of Online Games in 2010, which stipulate that 'online game operators should keep user registration data, operation data, maintenance logs, etc. in accordance with the law to protect state secret[s], commercial secrets, and users' personal information'.[46] The State Administration for Industry and Commerce enacted Tentative Measures for the Administration of Online Commodity Transactions and Related Services in the same year, defining the obligations of online commodity business operators and online service operators towards consumers in relation to the data collected from them, including the safe custody, reasonable use, limited retention period and proper destruction of those data.[47] In the following year, the Ministry of Commerce released Regulations on Administration of Platforms for Online Transactions with Third Parties, which stipulate in clear wording that 'without the users' consent, the platform operators shall not disclose or transfer to any third party the user list, transaction records and other data'.[48]

The foregoing survey of national legislation demonstrates that China already has in place a number of rules dealing with privacy protection. Also, the position of the Tort Law, the most important national law in this arena, is very clear in defining privacy as an independent right. An ISP may be held jointly liable with an Internet user if it 'ignores a notice of ... harmful comment posted online and fail[s] to undertake any reasonable response'.[49] However, when it comes to personal data protection, the situation before 2011 was rather disappointing. The relevant rules were at the ministerial level, and no systematic regime was established concerning the collection, storage and use of personal data.

4 Recent Developments in Data Protection in China

China's legal regime for personal data protection lags behind that of other countries. However, we cannot disregard the fact that China has

---

[46] Interim Measures for the Administration of Online Games, Ministry of Culture, article 28, 3 June 2010.

[47] Tentative Measures for the Administration of Online Commodity Transactions and Related Services, State Administration for Industry and Commerce, article 16, 31 May 2010.

[48] Regulations on Administration of Platforms for Online Transactions with Third Parties, Ministry of Commerce, article 7(1), 12 April 2011.

[49] Tort Law, articles 8–9. Qingxiu Bu, '"Human flesh search" in China: the double-edged sword' (2013) 3 *International Data Privacy Law*, 181, 191.

recognised the importance of such protection and that efforts have been made to rectify the situation in both academic and governmental circles. As early as 2005, for example, a scholarly version of personal data protection regulations was tabled at the State Council.[50] Unfortunately, little progress was made until 2012, which proved to be a fruitful year that witnessed several important initiatives taken to regulate the protection of personal data. In that year alone, the MIIT released two important documents specifically targeting such protection.

4.1   MIIT Provisions on Regulating the Market Order of Internet Information Services

On 15 March 2012, the MIIT's Several Provisions on Regulating the Market Order of Internet Information Services took effect. For the first time, the concept of personal data was defined as 'information relating to an online platform user which, when used either alone or in combination with other information, can identify that person'.[51] Accordingly, the standard of 'personal identifier', as also applied by the EU,[52] was officially adopted in China to define personal data. Whilst there has been no further elaboration of the scope of possible personal data covered by the MIIT document, this definition can be viewed as an important breakthrough in the regulation of personal data protection.

In addition, and also for the first time, this document acknowledges five fundamental data protection principles that are widely accepted internationally. The first is the principle of consent: users' consent is required for Internet Information Service Providers (IISPs) to collect their data and provide those data to a third party.[53] Privacy is compromised if personal data are used without users' consent.[54] The second is the purpose specification principle: IISPs 'have the duty to stipulate the manner, purpose and content of collecting and processing data and

---

[50] See, generally, Hanhua Zhou, *Personal Data Protection Law (Expert Draft) and Legislation Research Report* (Beijing: Law Press, 2006) p. 1.

[51] The MIIT Several Provisions on Regulating the Market Order of Internet Information Services, Article 11(1).

[52] Article 2 of Directive 95/46/EC of the European Parliament and the Council (EU Data Protection Directive), 24 October 1995, defines 'personal data' as 'any information relating to an identified or identifiable natural person'.

[53] MIIT Several Provisions on Regulating, article 11(1).

[54] Evelyne Cleff, 'Privacy issues in mobile advertising' (2007) 21 *International Review of Law, Computers & Technology*, 225.

not to use these data for any purpose beyond those consented [to] by ... users'.[55] The third principle is collection limitation: IISPs 'can only collect data that [are] essential for providing the services' in question.[56] The fourth is the use limitation principle: IISPs 'should not use data other than for the purpose of providing the [given] services'.[57] The fifth and final principle is the safeguard principle: IISPs 'should keep [users'] data in safe custody and take immediate remedial measures to safeguard data in [the] case of an illegal disclosure or potential illegal disclosure'.[58]

4.2 2012 MIIT Guidelines

Later in the same year, the MIIT issued another important document entitled Information Security Technology – Guidelines of Personal Information Protection in Public and Commercial Service Information System (MIIT Guidelines hereafter). Similar to the OECD Guidelines, the MIIT Guidelines provide detailed rules on the scope of personal information and the principles for the collection and use of that information. We may note that the definition of personal information is quite similar to that identified in the earlier document. This subsequent document goes one step further, however, by differentiating personal information into two categories: sensitive personal information and general personal information.[59] Two types of consent are also differentiated with respect to these two categories of information: tacit consent[60] and expressed consent.[61] The MIIT Guidelines also exemplify some of the information that can be considered as sensitive personal information, namely, such information as identification card numbers, mobile numbers, race, political views and religious beliefs.[62]

Furthermore, MIIT Guidelines also acknowledge the concept of 'users' rights' and provide eight general principles that should guide the processing of personal information.[63] These principles are further elaborated in detail concerning how they are to be implemented in practice, and it is stipulated that personal information administrators should comply

---

[55] MIIT Several Provisions on Regulating, article 11(2).   [56] Ibid. article 11(2).
[57] Ibid., article 11(2).   [58] Ibid., article 12.
[59] Information Security Technology – Guidelines of Personal Information Protection in Public and Commercial Service Information System, MIIT (MIIT Guidelines), article 3.2.
[60] Ibid., article 3(10).   [61] Ibid., article 3(11).   [62] Ibid., article 3(7).
[63] Ibid., article 4(2).

with them to protect users' rights.[64] Four stages are identified for the protection of personal information – collection, processing, transfer and deletion – with guidelines provided for the protection of personal information at each stage.[65]

In summary, the 2012 MIIT Guidelines, defined as a technical document with the nature of guidelines, lays down for the first time a set of national standards on a comprehensive basis. They can thus be taken effectively to promote personal information protection in China and to encourage the proper use of personal information within Chinese society. However, it must be noted that they are only guidelines, not a legally binding document. Despite their non-binding nature, the enactment by the MIIT of both the MIIT Guidelines and Provisions on Regulating the Market Order of Internet Information Services represents a milestone in the history of personal data protection in China. Never before had the Chinese government taken such a serious attitude towards personal data protection in an official manner. The extensive rules in the former document, in particular, encourage and offer a useful direction for self-regulatory efforts on the part of industry. More importantly, the document serves as a foundation for a more comprehensive personal data protection law in future.

4.3   Proposed Amendment to Administrative Regulations on Internet Information Services

Whilst the two important documents discussed previously were enacted only at the ministerial level, 2012 also witnessed two related initiatives taken to strengthen personal data protection at higher government levels. Almost twelve years after their initial enactment by the State Council, the Administrative Regulations on Internet Information Services were put forward for possible revision, with an amendment draft released for public consultation on 7 June 2012. The draft included one important provision concerning the duty of confidentiality that ISPs and interconnection service providers owed users with respect to personal data, including identity information and log records.[66] The amendment draft also strengthened the enforcement power of the government, with a new

[64] Graham Greenleaf, *Asian Data Privacy Laws: Trade & Human Rights Perspectives* (Oxford: Oxford University Press, 2014), p. 207.
[65] MIIT Guidelines, article 5.
[66] Administrative Regulations on Internet Information Services (Consultation), article 17.

provision defining the government's power to take punitive measures against offenders, including the issuance of rectification orders, confiscation of illegal profits, imposition of fines and termination of licences.[67]

4.4   2012 NPCSC Decision

Towards the end of 2012, the NPCSC released a Decision to Strengthen Network Information Protection, the aim of which was to protect electronic information that can be used to identify an individual citizen or that concerns the privacy of an individual citizen. The decision emphasises the importance of protecting electronic information related to personal information and privacy.[68] Similar to the OECD Guidelines, the NPCSC Decision also reiterates several general principles regarding the collection, storage and use of information. Data collectors are required to publish their reasons for collecting personal data, as well as the way in which and extent to which those data will be collected and used, and they need to obtain consent from the data subjects and use their personal data only for their stated purposes.[69]

The decision also stipulates that data subjects may take legal action to protect their personal data.[70] This right is further supplemented by the 2014 SPC judicial interpretation entitled Provisions of the Supreme People's Court on Several Issues Concerning the Application of Law in the Trial of Cases involving Civil Disputes over Infringement upon Personal Rights and Interests through Information Networks. According to this document, an individual can commence legal action against a network user or network service provider that infringes upon his or her right to personal privacy.[71] The document also lists several types of information that can be considered personal information, the infringement of which imposes tortious liability.[72] The infringed party may seek compensation for property damage or serious mental distress.[73] The 2012 NPCSC Decision can also be considered a breakthrough in the personal data protection arena. However, it provides only general principles and rather vague provisions. Furthermore, the legal effect of

---

[67] Ibid., article 29.
[68] The Decision of the NPCSC on Strengthening Network Information Protection (2012 NPCSC Decision), article 1, 28 December 2012.
[69] Ibid., article 2.   [70] Ibid., article 9.   [71] SPC 2014 Judicial Interpretation, article 12.
[72] Ibid. Such information includes genetic information, medical materials, materials on healthy conditions, criminal records, family address and private activities.
[73] Ibid., article 17.

NPCSC decisions is in doubt, with some practitioners believing that they constitute only normative documents that would be difficult to enforce in practice.[74]

4.5   2013 MIIT Rules

The foregoing discussion documents the efforts that the Chinese government took to promote the protection of personal data in 2012. Within that single year, many important documents were adopted in this arena. By contrast, 2013 was relatively quiet, witnessing only the enactment by the MIIT of Rules Regarding the Protection of Personal Information of Telecommunications and Internet Users on 16 July (2013 MIIT Rules hereafter). This document again adopts the personal identifier standard to define the concept of personal information,[75] but it extends the concept to include 'the time and place of the user using the service and other information',[76] which was not previously considered a component of personal information. The phrase 'other information' provides the 2013 MIIT Rules with the further flexibility to include additional types of information. The rules apply to the collection and use of personal electronic information by telecommunications service operators and IISPs. Hence, their scope is quite broad, applying to any entity that provides information through the Internet to online users.

In compliance with the 2012 NPCSC Decision, the 2013 document also outlines standards for the collection and use of information, safety measures, supervision and inspection, and legal liability. Building on that decision, the 2013 MIIT Rules are broadly based on the 1980 OECD Guidelines, which serve as minimum standards for personal data collection. They enshrine several international principles: 1) the principle of voluntariness in seeking an individual's consent before data collection/ use and of duly notifying individuals of any personal information collection;[77] 2) the principle of transparency: service providers must disclose the objective, scope and methods of collection and use;[78] 3) the principle of necessity: information collection should not be excessive and should be

---

[74] 'China turns up the heat in the battle against abuses of personal data', Hogan Lovells, 20 August 2013, accessed 4 May 2016, www.hoganlovells.com/en/publications/china-turns-up-the-heat-in-the-battle-against-abuses-of-personal-data.

[75] Rules Regarding the Protection of Personal Information of Telecommunications and Internet Users, MIIT (2013 MIIT Rules), article 4.

[76] Ibid.   [77] Ibid., article 9(1).   [78] Ibid., article 9(2).

in line with its stated objective[79] and 4) the principle of security: service providers have an obligation to take such measures as implementing clear management systems and security protocols and the ongoing supervision of third-party data processors to strengthen IT security.[80] A number of internal management procedures are provided to reduce the operational risks of entities dealing with a large amount of personal data on a daily basis.

Several differences between the 2013 MIIT Rules and 2012 MIIT Guidelines should be noted, especially with regard to the concept of personal information and the requirement of expressed and tacit consent.[81] The former make it clear that the provisions concerning users' notification and consent do not take the place of any other laws or regulations on the same issue that could help to clarify and reconcile the divergence among different laws and regulations.[82] However, this 'clarification' will no doubt result in the coexistence of different regimes in this area and cause confusion to users. Compared with the earlier document, the 2013 MIIT Rules also display several important improvements. For example, the concept of personal information is given an explicit definition, and, more importantly, the document outlines clear rules on the enforcement issue and possible liability. This can be considered an important step forward in ensuring realisation of the document's purpose and goal in reality. Furthermore, the 2013 Rules impose several requirements that are above and beyond those that typically exist elsewhere. For example, they provide for a mandatory data breach notification procedure, which requires the service provider to notify the MIIT and other regulators in the case of serious data security breaches and to cooperate in remedying the situation.[83] Accordingly, some commentators believe that the 2013 MIIT Rules represent 'a shift to focused, binding regulation, more in line with regulations seen in Europe and in Asian jurisdictions which have also adopted OECD standards based regulations'.[84]

---

[79] Ibid., article 9(3).   [80] Ibid., article 13.
[81] Ibid., article 9; MIIT Guidelines, article 5(1.1).   [82] 2013 MIIT Rules, article 9(5).
[83] Ibid., article 14(1).
[84] Mark Parsons and Xun Yang, 'New rules for online personal privacy in force 1 September 2013: implications for doing business in China', Freshfields Bruckhaus Deringer, 16 August 2013, accessed 4 May 2016, www.freshfields.com/uploadedFiles/SiteWide/Knowledge/August%202013_New%20rules%20for%20online%20personal%20privacy%20in%20force%201%20September%202013.PDF.

Nevertheless, we must be mindful of the problems in the current legal framework for personal data protection. First of all, there are different ways of defining the term 'personal data' among the different documents. The MIIT Guidelines, for instance, draw a distinction between sensitive and general personal data, which require different types of consent (tacit or express), a distinction that does not appear in other documents. A consistent definition would be helpful in enforcing the existing rules. In addition, the term 'necessary' in article 9 of the Guidelines also raises concerns over the scope of personal data for collection and the type of consent required.

Second, the 2012 NPCSC Decision and 2013 MIIT Rules explicitly prohibit selling, divulging or illegally providing personal data to a third party, whereas the 2012 MIIT Guidelines allow such transfer subject to certain conditions, including that 1) the data subject is informed of the transfer; 2) the recipient of the data is a qualified recipient who meets the requirements set out in the Guidelines and 3) the transferor ensures that the data will not be obtained by any individuals or entities other than the intended recipient.[85] The provision of such conditions helps to clarify the simple provisions in the two former documents, but it would be helpful if those documents added relevant rules regarding the illegal or legal transfer of personal data.

Third, as noted previously, a list of security measures is provided in the 2013 MIIT Rules. However, these measures are simply actions/behaviour that the service providers should take/engage in.[86] No minimum security standards are provided, leaving service providers with wide discretionary power in determining a specific action or behaviour. Finally, the rules provide for relatively light penalties, which may not provide sufficient incentives for compliance. For example, the maximum fine for the misuse of personal data is between RMB10,000 and RMB30,000.[87]

4.6   Amendments to Consumer Protection Law

The year 2013 also witnessed important amendments to the Consumer Protection Law, which complements the 2013 MIIT Rules in the area of personal data protection. The amendments, introduced in October 2013, add provisions governing the collection and use of personal data by online retailers, stipulating that the legality, rationality and necessity

---

[85] MIIT Guidelines, article 5.4.   [86] Greenleaf, *Asian Data Privacy Laws*, p. 213.
[87] 2013 MIIT Rules, article 23.

principles are to be strictly followed in such collection and use.[88] Other principles regarding user disclosure and data quality requirements largely follow those stipulated in the 2012 NPCSC Decision. The Consumer Protection Law amendments explicitly acknowledge consumers' rights to their personal data, rights that exist in both the online and offline environments. In contrast to the 2013 MIIT Rules, the law provides for tougher legal and administrative sanctions, including a fine of up to ten times the illegal gain and termination of a company's business licence in the event of a serious violation.[89] However, it is unclear with regard to the application of an 'opt-in' or 'opt-out' mechanism. According to the law, commercial information should not be sent to consumers without their consent or with their explicit refusal.[90] It thus appears that both the opt-in and opt-out mechanisms apply, although no detailed rules are provided. As a result, problems may arise concerning the proper time to inform consumers of their right to opt-out and the period in which they must indicate any objection.

5 Future Development of the Data Protection Legal Regime in China

We have witnessed encouraging progress over the past few years with respect to the regulation of privacy protection in China.[91] However, the situation is not yet fully satisfactory. Most existing rules are piecemeal and at the ministerial level.[92] The MIIT alone has enacted several documents, which may cause confusion and complexity in understanding and applying the rules therein. The work on producing a comprehensive law faces a number of difficulties, and at the same time reveals the cautious attitude adopted by the Chinese government. Discussions are ongoing, and many proposals have been put forward calling for possible legislation on personal data protection at the level of national law. One major issue is how to balance the relationship between privacy protection and Chinese ideologies and values. As noted at the chapter's outset, China is not a state that has traditionally emphasised privacy protection. However, the

---

[88] Consumer Protection Law, article 29(1).   [89] Ibid., article 56.
[90] Ibid., article 29(3).
[91] Graham Greenleaf, 'China's internet data privacy regulations 2012: 80 percent of a great leap forward?' (2012) 116 *Privacy Laws & Business International Report*, 1.
[92] Ding Chunyan, 'Patient privacy protection in China in the age of electronic health records' (2013) 43 *Hong Kong Law Journal*, 245.

issues of respect for the right to privacy in networks and the need to protect privacy are receiving worldwide attention. China's former approach of reliance on ethical standards and social rectification of infringements of the right to privacy is no longer adequate or justifiable. This is especially so in view of the current EU regime concerning transborder data transfer. China needs to meet the so-called 'minimum standards' to carry out international standards. What then is the way forward for China in the years to come?

First of all, a comprehensive data protection law is a must. Self-regulation has been advocated for legal issues in the Internet industry. However, in Chinese society the need for privacy protection is not widely accepted, and only a minority of Internet users in China realise the need for or understand how to protect online privacy and prevent privacy violations. For example, one empirical study shows that the privacy statements displayed on many Chinese websites fail to comply with the generally accepted principles of privacy protection.[93] Moreover, the industry's self-regulatory standards are observed to be relatively weak in China.[94] It would be useful to have national legislation promoting privacy protection and calling on service providers to take measures to combat privacy violations. Discussions in this regard are well underway, and we can optimistically expect such legislation to be in place sooner rather than later. At present, we need to consider several issues involved in the regulation of personal data. First, which regulatory approach would work best for China: technology-neutral or technology-specific? Drawing on China's legislative experience, we can easily identify the advantages of the technology-neutral approach. The Electronic Signature Law offers an excellent example. In view of today's rapid technological developments, a neutral approach seems to work best in balancing the flexibility and stability required for national legislation.

Second, we need to differentiate among three closely related terms: 'privacy', 'personal information' and 'personal data'. One needs to be selected for the forthcoming legislation. Privacy is a relatively broad concept, and China's Tort Law acknowledges the right to privacy. In the electronic age, we are more concerned with information privacy.

---

[93] Lingjie Kong, 'Online privacy in China: a survey on information practices of Chinese websites' (2007) 6 *Chinese Journal of International Law*, 157.

[94] Kai P. Purnhagen and Jörg Binding, 'Regulations on e-commerce consumer protection rules in China and Europe compared – same same but different?' (2011) 2 *Journal of Intellectual Property, Information Technology and E-Commerce Law*, 186.

Generally speaking, personal data, as opposed to personal information, is more widely referenced in international legislation, and, indeed, has been adopted in several of the documents enacted by the MIIT. Adoption of the term 'personal data' would thus be consistent with both international practice and existing Chinese legislation, and our future national law would be advised to adopt it.

Third, we need to consider the scope of personal data and concept of sensitive data. The issue has been partly resolved by the 2012 MIIT Guidelines and 2013 Rules. However, we should also take into account technological development. It would thus be advisable to include a generic definition for both terms, to be supplemented by enumerations of typical examples. For example, the EU Data Protection Directive provides that 'member states shall prohibit the processing of personal data revealing racial or ethnic origin, political opinions, religious or philosophical beliefs, trade-union membership, and the processing of data concerning health or sex life'.[95] The damages defined in our prospective law should be able to reflect the harm caused by the defendant, with the type of data being infringed applicable in this respect.

Fourth, personal data protection should not disregard the protection of national security and commercial secrets. Furthermore, whilst the proposed law will emphasise the importance of the right to privacy, freedom of speech should be respected as well. A proper balance should be struck between privacy and freedom of speech. In this regard, we need to consider seriously possible exemptions in balancing public interest considerations. Useful reference can be made to the Personal Data (Privacy) Ordinance in Hong Kong,[96] a whole section of which (Part 8) is devoted to exemptions, in the case of judicial functions, domestic purposes or crimes, for example.[97]

Fifth, enforcement is always a thorny issue in China regardless of the law concerned. It will be necessary to consider an appropriate regulatory authority to oversee the enforcement of the rules enacted. Which governmental authority is in the best position to enforce a comprehensive data protection law? The current regime relies on the actions of the MIIT and telecommunications bureaus at the provincial level. It is true that the MIIT is one option for the supervisory authority. However, it is doubtful

---

[95] EU Data Protection Directive, article 8.
[96] Cap. 486, Personal Data (Privacy) Ordinance, Gazette Number: E.R.1 of 2013, version date: 25 April 2013.
[97] Ibid., sections 51–63D.

whether such an arrangement would be suitable for personal data protection, given the ministry's multifaceted functions. We can again make reference to the supervisory arrangements in other jurisdictions. Taking Hong Kong as an example again, a Privacy Commissioner, the supervisory authority established under the Personal Data (Privacy) Ordinance, may offer a solution. Such an independent supervisory authority would be able to enforce the rules on personal data protection in a neutral and impartial manner. Such an arrangement, which would be strictly in compliance with the international regime, could strengthen enforcement of the relevant provisions and help to win the confidence of the public. China should seriously consider the possibility of establishing a specific regulatory authority for the purpose of personal data protection.

Last but not least, we should also emphasise the importance of education and promotional campaigns to raise public awareness of the need for personal data protection.[98] The existence of a comprehensive data protection law per se would be a good start. Various interest groups could be involved in promotional campaigns, and the aforementioned supervisory authority would also be an excellent entity for raising public awareness.

6   Conclusion

The new century has witnessed the rapid development of information technology and growing use of the Internet by Chinese citizens. Statistics show that by June 2014, 'the number of Internet users in China had topped 632 million, up by 14.42 million over the end of 2013, and the Internet penetration rate was 46.9%'.[99] The widespread use of the Internet has exposed users to security risks and privacy violations stemming from a lack of transparency and data manipulation.[100]

The right to privacy has long been a heated topic among human rights lawyers.[101] China only joined the debate two decades ago, but since then

---

[98] Matthew Sundquist, 'Online privacy protection: protecting privacy, the social contract, and the rule of law in the virtual world' (2012) 25 *Regent University Law Review*, 153, 182.

[99] 'CNNIC released its 34th statistical report on internet development in China', China Internet Network Information Center, 23 June 2014, accessed 4 May 2016, www1.cnnic.cn/AU/MediaC/rdxw/2014/201407/t20140723_47471.htm.

[100] Aimee Boram Yang, 'China in global trade: proposed data protection law and encryption standard dispute' (2008) 4 *International Journal of Law and Information Technology*, 897.

[101] Lynn Chuang Kramer, 'Private eyes are watching you: consumer online privacy protection – lessons from home and abroad' (2002) 37 *Texas International Law Journal*, 387.

its legal regime for privacy protection has developed fast. In the information age, information privacy is a major concern. Relevant rules, largely at the ministerial level, are in place to guide various parties in protecting personal data, but the situation is not entirely satisfactory. We need to consider seriously how best to promote the further development of a national personal data protection legal regime.

A comprehensive personal data protection law appears to be the best, and perhaps only, way to protect individuals from 'disturbance or intrusion'.[102] It is encouraging to see that progress is being made, and we are not starting from zero. A scholarly version of a personal data protection law has already been produced, and was tabled at the State Council as early as 2005. Furthermore, as outlined in this chapter, remarkable progress has been made since 2011, particularly in 2012 and 2013, paving the way for a national personal data protection law. For example, the MIIT Guidelines are largely in compliance with the international legal regime, giving us reasons for optimism concerning the future legislative process. That process and the future national law will further raise public awareness of the need for personal data protection. Such a law could also serve to strengthen China's links with international trading partners in conjunction with its WTO membership. In an increasingly globalised world, we have every reason to believe that the existence of a national personal data protection law would help China to integrate further into the international community.

---

[102] Hao Wang, *Protecting Privacy in China: A Research on China's Privacy Standards and the Possibility of Establishing the Right to Privacy and the Information Privacy Protection Legislation in Modern China* (Dordrecht: Springer Science & Business Media, 2011), p. 169.

PART II

The Back Matters

Historical Legal Reform in China

10

Traditionalising Chinese Law

Symbolic Epistemic Violence in the Discourse of Legal Reform and Modernity in Late Qing China

LI CHEN*

Over the past century, China has undertaken a series of legal reforms in order to establish a 'modern' legal system. Despite the efforts of several generations of reformers, many commentators and scholars continue to find the Chinese legal system lacking in elements they consider indispensable to a modern legal system or modern rule of law. The unsatisfactory outcome of China's century-long legal transformation is often attributed to incommensurability between Chinese tradition and modern values and institutions, as represented by those of the industrialised Western countries since the nineteenth century. Underlying this view is a widespread assumption that there exist *natural* boundaries between 'traditional' and 'modern' law and between Chinese and Western law.[1] To understand the history of Chinese legal modernity better, this chapter argues that it is important to examine the question of how and why the

---

* An earlier version of this chapter was presented at Columbia University in September 2014 and at the University of Hong Kong in May 2015. The author is grateful to the organisers of those events, and for all of the feedback received. Research for this chapter (and a larger project on the late Qing legal reform) was conducted at libraries and archives in New York, Taipei and Beijing in 2004 and 2005. Due to space limitations, only a small portion of the materials collected is cited here.
[1] For studies influenced to varying degrees by this view, see, e.g. Jianfu Chen, *Chinese Law: Context and Transformation* (Leiden: Brill, 2008), pp. 1–30; Yongming Ai, 'Why did the attempt to modernise the legal system in late Qing China fail? A Sino–Japanese comparative study' (2004) 16(1) *Bond Law Review*, 72–91. For earlier but influential studies sharing this view, see Joseph K. Cheng, 'Chinese law in transition: the late Ch'ing law reform, 1901–1911', PhD thesis, Brown University (1976); Marinus Meijer, *The Introduction to Modern Criminal Law in China* (Batavia: De Unie, 1950). For an insightful critique of the contemporary dismissal of Chinese law, see Teemu Ruskola, *Legal Orientalism: China, the United States, and Modern Law* (Cambridge, MA: Harvard University Press, 2013).

Chinese legal system was labelled traditional (and hence presumably incompatible with modern or Western law) in the first place.

As the first stage of China's efforts to restructure its legal institutions in line with Western models (often through Japanese interlocutors), the late Qing legal reform of 1902–1911 provides an ideal example for demonstrating how Chinese law was turned into the traditional, inferior 'other' of both Western and modern law.[2] To understand the relevant processes and implications, we need to explore at least three questions: (1) How was Chinese law Orientalised or self-Orientalised and made incompatible with modern law? (2) How did the Chinese negotiate with the Euroamericentric notions of tradition and modernity? (3) How did the late Qing legal reform project contest or contribute to the traditionalisation (*chuantong hua*) of Chinese law?

By re-examining the changing sentiments and debates among the late Qing literati and officials during the last four decades of the Qing era, including the New Policy period of 1902–1911, this chapter shows that the traditionalisation of indigenous Chinese legal culture was both a cause and a product of the legal reform movement over the past century. It also calls for more attention to the frequently overlooked symbolic epistemic violence that accompanied the Euroamericentric discourses of modern law and civilisation and conditioned the Chinese legal reforms of the late nineteenth and early twentieth centuries. I believe that instead of debating whether China has succeeded in modernising its legal system, it would be more fruitful to understand the historical specificities and complexities of the Chinese experience and to problematise the normative assumptions of the dominant discourse of legal modernity.

I first trace how the dominant narrative of modern law came to affect the late Qing understanding of Chinese and Western law and culture in the 1870s to 1890s. I then re-examine the debates in the Qing legal reform of 1902–1911 to analyse how a Chinese legal tradition was constructed in contradistinction to Western or modern law. I offer brief observations and concluding remarks in the final section of the chapter. In addition to exploring the aforementioned issues, the chapter illustrates how real or constructed differences between Chinese and Western law were represented,

---

[2] For more recent and more nuanced studies, see Jerome Bourgon, 'Abolishing "cruel punishments": a reappraisal of the Chinese roots and long term efficiency of the Xinzheng legal reforms' (2003) 27(4) *Modern Asian Studies*, 851–862; Frank Dikötter, *Crime, Punishment and the Prison in Modern China* (Hong Kong: Hong Kong University Press, 2002); Xiaoqun Xu, *Trial of Modernity: Judicial Reform in Early Twentieth-Century China, 1901–1937* (Stanford, CA: Stanford University Press, 2008). See also the Chinese publications cited below.

politicised and institutionalised through the discourse of and debate on legal reform in the Sino–foreign contact zones during the late nineteenth and early twentieth centuries. It is worth emphasising that real or perceived differences between two cultures, civilisations or legal systems do not and should not mean incommensurability or a hierarchy between them unless people choose to endow such differences with normative, ideological implications. The story of the traditionalisation of late imperial Chinese law in the early twentieth century is a case in point.

1 Political Genealogy of the Global Discourse of Legal Modernity

Although the desire to abolish foreign extraterritoriality has been frequently cited as a *direct* cause of the late Qing legal reform, the reform movement cannot be fully understood by focusing solely on that issue or even on the larger context of Sino–Western relations after the two Opium Wars (1839–1842, 1856–1860). Instead, we need to view that reform project in a longer time-frame and against the global history of transcultural encounters, modernity, colonialism and Orientalism preceding it by two to three centuries. A brief overview of the genealogy of earlier Western representations of China and Chinese law is thus in order here.

As I have recently discussed elsewhere, Western knowledge of China and Chinese law grew over the course of the sixteenth to nineteenth centuries through the work of Western missionaries, diplomats and early Sinologists (including Sir George Thomas Staunton, who published the first English translation of the Qing Code without most of its substatutes in 1810).[3] Such knowledge played an important role, both as a positive inspiration and as a negative foil, in shaping the emerging debates on modernity in the West. Leading Enlightenment intellectuals such as Montesquieu, Voltaire, Cesare Beccaria and Jeremy Bentham all engaged, either explicitly or implicitly, with the China cipher as a crucial reference point in developing theories of the modern legal or political system. Their influential writings on the rule of law, rational and humane criminal justice, or systematic codification inspired widespread interest in legal reform and a series of attempts to modernise Western judicial systems beginning in the late eighteenth century. Although actual progress in legal reform was uneven among Western countries, and rather limited in Britain and the United States, the discourse of legal modernity itself influenced many people in Euroamerica and was soon deployed as a

---

[3] Li Chen, *Chinese Law in Imperial Eyes: Sovereignty, Justice, and Transcultural Politics* (New York: Columbia University Press, 2016), pp. 69–155.

master narrative to help to legitimate Western colonial expansion as a civilising mission in the Orient.[4]

At the same time, the European empires' desire for extraterritoriality in the Orient led to a global discourse of China as an Oriental despotism ruled by a backward tradition of arbitrary, irrational, and barbaric laws and institutions. The wide circulation of sensational accounts of Sino–Western legal disputes and memorable images of real or imagined Chinese judicial brutality in the eighteenth and nineteenth centuries provided fodder for this Orientalist discourse. In granting the Western powers extraterritorial privileges in China, the series of unequal treaties signed after the First Opium War served to validate and codify the earlier Western representations of Chinese law as incommensurable with that of the 'civilised' Western nations.[5] By 1900, the aforementioned Euroamericentric discourse of modern law and civilisation and the Orientalist discourse of China had merged into the dominant discourse of legal modernity in late Qing China.

That dominant discourse did not gain complete hegemony, however. A number of non-Western countries, including Japan and China, restructured their legal and political institutions in the late nineteenth and early twentieth centuries, and, in the process, various 'native' institutions and practices were stigmatised and relegated to a supposedly stationary, pre-modern tradition. But this process of transculturation was not unilaterally controlled by foreign ideas or actors. Like their counterparts in other Asian countries, the late Qing Chinese appropriated or negotiated with the prevailing foreign discourses to reclaim Chinese agency and cultural identity even as they embraced some foreign ideas and practices. Drawing upon the concepts of Gayatri Spivak and Pierre Bourdieu, I use the term 'symbolic epistemic violence' in this chapter to highlight the normative and epistemic pressure exerted by the dominant cultures and discourses on the Chinese imagining of legal modernity on the one hand and the contribution of Chinese actors to 'producing the efficacy' of those discourses on the other.[6] My purpose is

---

[4] Ibid. See also Ruskola, *Legal Orientalism*.

[5] Chen, *Chinese Law in Imperial Eyes*, pp. 25–68, 156–242. For Western representations of Chinese criminal justice, see also Timothy Brook, Jérôme Bourgon and Gregory Blue, *Death by a Thousand Cuts* (Cambridge, MA: Harvard University Press, 2008), pp. 152–202.

[6] For the term 'epistemic violence', see Gayatri C. Spivak, 'Can the subaltern speak?', in Cary Nelson and Lawrence Grossberg (eds.), *Marxism and the Interpretation of Culture* (Urbana: University of Illinois Press, 1988), 277–316. For the term 'symbolic violence',

partly to highlight the fact that the Chinese themselves played a part in traditionalising or Orientalising Chinese law and culture.

2 Reimagining modernity and tradition, 1872-1902

The print media and other publications were indispensable to the global spread of Western ideas of modernity, law and China. Building upon the work of earlier authors and periodicals, such as the *Indo-Chinese Gleaner* (1817–1822), *Canton Register* (1827–1843) and *Chinese Repository* (1832–1851), the Shanghai-based *North China Herald* (1850–1943) and other China-focused media worked closely with their metropolitan counterparts, such as the London *Times*, *Boston Recorder*, *Chicago Tribune* and *Washington Post*, often preaching Western material, cultural or racial superiority.[7] By the end of the nineteenth century, many of their ideas and cultural assumptions had reached Chinese commoners and elites alike through translated works and such Chinese-language newspapers as the Hong Kong–based *Huazi Ribao* (*Chinese Mail*, 1872–1941) and *Xunhuan Ribao* (*Universal Circulating Herald*, 1874–1947) and influential Shanghai-based *Shenbao* (1872–1949). In this section, I analyse *Shenbao* to provide a glimpse of how late Qing literati and writers engaged with the foreign discourses in the last three decades of the nineteenth century. Whilst space limitations allow me to touch upon only a small number of samples, my analysis is informed by examination of the newspaper's editorials and main news items from 1872 to 1912.

Scholars have shown that despite its foreign ownership, *Shenbao* was a *Chinese* newspaper in content, authorship and readership, and played an important role in shaping the incipient 'public sphere' of the late Qing era.[8] As the most influential Chinese-language newspaper in this period, its reports on current affairs and legal matters captured the epistemic

---

understood as 'the violence which is exercised upon a social agent with his or her complicity', see Pierre Bourdieu and Loïc J. D. Wacquant, *An Invitation to Reflexive Sociology* (Chicago: University of Chicago Press, 1992), p. 167.

[7] On the impact of foreign media on the image of Chinese law and society, see Chen, *Chinese Law in Imperial Eyes*, pp. 156–242.

[8] For recent studies of *Shenbao*, see Natascha Vittinghoff, 'Readers, publishers and officials in the contest for a public voice and the rise of a modern press in late Qing China (1860–1880)' (2002) 87(4/5) *T'oung Pao*, 399; Barbara Mittler, *A Newspaper for China? Power, Identity, and Change in Shanghai's News Media, 1872–1912* (Cambridge, MA: Harvard University Asia Center, 2004); Rudolf G. Wagner (ed.), *Joining the Global Public: Word, Image and City in Early Chinese Newspapers, 1870–1910* (Albany: State University of New York Press, 2007).

transformation of the late Qing, as educated Chinese began to reassess their own institutions and culture in relation to those of Western nations and other countries. The reports on two controversial legal cases in the 1870s illustrate this. In 1873, Yang Yuelou, an actor in Shanghai, was convicted, under judicial torture, of abducting the daughter of a Cantonese comprador. In 1875–1876, Yang Naiwu and Xiao Baicai (Little Cabbage, or Mrs Guo née Bi) from Zhejiang province were also coerced into confessing to adultery and the murder of the latter's husband. Their death sentence was reversed after Empress Dowager Cixi intervened and ordered the Ministry of Justice (*Xingbu*) to retry the case in Beijing.[9] The harsh treatment of the suspects in these cases was criticised in a series of reports by *Shenbao* and the *North China Herald.*

In depicting Yang Yuelou as someone fighting against Chinese social oppression for individual freedom and romantic love, the *North China Herald* viewed the case as more 'proof that the Chinese – mandarins at least – hardly deserve credit for semi-civilization'.[10] Commenting on the case again six months later, the same paper concluded, 'Let the merits of the case be what they may, the brutality of the proceedings alone is enough to relegate Chinese boasted civilization to the category of barbarism.' In other words, regardless of the legal or factual basis of the judicial proceedings, the way that China administered its law and punishments rendered it a barbarous country.[11] Similarly, the Yang Naiwu case and other reported instances of judicial abuse were cited to confirm that the Chinese legal system was unsuitable for governing people of the civilised (Western) nations.[12] *Shenbao* also followed these cases closely, and it has been credited by modern scholars with helping to reverse the conviction of Yang Naiwu and Xiao Baicai. Although its commentaries generally did not dismiss the entire Chinese legal system as foreigners tended to do, they appropriated certain foreign ideas in calling for the reform of

---

[9] For more about the Yang Naiwu case and its media coverage, see William P. Alford, 'Of arsenic and old laws: looking anew at criminal justice in late imperial China' (1984) 72 *California Law Review*, 1180–1250; Madeleine Yue Dong, 'Communities and communication: a study of the case of Yang Naiwu, 1873–1877' (1995) 16(1) *Late Imperial China*, 79–119.

[10] 'The romance of real life', *North China Herald*, 1 January 1874.

[11] 'The Yang Yeh-Liu case', *North China Herald*, 6 June 1874.

[12] Also see 'A Chinese inquest' [about the Yang Naiwu Case], *North China Herald*, 15 March 1877; 'The administration of justice in China', *North China Herald*, 28 April 1877. For similar reports of Chinese punishments, see, e.g. 'Decapitated by dozens', *Chicago Daily Tribune*, 28 July 1877.

Chinese institutions. For instance, a *Shenbao* editorial in early 1876 noted that the egregious misconduct of the judges in this case indicated that the imperial government had to find more effective ways to enforce the established laws and improve the methods and procedures of adjudication if it was serious about its mission of 'cherishing people's lives' (*aixi minming*). The editor expressed the belief that judicial reform should be prioritised over the introduction of Western science and technology, citing Turkey as a cautionary example. Turkey's importation of new European technology and machinery did not prevent foreign domination because the country stuck to 'Asiatic customs' (*yaxiya chengxi*) and failed to reform its legal system. 'Nothing would prosper if the people were not given [proper] legal protection or guidance', the editor stated. To follow the Western 'path to prosperity' and avoid Turkey's fate, China had to reform.[13]

Such commentaries indicate that many late Qing observers attributed the domination of the treaty powers to the relative advantages of their institutions, which partly explains why valorising accounts of Western law and culture were sometimes taken at face value during that period. For instance, the aforementioned *Shenbao* editorial recommended the adoption of certain aspects of European criminal justice because the European judicial systems 'never lead to wrongful convictions or let the guilty get away'.[14] Overestimation of the professional competency and integrity of Western lawyers led *Shenbao* to contend, in 1873 and 1880, that the lack of similar legal professionals was a serious defect of the Chinese judicial system. In contrast to Chinese pettifoggers (*songgun*), who were lambasted for instigating frivolous litigation, falsifying evidence and colluding with *yamen* clerks at the expense of commoners (*xiaomin*), Western lawyers (*xiguo zhuangshi*) were lauded for their expertise, impartiality and fearless defence of clients in courts of law. The service of lawyers would help to eliminate the use of judicial torture to extort confessions and enable judges to adjudicate cases 'always strictly' according to the law and evidence. The use of legal counsel in trials was therefore recommended as a 'wise measure' (*shanju*) that would 'protect the people from corrupt officials'.[15]

---

[13] 'Another note on the public petition of Zhejiang gentry' ('*Zailun zheshen gongbin shi*'), *Shenbao*, 9 February 1876.

[14] Ibid.

[15] 'About lawyers' ('*Zhuangshi lun*'), *Shenbao*, 16 September 1873; see also 'About the hiring of lawyers' ('*Lun yaoqing zhuangshi*'), *Shenbao*, 16 March 1880. A *Shenbao* editorial in

The idea of 'protecting the people' (*minbi*) was emphasised because these late Qing writers knew more about international politics and history than their predecessors. In urging various social reforms, including the prohibition of foot-binding, *Shenbao* observed in late 1874 that in light of the history of the European powers, the people would suffer and wither, and the country decline, if both ruler and ruled did not observe the law and if the people were not protected and thus empowered to strengthen their nation. The implied causal relationship among the rule of law, protection of the people and fate of the nation was considered 'a natural principle' (*ziran zhili*). To illustrate, the newspaper pointed out that Britain was more prosperous and powerful than other European states because it had done a better job of safeguarding its people.[16] In the same vein, several *Shenbao* commentaries in the 1880s and 1890s urged the Chinese government to moderate harsh punishments, encourage talented youths to study foreign and Chinese laws, and allow lawyers to represent litigants and use a jury for fact finding in judicial hearings.[17]

The tendency to romanticise Western law and society can be attributed partly to foreign propaganda and imperial pedagogy. In response to criticism of the British jury system as an outdated and perjury-prone institution, for instance, the *North China Herald* defended it as a guardian of 'public liberty' and as an institution that made the British people and culture unique and superior. In contrast, the Chinese people and legal system were depicted as singular and antithetical to those of the Western nations.[18] The Yang Yuelou case of 1874 was described as 'illustrating some peculiar Chinese customs – so peculiar in fact, and so essentially Chinese, that home [European] readers will be strengthened in the prevalent conviction that everything Celestial is in contradiction to everything European'.[19]

What was rarely mentioned in the foreign media, and little known to Chinese commentators, was the fact that the arbitrariness of the criminal

---

1876 also suggested that judicial hearings should be open to the people and amenable to public scrutiny. See 'Another note on the public petition', *Shenbao*.

[16] 'Another note on the public petition', *Shenbao*.

[17] 'Lawyers for Sino–foreign disputes' ('*Lun huayang jiaoshe guanyuan zhuangshi*'), *Shenbao*, 27 July 1883; 'Chinese ought to study Western law' ('*Huaren yixi xilü shuo*'), *Shenbao*, 9 March 1891; 'China ought to use Western law' ('*Zhongguo yi canyong Taixi lüfa lun*'), *Shenbao*, 8 November 1898.

[18] 'Execution by strangulation', *North China Herald*, 6 May 1876.

[19] 'Thoughts on reports from the *Huibao*' ('*Shu Huibao gelun hou*'), *Shenbao*, 23 November 1874.

justice system, rampant perjury by jurors and excessive discretion on the part of judges had prompted British reformers to call for codification and other legal reforms in the 1810s to 1830s. The ensuing legislative debates often boiled down to whether the proposed reforms were suited to the legal and cultural tradition and national character of the British people. Ironically, the recently translated Qing Code was cited by supporters of the legal reforms as a source of inspiration for improving the British legal system and by their opponents as a negative example of a codified legal system unsuitable to a free and 'modern' nation such as Britain. Although efforts to codify or 'modernise' the British common-law tradition over the next two centuries have largely failed, Britain's status as a global empire and its famed codification for India and other colonies led the founders of modern comparative law and society such as Sir Henry Maine and Max Weber to claim the British legal system as part of the family of most advanced modern law.[20] In other words, the centuries-old British legal tradition by and large survived the modernising impulse of the nineteenth century to emerge triumphant as a exemplary modern legal system in the twentieth and twenty-first centuries. This is in sharp contrast to the fate of the legal system of late imperial China, as further discussed in the following sections.

2.1 Bifurcation Strategies and Negotiation with the Dominant Discourse

From the *Shenbao* commentaries and other texts of the period, one could argue that the late Qing Chinese themselves contributed to the process of the Orientalisation or traditionalisation of Chinese law and culture. Nevertheless, many Chinese, including some of the commentators cited previously, did make efforts to counter or negotiate with the dominant discourse of modernity by adopting a strategy of bifurcation, among other tactics. They often distinguished the practical advantages of a Western legal practice or institution from the alleged superiority of Western legal or cultural tradition as a whole. At the same time, they separated a lamentable aspect or instance of Chinese judicial practices from the entire Chinese legal or cultural tradition. This is similar to the well-known dichotomy of essence (*ti*) and function (*yong*) used by late imperial Chinese intellectuals when dealing with Western learning and

---

[20] Chen, *Chinese Law in Imperial Eyes*, pp. 139–155.

science.[21] As a result, they could recommend the adoption of some Western institution (i.e. function) to serve Chinese purposes (i.e. essence) without fully endorsing the Orientalist discourse or admitting Chinese cultural or racial inferiority. Other strategies of bifurcation included emphasising the difference between the theory and practice of Western or Chinese law and the difference between the Western metropolitan rule of law and the judicial systems in Western colonies or extraterritorial courts. These strategies allowed them to acknowledge the merits of some Western theories of the modern rule of law while pointing out the gap between those theories and Western legal practices. Frequently reported discrimination against local litigants and offenders by the treaty powers' consular officials or judges in China led some late Qing commentators to become increasingly cynical about the presumably race-blind impartiality and justice of Western legal systems.[22] In early 1881, a *Shenbao* editorial pointed out that although lawyers' representation of litigants in Western countries minimised the manipulation of the corrupt judicial clerks (*xuli*) who plagued the Chinese judicial system, Western lawyers were not always guided by impartiality or the public interest. As the lawyers for both the plaintiff and defendant attempted to serve the interests of their own clients, the outcome of a lawsuit could be completely determined by the relative competency of the lawyers. A Western lawyer could thus manipulate laws or judicial proceedings to distort facts and determine the outcome of a lawsuit, just as corrupt judicial clerks could in China.[23] Interestingly, when evaluating Chinese law in the early nineteenth century, British and other European commentators often resorted to a similar set of bifurcation strategies, pointing to the differences between the theory and practice of Chinese law, between legal rationality and civil liberty, and between Chinese and

---

[21] For the attitude of the Ming and Qing literati and officials towards Western learning, see Benjamin A. Elman, *On Their Own Terms: Science in China: 1550–1900* (Cambridge, MA: Harvard University Press, 2005). Shumei Shih has discussed another kind of bifurcation between 'the metropolitan West (Western cultures in the West) and the colonial West (the cultures of Western colonizers in China)', which allowed the borrowing of Western cultural elements without being accused of collaboration with foreign imperialism in China. See Shumei Shih, *The Lure of the Modern: Writing Modernism in Semicolonial China, 1917–1937* (Berkeley: University of California Press, 2001), pp. 32–37.

[22] See, e.g. 'On Western adjudication' ('*Lun taixi ban'an*'), *Shenbao*, 8 December 1881; 'On the relationship between rulers and ruled in the West' ('*Lun taixi junchen zhiyi*'), *Shenbao*, 9 July 1881.

[23] 'Comparing Chinese and Western criminal law' ('*Zhongxi xinglü yitong shuo*'), *Shenbao*, 9 February 1881.

Western law.[24] In this sense, Qing literati and officials were not that different from their Western counterparts in utilising such strategies to appropriate certain foreign ideas and technologies while fending off perceived threats to their cultural identity and/or cherished values.

By such means, late Qing authors often chose to highlight commonalities rather than incommensurability or hierarchy between the Chinese and Western civilisations. They sometimes claimed that the spirit or essence of certain desirable Western judicial practices was not exclusively Western in origin but shared by the Chinese as well.[25] Their criticism of abusive officials or judicial practices in particular cases seldom resulted in wholesale condemnation of Chinese law or culture. For instance, Shenbao repeatedly argued that the sentiments of humane justice underlying modern Western legal systems also informed Chinese laws and procedures. For Chinese commentators, the rationale behind the procedural safeguards of Anglo-American jury trials was similar to the ancient Chinese adage that 'it is the hardest task and requires maximum care to find the truth and do justice'. Deviation from age-old practice had caused the proliferation of harsh punishments and torture, and the use of illegal torture by local officials was attributed to the lack of talented judges in recent years rather than to the imputed barbarity of the Chinese people or culture.[26] The eventual punishment of abusive judicial officials in such cases also testified to the continuing value of the longstanding Chinese emphasis on justice and benevolence. Moreover, allowing lawyers to represent litigants in the West might indeed afford better protection from official oppression, but the practice itself implied that 'crafty and corrupt officials existed in all countries'. Despite its advantages, the heavy reliance upon jury trials and lawyers also indicated a universal failing of humanity.[27]

In their attempts to balance the desire to appropriate foreign ideas and institutions with the desire to claim Chinese agency and civilisational equality, late Qing commentators sometimes ended up essentialising Chinese legal culture as well as its Western counterpart. According to one of the Shenbao editorials, li (ritual propriety or moral norms) and

---

[24] Chen, Chinese Law in Imperial Eyes, pp. 134–139.
[25] See, e.g. 'Comparing Chinese and Western criminal law', Shenbao.
[26] 'After reading the history of Franco-Prussian War' ('Du Pufa zhanji shu Ho'), Shenbao, 23 January 1873; 'On judicial leniency for avoiding disasters' ('Xuxing suoyi mizhai shuo'), Shenbao, 20 September 1882.
[27] 'About lawyers', Shenbao; 'About the hiring of lawyers', Shenbao.

xing (law or punishment) were the twin pillars of the universal Way of governance. The Way was missing 'if *li* was too rigid and *xing* was too harsh'. According to the prevailing norms of the time, officials had to kneel before the throne when memorialising and litigants had to kneel before the judge. Such practices had reified and widened 'the gap between the superior and the inferior, making it difficult for them to have affection for each other'. Illegal judicial torture by abusive officials made matters worse. The absence of public support for the Qing government in the recent Sino–Japanese dispute over Liuqiu evidenced the deficiency of existing ritual and judicial practices in cultivating loyalty and patriotism among the people. This was considered a major difference between the contemporary Chinese and their Western counterparts. If China was to become wealthy and powerful again, the country needed to follow the Way of governance, as the Western powers had done, by relaxing its rigid social hierarchy, reforming its laws and penal practices, and improving its bureaucracy and economy. In this way, late Qing authors endowed the ancient Chinese duality of *li* and *xing/fa* with a new meaning and political potency, informed by awareness of international power politics and couched in the Western language of individualism, modernity and nationalism.[28] In so doing, they neutralised some of the Eurocentric prejudices of the dominant discourses of legal reform and repackaged classical Chinese ideas of governance as *universal* values even in the modern era. Their strategic articulations of Sino–Western commensurability allowed China to borrow certain Western ideas and practices without forfeiting its claim to be an ancient *and* potentially modernising civilisation. In the process, however, their arguments had the effect of oversimplifying the long history and changing complexities of Chinese law and culture into essentialist concepts or categories.[29] As discussed later, this tendency continued into the twentieth century.

As the national crisis deepened over the last few decades of the Qing era, more and more people came to accept the necessity of major changes to promote justice, improve governance, win the people's hearts and rejuvenate the nation, leading to the short-lived Hundred Days' Reform in 1898.[30] By 1902, many of the *Shenbao* commentaries had been

---

[28] 'Thoughts on reports from the *Huibao*', *Shenbao*.

[29] 'On harshness and leniency of Chinese and Western criminal law' ('*Zhongxi xinglü kuanyan deshi lun*'), *Shenbao*, 30 April 1894.

[30] See, e.g. 'On illegal torture' ('*Jie shixing lu*'), *Shenbao*, 11 February 1881; 'On Yunnan governor's impeachment of an abusive magistrate' ('*Shu dianfu zoucan lanxing zhixian*

circulated widely among Chinese literati and scholar–officials, especially after they were reprinted in a series of influential compendia of statecraft literature.[31] In the meantime, late Qing literati or scholars such as Liang Qichao had already begun quoting leading European thinkers extensively, including Montesquieu, Jeremy Bentham, Cesare Beccaria and Henry Maine, to suggest that the Chinese political and legal systems were backward and incompatible with a modern civilised state.[32] Thanks to weakened governmental control and the rising influence of the mass media, the 1901–1911 decade witnessed the rapid spread of new and diverse ideas ranging from constitutional politics to social and gender equity.[33] It is within this larger context and prevailing global processes and discourses that the late Qing legal reform took place.

3 Debates on Legal Modernity and Tradition in the Late Qing Era

Scholars have written extensively about the legal reform of 1902–1911, so a summary shall suffice here. After the eight foreign powers suppressed

zhe hou'), Shenbao, 6 July 1881; 'On "adjudicate to prevent litigation"' ('Tingsong qiyu wusong shuo'), Shenbao, 26 June 1881; 'Words for remedying the evils of adjudication' ('Xun'an bianyan'), Shenbao, 17 September 1881; 'On the unreliability of judicial torture: reflections on the Sanpailou case of Jinling' ('Lun xingxun nanshi: shu Jinling sanpailou jiu'an'), Shenbao, 4 November 1881.

[31] See, e.g. Chen Zhongyi (ed.), The Third Anthology of Statecraft Writings of the August Dynasty (Huangchao Jingshiwen Sanbian) (Shanghai: Shanghai Shuju, 1901 [1898]). This anthology includes some prize-winning essays from the Shanghai Polytechnic Institute, which were based on some of the Shenbao editorials discussed herein. Compare the essays by Li Jingbang in Wang Tao (ed.), Examination Papers of the Polytechnic Institute (Gezhi shuyuan keyi) (Shanghai: Tushu jicheng yinshuju, 1893).

[32] Liang Qichao, 'History of the development of Chinese jurisprudence' ('Zhongguo fali xue fada shilun') and 'On the merits and demerits of China's legal codification in history' ('Lun zhongguo chengwenfa bianzhi zhi yan'ge deshi'), in Fan Zhongxin (ed.), Liang Qichao's Essays on Jurisprudence (Liang Qichao faxue wenji) (Beijing: Zhongguo zhengfa daxue chubanshe, 1997 [1904]), pp. 68–182.

[33] A glance at the issues of Shenbao, Dongfang zazhi (Eastern Miscellany) and Dagong bao (Impartial Daily) published from 1902 to 1912 provides ample illustration of this. For a collection of articles from Chinese periodicals authored by such people as Liang Qichao, Yan Fu, Wang Jingwei, Lu Xun and Zhang Binglin, see Zhang Dan and Wang Renzhi (eds.), Selected Essays on Current Affairs in the Decade before the 1911 Revolution (Xinhai geming qian shinian shilun xuanji) (Beijing: Sanlian shudian, 1977), vol. 3. For the sentiments of overseas Chinese students regarding Chinese law and reform, see, e.g. 'Letters from overseas Qing students to Duanfang' ('Chuguo youxuesheng deng zhi Duanfang hanzha'), in Series of Qing Archival Material (Qingdai dang'an shiliao congbian) (Beijing: Zhonghua shuju, 1990), vol. 14, pp. 245–396, esp. 279–280, 359–363.

the Boxer Uprising and occupied Beijing in 1900, the Manchu ruling house under Empress Dowager Cixi (1835–1908) and the Guangxu Emperor (r. 1875–1908) fled to Xi'an and issued an edict in early 1901 to solicit ideas from senior officials on how to save the beleaguered empire. Three memorials, submitted jointly in 1902 by Huguang Governor-General Zhang Zhidong (1837–1909) and Liangjiang Governor-General Liu Kunyi (1830–1902) and calling for comprehensive reforms in politics, the military, industry, bureaucracy, education and law, were approved. The recommended changes concerning the legal system were to reduce litigation and red tape, mitigate punishments, build prisons, convert bodily punishments into monetary fines, and separate administrative from judicial duties.[34] Over the next decade, the Law Revision Commission (*Xiuding falü guan*, established in 1904) and Constitution Compilation Commission (*Xianzheng biancha guan*, renamed from *Kaocha zhengzhi guan* in 1907) ushered in a series of reform programmes. Study of foreign legal systems was promoted by sending students overseas and establishing law schools in China; foreign lawyers and foreign-trained Chinese lawyers were recruited to implement the legal reform; and a number of foreign law codes and treatises were translated into Chinese for the benefit of the legal reformers. By 1911, these initiatives had resulted in a series of draft codes of civil law, criminal law, civil and criminal procedural law, nationality law, press law, copyright law and so on.[35]

---

[34] For the original edict, see *Veritable Records of the Guangxu Emperor* (*Dezong [Jing] Huangdi shilu*), 60 vols. (Beijing: Zhonghua shuju, 1987), pp. 273–274 (juan 476, GX26/12/12); Zhu Shoupeng (ed.), *Donghua Records of the Guangxu Reign* (*Guangxuchao Donghua lu*), 5 vols. (Beijing: Zhonghua shuju, 1903 [1984]), vol. 5, p. 17. According to Xu Tongxin, who graduated from the predecessor of Hosei University (*Riben fazheng daxue*) and was a member of the Constitution Compilation Commission (see *Zhengzhi guanbao*, 23 May 1909, 562, 5 (XT1/4/5), it was Yuan Shikai who originally drafted the various memorials, including the one about reforming the legal system, and recommended Shen Jiaben and Wu Tingfang before his ideas were endorsed and submitted by Liu and Zhang. See the handwritten letter by Xu Tongxin to Wang Shitong (h. Zhian) in *Archives of the Memorials of the Law Revision Commission* (*Falüguan zougao bu*) (Beijing: Library of the Legal Institute of Chinese Academy of Social Sciences, c. 1904–1911).

[35] For primary sources and details of these reform initiatives, see *Archival Sources on Late Qing Preparation for Constitutional Monarchy* (*Falüguan zougao bu; Gugong bowuyuan Ming Qing dang'an bu*, comp., *Qingmo choubei lixian dang'an shiliao*) (Beijing: Zhonghua shuju, 1979), vol. 2. For influential studies of the late Qing legal reform, see Zhang Jinfan, *Tradition and Modern Transition of Chinese Law* (*Zhongguo falü de chuantong yu jindai zhuanxing*), 2nd edn. (Beijing: Falü chubanshe, 2005 [1997]); Li Guilian, *A Biography of*

3.1 Foreign Extraterritoriality and Treaty Obligation of Legal Reform

Against the backdrop of considerable social and cultural change, the desire to abolish foreign extraterritoriality remained one of the main driving forces behind the late Qing legal reform. Contrary to the received wisdom in modern historiography, the demand for extraterritoriality by Britain and later by other treaty powers had little to do with the Chinese legal system itself; however, the foreign powers justified extraterritoriality by representing Chinese law and justice as uncivilised or incompatible with their own notions of justice.[36] It was not until the 1860s that the treaty powers explicitly made the Westernisation of Chinese law a precondition of their formal commitment to relinquishing extraterritoriality. When the Anglo–American governments insisted that their citizens should enjoy the same privileges as native Chinese to travel, trade and reside in inland China beyond the treaty ports freely, Prince Gong, the Minister of Foreign Affairs (*Zongli yamen*), and his colleagues responded in late 1868 that foreigners could have those privileges if they agreed to subject themselves to Chinese law as Chinese subjects did. American Minister to China Ross Browne insisted that China should first put in place 'a code of laws based on principles of justice, recognized and accepted by the comity of western nations, and to which the Government of the United States can safely give its assent'. British Minister to China Sir Rutherford Alcock echoed this request.[37] In December 1868, in

---

Shen Jiaben (*Shen Jiaben zhuan*) (Beijing: Falü chubanshe, 2000); Li Guilian, *Modern Chinese Law and Jurisprudence* (*Jindai zhongguo fazhi yu faxue*) (Beijing: Beijing daxue chubanshe, 2002); Huang Yuansheng, 'Legal thought of Shen Jiaben and late Qing reform of criminal law' ('*Shen Jiaben falü sixiang yu wan Qing xinglü bianjian*'), PhD thesis, National University of Taiwan (1991); Chen Yu, *The Legal Revision Commission in the late Qing New Policy Period* (*Qingmo xinzheng zhong de Xiuding falüguan*) (Beijing: Zhongguo zhengfa daxue chubanshe, 2005). For late Qing legal education and its influence, see Cheng Liaoyuan, *The World of the People in Law and Politics during the Late Qing* (*Qingmo fazheng ren de shijie*) (Beijing: Falü chubanshe, 2003).

[36] Chen, *Chinese Law in Imperial Eyes*, pp. 25–68.

[37] Mr. Browne to Prince Kung, 23 November 1868, in *Papers Relating to the Foreign Relations of the United States* (Washington, DC: United States Department of State, 1870), p. 318. In paraphrasing Browne's point, Sir Rutherford Alcock, the British Minister to China, stated that 'there was no code of laws in China which could be accepted by western states' and that extraterritoriality might be relinquished only if China adopted a written code 'based on the same general principles as those constituting the law with minor modifications of the western world'. See Sir Rutherford Alcock to Prince Kung, 9 November 1868, in *Papers Relating to the Foreign Relations of the United States*, p. 312.

addition to agreeing to open up China, the Qing government promised to 'adopt a written code of commercial law, and fixed rules of procedure and practice, and a better constitution of mixed courts for its administration in all mixed cases of civil suit between foreigners and natives'.[38] In the words of the American minister, it was necessary to 'force our civilization upon them ... to advance them to a higher civilization'. The message for the Chinese was loud and clear: 'There must be a fixed code of laws and a radical change in the system of administering justice in this country before extraterritorial protection can find a substitute in native courts.'[39]

After the Qing government was compelled to sign the Boxer Protocol in 1901, its promise of 1868 was turned into a legal commitment through international treaties, couched in language giving the impression that China voluntarily sought to Westernise its legal system. Article XII of the 1902 Sino–British treaty on commercial relations declared:

> China having expressed a strong desire to reform her judicial system and to bring it into accord with that of Western nations, Great Britain agrees to give every assistance to such reform, and she will also be prepared to relinquish her extra-territorial rights when she is satisfied that the state of the Chinese laws, the arrangement for their administration, and other considerations warrant her in so doing.[40]

A similar article was included in other treaties signed between China and foreign powers around the same time. These treaties made it clear that the existing Chinese legal system had to be transformed into something resembling that of the Western nations and that the foreign powers themselves would determine whether and when to relinquish extraterritoriality. Indeed, despite enormous changes in the Chinese legal system in the next two decades, the treaty powers continued to express dissatisfaction and refused to give up extraterritoriality until the Second World War necessitated its abolition in 1943. In any event, before the Qing

---

[38] 'Bases of revision of the Treaty of Tien-tsin, accepted by the Chinese Government', 8 December 1868, in *Papers Relating to the Foreign Relations of the United States*, p. 320.

[39] Browne to Alcock, 17 December 1868, in *Papers Relating to the Foreign Relations of the United States*, pp. 320–321. For Anglo–American demands, see ibid., pp. 312–319.

[40] See Article XII of Treaty between Great Britain and China Respecting Commercial Relations, &c., signed at Shanghai, 5 September 1902, in Edward Hertslet and Godfrey E. P. Hertslet (eds.), *Treaties, &C., between Great Britain and China; and between China and Foreign Powers*, 3rd edn. (London: His Majesty's Stationery Office, 1908), p. 182. For the Sino–American treaty, see Article XV of the Treaty between China and the United States Respecting Commercial Relations, signed on 8 October 1903, in ibid., p. 575.

government initiated the New Policy reforms in 1902, it had already appeared almost inevitable that the Chinese legal system would be recast as the traditional opposite of modern (Western) law.

3.2 Debates during the Legal Reform

Most of the draft law codes had not yet been promulgated by the time the Qing dynasty collapsed in 1911, but their contents did generate great interest and lively debates across China. Ideas about the separation of powers, judicial independence, private property, natural rights and parliamentary democracy were introduced or reinterpreted.[41] An enduring legacy of the late Qing debates was that more and more Chinese came to accept the idea that the pre-existing Chinese legal system was incompatible with a modern nation or society in the twentieth century largely because it was different from the supposedly civilised and superior legal systems of the dominant foreign powers.

In the edict of May 1902 that appointed Shen Jiaben (a leading Qing jurist) and Wu Tingfang (the first Chinese barrister trained in England) as Commissioners of Law Revision, the Qing imperial court explicitly noted that the reform project was primarily designed to resolve difficulties arising from 'increased international contact and trade'. Shen and Wu were instructed to keep these considerations in mind and 'study the laws of all countries' (*canzhuo geguo falü*) to develop a legal system that could be 'applicable to both Chinese and foreigners' (*wuqi zhongwai tongxing*) and conducive to governance.[42] To achieve this goal, the reformed legal system would have to address the treaty powers' concerns

---

[41] See the debates over the draft codes of procedural law, civil law and criminal law and the related discussions in such newspapers as *Shenbao, Dagong Bao, Diguo Ribao, Shuntian Shibao* and *Shibao* from 1906 to 1911. For the official debates and commentaries on the draft procedural codes, see Zhao Bin (comp.), *Collected Comments and Criticism on the Criminal and Civil Procedural Codes (Xingshi minshi susongfa boyi buju)* (Beijing: Beixin shuju, 1908); Zhang Sanquan, *Commentary on the Draft Criminal Code of the Great Qing (Da Qing xinglü cao'an jianzhu)*, 2 vols. (Henan: n.p., 1908). About the commercial code, see Jin Bangping, *Doubtful Points about the Commercial Code of the Great Qing (Da Qing shanglü cunyi)* (Tokyo: Library of Waseda University, c. 1908).

[42] For the edict (GX28/4/6), see *Copies of Memorials on Legal Reform in the late Qing (Qingji xiuding falü zougao ji shuotie chaojian)*, M.S. (Beijing: Library of the Legal Institute of the Chinese Academy of Social Sciences, 1902–1911), p. 1. Also see 'Canzhuo falü ni dagai banfa' (GX29/12/7), in *Grand Council Copies of Memorials (Junjichu lufu zouzhe)* (Beijing: First National Historical Archives), 539–7227-57. Wu Tingfang studied law at University College London in 1874, was called to the bar at Lincoln's Inn in 1876 and received his LLD in 1877.

satisfactorily. Hence, foreign representation and criticism of Chinese law and justice exerted enormous influence on the guiding principles of the late Qing legal reform.

One of the most notable changes made during the late Qing reform was that the centuries-old practice of organising the contents of the dynastic law codes by the six ministries of the central government was replaced by the Western-style departmentalisation of the legal system into civil, procedural, criminal, commercial, constitutional law and so on. Western commentators who reviewed Staunton's 1810 translation of the Qing Code criticised the Chinese legal system for its supposedly irrational structure and lack of civil law, rights consciousness and individual liberty as understood in the West.[43] Anxious to meet foreigners' expectations, the late Qing legal reformers often made such stereotypical characterisations appear both indisputable and self-fulfilling.

Moreover, in early 1902, the legal reformers took the first available opportunity to abolish the three severest forms of punishment – slicing (*lingchi*), gibbeting (*xiaoshou*) and desecration of the corpse (*lushi*) – as well as the laws on tattooing and vicarious criminal responsibility (*yuanzuo*). Judicial torture was also banned except in capital cases when multiple witnesses had already proved the guilt of the accused.[44] As noted earlier, Euroamericans had cited these practices to stigmatise Chinese law and government since at least the eighteenth century, often *retrospectively* to justify their longstanding defiance of Chinese law and jurisdiction. Likewise, the New Draft Criminal Code (*Xin xinglü cao'an*), first presented to the throne in 1906, sought to change the forms of Chinese corporal punishment into the death penalty (only by

---

[43] See Chen, *Chinese Law in Imperial Eyes*, chaps. 2–3. For the structural change to the existing Qing Code, see *Archival Sources on Late Qing Preparation*, pp. 851–852. Interestingly, in support of the Law Revision Commission's efforts to restructure the current Qing Code, Wang Rongbao cited all Chinese examples to justify the change. See Wang Rongbao, 'On the Law Revision Minister's list of statutes deleted for compiling the currently effective criminal law' ('*Xiuding falü dachen bianzhuan xianxing xinglü shanchu zongmu yi*'), in Wang Rongbao, *Writings Preserved at the Jinxie Linlang Studio* (*Jinxie linlangzhai wencun*), reprinted in Shen Yunlong (ed.), *Collection of Primary Sources on Chinese History from the Late Eighteenth Century* (*Jindai Zhongguo shiliao congkan di liushi ji*) (Taipei: Wenhai chubanshe, 1970), vol. 60, pp. 93–95.

[44] 'Several harsh laws should be changed' ('*Biantong lüli nei zhongfa shuduan zhe*') (GX31/3/29) in *Grand Council Copies*, 539–7226–64; also included in *Collections of the Memorials* (Beijing: National Library, c. 1905–1996). The memorial was approved by the throne on 24 April 1905 (GX31/3/20). For the imperial edict approving the abolition of judicial torture and beating with bamboo, see Zhu, *Donghua Records* (GX31/3/25, 25 April 1905), vol. 5, p. 48.

strangulation), imprisonment, detention and fines; reduce the number of capital statutes; abolish adjudication by analogy (*bifu*) where no applicable statutes existed; and build juvenile correctional facilities. Shen Jiaben justified these changes by citing examples from Chinese law in *earlier* dynastic periods and from contemporary Western legal systems, recasting existing laws as repugnant to both the better tradition of Chinese law and the 'universal' practice of the modern world. Although he appeared to be more sympathetic to the preservation of indigenous Chinese legal culture, Shen was fully aware that the extraterritorial powers, now including Japan, would not be satisfied with piecemeal changes to the legal system. As he explained to the imperial court (and to the general public):

> An independent state shall have exclusive jurisdiction (*duli faquan*) within its territory (*lingdi*). Except for foreign sovereigns, diplomats, and certain military forces, all foreign sojourners shall be subject to the law of the country under international norms. However, consular jurisdiction was [imposed by foreign powers] in China under the pretext that our judicial system was defective. Britain started it and was later followed by Germany while Japan even set up courts of law in the ancestral home [of the Qing rulers in Manchuria]. Our sovereignty (*zhuquan*) has been undermined day by day. The current situation makes it imperative to reform our legal system.

For Shen and advocates of the proposed reforms, in an age when the law and government of all countries were becoming increasingly similar or 'universalised' (*fangjin geguo zhengzhi ri jiyu datong*), borrowing Western and Japanese ideas and institutions was both inevitable and necessary to establish a legal system that would help China become 'civilised'.[45]

Like many of the earlier commentators in *Shenbao*, Shen Jiaben and other moderate reformers took pains to find a middle ground between clinging to the existing Chinese legal system and taking for granted a Westernised legal system (often mediated by the Japanese experience). They did this by citing precedents in Chinese legal history to justify proposed laws or changes.[46] Ji Tongjun (1854–1936), another learned jurist and important member of the Law Revision Commission, was reportedly the first to recommend the abolition of the harsh corporal

---

[45] *Archival Sources on Late Qing Preparation* (Shen Jiaben, GX44/8/26), pp. 846–929; *Grand Council Copies*, 539-7227-57 (GX29/12/7), 539-7228-5 (GX32/4/2). See also Zhu, *Donghua Records* (GX31/4/8, 8 May 1905), vol. 5, pp. 56–57.

[46] See the preambles to the different draft codes and memorials calling for the abolition of severe punishments.

punishments noted earlier, but his ideal solution was to revise and reform
the Qing legal system without abandoning its substance and essence.
Towards that goal, he convinced the Law Revision Commission to amend
and update the Qing Code into Currently Effective Criminal Law (*Xianxing Xinglü*).[47] Although men like Shen and Ji might have held different
views on precisely how to achieve their goals, they agreed in principle
that the essence of Chinese law was not incommensurable with that of
Western or modern law and that Chinese modernity could not and
should not be constituted through total deconstruction or destruction
of the Chinese legal tradition.

However, the growing fear of foreign colonisation after 1900 led more
and more educated Chinese, especially those who had studied in Japan,
to prefer a more radical break with the past and the establishment of a
brand-new political and legal system to save the country. Their proposals
in turn radicalised other people in various quarters of late Qing official-
dom and society. The resulting competition to impose their own vision of
Chinese modernity on the late Qing reforms led people on both sides to
deploy reductionist or essentialising language to characterise Chinese
law, society and civilisation in contradistinction to their Western or
modern counterparts. To a large extent, these debates invented, propa-
gated or reinforced many of the still-popular Orientalist and Occidental-
ist stereotypes about China and the West. The resulting Sino–Western
dichotomy and traditionalisation of Chinese law had as much to do with
critics of the proposed reforms as with their supporters. In the remainder

[47] Ji Tongjun, 'Preface', in Ji Tongjun (ed.), *Class Essays of the Law School of the Ministry of
Justice (Fabu Lüxue guan kejuan disiji)* (Beijing: Fabu lüxue guan, 1911), vol. 4. Although
Dong Kang tried to take credit, Ji Tongjun's writings indicated that Ji's memorandum
inspired the memorials of Shen Jiaben and Wu Tingfang concerning the abolition of
slicing, gibbeting, desecration of the corpse and vicarious criminal responsibility, reduction of capital punishment and beatings with bamboo, and increased use of monetary
fines and imprisonment. See Ji Tongjun, 'Memorandum to the minister of law revision on
abolishing severe punishments' ('*Shang xiulü dachen zhuochu zhongfa shuotie*), in *Essential Advice for Adjudication (Shenpan yaolüe)*, appended to Ji Tongjun, *Lecture Notes on
the Currently Effective Criminal Law of the Great Qing (Da Qing xianxing xinglü jiangyi)*,
8 vols. (Beijing: Fabu lüxueguan, 1910), and also reprinted in Yan Xiaojun and Chen Tao
(eds.), *Collections of Lesu Hall (Lesutang wenji)* (Beijing: Zhongguo falü chubanshe,
2014). See also Dong Kang, 'Process of Chinese legal reform' ('*Zhongguo xiuding falü
zhi jingguo*'), in He Qinhua and Wei Qiong (eds.), *Anthology of Dong Kang's Writings on
Law (Dong Kang faxue wenji)* (Beijing: Zhongguo zhengfa daxue chubanshe, 2005),
p. 461. In this period, Ji Tongjun was a senior member (*zuanxiu*) of the Compilation
Department (*bian'an chu*) of the Law Revision Commission, and was in charge of
deleting old statutes and compiling various regulations (*zhangcheng*).

of this chapter, I briefly discuss the major controversies over the New Draft Criminal Code to illustrate this.

Given the strong reaction to the earlier draft codes of procedural and civil law, it is not surprising that a number of Qing officials expressed serious reservations about the New Draft Criminal Code once it was circulated for public comment in late 1907.[48] Like the few Japanese lawyers who helped draft other law codes in this period, Okada Asataro (1868–1936), a prominent scholar of criminal law and a professor at Tokyo Imperial University, was hired by the Law Revision Commission in 1906, and spent the next year putting together the draft code, patterning it after the Japanese criminal code, which in turn had been modelled on Western law codes.[49] Several other important drafters who helped Okada and Shen Jiaben polish or defend the draft code were also graduates of Japanese law schools, including Wang Rongbao (1878–1933), Dong Kang (1867–1947, jingshi in 1890), Zhang Zongxiang (1879–1962), Cao Rulin (1877–1966), Jiang Yong (1878–1960), Lu Zongyu (1876–1941) and Xu Tongxin (1878–?).[50] Contemporary observers noticed that the New Draft Criminal Code was vastly different from the existing Qing Code and Chinese legal system, although the drafters later attempted to restore some concepts or features from the latter. About two dozen memorials commenting on the draft code were submitted between 1908 and 1910. Although memorialists and commentators in the media shared the drafters' sense of urgency about reforming the legal system and borrowing the good elements of Western and Japanese law codes, many of them felt that the drafters had gone too far in adopting a

---

[48] The part entitled 'General principle' (Zongze) was presented on 3 October 1907 (GX33/8/26), and the other parts (Fenze) were presented on 30 December 1907 (GX33/11/26). For the relevant memorials and edicts, see, e.g. Lao Naixuan (ed.), 'Collected commentaries on the New Criminal Code' ('Xin xinglü xiuzheng an huilu'), in Writings Bequeathed by Mr Lao Naixuan (Tongxiang Lao Xiansheng (Naixuan) Yigao), reprinted in Shen, Collection of Primary Sources on Chinese History, vol. 36, pp. 879–884.

[49] In addition to Okada Asataro, a few other Japanese lawyers also helped, including Shida Taro (1868–1950) with procedural law, Matsuoka Yoshimasa (1870–?) with civil law and Ogawa Shigejiro (1863–1925) with prison reform. See Archival Sources on Late Qing Preparation, vol. 2.

[50] On the drafting process of the New Criminal Code, see Wang Rongbao, Diary of Wang Rongbao (Wang Rongbao riji) (Tianjin: Tianjin guji chubanshe, 1987). Other Japanese-educated drafters included Zhang Zongxiang (Imperial University), Cao Rulin (Tokyo University), Jiang Yong and Lu Zongyu (Kyoto University), and Xu Tongxin (Japanese University of Law and Politics). See Wang Rongbao, 'Preface to Zhao Xinbo's commentary on the Criminal Code of the Republic of China' ('Zhao Xinbo zhonghua minguo xinglü lun xu'), in Wang, Writings Preserved at the Jinxie, p. 227.

foreign-style code with little regard for what they considered the Way of Chinese society and civilisation: the hierarchical social and political order (*sangang wuchang*) and moral norms (*lijiao*).[51] A memorial from the Ministry of Education (*Xuebu*) headed by Zhang Zhidong was particularly harsh on the New Criminal Code for eliminating the differential legal treatments for people of different social, familial and gender statuses, a sentiment echoed by a number of other official memorials.[52] The strong backlash led the Qing court to order the Law Revision Commission and Constitution Compilation Commission to preserve essential Chinese customs and moral norms in the new law codes. To reflect critics' concerns, some minor changes were made, and five articles were appended to the New Criminal Code. The revised version was submitted in early 1910 to the Constitution Compilation Commission and, later that year, to the newly established Imperial Council of Political Consultation (*Zizhengyuan*) for deliberation.[53] Lao Naixuan, appointed to both of these institutions because of his scholarly erudition, became a leading critical voice after publishing two memoranda demanding amendments to the draft code. The next few months saw a series of intense debates both within the Imperial Council and far beyond.

The debates eventually boiled down to the question of how to define the nature of Chinese law and civilisation in relation to Western or modern law and civilisation. Explaining the legislative rationale of the New Criminal Code to the Imperial Council, Yang Du (1875–1931), a native of Hunan who had studied law and politics in Japan before being appointed to the Constitution Compilation Commission, famously argued that the debate was not just over the New Criminal Code but over whether China should replace its old 'familism' (*jiating zhuyi*) with 'statism' (*guojia zhuyi*) that prevailed in other countries. For him, China's crisis and weakness were the result of its laws (*falü*) and moral norms (*lijiao*) being rooted in familism, under which every individual's rights

---

[51] For these memorials and the commentaries therein on specific articles of the draft codes, see, e.g. Liu Jinzao (ed.), *Continued Documentary History of the Qing Dynasty* (*Qingchao xuwenxian tongkao*), 12 vols. (Taipei: Xinxing shuju, 1959), 9883–10008.

[52] Zhu, *Donghua Records*, vol. 5, p. 5509. For reactions to the New Criminal Code from various ministries and provincial officials, see Xianzheng Biancha Guan (comp.), *Commentaries on the Draft Criminal Code* (*Xinglü caoan qianzhu*), 3 vols. (Beijing: Xianzheng biancha guan, c.1910); Gao Hancheng (ed.), *Collection of Legislative Materials of the New Criminal Code of the Great Qing* ('*Daqing xin xinglü lifa ziliao huibian*') (Beijing: Shehui kexue wenxian chubanshe, 2013).

[53] For some of the details regarding the drafting and revision processes, see *Archives of the Constitutional Compilation Commission* (*Xianzheng biancha guan dang'an*) (Beijing: First National Historical Archives), no. 52.

and obligations were tied up with the family instead of the state or country. In contrast, he continued, other countries' laws and morality were rooted in statism, under which every adult became a citizen of the country (*guomin*), and individual wealth and ability were translated into national strength. The existing Chinese legal system was found to be 'incapable of developing its citizens' (*fada qi guomin*) or 'strengthening the state' (*zhengxing qi guojia*).[54] These arguments were reductive of both Chinese and foreign laws and cultures. Yang Du may have come across a translation of Sir Henry Maine's famous *Ancient Law* (1861), which Liang Qichao explicitly quoted in the same period. In addition to asserting that China had never moved beyond a status-based society into a contract-based modern society, Maine claimed that although the law helped other societies advance, Chinese laws had actually kept that country backward.[55]

Yang Du was far from alone in attributing China's political subordination to its legal system and ultimately to its cultural tradition and national consciousness. Other supporters of the legal reform programme echoed this argument enthusiastically. For instance, Wu Tingkui, another advisor to the Constitution Compilation Commission, pointed to China's history since the First Opium War to show that adherence to the 'old ideas' (*jiushuo*) (that is, the old Chinese way of thinking or epistemology) was inappropriate when discussing the New Criminal Code, and would 'breach the [Sino–foreign] commercial treaties, undermine constitutionalism, and prevent China's progress'. Seeing law as the essence and foundation of the state, he believed that fundamental legal reform was required for China's revival[56] and that it should be patterned on Western and Japanese models.[57] In fact, some commentators equated the existing

---

[54] Yang Du, 'Yang Du on statism and familism' ('*Yang Jinqing lun guojia zhuyi yu jiazu zhuyi*'), in *Collected Commentaries on the Criminal Code* (*Xinglü pingyi huibian*) (Beijing: n.p., c. 1910), pp. 8a–11b, reprinted in *Shibao* 2 December 1910 (XT2/11/1) and *Shuntian Shibao* 2 December 1910 (XT2/11/1). See also 'Opinions of the Compilation Bureau on how to revise the New Criminal Code' ('*Bianzhiju jiaoding xin xinglü yijianshu*'), in *Collected Commentaries on the Criminal Code*, pp. 12a–14b, reprinted on 19 December 1910, by *Shenbao*, *Shibao* and *Guofeng Bao*.

[55] Henry Sumner Maine, *Ancient Law: Its Connection with the Early History of Society, and Its Relation to Modern Ideas*, 2nd edn. (New York: Charles Scribner, 1864 [1861]); see also Chen, *Chinese Law in Imperial Eyes*, chap. 2.

[56] Wu Tingkui, 'Councillor Wu's critique of the use of old ideas to assess the draft law code' ('*Wu Canyi yong jiushuo yi lü bian*'), in *Collected Commentaries on the Criminal Code*, pp. 7a–7b.

[57] Wu Tingkui, 'Councillor Wu's comments on making the law similar to foreign laws according to the agreement on treaty revision', in *Collected Commentaries on the Criminal Code*, pp. 6a–6b; also printed as 'Councillor Wu Tingkui on the commercial treaties'

Qing legal system with the Manchu-style pigtails that they desperately urged people to cut off in order to get rid of all signs and causes of China's 'backwardness'.[58]

Lao Naixuan and his supporters, who accounted for over half of the Imperial Council's members, have often been criticised or derided over the past century as irrational conservatives who clung stubbornly to a backward Chinese tradition. This dismissive label misses the complexities of China's experience with modernity. Examination of their arguments shows that Lao and his supporters did not actually oppose most parts of the New Criminal Code or the legal reform movement itself. In his widely circulated memoranda on the Draft New Criminal Code, Lao agreed with the drafters on the necessity of reforming the legal system in order to abolish extraterritoriality. However, he disputed the assertion of Yang Du and others that China had to adopt the same kind of legal system as those of Japan and Western countries, particularly in defining crimes and punishments. He was not opposed to abolishing corporal punishment by bamboo and judicial torture or to establishing judicial independence and a prison system. After these reforms had been under-taken, he argued, China would have met the preconditions for ending extraterritoriality stipulated in the recent Sino–Western commercial treaties, as long as the reformed legal system was 'comparable in general' (*dati xiangtong*) to that of the extraterritorial powers. To those who argued that nearly every article of the new law codes had to be satisfac-tory to foreigners in order to abolish extraterritoriality, Lao countered that the extraterritorial powers differed from one another in various aspects of their own legal systems, making it impossible for any Chinese legal system to satisfy all foreign countries. Moreover, he pointed out that among the treaty powers, the nationals of one country could not deny the jurisdiction of another country just because they found that country's law to differ from their own. Based on his own experience of dealing with foreign governments, Lao also noted that legal reform itself would not determine whether foreign extraterritoriality was abolished.[59] Regardless

---

requirement for all countries to make laws similar' ('*Wu Canyi Tingkui shangyue gaitong geguo lüli yilü shuo*'), *Diguo Ribao*, 15 December 1910.

[58] See, e.g. 'Signs of improved knowledge of parliamentarians' ('*Yiyuan zhishi jinbu zhi tezheng*'), *Diguo Ribao*, 16 December 1910; see also *Diguo Ribao* on 19 and 21 Decem-ber 1910.

[59] Lao Naixuan, 'Memorandum on the revised draft criminal code' ('*Xiuzheng xinglü cao'an shuotie*'), which was submitted to the Constitutional Compilation Commission, in Lao, 'Collected commentaries on the New Criminal Code', 884–928, esp. 885–900, 942. On his

of whether one likes or dislikes Lao and his supporters, many of these arguments sound quite reasonable. Among other things, he was right about the issue of foreign extraterritoriality, which did not end until three decades after the late Qing legal reform.

What is more interesting for our purposes is that, like Yang Du and other vocal supporters of the new codes, Lao Naixuan also resorted to essentialisation in trying to preserve what he considered to be the core values of imperial Chinese law and culture. Instead of attacking the New Criminal Code for its foreign roots, he tried to reinsert into the new code several Qing statutes related to crimes committed between relatives, the digging of others' graves, adultery by unmarried women (wu fu jian) and the right to discipline children or grandchildren. These statutes were assumed to be fundamental to social order and moral norms (lunji lijiao), and thus indispensable to the criminal code. Unlike Yang Du and others, Lao and his sympathisers did not think that law and morality could be fully separated, especially given that the Qing court had just ordered the drafters to preserve time-honoured moral values as the foundation of the country.[60] Lao accepted Yang's assertion that China was founded on the spirit of familism, but he attributed the lack of national consciousness and patriotism not to the country's law or familism but to its political institutions of 'despotism' (zhuanzhi zhuyi). Contrasting China as an agricultural society with the Western industrialised nations, Lao concluded that the lifestyle and living conditions of a nation determined its customs, moral norms and polity, and then its laws.[61] For him, the social and gender hierarchy, as epitomised by the statutes he tried to retain, had to be maintained to prevent China from losing its 'national essence (guochui) for a few thousand years and the foundation of the country (liguo zhiben)'.[62] By the end of the first reading of the Revised New Criminal Code in the Imperial Council, the focus of the debate was

---

experience of dealing with the Western powers, see Lao Naixuan, Manuscripts of Lao Naixuan's Official Correspondence (Lao Naixuan gongdu shougao) (Tianjin: Tianjin guji chubanshe, 1988).

[60] Lao, 'Collected commentaries on the New Criminal Code', 886–887. In response to the earlier criticism of Lao and others on the Constitution Compilation Commission, the Law Revision Commission agreed to place in an appendix to the code several related articles applicable only to Chinese people. Lao criticised this creation of separate laws for the Chinese as contrary to the original purpose of regaining full and uniform jurisdiction by enacting a new criminal code (ibid., 887).

[61] Ibid., 867–876. He classified human societies into three types: agricultural (ruled by family law), nomadic (ruled by military law) and industrial (ruled by commercial law).

[62] Ibid., 925–926.

further reduced to two issues: (1) whether the code should criminalise adultery by unmarried women and (2) whether the code should punish someone for injuring a child or grandchild in the course of disciplining the latter as though the injury had occurred between social equals (*zisun weifan jiaoling*). Whereas Shen Jiaben and others contended that these were not legal but moral issues and should therefore be dealt with through education or correctional facilities, Lao and his sympathizers such as Chen Baochen considered them crucial to social customs and public morality, and hence worthy of the intervention of the state and legislators.[63]

For a few weeks, the debate over these issues fired the public imagination across many Chinese urban centres, including Tianjin, Shanghai and Beijing. Numerous newspapers and periodicals followed it closely and published passionate commentaries that generally castigated Lao's 'faction' as representing the reactionary elements of traditional Chinese society and constituting an obstacle to Chinese progress and modernity.[64] At one point, tensions ran so high that Gao Lingxiao, a vocal supporter of Lao in the Imperial Council, even traded blows with supporters of the new code outside the council.[65] Contrary to popular

---

[63] For the debate between Lao and Shen Jiaben, see ibid., 929–942, esp. 940–942. See also 'Chen Baochen on the commentaries of Lao Naixuan and Shen Jiaben on the New Criminal Code' (*'Chen Gexue du Lao Tixue ji Shen Dachen lun xinglü cao'an pingyi'*) and 'Chen Baochen on criminalisation of adultery of unmarried women' (*'Chen Gexue xin xinglü wufujian zui shuo'*), in ibid., 945–965; Yang Zhongjue, 'Mr Yang's petition on the need to revise the New Criminal Code to maintain social norms' (*'Yang shi chenqing biandong xin xinglü yiwei fenghua chengwen'*) and 'Mr Yang urges amendment of the New Criminal Code for its failure to criminalise adultery of unmarried women' (*'Yang shi xin xinglü jian fei zui niqing xiugai shuo'*), in ibid., 1011–1026. For a rebuttal to Yang Du, see Lin Zhiping, 'Mr Lin argues that statism and familism should not be dichotomised' (*'Lin shi bianming guojia zhuyi yu jiazu zhuyi burong liangli shuo'*) in ibid., 991–999. For recent studies on these debates, see, e.g. Li, *Modern Chinese Law*; Alison Sau-chu Yeung, 'Fornication in the late Qing legal reforms: moral teachings and legal principles' (2003) 29(3) *Modern China*, 297–328.

[64] For the debate in the Imperial Council, see *Minutes of the First Year of the Imperial Council of Political Consultation* (*Zizhengyuan diyici changnian huiyi jilu*) (Beijing: n.p., 1911), sess. 23, pp. 45–70, sess. 37, pp. 39–92, sess. 38, pp. 25–59, sess, 39, pp. 63–119, sess. 40, pp. 9–15. For reports by the media, see, e.g. 'Society for the New Criminal Code' (*'Xinlü weichihui'*), Shibao, 11 December 1910; 'The New Criminal Code unlikely to pass' (*'Lun xinlü zhi kongnan tongguo'*), Shibao, 16 December 1910; 'Struggle between the old and the new' (*'Xinjiu zhizheng'*), Shibao, 29 December 1910.

[65] See, e.g. 'The New Criminal Code and parliamentarians' (*'Xin xinglü yu yiyuan'*), Diguo Ribao, 19 December 1910; 'Three animals in the parliament' (*'Zizhengyuan sansheng'*), Minli Bao, 14 December 1910. See also the relevant reports and editorials in Shenbao, 13, 15 and 23 December 1910, 13–17 and 23 January 1911; Shuntian Shibao, 22 December 1910, 22 January 1911.

perception and conventional interpretations, however, the disagreement between the two sides was narrowly framed and limited to a relatively small number of specific statutes. Lao Naixuan felt himself wrongfully attacked by the media as the public enemy of the New Criminal Code, given that, in his words, he actually supported over 97 per cent of the four hundred or so articles of the new code.[66] Even those who had reservations about the New Criminal Code and other draft law codes found it necessary to cite Western ideas or theories to legitimate their arguments. For instance, Ji Tongjun cited British philosopher Herbert Spencer in arguing that the law must be 'suited to the history and national character (*guoti*) of the country' to prevent endless problems in its actual implementation.[67]

At the end of the Qing era, ironically, it was lawyers from the foreign treaty powers who acknowledged the value of the dying Chinese legal tradition. For instance, Dr Harald Gutherz, a German jurist and lecturer at the German-Chinese Institute in Qingdao, wrote a famous critique of the New Criminal Code while it was being debated by Chinese legislators in 1910, cautioning that the Chinese should not completely abandon their own legal system in favour of a foreign one because even European jurists had recognised the merits of the Qing Code since its translation by Staunton in 1810.[68] Similarly, in 1908, Charles Sumner Lobinger, a judge of the American extraterritorial court in Shanghai, reminded readers of the forgotten fact that China had a highly sophisticated legal system and by far the world's oldest law code in continuous operation, noting that if the Roman Empire's Code of Justinian had been in force since it was first promulgated in the sixth century, it would still be very young in comparison.[69]

---

[66] Lao, 'Collected commentaries on the New Criminal Code', 1056–1057. Lao noted that he had asked only to restore or revise five or six articles and add eight or nine others. Wang Rongbao also noted that the opponents had missed the point and focused on 'one or two trivial (*xianxi*) aspects'. See Wang, 'Preface to Zhao Xinbo's commentary', 227.

[67] Ji, 'Preface'.

[68] Harald Gutherz, 'On the Chinese New Criminal Code' ('*Zhongguo xin xinglü lun*'), in Lao, 'Collected commentaries on the New Criminal Code'. On his attempt to influence Chinese legal reform, see Harald Gutherz and Hans Wirtz (trans.), *General Principles of the Draft New Criminal Code of the German Empire* (*Deyizhi diguo xin xinglü cao'an zongze*) (Qingdao: Qingdao Dehua tebie gaodeng zhuanmen xuetang, 1910).

[69] Charles Sumner Lobinger, 'The need of law reform in China' (1908) 37 *American Review of Reviews*, 218–219. Lobinger also cites the *Edinburgh Review*'s commentaries on Staunton's 1810 translation.

4 Conclusion

Although some of the self-Orientalising ideas and images discussed in this chapter still influence Chinese legal scholars and reformers today, even the most enthusiastic supporters of the New Criminal Code in the late Qing era soon recognised the problems of wholesale Westernisation or the uncritical embrace of the dominant foreign discourses. In 1927, Wang Rongbao, a code drafter and advocate, effectively admitted his and other legal reformers' mistakes of seventeen years earlier. He realised that late imperial Chinese law had grown organically out of a long history and had already developed into a distinctly sophisticated legal system by the Tang period (in the seventh century) comparable to that of the West (presumably referring to the Roman legal system codified in the sixth century). The reason he offered for his eager support of the New Criminal Code in 1910 is very instructive:

> The New Criminal Code adopted a lot of Western legal ideas, in sharp contrast with the old Chinese law. I often found that problematic (*chang yiwei bin*), but I could not disagree with others even if I had wanted to because that [the desire to Westernise Chinese law] resulted from the prevailing sentiment (*fenghui*) at the time and the examples of numerous foreign countries.[70]

In other words, his views of legal reform in the last decade of the Qing were influenced primarily by public opinion and the dominant foreign cultures and discourses of the time. Elsewhere, Wang Rongbao echoed in 1926 the arguments that Lao Naixuan and others had made in 1910: *fa* and *li* were different sides of the same coin and 'interchangeable (*xiangwei zhuanhuan*)', he said. Wang even went a step further than Lao in contending that the rule of law was in essence the rule of *li* and that the foreign-educated Chinese had insisted on separating *fa* and *li* because their knowledge was superficial and they did not understand the origins of law. For him, law could be revised but morality and customs could not be so easily changed, and thus legislators should search for the roots of law, that is, 'study social morality and people's customs'.[71]

Dong Kang, another advocate of the New Criminal Code in 1910, also later changed his mind. In 1910, he argued, *inter alia*, that despite its distinctiveness, the existing Chinese legal system (*faxi*) could not be

---

[70] See Wang, 'Preface to Zhao Xinbo's commentary', 228.
[71] Wang Rongbao, 'Preface to Zhao Xinbo's study of legal philosophy' ('*Zhao Xinbo falü zhexue cijie xu*'), in Wang, *Writings Preserved at the Jinxie*, 211–213.

preserved if China wanted to 'progress and prosper' (*jinbu fada*) and avoid the lamentable fate of Turkey and India.[72] Ten years later, he blamed the influence of Western ideas for his earlier dismissive attitude towards China's own legal culture. He concluded that Chinese legal reform could not be carried out by abandoning Chinese *lijiao* (moral norms), which would be like 'cutting feet to suit shoes'. In light of the 'moral decay' in 1920s China, he was convinced that 'the family system should be preserved' and that '*lijiao* was the only possible means' of doing that.[73]

Both Wang Rongbao and Dong Kang in the 1920s accepted most of the arguments made by Lao Naixuan and others whom they had once attacked as irrational conservatives. They also acknowledged that their understanding of Chinese legal tradition and modernity around 1910 had been shaped by foreign ideas and cultures whose epistemic authority was mostly derived from the political domination of the treaty powers. Ironically, even in these self-reflections years later, Wang and Dong still showed the effects of the symbolic violence of cultural imperialism, as they continued to use self-Orientalising language that reduced the Chinese legal tradition and social realities into just *lijiao*, the family and social hierarchy. Although this kind of essentialism was designed to fend off total Westernisation, as China historian Arif Dirlik has observed, 'in the very process it also consolidate[d] "Western" ideological hegemony by internalizing the historical assumptions of Orientalism'.[74]

Although some of the late Qing reformers later changed their minds, they had already cast the die for Chinese law by turning it into an Oriental legal tradition that was presumed to be antithetical to modern law. By the early 1930s, the legal system that had governed imperial China for more than a thousand years could claim barely any legitimate role in the now 'modern' country even though some of its concepts and

[72] 'Dong Kang's rebuttal to the memoranda of Professor Harald Gutherz of Qingdao' ('*Dong Keyuan Qingdao He Jiaoxi shoutie boyi*'), in *Collected Commentaries on the Criminal Code*, pp. 33a–37b, 36b (for the quotations). See also 'Dong Kang refutes the idea that the New Criminal Code should not be modelled after foreign law') ('*Dong Keyuan bian xinglü cao'an bubi mofan waiguo*'), in ibid., pp. 38a–39b; 'Dong Kang's response to Lao Naixuan's commentary on the new code' ('*Dong Keyuan da Lao Yiyuan lun xinxinglü*'), *Diguo Ribao*, 9 December 1910.
[73] Dong Kang, 'Humble opinion on why criminal law ought to emphasise moral norms' ('Xingfa yi zhuzhong lijiao zhi chuyi'), in Qinhua and Qiong, *Anthology of Dong Kang's Writings*, 626–637, esp. 626, 637.
[74] Arif Dirlik, 'Chinese history and the question of Orientalism' (1996) 35(4) *History and Theory*, 114.

practices might still be used without explicit admission in certain areas of Republican judicial practice.[75] In contrast, the Anglo–American legal tradition whose history spans many centuries has become part of the universal standard defining modern law even in the twenty-first century.

In this chapter, I have shown that the history of Chinese legal reforms over the past century cannot be reduced to a set of neat dichotomies between tradition and modernity, China and the West, success and failure or conservative and progressive. The late Qing Chinese resorted to various strategies to appropriate new ideas and discourses in developing their own vision of what modern Chinese law and the modern Chinese nation should be like. The so-called 'conservatives' and 'reformers' actually had more common ground than has been recognised in earlier historiography. Influenced by the dominant foreign discourses of modernity and China, both sides made essentialising characterisations of Chinese, Western and modern laws and societies.[76] The history of Chinese legal modernity since the late Qing period should also be understood as a constant struggle among the Chinese for balance between anxiety about cultural identity and a yearning for international recognition by the dominant powers. Until that subtle or illusive balance can be achieved, the Chinese legal system will continue to appear too foreign to the Chinese and too Chinese to foreigners. To understand modern Chinese law better, it is important to keep in mind the tensions, ambivalence and intercultural politics that have shaped its trajectory over the past century.

---

[75] For a recent study of how early Republican legal professionals tried to make selective use of imperial Chinese legal concepts and/or practices from 1911 to 1930, see Michael H. K. Ng, *Legal Transplantation in Early Twentieth-Century China: Practicing Law in Republican Beijing (1910s–1930s)* (New York: Routledge, 2014).

[76] In addition to the source cited above, see also Dong Kang, 'Dong Kang's response to Lao Naixuan's commentary on the new code' ('*Dong Keyuan da Lao Yiyuan lun xinlü*'), *Shibao*, 13 December 1910; Okada Asataro, 'Why the New Criminal Code should not criminalise consensual sex between unmarried people' ('*Lun xinglü buyi zengru hejianzui zhi faze*'), *Shenbao*, 11 January 1911, also reprinted in *Collected Commentaries on the Criminal Code*, pp. 19a–21b; Okada Asataro, 'Dr Okada explains why the law on disciplining children or grandchildren should be deleted' ('*Gangtian boshi lun zisun weifan jiaoling yitiao ying shanqu*'), *Shuntian Ribao*, 6 December 1910, also reprinted in *Collected Commentaries on the Criminal Code*, pp. 22a–22b; 'Judge Matsuoka responds to Lao Naixuan's memorandum' ('*Songgang Panshi shu Lao Tixue xin xinglü shuotie hou*'), in *Collected Commentaries on the Criminal Code*, pp. 32a–32b.

11

Judicial Orientalism
Imaginaries of Chinese Legal Transplantation in Common Law

MICHAEL NG

1 Introduction

Hong Kong, a common law jurisdiction with a predominantly Chinese population of mainland ancestry, offers an ideal site in which to investigate the historical laws of China from a comparative perspective. Since the early twentieth century, Hong Kong courts have accumulated more than one hundred years of experience dealing with cases of historical Chinese marriage that took place in Mainland China during the Republican era (1912–1949), forming a common law narrative of the historical changes that the law underwent from the imperial to modern legal systems.[1] Into the twenty-first century, a considerable number of family and succession law cases that touch upon the issues involved in these historical marriages continue to be brought before the courts of Hong Kong every year. This chapter challenges the century-old approach to narrating how family law changed in Republican China and raises wider methodological concerns about the tendency of common law–trained judges to follow judicial precedents based on archaic documentary sources and to adopt abandoned historiography in their investigations of Chinese legal transplantation.

---

[1] For the statutory basis on which historical Chinese law and custom were applied by the Hong Kong courts and a snapshot of relevant decisions, see E. S. Haydon, 'The choice of Chinese customary law in Hong Kong' (1962) 11(1) *The International and Comparative Quarterly Law*, 231; Anne Cheung, 'The paradox of Hong Kong colonialism: inclusion as exclusion' (1996) 11 *Canadian Journal of Law and Society* 63; Yigong Su, 'The application of Chinese law and custom in Hong Kong' (1999) 29 *Hong Kong Law Journal*, 267. For the choice of law in family law cases, see Keith Hotten, Azan Marwah and Shaphan Marwah, *Hong Kong Family Court Practice* (Hong Kong: LexisNexis, 2015), p. 50.

In deciding how to ascertain the meaning of the law governing these matters, the Hong Kong court (and apparently also the court of Singapore) demarcates historical China by the effective dates of the various books of the Republican Civil Code transplanted from the West from 1929 to 1931.[2] Cases concerning matters that took place prior to 1929 (primarily those dating to the late Qing [mid-nineteenth century to 1911] and Beiyang [1912–1928, also known as warlords period] eras) are decided with reference to the Qing Code and Chinese custom, whereas those concerning matters that took place in the Nationalist era (1928–1949) are decided solely on the basis of transplanted legal codes modelled on European templates.[3] Hence, traditional Chinese law and custom are ignored.

This conventional judicial practice of demarcating the Chinese legal past has gone largely unchallenged for the past hundred years in both common law courts and in legal scholarship in Hong Kong or other former British colonies in which Chinese law remains relevant to civil lawsuits. However this chapter argues, through a critique of a Hong Kong Court of Final Appeal (CFA) case important to understanding Chinese family law, that this century-old judicial approach is flawed and indeed Orientalist, particularly in its understanding of how historical legal transplantation took place in China.[4] Such an approach, if not corrected, will remain the authority in directing judges in deciding family law cases not only in Hong Kong but also in other former British colonies populated by indigenous Chinese such as Malaysia and Singapore. More importantly, this chapter also argues that such a judicial approach is but one example of the Orientalist knowledge system governing

---

[2] A similar demarcation approach was adopted by the Singaporean High Court. See *Wong Kai Woon alias Wong Kai Boon and another v Wong Kong Hom alias Ng Kong Hom and others* (2000) SGHC 176.

[3] The Republican Civil Code was primarily modelled on the Japanese Civil Code of 1898, which followed the template of the German Civil Code of 1896. It also took into consideration the civil codes of Switzerland and France.

[4] The 'Orientalist approach' is used here under the framework of legal Orientalism proposed by Teemu Ruskola to refer to the prejudicial construction of Chinese historical legal thoughts and practices as pre-modern. For such an analytical framework and related case studies of Euro–American representations of Chinese law, see Teemu Ruskola, *Legal Orientalism – China, the United States, and Modern Law* (Cambridge, MA: Harvard University Press, 2013), 'Legal orientalism' (2002) 101(1) *Michigan Law Review*, 179. For a recent detailed review of the framework, see Carol Tan, 'How a "lawless" China made modern America: an epic told in orientalism' (2015) 128 *Harvard Law Review*, 1677. For a response to her review, see Teemu Ruskola, 'A response to Professor Tan's review of *Legal Orientalism*' (2015) 128 *Harvard Law Review Forum*, 220.

Chinese legal traditions and legal culture in general, family law and custom included, within common law. Here, drawing on Teemu Ruskola's work on legal Orientalism, judicial Orientalism is defined as an epistemological representation of traditional Chinese law and legal culture produced and recycled in the courtroom and common law knowledge system. Such a representation for the past century distinguishes traditional Chinese jurisprudence from modern (by default Western) law, thereby 'othering' it. The resulting knowledge system cements the cultural distance between the modern West and the traditional Orient in law, as this study shows.[5]

The case analysed here concerns two women who became concubines in Nationalist China. The CFA imagines a binary division between pre-transplant customary Chinese law on the one hand and post-transplant modern Chinese law on the other, and presumes that traditional Chinese jurisprudence is irrelevant in understanding the legal meanings ascribed to the new legal codes imported from the West. Such a simplistic presumption and binary division has produced incorrect judgments on statutory interpretation of the transplanted legal codes practised in Republican China, as well as huge injustices to litigants, as the following landmark 2001 CFA judgment on the status of the two Nationalist-era concubines, *Suen Toi Lee v Yau Yee Ping*, shows.[6]

The chapter begins with the story of two deceased women, Sung So Chun and Chu Lee, whom a man named Sung Chuen Pao took as concubines in Shanghai in 1933 and 1945, respectively, following his marriage in 1929. Both Mr Sung's wife and other family members openly accepted and recognised the two women as his concubines. In 1951, Mr Sung moved to Hong Kong, where Mrs Chu joined him in 1952. Mrs Sung and Mr Sung's wife remained in Mainland China until their deaths in 1983 and 2000, respectively. Mr Sung and Mrs Chu died in 1985 and 1987, respectively.

The appeal before the CFA in 2001 concerned Mrs Chu's estate, with the court asked to determine who was entitled to it. The appellant, Suen Toi Lee, was Mrs Sung's daughter by Mr Sung. If both Mrs Sung and Mrs Chu had been Mr Sung's concubines, then the appellant was entitled to a share of Mrs Chu's estate as an 'issue' under the definitions

---

[5] Ruskola, *Legal Orientalism*, pp. 8–16. In addition to Ruskola's work, this study is also indebted to the work of Edward W. Said, particularly, *Orientalism* (New York: Pantheon, 1978).

[6] *Suen Toi Lee v Yau Yee Ping* (2002) 1 HKLRD 197 (CFA).

provided by the Intestate Estate Ordinance of Hong Kong. If neither woman had been a concubine, then none of Mr Sung's children were entitled to any of Mrs Chu's estate, which would instead remain in her own family. Because she had no children herself, in this case her estate would pass to her siblings, whose interests in the case were looked after by Mrs Chu's niece, the respondent Yau Yee Ping.

The two women's union with Mr Sung was openly accepted by the man's family, including his wife, and one of them bore him a number of children. Yet, after their deaths, the women were ruled by the CFA in 2001 to have, at best, enjoyed the status of mistress, thereby causing their issue to lose her right to succession within Sung's family under Hong Kong law. The critical issue that the CFA had to consider in this case was whether, as a matter of historical fact, the *Book of Family of the Republican Civil Code* (Book of Family hereafter), which came into effect on 5 May 1931, *abolished* the system of concubinage in Mainland China, rendering any union of concubinage created after that date (such as that of Sung and Chu) unlawful or invalid. The CFA judges ruled unanimously that the Book of Family had indeed abolished the system of concubinage, and therefore that it was unlawful for any union of concubinage to take place thereafter. This deprived the two now-deceased women of their legal status as concubines.

The CFA's judgment was based on three lines of reasoning: first, that the express provision against bigamy in the Civil Code was meant to prohibit the taking of concubines; second, that the Civil Code had created a new institution known as the 'household' to replace the old institution of 'concubinage', and through such creation concubinage was meant to have been abolished; and, third, that a published statement by the law drafter pointed to his intention that the transplanted Civil Code be used to uphold gender equality and eliminate concubinage in China by no longer mentioning concubines in the code. This view has become common law authority on the interpretation of the transplanted modern marriage law of Republican China, and will remain so until overruled by the CFA or a common law court of similar standing in the future.

Drawing on the latest scholarship of historians of the marriage regime in Republican China (1912–1949) and archival materials, this chapter argues that such judicial representation not only does not stand up to historical scrutiny; it actually distorts the way in which the marriage law was intended, understood and practised in the Republican era. More importantly, it demonstrates that it was the Orientalist image of traditional Chinese law and custom that has been continuously produced and recycled in the common law knowledge system over the past century that contributed to the anomalies of the CFA judgment. In the following sections, the chapter rebuts each of the three lines of reasoning offered by the CFA in its ruling in *Suen Toi Lee v Yau Yee Ping*, before turning to a succinct history of the common law knowledge system on traditional Chinese law exhibited in a set of judicial decisions, colonial reports and publications on Chinese law and custom relied on by the courts, as well as in common law textbooks that are still in use in law schools today. This analysis suggests the need for a revision of the judicial approach of Orientalising, and thus the neglecting of traditional Chinese jurisprudence in interpreting modern Chinese law. This chapter argues for a 'thicker description' of the legal reform process in China and perhaps in other parts of Asia. Such a description requires that imported legal codes and systems no longer be analysed as the simple displacement of old, traditional institutions by the implementation of Western-inspired and modern legal regimes. Instead they ought to be understood as the outcome of a more complex interplay between indigenous and foreign legal ideas and the way in which those ideas were discussed, interpreted and practised in their historical context. In that process, traditional ideas and practices were assimilated with the borrowed legal regime in a quest for legal modernity that fit particular political and societal needs.

2 Monogamy, Polygamy and Bigamy in China

One of the most important reasons for the CFA judges' decision that a relationship with a concubine could no longer be created under the law in the period in question was passage of the Book of Family, which was promulgated on 26 December 1930 and came into effect on 5 May 1931. The judges paid particular attention to Article 985 of the Book of Family, which states: 'A person who has a spouse may not contract another marriage.'[7] The court took the view that such an express prohibition of multiple marriages abolished concubinage in Mainland China. The CFA judges came to that conclusion because they regarded a concubine and a wife as similar in nature and saw Article 985 as upholding the modern conception of monogamy. Hence, the prohibition was seen as a logical bar to taking a concubine under the newly transplanted civil law of Republican China.

---

[7] Lixin Yang, *The Compilation of Chinese Civil Codes for One Hundred Years (Zhongguo Bainian Minfadian Huibian)* (Beijing: China Legal Publishing House, 2013), p. 495.

In the CFA's judgment, Justice Bokhary, citing the leading English marriage case of *Hyde v Hyde* to guide his argument, stated that a monogamous marriage is 'the voluntary union for life of one man and one woman, to the exclusion of all others', further commenting, 'I think the potential of the inclusion of a concubine renders a marriage potentially polygamous and that the actual inclusion of a concubine would render a marriage actually polygamous.'[8] Based on this Westernised notion of monogamy, he ruled that taking a concubine would render a marriage polygamous: 'We have seen the way in which the RCC [Republican Civil Code] abolished concubinage. It was by providing that a person who has a spouse may not contract another marriage.'[9]

This conception of marriage assumed that the transplanted Civil Code, modelled on legal codes from the West, also adopted its donors' legal definitions of monogamy, bigamy and polygamy. In *Suen Toi Lee v Yau Yee Ping*, the CFA judges viewed Chinese legal transplantation through the lens of modern Western jurists and did not realise that the Republican Civil Code assimilated the legal meanings of imperial China with regard to marriage and bigamy.

2.1   Differentiation of Concubinage and Bigamy in Chinese Law

The important archival study of Kathryn Bernhardt and Lisa Tran concerning how concubinage fit into the Chinese concept of monogamy shows such an assumption to be wrong.[10] In fact, the criminal codes of both the Beiyang and Qing eras (as well as those of earlier imperial eras) prohibited bigamy, but viewed concubinage as lawful. The Provisional Criminal Code promulgated in 1912 and Republican Criminal Codes promulgated in 1928 and 1935 adopted similar wording with regard to culpability in bigamy offences. Article 291 of the former states: 'One [who] contract[s] another marriage when he has a spouse will be punishable by level-4 imprisonment or less. . .'[11] Bigamy had been an offence under China's imperial codes for centuries. Under the Qing Code, a man

---

[8] *Hyde v Hyde* (1866) LR 1 P&D 130, cited in *Suen Toi Lee*, para. 7.

[9] *Suen Toi Lee*, para. 49.

[10] Kathryn Bernhardt, *Women and Property in China, 960–1949* (Stanford, CA: Stanford University Press, 1999), Chapter 7; Lisa Tran, *Concubines in Court: Marriage and Monogamy in Twentieth-Century China* (Lanham, MD: Rowman & Littlefield, 2015), chapters 1–3.

[11] Hongda Zhu (ed.), *The Compilation of New Criminal Law (Xinxinglu Huibian)* (Shanghai: Shijie Shuju, 1933), p. 401.

was subject to punishment of ninety strokes of the cane if he married while his first wife was alive. However, taking a concubine was lawful in both eras.[12]

How can we reconcile the apparently contradictory objectives of prohibiting bigamy while allowing concubinage? The issue can be elucidated in the context of Chinese conceptions of marriage. In Chinese tradition, marriage was both a union between husband and wife and a union between their respective families. Hence, marital union also constituted the establishment of kinship ties between families. However, those ties could be established only between the man's family and that of his one wife.[13] Kinship ties formed through marriage imposed unique rights and duties on married couples. One of the most important duties was performing mourning services for the extended family members of either spouse following their deaths. These services, which required the donning of specific types of dress and refraining from holding celebrations and other rituals, could last from several months to several years depending on the relationship proximity of the deceased and the mourning couple. Known collectively as the system of mourning (*fu zhi*), these responsibilities were very important in Chinese society and were prescribed in the Qing Code.[14]

The union between a man and a concubine, in contrast, was regarded by Chinese custom and law as a personal union. It did not involve any linkage between the couple's families. Hence, the concubine was required to fulfil mourning responsibilities for a very limited number of close family members of the man, and the man had no such responsibilities to his concubine's family members under Qing law. There was a clear

---

[12] Tao Tian and Qin Zheng (eds.), *The Qing Code (Daqing luli)* (Beijing: Law Press China, 1999), p. 206.

[13] The taking of an additional wife was permitted only in exceptional circumstances, such as the death of the first wife, or a situation in which the brother of the man's father had no son and the man thus had to take another wife on his paternal uncle's behalf to bear children to continue the uncle's family line. This was a customary practice known as *Jian Tiao*, which had been recognised by magistrates in legal rulings since the imperial era. For a succinct summary of the practices and issues involved, see Su, 'The application of Chinese law', 276–285. The practice continued into the Republican period; see *Investigation Report on Civil Practices (Minshi Xiguan Diaocha Baogaolu)* (Beijing: Ministry of Justice of Nationalist Government, 1930; Reprint: Beijing: China University of Political Science and Law Press, 2000). See in particular section 4 of such report on family and succession. For the legal treatment of the *Jian Tiao* relationship by the Republican Chinese courts, see Bernhardt, *Women and Property*.

[14] For a complete illustration of the traditional mourning system amongst Chinese family members under the Qing Code, see Tian and Zheng, *The Qing Code*, 64–79.

distinction in Chinese tradition between a union with a wife, which bore with it kinship relations and a variety of ceremonial rituals, and a union with a concubine, which bore only personal relations and much fewer rituals. Accordingly, bigamy referred only to the marrying of another wife; it did not apply to, nor prohibit, taking a concubine.

Although the Provisional Criminal Code and its provisions concerning bigamy were transplants from the West, the underlying legal meanings assimilated concepts of China's imperial legal past. The Draft Civil Code of the Qing era and its provisions on bigamy, which the Beiyang judiciary applied in civil cases together with the Qing's code on civil matters, and from which the Book of Family was largely copied, were also Continental European transplants. However, the Code was interpreted by the Republican era Supreme Court in deciding cases based on traditional Chinese concepts of the relationship amongst marriage, concubinage and bigamy. That interpretation is manifest in the following criminal and civil case decision directives issued by the Republican Supreme Court in the 1930s.

For example, in December 1931 (roughly seven months after the Book of Family took effect), the Ministry of Justice issued a statutory interpretation in response to a request from the High Court of Fujian Province to explain the law with regard to a case concerning succession. It read in part, 'Taking a concubine is not a marriage and therefore cannot be regarded as a ground for divorce under Article 1052(1) of the Civil Code.'[15] Article 1052 of the Civil Code reads, 'A husband or a wife can petition the court for divorce if the other party does the following[:] (1) Bigamy...'[16]

It is clear from the decisions cited that the distinction between a wife and a concubine, the exclusion of concubines from the marital relationship and the inapplicability of bigamy to the concubinage relationship persisted from the imperial era through the Beiyang and then Nationalist periods in both the civil and criminal law regimes despite the large-scale legal transplantation modelled on the West that took place after the Qing dynasty had been overthrown. As Lisa Tran notes: 'The greater the distance between concubinage and marriage,

---

[15] Wei Guo, ed., *Interpretations issued by Ministry of Justice (Sifayuan Jieshi Li Quanwen)* (Shanghai: Huiwentang Chubanshe, 1946), p. 513; see in particular interpretation no. 647 of 1931. Jingxiong Wu and Wei Guo, eds., *Reasons of Decisions and Interpretations on the Six Books of Law of the Republic of China(Zhonghua Minguo Liufa Quanshu Panjie Liyou Huibian)*. Vol. 2: *Civil Law* (Shanghai: Huiwentang Xinji Shuju, 1947); 546, interpretation no. 647 of 1931.

[16] Yang, *The Compilation of Chinese Civil Codes*, p. 502, art. 1052(1).

the easier it was for jurists to present the custom of concubinage as compatible with the principle of monogamy.'[17]

3 Household Member (*Jiashu*) or Concubine?

Another line of reasoning relied upon by the CFA judges in ruling that concubinage had been abolished under the law following promulgation of the Book of Family in 1931 was that a statutory institution called 'the house' (or household) had been *created* and provided for by other articles in the Book of Family. Justice (Non-Permanent) Lord Millet stated:

> The Civil Code replaced the institution of concubinage by the institution of 'the household'. Permanent members of a household were to be entitled to be maintained by the head of the household whether they consorted with him or not . . . By providing an alternative legal mechanism for the protection of women who were concubines in a factual sense after 1931 the Civil Code recognized that the former legal status of the concubine and its incidents had been abolished.[18]

Again, the CFA regarded household membership as a new legal creation in the newly transplanted civil law of Republican China expressly designed to replace and abolish concubinage. Assuming 'newness' and modernity to lie on the exit side of the legal transplantation door, the CFA judges failed to trace the origin of the concepts of household and household membership to traditional Chinese law and custom, and thus erred in regarding the household as a modern institution implemented to eliminate concubinage. The concepts of the household (*jia*) and a concubine's status as a member of the household (*jia shu*) can be traced back to the Ming and Qing Codes. In Chinese tradition, a wife should call her spouse 'husband' (*fu*) and a concubine should call that spouse 'household head' (*jia chang*).[19]

---

[17] Tran, *Concubines in Court*, p. 33.

[18] *Suen Toi Lee*, paras. 63 and 64. Justice Bokhary held a similar view: 'we have seen how the RCC dealt with the social problem resulting from the abolition of concubinage. This was by creating "the house" and providing that a woman who cohabited on a permanent basis other than as a wife with the head of the house or any other male member of the house qualified as a "member of the house" and was as such entitled to maintenance.' See *Suen Toi Lee*, para. 49.

[19] Fengjie Zhao, *The Legal Status of Chinese Women* (*Zhongguo Funu Zai Falu Shang Zhi Diwei*) (Taipei: Shihuo Chubanshe, 1973), p. 89; Jiguang Xue, 'A critique on the judicial decisions and interpretations regarding concubines' (*'Guanyu Qie Zhi Jieshi Panli Zhi Piping'*) (1933) 4(8) *Social Science Review* (*Shehui Kexue Luncong*), 74.

3.1 The Household: An Imperial Concept That
Survives into the Republic

The different terminology served to distinguish a concubine, who was a member of the household, from a wife, who was a member of the kinship (*qinshu*) relation under the matrimonial and familial concepts of traditional Chinese society. As previously noted, only the union with the wife was regarded as a union between the man and woman's families, tying them together in a kinship relationship. A union with a concubine, in contrast, was merely a personal relationship between the woman and the man and his immediate family members. Therefore, a concubine was a member of the man's immediate family but not a member of his clan.

These two types of membership entailed different rights and duties to a wife and a concubine within the Chinese familial hierarchy. One such difference was the aforementioned mourning services. The traditional mourning duties for a wife were called the 'wife's kinship (*qin*) mourning services' and the 'wife's mourning service towards husband's kinship (*fu ju*)'. That for a concubine was known as the 'concubine's household (*jia*) head mourning services'. The names of these services mark the important distinction between a wife's status as *qinshu* and a concubine's as *jiashu* by excluding the latter from kinship but placing her within the household. Although a concubine's inferior status entitled her to fewer rights than a wife, she nevertheless enjoyed the right to receive maintenance, as well as several other limited rights under imperial Chinese law.[20]

After the collapse of the Qing dynasty, the imperial legal system was replaced by a transplanted system. In civil matters, the post-Qing courts drew upon the regulations of the Qing Code, local custom and the late Qing era Draft Civil Code in deciding cases. The Republican Supreme Court frequently issued directives on how to select and adapt conflicting principles amongst these codes and custom.[21] On the matter of concubinage, although gender equality and monogamy were amongst the many political and legal ideals the Republicans referenced in appealing for public support for the revolution against imperial authority, concubinage

---

[20] Yu Cheng, *The Change in Law and Custom of Taking a Concubine (Xuqie Xixu Ji Fagui Zhi Bianqian)* (Shanghai: Renmin Chubanshe, 2013), pp. 169–198.

[21] As a result, the Supreme Court's statutory interpretation notes and case decision directives became part of the legal principles followed by the Republican courts in understanding the legal meanings of various statutes. See Li Xu, *Study on the Book of Family of the Civil Code of the Republic of China (Zhonghuaminguo Minfa Qinshu Yanjiu)* (Beijing: Law Press China, 2009), pp. 26–28.

continued to be practised after the Xin Hai revolution of 1911, as shown by the respective studies of Nationalist period concubines by Bernhard and Tran. Further, concubines' traditional household membership was reaffirmed in numerous Supreme Court case decision directives during the Beiyang era, well before the Nationalist Government's promulgation of the Book of Family in 1931. For example, the Supreme Court ruled that 'a person as a concubine under the law currently in force is recognised as a member of the household...'[22] In Chinese tradition, as a member of the household, a concubine is entitled to be maintained by the household as long as she does not contract a union of concubinage with another man or become another man's wife.[23] Such traditional entitlements as household maintenance were also recognised by the Supreme Court of the Beiyang era.[24]

It is clear from the cited examples that the institution of household was not a creation of the 1931 Book of Family for the purpose of abolishing concubinage. Rather, the 1931 Book of Family under the Nationalist Government further formalised the Supreme Court's directives by codifying them into a statutory provision of the Civil Code. By virtue of such codification of previously available rights, a woman who cohabitated on a permanent basis with the household head other than as a wife qualified as a member of the household and was entitled to maintenance. As a result, the Book of Family states: 'Although one is not a kinship member [qin-shu], if one cohabits on a permanent basis with the household head one qualifies as a member of the household [jiashu].' That provision closely follows the Supreme Court's case decision directive issued in 1916 during the Beiyang period: 'A concubine's identity is as a member of the household who cohabits on a permanent basis with the household head.'[25]

4   An Imagined Binary of Modern and Traditional Chinese Law

The CFA made, I argue, at least two mistakes in investigating China's legal past. First, it forcefully and erroneously imposed modern

---

[22] Wei Guo (ed), *Judgment of the Supreme Court (Daliyuan Panjueli Quanshu)* (Taipei: Chengwen Chubanshe 1972) case decision directive 1915, no. 2052.

[23] Yu, *The Change in Law and Custom*, pp. 169–198.

[24] For the range of rights affirmed by the court in favour of concubines, see Bernhardt, *Women and Property*, pp. 188–195; Tran, *Concubines in Court*, pp. 68–75. See also Jingli Xu, *Study of Changes of Women's Rights in Early Republican China (Minchu Nuxing Quanli Bianhua Yanjiu* (Beijing: Law Press China, 2010), pp. 221–222.

[25] Guo 209, case decision directive 1916, no. 1534.

common law jurisprudence on Chinese legal traditions and, in doing so, invented an imaginary modern Chinese marriage law that fit the aspiration of the common law that a man cannot marry two women if monogamy is to be upheld.

Second, it mistakenly imagined an Orientalist binary division of modern and traditional Chinese law, and believed that through that division lay a door marked legal transplantation. On the entrance side of the door could be found traditional Chinese laws that were reasoned on the basis of Chinese imperial codes and customs, whilst on the exit side lay the modern transplant, which should be interpreted only with reference to modern (by default Western) jurisprudence. It was beyond the CFA judges' comprehension that the entrance (pre-transplantation) side of the door contained elements of what they considered to be modern law (such as the law governing monogamy and bigamy) or that the exit (post-transplantation) side contained laws that carried elements of imperial Chinese jurisprudence (such as the exclusion of concubinage from bigamy prohibitions).

The transplantation door paradigm adopted by the CFA in the case under study here Orientalised Chinese law and Chinese legal reform. That Orientalising view effectively blinded the CFA judges, preventing them from asking the right questions, and from inquiring into both legal changes and legal continuities in the process of legal transplantation, thereby leading them to an incorrect conclusion concerning the relationship amongst marriage, bigamy and concubinage in Republican China.

In addition, applying the common law technique of statutory interpretation to their understanding of China's history of legal reform, the CFA judges also concluded that the system of concubinage had been abolished on 5 May 1931 because that system had been openly condemned by certain law drafters who said that it would no longer be recognised in law, and hence that the new Civil Code would no longer mention concubines. If one also takes into account what Foo Ping Sheung says in the memoir he wrote in Taiwan upon his retirement in the 1960s (discussed later in this section), it becomes doubtful whether such condemnation truly represented the Guomindang (GMD, the Nationalist Party, also known as Kuomintang) law drafters' intentions rather than an attempt to convince the Western legal powers that the GMD was keeping its promise to improve gender equality. In discussing his work on codifying the civil law for the Nationalist Government in this memoir, Foo specifically refers to the case of concubinage to highlight the difficulty of formulating a civil code modelled upon a European template to fit the needs of China:

> The process of drafting the civil code really involved much pressure and took a lot of efforts. Many difficulties were encountered. A few real examples here: 1. Status of concubines ... If an express statutory provision was used to recognise it, we would lose face and cause laughter in front of other countries. If we completely denied the status of concubines, how could the law ... cope with the extremely widespread fact of taking concubines in contemporary Chinese society? I thought extremely hard for over two weeks before deciding how to handle this issue...[26]

It is clear from Foo's recollection here that in drafting the law he and his colleagues deliberately refrained from criminalising concubinage in the Criminal Code and from mentioning its abolition in the Civil Code so as not to deny completely its continuation in practice. At the same time, they hoped that such ambiguous treatment would satisfy supporters of gender equality and garner praise from Western countries pressing for the modernisation (by default Westernisation) of Chinese law. It seems from the CFA decision in 2001 that those hopes were realised.[27]

In fact, the general disbelief that concubinage had truly been abolished is also made clear by the open practice of senior government officials and prominent entrepreneurs contracting concubines after promulgation of the Book of Family. Not only were these practices well known to the public; they were openly publicised in newspapers. News reports from *Shen Bao*, one of the most widely circulated Chinese newspapers of the day, testify to the ubiquity of concubinage. In the 1930s, it was not difficult for readers of *Shen Bao* to find conspicuously placed newspaper advertisements announcing run-away concubines. Some of these announcements were even posted by lawyers on behalf of their clients.

---

[26] Winston Hsieh, ed., *Record of Interview with Foo Ping Sheung* (Taipei: Institute of Modern History, Academia Sinica, 1993), pp. 75–76. Foo ping Sheung was a famous and influential jurist and politician of the Republican period. He led the work on drafting the new Civil Code.

[27] Foo's intention was made even clearer when Mainland women's groups, in frustration over the disappointing development of the Civil Code on the concubinage issue, pressed GMD legislators to criminalise adultery committed by men when the Criminal code was undergoing revision in the 1930s. Concerning the frustrations of women's groups over the disappointing civil law and their subsequent actions pressing for an egalitarian adultery law in the revised Criminal Code, see Tran, *Concubines in Court*, pp. 39–43.

On 1 June 1937, for example, Shanghai lawyer Yu Enliang posted the following declaration in *Shen Bao*:

> Announcement by Lawyer Yu Enliang representing the family of Dai Yishi to warn of the run-away concubine Wu Shunhao:
>
> My client took Wu Shunhao, the daughter of Wu Dieming, as a concubine in June of the 24th year of the Republic (1935). They got along well in the beginning. But recently she was not comfortable staying in [my client's] home and ran away with ten odd pieces of clothing on 30 May [1937]...[28]

Had a qualified lawyer regarded the Book of Family in the Civil Code and the revised Criminal Code as having abolished concubinage, he would never have made public the fact that his client had taken a concubine after those codes had come into effect. In fact, similar announcements filed by lawyers were relatively frequent in the newspapers of major Chinese cities such as Shanghai in the 1930s and 1940s.

More importantly, unlike the Book of Family, which purposely refrained from mentioning concubines to create the legal fiction that the law no longer recognised the concubinage system, in dealing with actual cases, the Republican Supreme Court did not have the luxury of maintaining that fiction. It had to face the facts directly by not only expressly mentioning the word 'concubine', but also by expressly recognising a woman's rights in maintenance, inheritance and separation as a concubine despite the omission of those rights from the codified law.[29] As Lisa Tran notes concerning the real intention of the law dealing with concubinage: 'Early Republican lawmakers still operat [ed] under the Qing logic on concubinage ... [and] the GMD lawmakers shared with their predecessors the goal of continuing the legal tolerance of concubinage without openly betraying their promise to uphold monogamy.'[30]

5   Modern West and the Backward Rest: Common Law Knowledge of Traditional Chinese Law

Justice Lord Millet states at the beginning of his analysis of concubinage in the CFA case under study: 'Concubinage is an institution peculiar to Oriental societies ... and is out of step with modern ideas.'[31] Considering

---

[28] *Shen Bao*, 2 June 1937
[29] Bernhardt, *Women and Property*, pp. 188–195; Tran, *Concubines in Court*, pp. 68–75.
[30] Tran, *Concubines in Court*, p. 33.   [31] *Suen Toi Lee*, para. 56.

a practice to be 'Oriental' leads to the assumption that it is also outdated and customary, and hence irrelevant to and incompatible with any understanding of 'modern' ideas and laws.[32] Such a prejudicial dichotomy between the modern West and the pre-modern Oriental contributed to the anomalous CFA judgment in this case. Perhaps the CFA judges involved were not entirely to blame. They had been given the task of ascertaining something that seems to have been unascertainable within their common law–informed cognitive boundaries even with the help of expert witnesses. Those boundaries made it difficult, if not impossible, for them to know what about the Chinese legal past should have been, but was not, raised by those witnesses.

Common law judges were also epistemologically bound by the English legal principle of *stare decisis* to maintain the prejudicial divide that segregates modern law and traditional Chinese legal practices. The legal principle of *stare decisis*, whereby the courts must follow higher courts' previous decisions involving similar legal issues, is an important characteristic of common law that aims to produce judicial decisions that are as consistent and predictable as possible. However, the principle has also produced an epistemological system of judicial knowledge concerning historical Chinese law and custom regardless of whether the decisions made within that system can now be proved wrong by the latest archival research performed outside the courtroom. The system's origins can be traced back to the heyday of global imperialism in the early twentieth century when colonial judges decided family law cases involving the colonised Chinese community.

One of the earliest precedents forming the backbone of the common law knowledge system of Chinese law and custom is *Ho Tsz Tsun v Ho Au Shi and Others*, heard in 1915, a decision that is often cited in contemporary judicial decisions concerning Chinese law and custom in Hong Kong and other former colonies, including the CFA case under study. The court in *Ho Tsz Tsun v Ho Au Shi and Others* expressed a clear view about the incompatibility of polygamous traditional Chinese marriage law with modern English law, which recognises monogamous marriage alone:

---

[32] Here, I borrow the phrase 'modern West and the backward rest' from the discussion of the prejudicial cultural construction of the rest of the world as opposed to Western modernity in Martin Fougère and Agneta Moulettes, 'The construction of the modern West and the backward rest: studying the discourse of Hofstede's culture's consequences' (2007) 2(1) *Journal of Multicultural Discourses*, 1.

It is clear ...that China is a polygamous country; that the first wife has
precedence, but that the other wives are wives and not merely
concubines...[33]
    What is in fact a matter of *common knowledge*, that polygamy is
expressly recognized by Chinese law, that the children of the principal
wife ("Tsai") and those of the secondary wife or concubine ("Tsip") are
treated alike as the lawful children, and that an adopted son is treated in
all respects as if he were the natural and lawful son of the person to whom
he is adopted. Now a law which permits polygamy, recognizes the rights
of the issue of such marriages, and gives an equal status to an adopted son,
is clearly so much at variance with the English law relating to marriage...
[Emphasis added][34]

The court produced, through judicial discourse, a 'common knowledge'
that was not only taken seriously in subsequent judicial decisions, but was
further reproduced through family law textbooks that in turn formed an
important source of information on which subsequent court decisions on
Chinese law and custom relied. For example, one such textbook that is very
often cited in family law judgments concerning Chinese customary marriage is *Family Law in Hong Kong*, first published in 1981. This textbook
reinforces the divide between legal modernity and traditional Chinese
practices and institutionalises the self-fulfilling 'common knowledge'
about traditional Chinese family law into the common law curriculum:
'We have seen also that concubines added to a modern [Chinese]
marriage ... have no legal status. The status of concubines therefore is
confined to women added to Chinese customary marriages.'[35]
    In its discussion of whether customary Chinese marriage constitutes
monogamy or polygamy, another popular family law textbook, *Family
Law for the Hong Kong SAR*, published in 1999, reproduces the
aforementioned quotes from *Ho Tsz Tsun and Others* and states:
'From this point of view, when a husband exercised his right to take
a concubine his customary marriage became actually polygamous.'[36]
Not only is monogamy thought to be exclusive to modern law in this
system of judicial knowledge, and thus excluded from traditional
Chinese law, another important family law concept, that of the legitimacy of children, is similarly conceptualised as a modern notion of

[33] *Ho Tsz Tsun v Ho Au Shi and Others* (1915) 10 HKLR 69, para. 73.
[34] *Ho Tsz Tsun v Ho Au Shi and Others*, para. 80.
[35] Leonard Pegg, *Family Law in Hong Kong* (Hong Kong: Butterworths, 1994), p. 31.
[36] Athena Nga Chee Liu, *Family Law for the Hong Kong SAR* (Hong Kong: HKU Press, 1999), p. 30.

morality afforded solely by modern law. In its 1967 decision in *Wong Kam Ying*, for example, the court opines that

> the taking of a concubine tends to produce conduct which violates the solemn obligations of married life... Under the old Chinese customary law legitimacy as we understand it (i.e. the status of a child born in wedlock) was an unknown concept and the only material question was whether the issue were born of such intercourse as was considered an offence: ... The recognition of the children offends neither legal principle nor morality – indeed many might say it best accords with modern notions of morality, since the children are innocent of any offence.[37]

Such a colonial view of the Chinese legal past has survived Hong Kong's reversion to China in the post-colonial era. Holding against the validity of taking a concubine by a man who married under 'modern' Chinese marriage law in 1944, the court in the *Estate of Wong Wong* in 1998 held that

> the right to take a concubine would only exist when the first marriage was a polygamous one according to the Chinese customary law. Accordingly, the personal law in Hong Kong was not available to the deceased to enable him to enter into a concubinage union when his original marriage was a monogamous one.[38]

Even as recently as 2014, a century after *Ho Tsz Tsun and Others* was decided, the High Court in *Ye Jinxiang v Kam Ping Kwong* recycled this reasoning, citing the aforementioned *Family Law in Hong Kong* and *Estate of Wong Wong*, as well as the case under study, and reaffirmed the 'common knowledge' that the taking of a concubine was no longer permitted once Chinese family law had been modernised from a polygamous conception of marriage to a monogamous one through the transplantation of Western family law.[39]

6 'The Chinese Are Our Opposites in Almost Every Action': Recycling Orientalist Knowledge

Not only has colonial-era judicial reasoning survived well into post-colonial Hong Kong, but the archaic documentary sources on Chinese law (both Qing and Republican) and custom that early colonial era judges relied on in reaching their decisions were still habitually relied

---

[37] *Wong Kam Ying and Ho Po Chun v Man Chi Tai* (1967) HKLR 201, para. 218.
[38] *In the Estate of Wong Wong* (1998) HKEC 164 (CFI).
[39] *Ye Jinxiang v Kam Ping Kwong* (2015) HKEC 302 (CFI).

on by judges of the later colonial period, and still are in the post-colonial courts, with inadequate attention paid to the growing scholarship on historical Chinese law and custom. Such archaic sources have generally not been trusted, if not entirely discounted, by historians because, as noted later, they not only lack adequate information on their historical sources by today's standards of historiography, but also very often contain prejudicial remarks on traditional Chinese law and even the Chinese race.

For example, in Hong Kong higher court judgments on Chinese law and custom regarding women, marriage and concubines, one rarely finds a citation of such prominent scholarly works as those by Philip Huang, Katherine Bernhardt, Matthew Sommer, Margaret Kuo and Lisa Tran, amongst others, who in the past two decades have together brought our understanding of Qing and Republican legal history to new heights based on the archival study of judgments reached by the county courts of Qing era China.[40] Their work also highlights the difference between representation in statutes and actual legal practice in the courtrooms of imperial China, as well as the continuities in and differences between imperial law in the Qing era and transplanted law in the Republican era, and hence argues against the view that concubines lost their legal status in 1931. Instead of relying on the latest scholarship, Hong Kong courts have chosen to follow their predecessors from the early colonial days and to cite books on Chinese law and custom published between the 1920s and 1960s, such as *Chinese Family and Commercial Law* (published in 1921), *Modern Chinese Family Law* (published in 1939) and *Marriage Laws and Customs of China* (published in 1966).[41]

---

[40] For example, Philip Huang, *Civil Justice in China: Representation and Practice in the Qing* (Stanford, CA: Stanford University Press, 1996), *Code, Custom, and Legal Practice in China: The Qing and the Republic Compared* (Stanford, CA: Stanford University Press, 2001); Bernhardt, *Women and Property*; Matthew Sommer, *Sex, Law, and Society in Late Imperial China* (Stanford, CA: Stanford University Press, 2000); Margaret Kuo, *Intolerable Cruelty: Marriage, Law, and Society in Early Twentieth-century China* (Lanham, MD: Rowman & Littlefield, 2012); Tran, *Concubines in Court*. For a succinct overview of the development of archive-based study of Chinese legal history by historians in the United States in the past two decades, see Chenjun You, 'How a "new legal history" might be possible: recent trends in Chinese legal history studies in the United States and their implications' (2013) 39 *Modern China*, 165.

[41] George Jamieson, *Chinese Family and Commercial Law* (Shanghai: Kelly and Walsh, 1921); Marc Van der Valk, *Modern Chinese Family Law* (Beijing: Henri Vetch, 1939); Vermier Chiu, *Marriage Laws and Customs of China* (Hong Kong: Institute of Advanced Chinese Studies and Research, New Asia College, 1966).

The reliability of these early books was sometimes questioned even by their authors. For example, *Chinese Family and Commercial Law* was based on the fraction of court cases heard in the mixed courts of Shanghai that were briefly reported in English language newspapers such as the *North China Herald*. The book's author thus alerts his readers to the following.

> None of these [newspaper] reports appear to have been officially revised, and being in many cases very brief, it is difficult to make sure that the facts are always fully stated... It is [a] matter of regret that so few of the purely native cases of which there must have been many, are recorded, because a better exposition of the Chines law proper might have been expected in these than in mixed [court] cases.[42]

Some of these authors' views on Chinese law show evidence of obvious prejudices or Orientalist perspectives. These perspectives generally fit into the 'lawlessness of China' theme. Popular prior to 1990s scholarship on Chinese legal history, this theme constitutes the view that the law is not important in the Chinese tradition and that to the extent that there was enforceable law in China, it was penal in nature, with civil law concerning individual rights simply not existing until Western law was introduced in the last few years of the Qing era.[43] A good example can be found in *Modern Chinese Family Law*, whose author notes the following in his preface.

> The Chinese mind was therefore bent upon finding the structural principles of the relationship existing in the universe, between man and man, man and society, society and nature... Western abstract categories such as time, space, quantity, quality, were non-existent in this trend of thought. It follows that the law of causation, being the connection of events separated in order of time in such a way that one is necessarily followed by the other, was also superfluous... To this [Chinese] concept the positive law, taken in the sense of a system of abstract rules, was wholly subservient. It was always liable to being overruled by the *li* [rites]... Law, being eminently criminal, was not used against those who were able to live according to the *li*, i.e. not against the higher classes, but against the common people...[44]

[42] Jamieson, *Chinese Family and Commercial Law*, p. 142.
[43] For the Western construction of a notion of Chinese lawlessness in understanding Chinese legal history, see Ruskola, *Legal Orientalism*, 3–8, chapter 2. See also William Alfred, 'Of arsenic and old laws: looking anew at criminal justice in late imperial China' (1984) 72(6) *California Law Review*, 1180.
[44] Van der Valk, *Modern Chinese Family Law*, pp. 8–9, 11–12.

In discussing traditional Chinese family law, the author further distinguishes between traditional China and the modern West through a narrative of the law:

> It should not be said that these characteristics, this lack of [a] system in our sense, this tendency to single out certain aspects, are due to the fact that the [Qing] Code was not set up as a systemic whole, but rather that it has to be considered as a historic code to which each dynasty added, thus gradually creating an impression of disorder... We shall now try to draw a short outline of the family law of China as it was just before the first efforts towards modernization were made. The fact must be borne in mind, and has been mentioned above, that this outline may not be strictly compared with an outline of the Western family law, as the law of the family in China was closely interwoven with other domains, such as morals, rites, etc., and was not clearly distinguished from them.[45]

The other important sources on which the common law court of Hong Kong has very often relied in seeking information on Chinese law and custom are several reports and publications prepared by former colonial officers (rather than trained historians). Amongst the most popular of these are the *Committee Report on Chinese Law and Custom*, published in 1953[46] and prepared under the leadership of George Strickland, the former Solicitor-General of Hong Kong (and thus more commonly known as the Strickland Report), and *History of the Laws and Courts of Hong Kong*,[47] published in 1898 and written by James Norton-Kyshe, who served as Hong Kong's Registrar General in the late nineteenth century. Both sources, which are still frequently cited by twenty-first-century Hong Kong courts in family and succession law cases (including the concubine-related case in question), are not only based on nineteenth-century historical knowledge, but also contain references and remarks that contemporary scholars have criticised for their Orientalist and prejudiced view of Chinese law and culture.

The Strickland Report, for example, which has been repeatedly relied upon in court decisions involving Chinese law and custom since 1965, references a book published in 1892 by James Dyer Ball, *Things Chinese: Being Notes on Various Subjects Connected with China*. In explaining Chinese customs, Ball makes such Orientalist remarks as

---

[45] Ibid., p. 17.
[46] Committee on Chinese Law and Custom, *Committee Report on Chinese Law and Custom* (Hong Kong: Government Printer, 1953) (*Strickland Report* hereafter).
[47] James William Norton-Kyshe, *History of the Laws and Courts of Hong Kong* (London: T. Fisher Unwin, 1898).

the Chinese are not only at our antipodes with regard to position on the globe, but they are our opposites in almost every action and thought... He [a Chinese man] asks you if you have eaten your rice, instead of saying, 'How do you do?'... He, perhaps, shows you with pride the set of coffin boards which his dutiful son has presented him.[48]

Moreover, the Hong Kong courts have repeatedly relied on both the Strickland Report and similar government reports as a guiding authority on the status of concubines despite their compilation constituting part of the colonial government's efforts, under pressure from Parliament, to abolish concubinage in Hong Kong.[49] It should therefore not be too surprising that in exploring the relationship and position of a concubine, the Strickland Reports states with a sceptical tone: 'It seems strange to the Westerner at first sight that a Chinese can even according to Chinese law be guilty of bigamy and strange to the Chinese to be called polygamous.'[50]

Another oft-cited government report, known as *Chinese Marriages in Hong Kong* and published in 1960 to make recommendations to the colonial government about reforming marriage law and abolishing concubinage, views concubines through the lens of English law, and thus treats them, erroneously, as being the same as mistresses:

Women who in Hong Kong have been tricked by men, and those who have tricked men, into being taken on as alleged concubines attached to a Chinese Modern Marriage are legally, and often socially and economically, nothing more nor less than mistresses... [The] feminine noun concubine has two meanings according to the Oxford English dictionary: either a mistress whose relationship has no lawful standing, or a secondary wife... A very large number if not the majority of so-called concubines in Hong Kong belong in fact to the first category...

---

[48] James Dyer Ball, *Things Chinese: Being Notes on Various Subjects Connected with China* (London: Sampson Low, 1892; Reprint: Hong Kong: Kelly & Walsh, 1903), pp. 717–718; see also similar note made by Teemu Ruskola, who criticised the Hong Kong court for expressly citing the *Strickland Report*'s references to 'such Orientalist gems as a social "history"' in 'Legal orientalism' (2002) 101(1) *Michigan Law Review* 226, note 201.

[49] On the colonial government's efforts to abolish concubinage in Hong Kong from the 1940s to 1970s, see Max Wong, '40 years after the abolition of concubinage' ('*Feiqie xishinian*') (2011) 19 *Reflexion (Sixiang)*. The *Strickland Report* has often been cited by Hong Kong courts since the early 1960s as offering guidance on Chinese law and custom. For recent cases citing the report in determining the issues of concubinage, Chinese customary marriage and succession, see *Re Estate of Ng Shum (No. 2)* [1990] 1 HKLR 67; *Leung Sai Lun & Others v Leung May Ling & Others* [1999] 1 HKLRD 649 (CFA); *Chan Chiu La & Others v Yau Yee Ping* [2000] 3 HKLRD 443 (CA); *Liu Ying Lan V Liu Tung Yiu & Another* [2003] 3 HKLRD 249.

[50] *Strickland Report*, p. 22.

[The] Government should expose the popular fallacy that mistresses
kept by men who have monogamously contracted a Chinese Modern
... Marriage have any of the hints or should have the status of a
lawfully married Concubine.[51]

It is also unsurprising that the report holds a view similar to that of the
CFA in the case under study: 'In this respect, the post 1930 Nationalist
Civil Code marriage code, and its derivative the Chinese Modern Marriage, bear no relation to the [marriage] which drew its inspiration direct
from old traditional customs.'[52] These reports' views on the issue of
concubinage should at the very least be treated with considerable caution,
if not outright scepticism.

The *History of the Laws and Courts of Hong Kong* is another popular
source used by the Hong Kong courts[53] despite its intellectual value and
Orientalist perspective being seriously questioned by scholars of Hong
Kong history. Christopher Munn, for example, who has written on the
suppressive nature of British colonial rule of the Hong Kong Chinese,
makes this critique:

The only analysis in this chronological plagiarism of the colony's early
[English] newspapers comes in the editorials and readers' letters that are
pasted into the narrative word for word yet without attribution. The vague
notion in the preface that Hong Kong was 'the starting point from whence
a civilizing power by its beneficent rule and humane laws was to endeavour to effect those reforms which an uncivilized power like China was
ever in need of' echoes [colonial historian E. J.] Eitel's view [of racial
destiny and imperial fulfilment in ruling Hong Kong], but the detailed
chronicle of scandal and mismanagement in the work's 1300 odd tightly
printed pages provides little support for these claims.[54]

[51] *Chinese Marriages in Hong Kong* (Hong Kong: Government Printer, 1960), pp. 6, 15, 22.
[52] Ibid., p. 26.
[53] The earliest citation of the book, as far as the author is aware, dates back to 1925 in a
probate case ruled by the Supreme Court of Hong Kong. It was still being cited in 2005 by
the Hong Kong CFA as a historical record of, for example, freedom of assembly existing
in early British rule of Hong Kong: 'There is nothing new about Hong Kong residents
gathering in public to discuss grievances and seek redress. We know that such a public
gathering was held on 4 January 1849. It is referred to in James William Norton-Kyshe,
The History of the Laws and Courts of Hong Kong From the Earliest Period to 1898 (1898),
Vol. 1 at pp. 217, 222, 224 and 257. That gathering seems to have been a somewhat elitist
affair. But these things have become far more broadly based since then.' See *Leung Kwok
Hung & Others v HKSAR* [2005] 3 HKLRD 164 (CFA), para. 120.
[54] Christopher Munn, *Anglo-China: Chinese People and British Rule in Hong Kong,
1841–1880* (Richmond: Curzon, 2001; Reprint: Hong Kong: Hong Kong University Press,
2009), p. 6.

7   Judicial Orientalism: Colonising Knowledge without a Colony

Regrettably, this system of knowledge and prejudices about the Chinese legal past is not restricted to family law. [55] In fact, the Orientalist view of traditional Chinese family law coincides with the larger common law knowledge system on traditional Chinese law and legal culture in general. A popular reference book for common law students in Hong Kong, entitled *The Common Law in Chinese Context* and published in 1992, discusses traditional Chinese law in a fashion not very different from that of the aforementioned *Chinese Family and Commercial Law*, which predates it by some seventy years:

> The judicial system in traditional China was based on the Confucian doctrine of rule by a morally educated elite class. This doctrine had the effect of subordinating the law to morality. The differences between the judicial systems of traditional Chinese legal culture and Common Law reflect the fundamental differences that exist in the historical development of the two civilizations... Civil law [in Chinese legal tradition] ... was not well developed. The need of the law to protect business interests and commercial transactions with formal legal machinery ... was previously not part of the custom. [56]
>
> There was no belief in a divine origin of law... The traditional Chinese looked on law with contempt and abhorrence... The trial procedures in traditional China did not encourage people to insist on their legal rights ... and to respect the legal rights of others... There are certain identifiable differences between the traditional Chinese attitude and the Common Law attitudes toward law. [57]

Whilst there are of course differences between cultures, the author's views on Chinese traditional law and legal ideas do not stand up to scrutiny of the archival study of traditional Chinese law over the past three decades spearheaded by a number of leading historians. [58] Those

---

[55] I draw insight from the title of chapter 6, 'Colonialism without Colonizers' in Ruskola's *Legal Orientalism*.

[56] Berry Hsu, *The Common Law in Chinese Context* (Hong Kong: HKU Press, 1992), pp. 28, 31. The book's popularity is evidenced by the fact that more than twenty copies are held and reserved at the libraries of the three universities in Hong Kong that run law. Another succinct summary of Western scholars' prejudices against Chinese legal tradition can be found in Albert H. Y. Chen, *Introduction to the Legal System of the People's Republic of China* (Hong Kong: Butterworths, 1992, 1998, 2004, 2011), pp. 18–22.

[57] Hsu, *The Common Law in Chinese Context*, pp. 38, 41, 48.

[58] On due process and procedural justice, see Alfred, 'Of arsenic and old laws'; on civil law, see Huang, *Civil Justice in China*; on business and property rights in the traditional

views feature what Ruskola calls 'legal Orientalism', which culturally distances the modern West from the pre-modern East of the post–cold war era through discourses of the law.[59]

As the foregoing discussion makes clear, such views have not only survived the end of the colonial era, but continue to dominate the common law knowledge system of Chinese law and custom. Even the most recently published textbook on the Hong Kong legal system, *Law and Justice in Hong Kong* (published in 2014), echoes the view of Lord Millet in discussing the application of Chinese customary law in Hong Kong, and it even adopts a similar tone in supporting the segregation of traditional Chinese law from modernity: 'Chinese customary law: "the law of a peasant community imbued with the culture of a bygone era" no longer suits the needs of urban ways of life.'[60] Somewhat ironically, such customary legal practices as the taking of concubines occurred more often in the relatively urbanised and affluent cities of China than in rural areas during the Republican era, and it is in those cities that transplanted marriage law from the West was most strictly enforced.

Historical judicial decisions, law textbooks and colonial documents reinforce one another to form the formidable authority of a common law knowledge system and historiography on traditional Chinese law vis-à-vis the modern (by default Western) world. Such a knowledge system serves as an authoritative source of information for everyone in the legal profession, ranging from senior judges and lawyers to law students researching the Chinese legal tradition and its relation to the modern legal world. It originates from the judicial views of the very early colonial era, but has managed to colonise the common law knowledge of post-colonial Hong Kong through self-citation and recycling in a legal system that relies on its own past judgments. Very few, if any, legal practitioners are able to subject such knowledge to scrutiny, as it has been endorsed by the higher appellate courts, including the HKCFA. In addition, the conventional academic disciplinary silo separating historical studies and legal studies renders the latest archival discoveries on Chinese law relatively inaccessible to jurists, making

---

Chinese legal regime, see Madeleine Zelin, *The Merchants of Zigong: Industrial Entrepreneurship in Early Modern China* (New York: Columbia University Press, 2005); Madeleine Zelin and Jonathan Ocko, eds., *Contract and Property in Early Modern China* (Stanford, CA: Stanford University Press, 2004).

[59] Ruskola, *Legal Orientalism*, p. 13.

[60] Eric Ip, *Law and Justice in Hong Kong* (Hong Kong: Sweet and Maxwell, 2014).

any challenge to the prevailing knowledge system even less likely. As Carol Tan notes in her critique of a Malaysian court decision: 'As Chinese customary law is a part of the law of the land it is not necessary to prove such law. It is a matter of precedent. The finding of a court of competent jurisdiction is the best evidence of such custom when it is in issue in subsequent cases.'[61] Common law courts' mission vis-à-vis Chinese customary law, until the general prejudice against traditional Chinese law is overturned, will likely remain one that uses modern law to cure the perceived injustices of Oriental societies, as suggested by the HKCFA in 1998 in one of its earliest cases concerning Chinese law and custom following Hong Kong's reversion to China: 'For whatever reason, an examination of the law in Hong Kong as it has developed shows more than a hint of a process moving towards providing remedies to what was perceived as injustices in Chinese law and custom.'[62] Such remarks on traditional Chinese law contrast sharply with those made on the common law tradition by Lord Anthony Mason, a former HKCFA judge:

> The common law also stands for a set of concepts, interests and values which it has protected during the course of its long history. They include the rule of law, the independence of the judiciary, access to the courts, the separation of the powers of government, liberty of the individual, freedom of expression, freedom of association... These values have both generated and informed legal principles including the rules of statutory interpretation ... The common law stands both as a symbol and as link between Hong Kong's past, its present and its future.[63]

Such a contrast, which is based on a flawed and Orientalist understanding of the history of legal transplantation in Republican China, contributed to the CFA's denial of the legal status of concubine to Mrs Sung and Mrs Chu. The court overlooked traditional Chinese laws concerning bigamy and the household membership of concubines, mistakenly

---

[61] Carol Tan, 'The twilight of Chinese customary law relating to marriage in Malaysia' (1993) 42(1) *International and Comparative Law Quarterly*, 155. On the difficulty relating to the use of judicial precedents in ascertaining the meaning of historical Chinese law and custom in the Hong Kong courts, see also Peter Wesley-Smith, *The Sources of Hong Kong Law* (Hong Kong: Hong Kong University Press, 1994), pp. 216–217.

[62] *Leung Sai Lun & others v Leung May Ling & others* (1999) 1 HKLRD (CFA) 649, para. 657.

[63] Anthony Mason, 'The role of the common law in Hong Kong', in Jessica Young and Rebecca Lee (eds.), *The Common Law Lectures Series 2005* (Hong Kong: Faculty of Law, University of Hong Kong, 2005), pp. 1–2.

believing that the laws that replaced them were new statutory institutions designed to replace concubinage. It ignored the historical context of the Book of Family's drafting and enactment, and took at face value the political manifesto made by politicians of the day. More importantly, the court relied solely on a textual interpretation of the law, neglecting how and why it was perceived, interpreted and practised as it was in the Republican court and society at large.

The CFA imagined legal transplantation as a straightforward process in which a legal system proceeded in linear fashion from discarding the old and customary to embracing the new and modern (and by default Western). In fact, as shown in the latest scholarship, legal transplantation in Republican China, and perhaps also in other Asian countries under the threat of colonialism in the early twentieth century, was a difficult and complex process in which new legal ideas were imported (from the West), but traditional practices were often not completely discarded.[64] Rather, they were reconciled with the new transplanted legal regime. Concubinage is but one example of such reconciliation during the first, and perhaps most important, legal transplantation in China.

It is clear, as demonstrated in this chapter, that the actual legal trajectory in China deserves a much thicker description than the simplistic view of old legal texts and institutions being straightforwardly displaced by new Western-inspired ones. Such a description, at the very least, would necessitate the abandonment of the century-old judicial approach of common law courts that demarcates the Chinese legal past by an imagined divide between traditional Chinese law and legal modernity to ensure that equal emphasis is placed on judicial practices and statutes; on pre-transplant legal ideas and imported ones; on how laws were intended from their drafters' viewpoint and how they were perceived and interpreted by users; and on legal changes and the wider historical context in which they took place.

It is hoped that this chapter alerts common law courts to the need for more nuanced studies, based on the latest developments in historical scholarship, of the role played by traditional legal ideas and the wider

[64] On civil law, see Huang, *Code, Custom, and Legal Practice in China*; on criminal law, see Michael Ng, *Legal Transplantation in Early Twentieth-Century China: Practicing Law in Republican Beijing (1910s-1930s)* (London: Routledge, 2014), chapter 1; Jennifer Neighbors, 'The long arm of Qing law? Qing dynasty homicide rulings in republican courts' (2009) 35 *Modern China*, 3.

historical context in which legal transplantation took place to ascertain the legal meanings of transplanted laws in modern China. It is after all safe to say that in the long history of legal transplantation in Asia, marriage law is certainly not the only example of such transplantation, and nor is China the only Asian country that saw it conflict, interact and reconcile with indigenous legal norms.

12

Commercial Arbitration Transplanted

A Tale of the Book Industry in Modern Shanghai

BILLY K. L. SO AND SUFUMI SO

This chapter[1] examines the Shanghai book industry[2] in the early twentieth century to elucidate how the industry players of the day negotiated the challenges of adapting to new legal institutions, from law courts to the alternative dispute resolution (ADR) system modelled on the Western legal approach to commercial dispute resolution. Focusing on arbitration in particular, the chapter is concerned with how these transplanted legal institutions evolved in the local environment and with the roles that those who acted as both local agents of change and the consumers of such institutions played in shaping the process of transplantation. It considers not only the normative dimension of legal modernisation but also the user perspective. The chapter is organised as follows. Section 1 provides background information on commercial dispute resolution reforms in China. Section 2 outlines the institutional development process of ADR in the Shanghai book industry under the new legal framework, and Section 3 presents six select cases to illustrate how people in the industry negotiated the legal norms of the new commercial dispute resolution methods. Finally, Section 4 offers some observations derived from the six cases, as well as a brief comparison with the book industry in Meiji Japan, and Section 5 concludes with a summary.

[1] This work is part of a research project supported by the Hong Kong General Research Fund (Project No. 643412). For their valuable comments on earlier drafts of the manuscript and useful suggestions for archival materials, we are happily indebted to Gabrielle Kaufmann-Kohler, Fan Kun, Xi Chao, Yu Xingzhong, Zhu Zheming, Michael Ng, Shiba Yoshinobu, Pearl Chih, Christian Lamouroux, Joe McDermott, Patrick O'Brien, Kent Deng, Wang Fei-hsien, Zou Zhenhuan, Ma Jun and Zhou Wu, among others.
[2] The term 'book industry' is used in this chapter to refer to an industry that comprises publishing, printing and bookselling, which was the most common pattern of book-related business in Shanghai in the early twentieth century.

1   Legal Reform of Commercial Dispute Resolution System

1.1   Commercial Dispute Resolution within the Traditional Legal Framework

Fan Jinmin succinctly explains the Ming–Qing legal framework as follows. When commercial disputes arose, they were first mediated by such extra-legal social institutions as kinship, village and religious organisations, as well as guilds. If such initial mediation failed, cases were brought to the law courts or judicial offices of the county presided over by an administrative head (i.e. magistrate or *zhixian*) for adjudication.[3] Fan offers ample evidence to show that merchants readily resorted to formal legal institutions for settlement of the numerous types of commercial disputes occurring in the Ming and Qing periods. Whilst judicial decisions were often based on *qingli* (which translates as 'accepted code of conduct'), taking into account the circumstances of the community in question and trade-specific conventional practices, a general legal framework was also considered in judicial decision-making. According to Fan, the court's priority was ensuring that disputes were speedily concluded and that the parties involved complied with the decisions reached. In reality, however, the parties frequently recanted their earlier consent and repeatedly applied to appeal against those decisions to prolong the litigation in the hope of ultimately winning. At the time, there was no mechanism for a final, binding and enforceable resolution of commercial disputes.[4]

1.2   New Legal Framework for Commercial Dispute Resolution

Starting with the judicial reform of the late Qing era, the court system of China gradually transformed into a Western-style law court system.[5]

---

[3] Fan Jinmin, *Ming-Qing shangshi jiufen yu shangye susong* (*Commercial Disputes and Litigation Cases in Ming-Qing China*) (Nanjing: Nanjing daxue chubanshe, 2007), chapters 1–3.

[4] Ibid. In addition to the large number of illuminating cases discussed by Fan, there is a sizable body of research on this topic. See, e.g. Philip C. C. Huang, *Civil Justice in China: Representation and Practice in the Qing* (Stanford, CA: Stanford University Press, 1996); *Code, Custom, and Legal Practice: The Qing and the Republican Compared* (Stanford, CA: Stanford University Press, 2001).

[5] A new hierarchy of law courts was established, but it was unstable between 1912 and 1937. It sometimes had four tiers, and at other times three. The central supreme court and provincial high courts were more stable, and the district and various courts of first

One feature of the new court system was the adoption of a three-trial appellate system,[6] which meant that merchants involved in commercial disputes could no longer prolong litigation indefinitely. They were required to accept the outcomes adjudicated in court. As the new law courts had the ultimate power to settle disputes, unlike the traditional magistrates' courts that preceded them, merchants had to consider the risk of having to accept unfavourable outcomes before taking cases to court. In addition, the transplanted modern legal concepts and principles were largely alien to local Chinese merchants, and often incompatible with their accustomed values and social conventions. Accordingly, they viewed the modern law court system as full of risk and uncertainty. The system also faced a lack of funding and well-trained personnel, which led to a growing backlog of cases. The new judicial system was thus placed under enormous pressure, and out-of-court settlements were encouraged.[7]

However, there is another side to the story. A new and lucrative legal profession emerged in the major cities of China, in treaty port cities such as Shanghai in particular. From around 1900, the number of both foreign and locally and overseas trained Chinese lawyers grew rapidly in these commercial hubs, and their presence helped to enhance the quality of the legal services on offer. Although legal costs were high,[8] merchants who could afford to pay them hired lawyers in the hope of increasing their chances of winning in court. The new court system thus appears to have attracted ample users.

---

instance or offices of trial and prosecution less stable, differing from place to place and from time to time. See Billy K. L. So, 'Law courts, 1800–1949', in David Pong (ed.), *Encyclopedia of Modern China* (Detroit, MI: Charles Scribner's Sons, 2009), vol. 2, pp. 438–440. For an explanation of the judicial reforms of the central government and Lower Yangzi Delta, see Xiaoqun Xu, *Trial of Modernity: Judicial Reform in Early Twentieth-century China, 1901–1937* (Stanford, CA: Stanford University Press, 2008), pp. 61–83; Tōa Dōbunkai, *Shina Keizai Zenshū (A Comprehensive Survey of the Chinese Economy)* (Tōkyō: Maruzen Kabushiki Kaisha, 1907), vol. 4, pp. 178–201.

[6] The appellate system in this three-trial system was stable, with each case allowed to be appealed to a higher judicial authority only twice. Xu, *Trial of Modernity*, pp. 81–82.

[7] Ibid., pp. 75–76.

[8] Chen Tong, *Jindai shehui bianqian zhong de Shanghai lüshi (Shanghai Lawyers in the Social Change of Modern China)* (Shanghai: Shanghai cishu chubanshe, 2008); Sun Huimin, *Zhiduyizhi: minchu Shanghai de Zhongguo lüshi (1912–1937) (Institutional Transplantation – The Chinese Lawyers in Republican Shanghai)* (Taipei: Zhongyang yanjiuyuan jindaishiyanjiusuo, 2012).

1.3 Significance of New ADR Framework for Commercial Dispute Resolution

Traditional forms of extra-judicial or community mediation were never integrated into the formal legal system, although some magistrates considered the use of mediation during the adjudication process. Arbitration transplantation accelerated in China in the 1900s. According to Fan Kun,[9] such transplantation constituted an incremental, longwinded and complicated process involving considerable confusion over translation and conceptualisation. The resultant Chinese version of arbitration failed to meet Western standards in terms of legislative rigour and implementation effectiveness. Fan Jinmin provides an interesting account of the commercial dispute cases resolved in chambers of commerce (*shanghui*) in the early twentieth century, illustrating the standards of judicial practice of the day.[10]

The introduction of law courts to Chinese society meant legal modernity. However, such modernity was not necessarily attractive to many Chinese merchants, as noted previously. As a result, merchants helped to implement a more palatable compromise system that was modelled on the Western legal framework but included many elements of traditional extra-legal practices in commercial dispute resolution. In practice, merchants' participation in arbitration processes resulted in the case-by-case adaptation and adoption of local practices in judicial decision-making. Arbitration commissions were established within chambers of commerce or the modern version of guilds in accordance with principles specified by statute. The process was democratic in the sense that Chinese merchants were allowed to participate in its establishment and implementation. Through such participation, merchants helped to shape the system. In fact, they were afforded the right to elect arbitrators while being users of the system themselves. The arbitration centres set up within chambers of commerce differed from the law courts, in which merchants had no say in the appointment of judges. This difference was almost certainly an important factor in merchants' decisions concerning whether to submit their disputes to arbitration or to the courts.

---

[9] Fan Kun, 'Glocalization of arbitration: transnational standards struggling with local norms through the lens of arbitration transplantation in China' (2013) 18 *Harvard Negotiation Law Review*, 175–219. See also Fan Kun, *Arbitration in China: A Legal and Cultural Analysis* (Oxford: Hart, 2013).

[10] Fan, *Ming-Qing shangshi*, chapters 4–5.

1.4 Salient Features of the Transplanted Arbitration System

Western-style arbitration was formally introduced into Chinese law in 1904, as part of the wider late Qing legal reform, as a newly established component of chambers of commerce whose statutory status was declared in that year's *Concise Regulations for Chambers of Commerce* (*Shanghui jianming zhangcheng; Concise Regulations* hereafter), article 15 of which is most relevant for our discussion:

> If any dispute shall arise between Chinese merchants, either party may report to a chamber of commerce. Regular meetings of a board of directors chaired by the chamber's chairman shall be held to resolve disputes in a fair and reasonable manner. Decisions by the directors shall be made by majority vote. If the outcome is unsatisfactory to the parties involved, either party shall be allowed to take the case to a local government for adjudication.[11]

Following the 1911 Revolution, the arbitration law was further articulated in the *Regulations on the Commercial Arbitration Tribunal* (*Shangshi gongduanchu zhangcheng; Regulations* hereafter) promulgated in 1913.[12] It was then further supplemented by *Detailed Regulations on the Commercial Arbitration Tribunal* (*Shangshi gongduanchu banshixize; Detailed Regulations* hereafter). Arbitration remained one of the major functions carried out by the chambers of commerce. Some characteristics of the arbitration mechanism can be found in the following provisions of the *Regulations*.[13]

- Arbitration tribunals shall be set up within chambers of commerce (article 1).
- The main role of an arbitration tribunal is to resolve commercial disputes in a conciliatory and amicable manner (article 2).
- Arbitral tribunal chairmen, arbitrators and investigators shall be honorary positions without pay, but they may receive honoraria. Each tribunal shall determine the secretary's salary based on the amount of work and local circumstances (article 7).

[11] Ibid., pp. 234–235. Note that article 16 describes how to carry out arbitration activities between Chinese and foreign parties under the chamber's supervision.
[12] Xu Baiji, *Zhonghua Minguo xianxing fagui daquan* (*A Complete Compilation of Current Laws and Regulations of the Republic of China*) (Shanghai: Shangwu Yinshuguan, 1937), vol. 5, pp. 805–812.
[13] Ibid.

- Arbitrators and investigators shall be elected from among the members of the chamber of commerce. No voting shall take place unless more than half of the members are present. Voting shall be by secret ballot, and decisions shall be made by majority vote (article 8).
- Arbitral awards must be accepted by all parties involved to ensure effective enforcement (article 17).
- Parties dissatisfied with arbitral awards may call upon the courts for a review (article 18).
- Arbitral awards accepted by all parties involved shall be reported to the courts in writing as 'settled', and the courts shall make official public announcements and enforce the awards (article 19).
- Decisions shall be made by a majority vote of all eligible members of the arbitration tribunal in attendance (article 29).
- The arbitral tribunal chairman shall appoint another arbitrator if a conflict of interest is presumed to arise or an appointment offer has been declined (article 33).
- If an arbitrator breaches any of his obligations and an unfair outcome has occurred in the arbitration as a result, then he is liable to pay compensation for any damage or loss suffered by the parties involved (article 36).

The system was further regulated in *Detailed Regulations* as follows.[14]

- Local commercial practices or locally accepted principles shall be honoured in arbitration. However, final arbitral awards cannot override existing laws, rules or regulations (article 5).
- Following the election of arbitrators, the chamber of commerce shall provide the local government in writing with the personal details of elected arbitrators, including their name, age, birthplace and profession, as well as the number of votes they each received. The local government shall then submit the information to the provincial government, which will store it. The Ministry of Commerce shall also be informed of the arbitrators' details. Where a law court exists, the court shall also be provided with the same information (article 10).
- If amicable settlements are reached earlier in the arbitration process, each party involved shall withdraw its petition separately. If such settlement occurs after litigation has commenced, withdrawal requests must be filed with the court through the chamber of commerce concerned (article 19).

---

[14] Ibid.

- Arbitral awards are legally binding only if they are accepted by all parties involved. Parties dissatisfied with the results may freely pursue litigation in court (article 48).
- Arbitral awards accepted by all parties shall be considered settled in accordance with generally accepted principles of reason (*lijie*). Once arbitration agreements have been signed by the parties involved, the awards become legally binding and no dispute shall be permitted thereafter unless factual errors are found to have occurred in the course of arbitration or new evidence that could undermine the finality of the awards emerges (article 49).

As is evident from article 49 of the *Detailed Regulations*, significant authority was afforded to the arbitral institutions. Once an arbitration agreement had been signed by all parties involved, the case was permanently and conclusively closed under the terms of that agreement. Whilst it was not impossible to reopen a case, there were stringent requirements for doing so. In short, the system effectively discouraged prolonged litigation.

When the Western arbitration model was first transplanted in China, some of its most important features were missing, including the contractual requirement that all parties must agree in advance to abide by the ultimate arbitration decision.[15] Fan Kun explains that such partial transplantation was an attempt to integrate two disparate cultures, namely, a legal culture that implied the risk of sanctions being imposed and a traditional local culture that valued settlement by amicable means to maintain social harmony. We will return briefly to this issue of cultural and legal boundaries in the Section 4 of the chapter. In the next section, we summarise the development of the arbitration system in the Shanghai book industry in the first two decades following its transplantation.

2   Institutional Development of ADR in the Shanghai Book Industry

In the early twentieth century, the Shanghai book industry comprised both traditional bookshops and modern book enterprises. Christopher Reed explains that print capitalism in the city was built on the adoption of Western technological and institutional advances, and shows how its development contributed to the transformation of old-style merchant guilds into modern trade guilds that worked for the collective interests of

---

[15] Fan, 'Glocalization of arbitration', pp. 205–207.

the industry's merchants in all matters, including the increasing number of copyright disputes they faced.[16] Furthering Reed's discussion, Wang Fei-hsien contends that the Shanghai publishers' guild provided an extra-legal self-governing mechanism for copyright protection and that copyright disputes were thus handled effectively outside the formal legal system.[17] Like the work of Reed and Wang, this chapter also examines the Shanghai book industry as an empirical case, although its focus differs from theirs. Here, we are concerned with how entrepreneurs in the Shanghai book industry used a new statutory body to resolve commercial disputes. We consider the arbitral centres attached to chambers of commerce as part of the legal reform effort of the late Qing and early Republican periods rather than as a modern version of traditional merchant guilds performing extra-legal mediation services.

Shanghai was among the first cities in China to see the creation of new-style chambers of commerce operated under the provisions of the new law governing Western-style business organisations. The Shanghai General Chamber of Commerce featured an elaborate system for administering arbitral proceedings in accordance with legal regulations.[18] It even hired non-Chinese legal advisors and lawyers to ensure high-quality implementation and to gain a good reputation for the new legal system.[19] At the same time, however, several legally established local trade associations were also allowed to set up their own arbitral tribunals, a situation that provides the context for our story here.

According to Reed, a guild-like organisation called *Shanghai shuye gongsuo* (which he translates as the Shanghai Booksellers' Guild) came into being in 1905 with a view to preserving such traditional functions of guilds as training apprentices, developing senior workers and perfecting experts. The organisation was also designed to deal with the technological, financial, social and legal challenges emerging from the new wave of educational reforms launched in 1905.[20] As a matter of

---

[16] For a succinct account of the industry, see Christopher A. Reed, *Gutenberg in Shanghai: Chinese Print Capitalism, 1876–1937* (Vancouver: UBC Press, 2004), chapters 4–5.

[17] Wang Fei-hsien, 'Creating a new order in the knowledge economy: the curious journey of copyright in China, 1868–1937', PhD dissertation, University of Chicago (2012), chapter 5.

[18] Xu Dingxin and Qian Xiaoming, *Shanghai zongshanghui shi* (*History of the Shanghai General Chamber of Commerce*), *1902–1929* (Shanghai: Shanghai shehuikexueyuan chubanshe, 1991).

[19] Tōa, *Shina Keizai Zenshū*, vol. 4, pp. 40–81.

[20] Reed, *Gutenberg in Shanghai*, pp. 174–181.

fact, its membership comprised not only booksellers but also publishers. Hence, we prefer the translation Shanghai Book Industry Guild (Guild hereafter). The Guild started operating officially upon its registration with the government in 1907.[21] Another trade association, called *Shanghai shuye shanghui* (Shanghai Booksellers' Trade Association in Reed's translation), was also formed in 1905. According to Reed, its objectives were similar to those of the Guild, and there was considerable overlap in their leadership.[22] However, the association's magazine, *Tushuyuebao* (Monthly Bulletin of Books),[23] states that its membership consisted primarily of publishers, although booksellers were included as well. Thus, we prefer the translation Shanghai Chamber of Commerce for the Book Industry (Chamber hereafter). As clearly stated in *Tushuyuebao*, the Chamber's primary role was the protection of its members' copyrights.[24] A tenth anniversary commemorative brochure published in 1914 notes that the Chamber arbitrated numerous copyright disputes in the course of assisting its members in copyright cases against non-member Chinese and foreigners.[25] In other words, the Chamber played a two-pronged role: resolving disputes among its members and assisting members involved in dispute settlement proceedings against non-members.

Although they performed similar functions, had similar qualities and were similar in nature, the Guild and Chamber operated separately, and

---

[21] Shanghai Municipal Archives (SMA), file no. S313-1-132-22.

[22] Reed explains that this association was first approved by the Ministries of Commerce and Education in 1906, but its operation was delayed until 1911 because additional approval from other government agencies was required. See Reed, *Gutenberg in Shanghai*, pp. 181–183. However, our perusal of the first issue of *Tushuyuebao* published in 1906 (reprinted in 2013), tells a different story, that is, that *Shanghai shuye shanghui* actually entered into operation after registering with the government in 1906. Based on our reading of the magazine, members of the association began discussions among themselves in late 1905 and the first board of directors was elected from among the members in early 1906. See *Tushuyuebao*, no. 1, 1906, reprinted in Wu Yonggui (ed.), *Minguo shiqi chubanshiliao huibian* (*A Compilation of Historical Materials on Publishing during China's Republican Era*) (Beijing: Guojiatushuguan chubanshe, 2013), vol. 16. For information on the first board of directors, see SMA, file no. S313-1-27.

[23] *Tushuyuebao*, no. 1, 1906.

[24] See *Tushuyuebao*, pp. 126–129, which also explains how the Chamber differed from the old-fashioned association of publisher-cum-bookseller merchants. The Chamber's genesis is also explained in the commemorative brochure *Shuyeshanghui shinian gaikuang* (*A 10-Year History of the Book Industry Association*) published by Zhonghua Book Company in 1914 (p. 1); see SMA, file no. S313-1-4-1.

[25] *Shuyeshanghui*, pp. 2–6; SMA, file no. S313-1-4-1.

there was no formal relation between the two.[26] The latter's leaders took pride in the Chamber's modern outlook and distinguished themselves markedly from the more traditional book merchants who made up the Guild's leadership. It is evident that each organisation had its own sense of identity and preferred to be dissociated from the other.[27] However, it appears that they did not compete against each other, and were willing to cooperate when necessary. On at least one occasion, the two organisations joined forces with other trade associations to draw up a petition calling for protection of the book industry's interests.[28] As noted, the Guild and Chamber had overlapping leaderships and memberships, which is unsurprising given that the board directors of both organisations included representatives of two publishers with relatively large capital assets, namely, the Commercial Press (*Shangwu yinshuguan*) and Zhonghua Book Company (*Zhonghua shuju*).[29] These representatives were able to exert their influence in book industry matters.[30] Understandably, the two publishers competed hard for board director positions in the Guild and Chamber, as they did in the book market.

The 1906 Regulations of the Guild state that the organisation was formed for the purposes of bringing its members together to formulate trade rules on such matters as the prohibition of copyright infringement,

---

[26] For a brief account of the evolution of the two organisations, see Wang, 'Creating a new order', pp. 228–229. Reed mistakenly believes that they merged in 1920. See Reed, *Gutenberg in Shanghai*, p. 181.

[27] SMA, file no. S313-1-4-24. A 1915 letter from the Chamber to the Shanghai General Chamber of Commerce makes it clear that the Chamber and Guild were separate organisations operating independently with no direct link between them.

[28] SMA, file no. S313-1-88.

[29] According to a municipal government survey report, for instance, the Enlightenment Bookstore (*Kaiming shudian*), the smallest of the top four publishing houses in Shanghai in 1932, had capital of 250,000 yuan and turnover of 425,000 yuan. In the same year, the World Journal Bookstore (*Shijie shuju*), the third largest, had capital of 735,000 yuan and turnover of 1.8 million yuan, whilst Zhonghua, the second largest, had capital of 2 million yuan and turnover of 4 million. The Commercial Press, the largest publishing house of the day, had 5 million yuan in capital in early 1932 and turnover of 5.5 million in the first eleven months of the year at its headquarters alone despite the heavy losses the company suffered during the 1932 Shanghai Incident, which saw a considerable number of their assets bombed into ashes by the Japanese army. By comparison, a well-known publisher called the Thousand Hectares Hall Bookstore (*Qianqingdang shuju*) had capital of a mere 10,000 yuan and turnover of 37,000 yuan. Other similar bookstores were in a similar financial situation. See SMA, file no. S313-1-128-67.

[30] See, for instance, SMA, file nos. S-313-1-4-1, S313-1-27 and S313-1-132-22. The Commercial Press had more than one representative on each of the two organisations' management teams.

banning and censorship of books and magazines, and arbitration of intra-industry disputes, the last of which is the most relevant to our discussion here. The regulations stipulate, for instance, that punishments for copyright infringement should be determined by a majority of the Guild's members and that disputes can be brought to the Guild for amicable settlement through mediation. In the latter instance, the Guild had no authority to make binding decisions for disputants; it could only suggest options for dispute settlement. If the Guild's suggestions were not acceptable to any of the disputants, the Guild was not authorised to take any further action.[31] Similar provisions can also be found in the Guild's 1913 Regulations,[32] which are in line with the aforementioned arbitration law of 1913. The Guild, however, had some leverage to impose informal sanctions on serious violators of its rules and regulations by, for example, depriving violators of their Guild membership and staging boycotts against their businesses.[33] The Chamber also had similar provisions, following the legal framework outlined in the 1904 *Concise Regulations*.[34]

3   Dispute Cases in the Shanghai Book Industry: The Choice between Litigation and Arbitration

Thanks to the recent publication of typed (rather than handwritten) documents on all book industry–related arbitration cases kept in the Shanghai Municipal Archives (SMA), those cases are readily accessible today. We have selected six dispute cases involving members of the Guild and Chamber for discussion in this chapter: four inter-member disputes (cases 1, 2, 5 and 6), including a defamation case and a case with unusual consequences, and two cases involving foreign companies (cases 3 and 4).[35] Although the SMA include other types of disputes, such as failures to meet contractual delivery dates, payment defaults and price wars,[36] the six cases discussed herein are sufficient to illustrate our point that entrepreneurs involved in business disputes in the early twentieth century resorted to either arbitral or litigation proceedings, two dispute resolution options that had recently become available to them.

---

[31] Song Yuanfang, *Zhongguo chuban shiliao, jindai bufen* (*Historical Documents on Chinese Publishing: The Modern Period*) (Wuhan: Hubei jiaoyu chubanshe, 2004), vol. 3, p. 502.
[32] SMA, file no. S-313-11.   [33] Ibid., article 45.   [34] SMA, file no. S-313-1-4-1.
[35] Zhuang Zhiling and Xu Shibo, 'Shanghai shuyegonghui guanyu banquanjiufen'an dang-anjilu (Records of copyright dispute cases preserved in the Shanghai Book Industry Guild archives) (1)' (2014) 17 *Shanghaishi dang'anshiliao yanjiu*, 189–214.
[36] SMA, file no. S313-1–120.

3.1 Copyright Disputes among Guild and Chamber Members

Case 1 (1923), *The Commercial Press v. World Journal Bookstore* (*Shijie shuju*), was a copyright complaint case brought before the Guild by the Commercial Press, which accused the World Journal Bookstore of infringing its copyright on a primary school geography textbook. The case was settled amicably through arbitration carried out by the Guild. The accused admitted to copyright infringement, and turned in all 2,668 pirated copies in stock to the Guild, which then destroyed them on behalf of the accuser.[37]

Case 2 (undated),[38] *The Dianshizhai Lithographic Bookstore* (*Dianshizhai*) v. *The Feiyingguan Bookstore* (*Feiyingguan*), was a copyright complaint case brought before the Chamber by the Dianshizhai Lithographic Bookstore, which accused the Feiyingguan Bookstore of reproducing its *Sanxidang Model Book of Calligraphy* (*Sanxidang fatie*) for sale without permission. The Chamber conducted an investigation, which found that the book in question was a book of stone rubbings based on the collection of Shi Ziqian. Hence, whilst the book contained the same material, it had a different source, and thus the accused had not committed copyright infringement. The two parties accepted the arbitration award, and the accuser withdrew the complaint, with the dispute thus settled amicably.[39]

3.2 Copyright Disputes between Chamber Members and Foreign Companies

Case 3 (1911), *Ginn & Company v. The Commercial Press*, was a case brought before the Shanghai Mixed Court.[40] Ginn & Company, an American publisher, accused the Commercial Press of copyright infringement, claiming that the defendant had, without permission, published and marketed in China a Chinese edition of a history book of which the plaintiff was the sole proprietor. The complainant argued its case on the ground of the protection that afforded the rights and interests of foreign copyright holders in China, as stipulated in the unequal treaties of commerce imposed on the Qing government by the Western

---

[37] SMA, file no. S313-1-121.

[38] It could have taken place anytime between 1906, the earliest case recordation year, and 1914, the year of the records' publication.

[39] *Shuyeshanghui*, p. 3, SMA, file no. S313-1-4-1.   [40] SMA, file no. S313-1-138.

powers, including the United States, at the turn of the twentieth century. The defendant, in contrast, argued that such protection, according to the provisions of the aforementioned treaties, extended only to foreign copyright holders' publications that were purposefully produced for consumption by Chinese readers in China and that there was no evidence to support the claim that the disputed material was intentionally produced for Chinese readers. The court accepted the defendant's argument, and the case ended in victory for the defendant.

Case 4 (1919),[41] *The American Textbook Publishing House*[42] *v. The Commercial Press*, was a case in which the US company complained to the Shanghai General Chamber of Commerce that the Commercial Press, without permission, had published and marketed in China a Chinese edition of a European history book of which the accuser was the sole proprietor. The plaintiff initially petitioned the American Chamber of Commerce in China concerning the case, which had then urged the Embassy of the United States in China to negotiate a settlement with China's Foreign Ministry. The petition was subsequently forwarded to the Shanghai General Chamber of Commerce for investigation and handling. The General Chamber then notified the accused, the Commercial Press, that a complaint had been filed against it on the ground of copyright infringement. Lawyers representing the accused rejected the complaint, citing *Ginn & Company v. The Commercial Press* (case 3), and demonstrated their firm stance against the accuser and willingness to resort to litigation to settle the dispute. In the end, the US publisher withdrew its petition, and the case never reached the litigation stage. It is noteworthy that the non-Chinese accuser sought amicable resolution whilst the Chinese company accused of copyright violation preferred litigation.

3.3   Defamation Dispute between Guild and Chamber Members

Case 5 (1919), *The Commercial Press v. Zhonghua Book Company*, was a case between the two most prominent publishers of the day.[43] A series of

---

[41] Zhang Jinglu, ed., *Zhongguo xiandai chuban shiliao jia bian* (*Historical Materials of Publishing in Contemporary China: Part 1*) (Beijing: Zhonghua shu ju, 1954), pp. 327–344.

[42] This is our English translation of the name *Meiguo keben chubanju* appearing in the Chinese source. We have not been able to verify its accuracy.

[43] Tarumoto Teruo, *Shōmuinshokan kenkyū ronshū* (*Collected Studies on the Commercial Press*) (Ōtsu: Shinmatsu shōsetsu kenkyūkai, 2006), pp. 68–111. For the negative advertising the two companies used against each other before the mid-1910s, see Sawamoto

allegations and counter-allegations by both parties, which were widely reported in the media in the 1910s, led to a defamation lawsuit against Zhonghua filed in the Shanghai Mixed Court by the Commercial Press in 1919. The plaintiff claimed that the defendant had damaged its reputation by publishing defamatory materials in newspapers in July 1919 and subsequently in book form for wider circulation. The proceedings lasted from late 1919 to early 1920. According to Tarumoto Teruo,[44] Zhonghua had long tried to portray its main competitor in a negative light by accusing it of failing to produce patriotic textbooks because of its partnership with a Japanese publishing company. Such a tactic worked well during the May Fourth Movement, when anti-Japanese nationalist sentiments were running high in Shanghai. In July 1919, Zhonghua published a Chinese translation of a Japanese magazine[45] article that had circulated in Tokyo a month earlier and stated, inaccurately, that the Commercial Press was still in partnership with a Japanese company and had been so throughout the year. In actual fact, the partnership had ended in early 1914. The Commercial Press suffered significant business losses as a result of Zhonghua's actions, the publication of the aforementioned article in particular. Upon learning that the negative news about it had come from Zhonghua, the Commercial Press took immediate action, demanding an open apology from Zhonghua, which promptly rejected the demand. At this point, a Guild member close to both companies suggested that they resolve their dispute amicably through private mediation or arbitration performed by the Guild. The Commercial Press rejected the proposal, and instead sued Zhonghua in the Shanghai Mixed Court for defamation and sought a civil remedy. Following a month-long trial and subsequent appeal, Zhonghua lost the lawsuit and was ordered to make a public apology and pay 10,000 yuan in compensation to the plaintiff, a fairly large amount of punitive damages given that the Commercial Press had capital of just 3 million yuan in 1920.[46]

Ikuma, 'Shōmuinshokan to Chūkashokyoku no kyōkasho sensō (A textbook war between the Commercial Press and Zhonghua Book Company)' (1996) 19 *Shinmatsu shōsetsu*, 65–101. The case was reported extensively in the Shanghai newspaper *Shenbao*.

[44] Tarumoto, *Shōmuinshokan*, p. 71.   [45] *Business Japan (Jitsugyō no nihon)*.

[46] Yamamoto Kiichirō, ed., *Chūka zenkoku chūnichi jitsugyōka kōshinroku (Shanhai no bu)* (*The Directory of Chinese and Japanese Entrepreneurs in China [Shanghai]*) (Shanghai: Shanhai kōshinjo, 1936), vol. 1, p. 386; reprinted in Fuji Shuppan (ed.), *Senzenki kaigai shōkō kōshinroku shūsei* (*A Collection of Pre-war Directories of Overseas Trade and Industrial Organisations*), vol. 5, *chūgoku hen* [China] 4 (Tokyo: Fuji Shuppan, 2010).

3.4 Commercial Dispute between Guild Members Involving Inappropriate and Hostile Behaviour

Case 6 (undated), *Li Difan v. The Commercial Press*, yet again involved the Commercial Press, this time in a case brought by a book trader. The charge was that two of the publishing house's staff members had subjected book trader Li Difan to unlawful and involuntary confinement. The two had happened upon Li's books in an opium den. Suspecting that the books were pirated, the men tricked Li into agreeing to sell them a cartload of the books in question and deliver them to a fake address. The street on which the Commercial Press was located was on the way to that address. As Li neared the publishing firm's front gate on his way to make the delivery, a couple of sturdy men dashed out and bundled Li and his goods into the premises by force. The books were then subjected to scrutiny for evidence of piracy, and no such evidence was found. Li, still under confinement, was interrogated about the books and forced to agree to go to the shop he had purchased them from, accompanied by two Commercial Press staff, to obtain a document attesting that the books had been produced lawfully for sale in the domestic market. Li's confinement was unquestionably unlawful. The case was handled by the Guild's arbitral tribunal, which appointed at least four investigators, all elected Guild members, to conduct thorough investigations independently. On the basis of their reports, the tribunal unanimously ruled that the fault lay with the Commercial Press. It appears that the two parties accepted the arbitral award and reached an amicable settlement.[47]

4 Putting the Shanghai Dispute Cases in Perspective: Some Observations

Adaptive flexibility is demonstrated in the six foregoing dispute cases of early twentieth-century Shanghai. All six commercial disputes were handled flexibly and adaptively using alternative settlement options within the newly introduced legal framework. It is clear that major companies within the Shanghai book industry were prepared to resort to such new legal institutions as law courts and arbitral tribunals in accordance with

---

[47] SMA, file no. S313-1-75. The written records in SMA in relation to this case are fragmentary, and some are illegible. However, the information is by and large consistent across the investigation reports, with the only differences lying in the fine details of what the investigators heard from witnesses. See Zhuang and Xu, 'Shanghai shuyegonghui', 201–206. See also Wang, 'Creating a new order', pp. 265–275.

their perceived best interests. Legal proceedings and their outcomes, whether before the courts or tribunals, were seen as fair. The arbitrators elected to the Guild's or Chamber's arbitral tribunal, who were often themselves members of the companies involved in disputes, were unable to exercise undue influence over the dispute resolution process to ensure a finding in their favour. The arbitration system, which was equipped with appropriate impartial mechanisms, was received positively, and the system largely enjoyed credibility. From our reading of the six dispute cases, it can be said that the passive transplantation of exogenous legal institutions, notions and values played a role in the theoretical and normative aspects of modern China's legal reform and that the norms and institutions of the transplanted legal system were not necessarily embraced in a wholesale manner, but rather adapted by the entrepreneurs of the day for effective implementation in a manner consistent with the local culture. In fact, entrepreneurs frequently used the system to pursue their own business interests, and were thus often its consumers. In the process, they also played the role of change agents in shaping the way in which the new legal system was implemented. The resulting pragmatic mix of old and new was akin to what is known as med-arb or arb-med in today's legal regime governing international commercial arbitration.[48] It is thus safe to say that the assumed contradictions between Western-style legal institutions and China's traditional legal resources can be overcome through adaptive flexibility and co-evolutionary dynamics.

The Western-style arbitration system was translated as *gongduan* in Chinese, which deserves a few words of explanation.[49] The character for *gong* can be associated with such words as fairness (*gongbing*), justice (*gongyi/gongzheng*), the right way (*gongdao*), people (*gongzhong*), the public (*gonggong*), the public interest (*gongsi zhi gong*), openness and transparency (*gongkai touming*), the ordinary feelings of human beings (*ren zhi changqing*), accepted codes of conduct (*qingli*), and customs (*xiguan*). *Gongduan* meant 'adjudication' in the magistrates' courts of the traditional Chinese legal system.[50] However, it received a new

---

[48] Fan, 'Glocalization of arbitration', 212–215.

[49] Su Jilang (Billy K. L. So) and Sufumi So, 'Qingmominchu jiejue shangye jiufen de fating caijue yu shanghui gongduan (Litigation versus arbitration conducted with the chamber of commerce for commercial dispute resolution in late Qing and early Republican China)', in Xu Zhangrun and Dao Kai (eds.), *Wenhua Zhongguo de fayixushi* (*A Jurisprudential Narrative of Cultural China*) (Beijing: Falü chubanshe, 2015), pp. 190–209.

[50] See, for instance, the case of *Zhou Yingqi v. Chen Wanxing* reported in *Shenbao* on 4 June 1889.

Western meaning in the late nineteenth century when it was used as a translation of the term 'arbitration' in international law.[51] When the modern legal system was established in the Republican China era, the term was formally distinguished from *caijue* or *caipan*, meaning court trial,[52] and ceased to mean international arbitration. It appears that the hybrid nature of Chinese-style arbitration, a non-judicial institution, was well captured in the term *gongduan* used in the early twentieth century.

It should be noted that during the Meiji period in Japan, many kanji-based Japanese words, or *wasei-kango*, were created through the translation of Western materials to suit the needs of modern society, among them such words as *keizai* (economy), *seiji* (politics) and *kagaku* (science), many of which found their way into contemporary Chinese. However, *gongduan* was not a *wasei-kango*. In Meiji Japan, *chūsai* was used to refer to arbitration. The term *chūsai saiban* was chosen to refer to arbitration judgment in the Meiji Civil Code after a lengthy discussion of such alternative terms as *saitei, saiketsu* and *bandan*.[53] As time passed, the Japanese term *chūsai* (or *zhongcai* in Chinese) came to be more commonly used in China, and eventually replaced *gongduan* altogether. Up until the 1920s, however, the use of *zhongcai* was limited, with the term used primarily for international arbitration or domestic labour disputes.[54]

One final note worth mentioning is that unlike the case in late Qing and early Republican China, the legal institution of arbitration was transplanted in Meiji Japan with little trace of hybridity. In Japan, the word 'arbitration' made its first appearance in the 1890 Code of Civil Procedure, which was based on the Civil Procedure Act of Germany because the Meiji government was compelled to make its codes acceptable to the world's great powers. The 1890 Code was further refined into what is now referred to as the Old Arbitration Act, which was promulgated in 1902.[55] For example, the arbitration rules and procedures

---

[51] See, for instance, the case of *U.S.A. v. Great Britain* reported in *Shenbao* on 16 November 1872.

[52] Fan, 'Glocalization of arbitration', 209–211.

[53] See Hōmu daijin kanbō shihō hōsei chōsa-bu, *Nihon kindai rippō shiryō sōsho (Japanese Modern Legislation Materials Series*. Vol. 22) (Tokyo: Shōjihōmu kenkyūkai, 1985); 'Hōritsu torishirabe iinkai minjisoshōhō sōan giji hikki' (Minutes of the drafting committee meeting on the code of civil procedure) no. 53, 600–602.

[54] For instance, most of the *zhongcai* cases in SMA are cases of international arbitration or local labour disputes, some of them involving foreign business interests.

[55] Kikui Tsunahiro, 'Meijiki chūsai kanken (My personal view on arbitration in the Meiji era)' (1982) 54(8) *Hōritsu jihō*, 8–15. See also Muramoto Kazuo, *Hōsō tsurezure gusa (Random Thoughts about Law)* (Tokyo: Sakai shoten, 1964); Koyama Noboru, 'Chūsaihō

established by the Booksellers Association of Tokyo (*Tōkyō shosekishō kumiai*) were akin to those in Europe.[56] The actual use of arbitration, however, was limited. Records reveal only a few arbitration cases concerning disputes over defaults on consignment sales.[57] In Meiji Japan, litigation, a newly established legal mechanism, or mediation, an extra-legal method, was considered more effective and was used more frequently for the resolution of civil and commercial disputes.[58] One plausible explanation for this is that the confrontational nature of the Western-style arbitration method did not sit well with the cultural norms and social practices long valued by the Japanese people. Disputants thus preferred such extra-legal methods as out-of-court private mediation in order to maintain a relationship with the other parties or to at least not make it any worse. Otherwise, they would rather resort to litigation than arbitration. The contrast between the ways in which Republican China and Meiji Japan responded to the newly implemented Western-style legal institutions reveals intriguing dimensions of legal transplantation, including the dichotomy between sentiment and reason.

5 Conclusion

In this chapter, we have discussed the transplantation of Western legal institutions into early twentieth-century China and the reception of such institutions by the Shanghai book industry. As we have explained, arbitral tribunals were established within such business associations as the Shanghai Book Industry Guild and Shanghai Chamber of Commerce for the Book Industry. In fact, newly introduced arbitration services were

no enkaku no gaikan to sono yokei' ('A historical survey of the arbitration law and its unexpected benefits') (1979) 29(3–4) *Hokudai hōgaku ronshū*, 349–400; Ishimoto Yasuo, 'Meijiki ni okeru chūsai saiban—jakkan no kōsatsu' ('Some thoughts on arbitration in the Meiji era') (1963) 9(3–4) *Hōgaku zasshi*, 168–183.

[56] Billy K. L. So and Sufumi So, 'Law court or alternative dispute resolution (ADR) for commercial disputes? The cases of the publishing industry in Shanghai in the modern era and Tokyo in the Meiji period', a paper presented at 17th World Economic History Congress, Kyoto, 4 August 2015.

[57] Ōshiba Shirō, 'Tōkyō shosekishō kumiai-shi (A history of the Booksellers Association of Tokyo)', in Tōkyō shosekishō kumiai (ed.), *Tōkyō shosekishō denkishūran* (A Collection of Tokyo Booksellers' Biographies) (originally published in Tokyo in 1912 by Tōkyō shosekishō kumiai; reprinted in Tokyo in 1978 by Seishōdō shoten), pp. 5–15. See earlier texts about the same association dated 1877 and 1890 in the Tokyo Municipal Archives, file nos. D320-RAM-617.D3.07 (002) and D327-RAM-619.A4.18 (001), respectively.

[58] Ōshiba, 'Tōkyō shosekishō kumiai-shi.'

used frequently to resolve the growing number of commercial disputes between Chinese parties and between Chinese and foreign parties, while such distinct features as non-binding arbitration rules were also created and maintained. Resorting to adjudication also seems to have been a common practice. The choice between arbitration and court proceedings was largely a matter of a rational calculation of self-interest, but it also rested on the historical and socio-cultural factors that had shaped Chinese business, which resulted in a preference for non-confrontational conflict resolution and distaste for the imposition of decisions reached by third parties. By comparison, the arbitral tribunal established within the Booksellers Association of Tokyo as a result of the transplantation of Western-style legal systems in Meiji Japan was seldom used in practice, with private mediation and litigation remaining the preferred methods of dispute resolution in commercial matters. We believe that the six dispute cases discussed herein illustrate the phenomena of adaptive flexibility and co-evolutionary dynamics in the process of transplanting new legal institutions.

13

China's Unilateral Abrogation of the Sino–Belgian Treaty

Case Study of an Instance of Deviant Transplantation

MARIA ADELE CARRAI

1 Introduction

The Second Opium War (1856–1860) marks a turning point in the history of the transplantation of Western legal concepts to China. When international law was initially transplanted to China as a new discipline in the mid-nineteenth century, the Chinese literati used it instrumentally as a way of dealing with foreign 'barbarians'. However, because of China's internal weaknesses and inability to strike back at the Western powers, in the years after that war the Qing literati and jurists gradually began replacing the country's no-longer-workable Sinocentric normative world-order with transplanted international law. By 1911, international law had replaced the traditional Chinese tribute system, and China was no longer in the hands of imperial dynastic rulers but was a sovereign state. One of the main assumptions of modern international law is sovereign equality. However, international society was highly unequal and hierarchical in the nineteenth century, and characterised by anti-pluralism, as it will be further defined in the next section.

In this chapter, I argue that because of China's different understanding of equal sovereignty, Chinese diplomats in the Republican period began to challenge the doctrine of juridical sovereignty as it was defined in the West. In particular, they opposed the dominant European doctrine of legal positivism, which promoted status and legalised hierarchies, with a concept of the sovereign equality of states that was grounded in a more pluralistic vision of the world. In this sense, the transplantation was partly deviant: it departed from the expectations of the Western powers and contributed to a renegotiation of the meaning of juridical sovereignty, placing it within a broader discourse that contributed at the same time to fulfil the more universalistic aspirations of international law, which were contained in the Western doctrine of that time. By adopting a pluralistic vision of international society, these diplomats defended China's existential equality against the legalised hierarchies of the West. By the 1940s, China was fully recognised as an equal member of international society, had gained control over its tariffs and had put an end to extraterritoriality.

China's different understanding of juridical equality, which emerged from its claims of existential equality, is particularly evident in the diplomacy surrounding the attempts at treaty revision in the 1920s and 1930s. In examining China's unilateral abrogation in 1926 of the Sino–Belgian Treaty of 1865, the aim of this chapter is not only to rehabilitate the history of Republican China, often dismissed as a period of chaos, but also to depart from Eurocentric histories of international law that relegate China to the status of passive receiver of international legal norms. In fact, China was far from being a passive receiver of international law, with the process of transplantation producing new hybrid legal notions.[1] For instance, the idea of sovereign equality, one of the key assumptions of the Western Westphalian system and of international law, was understood differently in China.

2   Sino–Belgian Treaty of 1865: A History of Unequal Treaties

Whilst treaties, together with customary international law and the general principles of international law, have long been one of the main sources of the Western international normative order, they did not play the same role in imperial China.[2] Before international law was transplanted to the country starting from the mid-nineteenth century, China's international normative order was grounded on a hierarchical Sinocentrism rather than equality.[3] The first treaty signed by imperial China with a Western country

---

[1] In this regard, see Lydia Liu, *Translingual Practice, Literature, National Culture, and Translated Modernity – China, 1900–1937* (Stanford, CA: Stanford University Press, 2005); Lydia Liu, *The Clash of Empires: The Invention of China in Modern World Making* (Cambridge, MA: Harvard University Press, 2004).

[2] According to article 38(1) of the International Court of Justice Statute, the sources of international law are (in non-hierarchical order) treaties, customary international law and the general principle of law (available at www.icj-cij.org/documents/? p1=4&p2=2).

[3] Angela Zito, *Of Body and Brush: Grand Sacrifice as Text/Performance in Eighteenth-Century China* (Chicago: University of Chicago Press, 1997); James Hevia, *Cherishing Men from Afar: Qing Guest Ritual and the Macartney Embassy of 1793* (Durham, NC: Duke University Press, 1995); James Hevia, 'Tribute, asymmetry, and imperial formations:

was the Treaty of Nipchu (Nerchinsk) agreed with Russia in 1689. That treaty, however, was not a treaty in the modern sense, and it did not mean that China accepted Western international law. Although it was formulated in terms of equality, for China the treaty was more a favour granted out of magnanimity or tolerance to an inferior Russia. It did not question the fundamental Sinocentric normative order.[4] Although China signed a number of other treaties with Russia during the eighteenth century, it is the Treaty of Nanjing with Britain in 1842 that truly marked the beginning of its socialisation with Western international society as it emerged, developed, and globalized through international law from its founding myth of the Peace of Westphalia (see Figure 13.1).[5]

The Western states, despite paying lip service to the principle of equality, supported a hierarchical and unequal world-order characterised by the divide between so-called 'civilised' and 'non-civilised' countries. With the imperialistic expansion of the Western powers, modern international law began increasingly to regulate other non-Western realities, but its declared universality continued to deny equality to non-Western states on the ground of the standard of 'civilisation'. The anti-pluralistic character of the Western world-order, as it will be further discussed, was reflected, for instance, in the very nature of the treaties signed by China and the Western powers from the mid-nineteenth century onwards. These were unequal by design in that they were characterised by an imbalance in China's obligations towards the other contracting powers. Those obligations were usually imposed upon China by force or the threat of force,[6] although it is not the case that all of the treaties were

Rethinking relations of power in East Asia' (2009)16 *Journal of American–East Asian Relations*, 69–83.

[4] For Joseph Sebes, the Sino–Russian treaties of Nerchinsk (1689) and Kiakhta (1727) are the first treaties in which the principle of equality is fully accepted by China: 'China gave up her traditional attitude and entered into treaty relations with Russia on the basis of equality and reciprocity as established by the law of nations.' See Joseph Sebes, *The Jesuits and the Sino–Russian Treaty of Nerchinsk (1689): The Diary of Thomas Pereira, S.J.* (Rome: Institutum Historicum S.I., 1961), vol. XVIII, p. 114. However, it is argued in this chapter that this was not really the case: not only was China unaware of the law of nations at that time, but its Sinocentric view was also preserved with regard to Russia until the end of the nineteenth century, as clearly reflected in its sacred geography. In this regard, see Takeshi Hamashita, *China, East Asia, and the Global Economy: Regional and Historical Perspective* (New York: Routledge, 2008), pp. 12–26.

[5] Andreas Osiander, 'Sovereignty, international relations, and the Westphalian myth' (2001) 55 *International Organization* (2001), 251–287.

[6] Anne Peters, 'Unequal treaties', in Rüdiger Wolfrum (ed.), *The Max Planck Encyclopedia of Public International Law* (Oxford: Oxford University Press online, 2007).

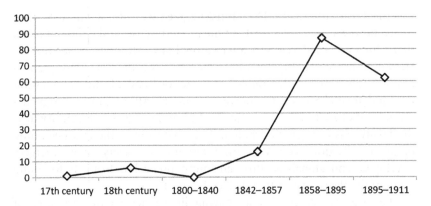

Figure 13.1   Number of treaties signed by imperial China from the seventeenth century to 1911
Source: Statistical Department of Inspectorate General Customs, Treaty, Convention, etc. between China and Foreign States (Shanghai: Kelly&Walsh, 1917), vol. II.

signed after the major defeats of the Qing Empire, that is, the Opium Wars (1839–1842, 1856–1860), Sino–Japanese War (1894–1895) and Boxer Rebellion (1900–1901).

If the Treaty of Nanjing of 1842 was the first unequal treaty, then the Tianjin Treaty of 1858 and the Beijing Convention of 1860 that ended the Second Opium War (1856–1860) brought to full maturity the system of unequal treaties, legalising Western encroachment of China's sovereignty. The Treaty of Nanjing opened China's doors to only a few Western powers, namely, Great Britain, France and the United States, whilst the Treaty of Tianjin and the Convention of Beijing opened them wider to allow the entry of most of the Western and other powers of the day: Russia, Belgium, Germany, Portugal, Denmark, the Netherlands, Spain, Italy, Austria-Hungary, Japan, Peru and Brazil.[7] China's territorial integrity and sovereignty were formally recognised, but in reality they were increasingly infringed upon by the treaties' terms.

---

[7] France (Treaty of Tianjin 1858, Convention of Beijing 1860), United States of America (Treaty of Tianjin 1858, Convention of Beijing 1868), Russia (Treaty of Tianjin 1858, Convention of Beijing 1860), Germany (Treaty of Tianjin 1861), Belgium (Treaty of Beijing 1865), Denmark (Treaty of Beijing 1863), Holland (Treaty of Tianjin 1863), Portugal (Treaty of Tianjin 1862), Spain (Treaty of Tianjin 1864), Italy (Treaty of Tianjin 1866), Austria–Hungary (Treaty of Beijing 1869), Japan (Treaty of Tianjin 1871) and Peru (Treaty of Tianjin 1874); see Statistical Department, *Treaty, Convention, etc.*, vols. I–II.

The Treaty of Friendship, Commerce, and Navigation between China and Belgium, signed in Peking (Beijing) on 2 November 1865 and ratified in Shanghai on 27 October of the following year, also belonged to the category of unequal treaties. It defined Sino–Belgian relations for the next sixty years, granting extraterritorial privileges to Belgian nationals and most-favoured-nation treatment to Belgium (article 45). Article 46, the interpretation of which was contested after China's unilateral denunciation of the treaty in 1926, afforded the possibility of reopening the negotiations at ten-year intervals if the modification of any clause of the treaty was considered useful by the Belgian government, and the Belgian government alone. Moreover, the treaty strictly regulated commerce and shipping. The attachment to the treaty of a list of tariffs on a variety of imports and exports, as well as a set of nine commercial rules, perpetuated China's lack of tariff autonomy.[8]

If, as US authority on Chinese affairs Harley Farnsworth MacNair noted in 1926, 'the causes of the Anglo–Chinese wars of the nineteenth century must be divided almost equally between the opium question and the struggle for equality',[9] in that they opposed the hierarchical Sino-centric system that placed the Western powers in an inferior position, then the treaties signed after those wars were clearly unequal towards China. Although the principle of sovereign equality is one of the most reiterated in modern international law, and is generally believed to be one of the fundamental assumptions underpinning its successful functioning since the Peace of Westphalia was concluded in 1648, Western international society and international law have functioned not only by assuming the principle of formal equality; hierarchies have been and continue to be equally important.[10] In particular, the positivist turn in international law doctrine at the end of the nineteenth century justified the difference in status between countries by distinguishing between sovereign and semi-sovereign states.[11]

---

[8] Ibid., vol. II, pp. 758–795.

[9] Harley Farnsworth MacNair, *China's International Relations & Other Essays* (Shanghai: Commercial Press, 1926), p. 35.

[10] Jack Donnelly, 'Sovereign inequalities and hierarchy in anarchy: American power and international society' (2006) 12 *European Journal of International Relations*, 139–170.

[11] Milos Vec, 'Universalization, particularization, and discrimination. European perspectives on a cultural history of nineteenth century international law' (2012) 2 *InterDisciplines*, 79–102, at 84–86; Luigi Nuzzo, *Origini di Una Scienza. Diritto Internazionale e Colonialismo nel XIX Secolo* (Frankfurt: Klostermann, 2012); Mónica García-Salmones Rovira, *The Project of Positivism in International Law* (Oxford: Oxford University Press,

In order to make sense of the difference in international society between formal equality and substantial inequalities, it is useful to recall Simpson's notion of juridical sovereignty, which is the product of the interaction of three different ideas of equality and two types of hierarchy. Juridical sovereignty has defined the Western legal order, but its content and meaning have continually changed, and not necessarily in the direction of the progressive establishment of sovereign equality. Simpson differentiated among three ideas of sovereign equality: 1) formal equality, that is, equality before the law; 2) legislative equality, which refers to states being bound only by the international legal norms to which they consent, as well as the equality of voting rights and representation in the decision-making process of international bodies and an equal role in the creation of international treaty and customary law and 3) existential equality, which refers to recognition on the part of the international community that an entity is entitled to sovereign statehood and consequently to be treated according to the principle of equality. Whilst formal equality has been mostly assumed and respected, legislative and existential equality have been influenced by two legalised hierarchies: 1) legalised hegemony, which is a force that opposes legislative equality and gives constitutional weight to one party or parties over another or others, and 2) anti-pluralism, which challenges existential equality by creating hierarchies based on culture and civilisation.[12] Juridical sovereignty is the result of the interaction of ideas of equality and types of hierarchy, which are in constant tension with one another.

With reference to the preceding distinction, unequal treaties were a sign of the anti-pluralism that denied the existential equality of China. Although they were sometimes defined in international law manuals, unequal treaties did not have a proper legal qualification. Jurist Henry Wager Halleck distinguished equal and unequal treaties thus at the beginning of the twentieth century: 'Equal treaties are where the contracting parties promise the same or equivalent things; and unequal treaties are where the things promised are neither the same nor equitably proportioned.'[13] If unequal treaties lacked a clear legal qualification, they

---

2013). The school of legal positivism is traditionally opposed to the school of natural law. Although such a distinction is an oversimplification and there are many overlaps between the two traditions, the distinction can be useful, and is used here for analytical purposes.

[12] Gerry Simpson, *Great Powers and Outlaw States, Unequal Sovereigns in the International Legal Order* (Cambridge: Cambridge University Press, 2004), pp. 3–24, 62–90.

[13] Henry Wager Halleck, *International Law, or Rules Regulating the Intercourse of States in Peace and War* (London: Kegan Paul, Trench, 1908), p. 304.

were nonetheless contemplated in international law, particularly given the notion of juridical sovereignty that was dominant in the nineteenth century: formal equality was granted but existential equality was hampered and limited by the non-pluralistic hierarchy of Western doctrine and practice.[14]

Contrary to the positivist doctrine that promoted different statuses according to the degree of civilisation, granting sovereign membership based on internal, moral and cultural elements, Chinese jurists, precisely because their country was denied equal sovereignty on these grounds, adopted a pluralistic attitude towards China's membership of international society. To oppose the anti-pluralism of Western diplomatic practice and international legal doctrine, Chinese diplomats and scholars began to promote and defend China's juridical sovereignty, characterising it through the idea of the right to exist (*shengcunquan*), from which derived a series of other rights such as equal sovereignty and reciprocity. This recharacterisation gave rise to Republican diplomatic activity around treaty revision, which led in 1926 to China's first unilateral denunciation of the Sino–Belgium Treaty of 1865.

3 Treaty Revision Diplomacy: China's Search for Existential Equality

The first systematic transplantation of international law did not take place until Martin's translation of Wheaton's *Elements of International Law* in 1864.[15] However, the role of the early treaties signed by China and the foreign powers between 1842 and 1860 should not be underestimated. They in fact already demonstrate the emergence of an awareness of the notions of sovereign equality and sovereign rights, which by the 1880s were already fully appropriated by Chinese intellectuals and diplomats. However, it is only at the beginning of the twentieth century that the term 'unequal treaties' was adopted in China. In the wake of Japan's successful

---

[14] The unequal treaties were recognised in international law beginning with Grotius, but their inequality was not used as grounds for justifying their illegality. At the end of the nineteenth century and beginning of the twentieth, their discussion was in decline. See Hungdah Chiu, 'Chinese views of unequal treaties', in Jerome Alan Cohen (ed.), *China's Practice of International Law: Some Case Studies* (Cambridge, MA: Harvard University Press, 1972), pp. 240–241.

[15] Rune Svarverud, *International Law a World Order in Late Imperial China, Translation, Reception and Discourse* (Leiden: Brill, 2007); William Alexander Parsons Martin, *Wanguo gongfa* (Taibei: Zhongguo guojifa xuehui 1998).

abrogation of unfavourable treaties signed with the Western powers in the nineteenth century, Chinese scholars and diplomats took up the rhetoric of unequal treaties (*bupingdeng tiaoyue*), calling for China's equal sovereignty to be recognised internationally. Father of the new Republic Sun Yat-sen used the term 'unequal treaties' for the first time in 1906.[16] The Nationalist Party, or Kuomintang, which in 1929 replaced the Beiyang government (which was recognised by various Western powers between 1912 and 1928), was equally resolute in redeeming Chinese existential equality as its predecessor, and it continued its 'diplomacy of treaty revision' (*Xiuyue waijiao*).[17]

The termination of unequal treaties also became a very popular theme in the academic and popular literature, animating the May Fourth Movement of 1919 and the protests that took place near the Belgian stock market in downtown Brussels on 27 October 1926. For instance, in 1925 the China Committee of the China Group published thousands of copies of a booklet about extraterritoriality, tariff autonomy and unequal treaties for the members of the Institute of Pacific Relations, which sold out immediately.[18] There followed *A Collection of Discussions on Unequal Treaties*, edited by Zhang Tinghao and published in 1928; Qiu Zuming's *On Lost Rights in the Negotiation of Treaties between China and Foreign Countries*, which appeared in 1929; and Wang Jiyuan's *History of Unequal Treaties* and Chen Jicheng's *An Introduction to the Unequal Treaties*, both published in 1935.[19]

---

[16] The Japanese were occupied with the revision of unequal treaties for more than two decades, from 1871 to 1894. Their main concern was the removal of extraterritorial consular jurisdiction and the clauses that deprived Japan of its tariff autonomy. Japan, after having defeated China in the First Sino–Japanese War, became recognised as an equal power. See Masujiro Honda, 'The evolution of Japanese diplomacy' 1912 3(2) *Journal of Race Development*, 188–200, at 195–198. See also Michael R. Auslin, *Negotiating with Imperialism: The Unequal Treaties and the Culture of Japanese Diplomacy* (Cambridge, MA: Harvard University Press, 2004). For the first use of the term *bupingdeng tiaoyue* by Sun Yat-sen, see Zhang Jianhua, 'Sun Zhongshan's idea of unequal treaties' ('*Sun Zhongshan yu bu pingdeng tiaoyue gainian*') (2002) 39(2) *Beijing daxue xuebao, zhexue shehui kexue ban*, 3.

[17] Tang Qihua, 'The origin of the treaty revision diplomacy of the Beijing Government of the early Republican period, 1912–1918' ('*Minguo chu nian Beijing zhengfu 'xiu yue waijiao' zhi mengya1912–1918*') (1998) 28 *Wenshi xue bao*, 118–143.

[18] J. Y. C. Yen, L. T. Chen, T. Z. Koo and Yau Tsit Law, 'Extracts from letters' (20 May 1926) *News Bulletin, Institute of Pacific Relations*, 3–8; Society for the Education of the People and for the Construction of China, *Unequal Treaties* (*Bupingdeng tiaoyue*) (Shanghai: Shangwu, 1927).

[19] Zhang Tinhao, *A Collection of Discussions on Unequal Treaties* (*Bu pingdeng tiaoyue taolun ji*) (Shanghai: Dadong shuju, 1928); Qiu Zuming, *On Lost Rights in the Negotiation*

One of the doctrinal reasons that scholars cited in promoting China's existential equality was the country's right to exist. Alfred Sze Sao-ke (Shi Zhaoji, 1877–1958), who before joining the Beiyang government and becoming a key diplomat in the Republican period studied at Cornell University, derived the right to exist from sovereign rights. He first discussed the origin of sovereignty through an analogy between the individual and the state:

> China does not ask for anything which does not rightfully belong to her as a sovereign and independent nation. The international jurisprudence of the world is built upon the premise that the independent members of the family of Nations are entitled to certain rights which are inherently theirs by reason of their several sovereignties; and these 'Rights of Nations' are themselves based upon the proposition that these Nations are political personalities which have a character similar to that accorded by ethics to human individuals. Since the time of Immanuel Kant it has been recognized that the human individual is, to use Kant's phrase, an end in himself, his welfare is an absolute good... Therefore, applying this same doctrine to sovereign political powers, that is, to the sovereign States of international law, it is clear that no Nation or group of Nations has either the ethical or the legal right to use the resources or markets of another State for the advancement of its or their own individualistic interests to the detriment of the welfare of the State whose resources or markets are thus utilized or controlled.[20]

Sze then justified China's right to exist by drawing on the idea of sovereignty:

> All international jurists concede that the rules governing the relations between sovereign States are themselves founded upon the rights and corresponding obligations which belong to, and, as it were, adhere to members of the family of nations as sovereign and independent entities or political persons. The chief of these rights, as in the case of individual human beings, is the right of existence... It means the right, in the case of a State, to protect its people in the enjoyment of those material and cultural interests which are deemed essential to the maintenance of a reasonably satisfactory life.[21]

of Treaties between China and Foreign Countries (Zhongwai ding yue shi quan) (Beijing: Beijing Zhing xian ta fang keji fazhan youxian gongsi, 1926); Chen Jicheng, An Introduction to the Unequal Treaties (Bu pingdeng tiayue qian) (Shanghai: Zhonghua shuju, 1935); Wang Jiyuan, A History of Unequal Treaties (Bu pingdeng tiaoyue shi) (Shanghai: Yaxiya shu ju, 1935).

[20] Alfred Sze Sao-ke, Addresses (Baltimore: Johns Hopkins University Press, 1926).
[21] Ibid., 120.

For Sze, given the originality of the right to exist and of sovereign rights, the conduct of states that pursued their own interests in China to the detriment of its territorial sovereignty was unethical and illegal, as reflected in particular in China's lack of tariff autonomy and extraterritoriality. He urged those states to 'seek to bring their several national policies into harmony with the requirements of the welfare of that larger unit, Humanity'.[22] Extraterritoriality and the lack of tariff autonomy constituted the 'most serious curtailment of China's sovereign right to use her fiscal power for the advancement of the welfare of her own people'.[23] By imposing non-reciprocal limitations upon China, undermining its sovereignty and limiting its national interests, the 'whole complex of unequal treaties which have been forced upon [China] by the other powers is without an ethical basis'.[24]

Chinese diplomat Qiu Zuming was another important contributor to the debate, adopting the right to exist as a justification against unequal treaties. He began his dissertation about such treaties in 1926 by referring to a country's right to exist, which comes before sovereignty. If, as he noted, the majority of publicists and writers identified sovereignty with the principle of independence, referring to internal and external independence, then Qiu, with reference to French jurist Paul Fauchille, argued that sovereignty should first of all be understood through the fundamental right of a state to exist, from which it derives the right to self-preservation and the right to freedom.[25] The principle of equality derives from the right to external sovereignty, which corresponds to the principles of independence and non-inference, which themselves derive from the right to freedom.[26] What was important for Qiu was that it is from the right to exist that all other rights derive. Although he did not qualify the right to exist – e.g. we do not know from his arguments whether it is an internal matter for a particular political regime or an external matter of recognition – it seems obvious from the context in which he discusses that right, that is, in the context of a dissertation denouncing unequal rights, that he saw China's right to exist as very much related to its existential equality.

As I have already noted, although the principle of equality was often declared by the Western powers and assumed as a working principle in many legal codes – as was the case with the very first unequal treaty formally promoting Chinese equality while in practice disregarding it – that

---

[22] Ibid., 56–57.   [23] Ibid., 78.   [24] Ibid., 109.
[25] Qiu, *On Lost Rights in the Negotiation*, pp. 11–12.   [26] Ibid., 17.

principle was not used in international law to contest unequal treaties. It was China, emphasising its existential equality based on its right to exist, that argued for the invalidity of unequal treaties.

4 Prodromes of Unilateral Denunciation: Paris and Washington

Chinese diplomat Wellington Koo, in his PhD dissertation for Columbia University published in 1912, provided the first account of the foreign rights granted by the unequal treaty system beginning with the Treaty of Nanjing in 1842. These innumerable rights of aliens, he wrote, 'were secured at the outset with the aid of the sword', and 'foreigners in China enjoy very many rights and privileges which are not accorded to aliens in other countries'.[27] After having adopted the naturalist tradition's analogy between the state and the individual, he continued as follows.

> If China, of any of the foreign states maintaining treaty relations with her, is bent upon getting something for nothing, little can be done to either recover territorial rights on the one hand or to obtain full commercial freedom on the other. Mutual forbearance and reciprocal concession are no less than the best policy in the intercourse between nations than in the intercourse between individuals.[28]

The idea of reciprocity expressed by Koo in 1912 became the grounds for the denunciation of unequal treaties at the Paris Conference of 1919. In a memorandum on the Abolition of Consular Jurisdiction, Chinese delegates in Paris argued that the lack of reciprocity in a treaty, such as in the treaties granting unilateral consular jurisdiction to Western powers, could be used to justify the unilateral abrogation of that treaty.[29] The formula used by the Chinese diplomats in Paris was that of *rebus sic*

---

[27] Wellington Koo, *The Status of Aliens in China* (London: P. S. King & Son, 1912), pp. 472, 350.

[28] Ibid. pp. 477, 355.

[29] Dong Wang, *China's Unequal Treaties, Narrating National History* (New York: Lexington Books, 2008), p. 49. There was also a minority of more conservative diplomats aligned with the previous diplomatic strategy of respecting the principle of *pacta sunt servanda* at any cost, such as Liu Shu Shun, China's first ambassador to Canada. He argued that the unequal treaties could be modified and eventually annulled only through diplomatic negotiations and mutual consent and that unilateral action legitimised by a lack of respect for the principle of reciprocity would not hold in international law. The end of extraterritoriality and reacquisition of full territorial sovereignty was for him just a matter of time because the theory of the principle of sovereign territoriality had already become dominant and because the Chinese legal system had already improved sufficiently to be compatible with the 'standard of civilisation' imposed by the West. See Liu Shih Shun,

stantibus,[30] according to which a treaty can become void if the circumstances in which it was signed have changed fundamentally. The use of this principle was quite uncommon in international law until it was included in the Vienna Convention in 1969.[31] Although some European jurists were already maintaining that a treaty became void as soon as it conflicted with the rights and welfare of the people concerned, the vast majority of the scholarship published at the beginning of the twentieth century took the view that a treaty could be declared void through the *rebus sic stantibus* formula only in very exceptional circumstances.[32] US President Woodrow Wilson, speaking at the Paris Conference, opposed the minority view, declaring that 'it would be better to live up to a bad treaty than to tear it [up]'.[33] In fighting for the restitution of Shandong along with the other delegate Lu Zhengxiang at the Vienna Convention, Koo used the principle of *rebus sic stantibus*. He argued that the agreements China had signed with Japan during the First World War had been agreed only through coercion. For China, those agreements were temporary in nature because they dealt with war-related issues and would be settled by the Peace Conference, Koo maintained.[34] Thus, given the change in circumstances, the general rule of *pacta sunt servanda* could be seen as having been suspended.[35] However, the other powers participating in the Paris Conference were indifferent to China's claims. According to article 119 of the Treaty of Versailles, Germany had to renounce its sovereignty over its former colonies. Although it agreed to the abrogation of leases from the Chinese government, restoring the full exercise of Chinese sovereignty in the German concessions of Hankou and Tianjin, article 156 of the Treaty ruled that Germany's rights, titles and privileges

---

Extraterritoriality: Its Rise and Its Decline, Studies in History, Economics and Public Law, vol. CXVIII, no. 2 (New York: Columbia University Press, 1925).

[30] Wang, *China's Unequal Treaties*, pp. 47–53.

[31] For instance, see the discussion on the history of the formula in Lester H. Woolsey, 'The unilateral termination of treaties' (1926) 20(2) *American Journal of International Law* 20, 346–353, at 347; James W. Garner, 'The doctrine of *rebus sic stantibus* and the termination of treaties' (1927) 21(3) *American Journal of International Law*, 509–516.

[32] See, for instance, August Heffter, *Le Droit International de l'Europe*, trans., F. H. Geffcken (Paris: A. Cotillon & Cie, 1883), pp. 189, 221–222.

[33] Wunsz King, *Woodrow Wilson, Wellington Koo, and the China Question at the Paris Conference* (Leyden: A. W. Sythoff, 1959), p. 16.

[34] Lau-King Quan, *China's Relations with the League of Nations, 1919–1936* (Hong Kong: The Asiatic Litho Printing Press, 1939), p.18.

[35] King, *Woodrow Wilson*. See also Xu Guoqi, 'The age of innocence: the First World War and China's quest for national identity', PhD thesis, Harvard University (1999), p. 342.

to its Shandong concession should go to Japan rather than China.[36] China opposed this ruling and refused to sign the treaty.

Given Chinese discontent and the many issues left unresolved at the Paris Conference, Wilson's successor, Warren G. Harding, sent invitations to nine world powers to discuss disarmament in the Pacific Ocean and East Asia at what was to become known as the Washington Naval Conference, held between November 1921 and February 1922. China was invited, together with the United States, Japan, France, Britain, Italy, Belgium and the Netherlands, and given an opportunity to express its frustrations concerning the Shandong question.[37] China's delegates were Wellington Koo, Chung-Hui Wang and Alfred Sze Sao-ke.[38] Koo believed that 'the existing treaty provisions [in relation to the lack of tariff autonomy] ... constitute not only a restriction on China's freedom of action but an infringement of her sovereignty'.[39] The Chinese delegates promoted the principle of sovereign equality, according to which, they argued, 'the Powers [should] engage to respect and observe the territorial integrity and administrative independence of the Chinese Republic', annulling their special privileges, immunities and rights so to remove any limitation over China's political and administrative freedom of action.[40]

Their resolution at the Washington Naval Conference resulted in a treaty settling the Shandong controversy that was signed by the Chinese and Japanese delegates on 4 February 1922, thereby putting an end to the discontent that had animated the May Fourth Movement.[41] Moreover, the eight other powers participating in the conference agreed that they would respect Chinese sovereignty and administrative autonomy.

---

[36] Norman A. Graebner and Edward M. Bennet, *The Versailles Treaty and Its Legacy: The Failure of the Wilsonian Vision* (Cambridge: Cambridge University Press, 2011).

[37] Westel Woodbury Willoughby, *China at the Conference: A Report* (Baltimore: Johns Hopkins University Press, 1922).

[38] 'Principles and policies concerning China (Nine-Power Treaty)', in Charles I. Bevans, *Treaties and Other International Agreements of the United States of America, 1776–1949*, vol. 2 (Washington, DC: Dept. of State, U.S. Govt. Print. Off., 1968–1976), p. 376.

[39] Wang, *China's Unequal Treaties*, p. 50.

[40] Willoughby, *China at the Conference*, pp. 34–35.

[41] 'A treaty between all nine powers relating to principles and policies to be followed in matters concerning China' (1922) 16(2) *American Journal of International Law*, 64–68. See also the work of the legal advisor to the Chinese Republic in the 1916–1917 period and the technical expert to the Chinese Delegation to the Conference on Limitation of Armament and Pacific and Far Eastern Questions at Washington, in Westel W. Willoughby, *Foreign Rights and Interests in China* (Baltimore: John Hopkins Press, 1927), vol. I, pp. 326–333.

The conference also established the Commission on Extraterritoriality, which was set up to examine the Chinese administration of criminal justice with the aim of the eventual relinquishment of extraterritoriality. Furthermore, in 1926 China managed to bring together delegates from various foreign powers to participate in a tariff revision conference, as provided for by the Washington Naval Conference. Although the tariff conference was inconclusive, the guidelines eventually adopted by the Nanjing government in its successful claims to tariff autonomy in 1928 were formulated during it, and it also influenced the scholarly debate over the issue of unequal treaties, prompting the American Society of International Law, for instance, to dedicate a meeting to the discussion of such treaties in 1927.[42] China's claims to sovereign equality had a strong impact. For example, Henry T. Hodgkin, the British secretary of the Friends' Foreign Missionary Association, in 1925 suggested to British foreign affairs scholars that China must be treated as an equal with full sovereign rights 'to let China know that we are not condescending to her but are giving her the respect and consideration due to any great power', which would 'be a great thing [that] must be shown in deeds as well as in polite phraseology'.[43]

Thanks to the treaty revision campaign that began in the 1920s, guided by the idea of promoting a less compromising sovereignty that entailed the principle of substantial equality, considerable progress was made with regard to treaty revisions. As historian Tang Qihua described it, diplomats of the Beiyang government not only managed to improve the terms of the Boxer Protocols negotiated with Germany, Japan and Russia, but also managed to negotiate new treaties and the revision of old ones, on the basis of equality and reciprocity.[44] As early as 1924, according to the terms of the Sino–Soviet Treaty, Russia had to give up extraterritoriality and its concessions in Tianjin and Hankou, as well as repay its share of the Boxer indemnity. However, throughout the 1920s the Western doctrine and practice of jurisdictional sovereignty, although challenged

---

[42] George A. Finch, 'The Chinese customs tariff conference' (1926) 20(1) *American Journal of International Law*, 12–27.

[43] Henry T. Hodgkin, 'Britain and China: a psycho-political study' (1925) 4(6) *Journal of the British Institute of International Affairs*, 255–285.

[44] This was the case with, for instance, such countries as Belgium, Britain, Finland, France, Greece, Mexico, Persia, Poland and Vietnam. See Tang Qihua, *The Hidden History of the Relinquishment of Unequal Treaties of the Beijing Government Treaty Revision Policy (1912–1928)* (*Bei 'feichu bu pingdeng tiaoyue' zhebi de beiyang xiu yue shi [1912–1928]*) (Beijing: Shehui kexue wenxian chuban she, 2010), chapters 7–8.

by China's assertiveness and its claims to equal sovereignty based on existential equality, continued to isolate China in the realm of semi-civilised nations. For instance, in 1926, the Commission on Extraterritoriality concluded that China was not yet ready for relinquishment of the unequal treaties. Matters were going to change in the next decade.

5 Equality and Reciprocity: China's Unilateral Termination of the Sino–Belgian Treaty

It was within the doctrinal and diplomatic context described previously that China unilaterally declared the Sino–Belgian Treaty of 1865 invalid. In April 1926, the Beiyang government informed Brussels that, upon its expiration on 27 October of that year, the treaty would be terminated and that a new agreement based on equality and reciprocity would have to be negotiated.[45] The importance of this case lies in the fact that it was the first in which the practice of the diplomacy of treaty revision, promoted by both the Beiyang and Nationalist governments, led to the successful termination of an unequal treaty, thereby promoting the pluralistic idea of juridical sovereignty against a hierarchical international legal order that perpetuated extraterritoriality while denying China tariff autonomy. Moreover, the preliminary treaty negotiated in 1928 provided a model for China's future treaties with other powers. It also became a major diplomatic event in China that spurred national and international debate and shaped and consolidated Chinese public opinion as an expression of a flourishing civil society.[46] China's unilateral denunciation of the Sino–Belgian Treaty was accompanied by the mobilisation of students and supported by emerging public opinion. Chinese students in Brussels protested against the treaty, calling for its revision, and the denunciation was also sparked by Chinese propaganda inspired by Wang Jingqi (1882–1941), the Chinese minister in Belgium, who often referred to the importance of Chinese public opinion.[47]

The main preoccupation of Chinese diplomats in their unilateral denunciation of the Sino–Belgian Treaty was the reassertion of China's

---

[45] Permanent Court of International Justice, The Hague, *Denunciation of the Treaty between China and Belgium* (series C, 16, 01) (Leyden: A. W. Sijthoff's, 1929), pp. 51–53.

[46] This was especially true in such cities as Shanghai and Beijing. See, for instance, Marie Claire Bergère, 'Civil society and urban change in Republican China' (1997) 150 *China Quarterly*, Special Issue: Reappraising Republic China, 309–328.

[47] John Patrick Martin, *Politics of Delay: Belgium Treaty Negotiations with China, 1926–29* (New York: St. John's University, 1980), p. 66.

existential equality, which would have coincided with the reacquisition of
tariff autonomy and elimination of extraterritorial jurisdiction. Referring
to article 19 of the Covenant of the League of Nations, which provided
for the possibility of revising treaties from time to time, the formula
called for by the Chinese diplomats was that of *rebus sic stantibus*.[48]
China's unilateral denunciation of the treaty was justified on the basis of
the altered circumstances; the fact that China had been coerced into
signing it; and the current Chinese desire and right to be part of the
family of nations on a footing of equality and reciprocity, which 'cannot
be consummated so long as there is in the relations between China and
other powers a lack of equality and mutual respect for territorial integrity'.[49] One of the reasons for that lack was explained in a Chinese note to
the Belgian government on 16 April 1926, according to which China now
qualified for full sovereignty, meaning that its existential equality should
be fully recognised:

> During the long period which has elapsed since its conclusion so many
> momentous political, social and commercial changes have taken place in
> both countries that, taking all circumstances into consideration, it is not
> only desirable but also essential to take the mutual interest of both parties
> concerned, to have the said treaty revised and replaced by one to be
> mutually agreed upon.[50]

Belgium was against China's unilateral denunciation and the abrogation
of the treaty. From its point of view, the Chinese legal system was not yet
modern enough, it would be imprudent to drop the protection of Belgian
citizens in China, and abrogation would be premature without the results
of the Commission on Extraterritoriality that met in 1926.[51] Belgium also
opposed the Chinese request for tariff autonomy because it did not want
to be put in a position that was unfavourable relative to other nations; it

---

[48] Permanent Court of International Justice, *Denunciation of the Treaty*, pp. 51–54.

[49] Wellington Koo, 'Statement explaining the termination of the Sino–Belgian treaty of
November 2, 1865, November 6, 1926', in Wunsz King (ed.), *V. K. Wellington Koo's
Foreign Policy, Some Selected Documents* (Shanghai: Kelly and Walsh, 1931), pp. 48–54,
at 48.

[50] Note to the Belgian Government dated 16 April 1926, in Permanent Court of International Justice, *Denunciation of the Treaty*, p. 52.

[51] Report of the Commission on Extraterritoriality in China, Peking, 16 September 1926,
being the report to the governments of the commission appointed in pursuance to
Resolution V of the Conference on the Limitation of Armaments, together with a brief
summary thereof (Washington, DC: US Govt. Print. Off.,1926).

awaited proof of Chinese fiscal reforms and the results of the tariff conference before abandoning any tariff agreement made in the past.[52] Belgium tried unsuccessfully to obtain support from other Western countries and to negotiate a new *modus vivendi* with China that would have replaced the treaty without relinquishing Belgian extraterritorial and tariff privileges. In September 1926, China proposed a possible *modus vivendi* based on the principles of equality and reciprocity that recognised the tariff autonomy of both countries and Chinese territorial jurisdiction. However, no agreement was reached, and on 27 October 1926 China declared that the treaty was no longer valid. In reaction, on 25 November of the same year, Belgium, under article 40 of the Statute of the newly formed Permanent Court of International Justice, submitted a unilateral application to it calling for the protection of its interests in China. According to Belgium, article 46 of the Sino–Belgian Treaty of 1865 granted Belgium alone the right to initiate treaty revisions. According to China, however, the problem did not reside in the interpretation of article 46: 'The real question at bottom is that of the application of the principle of equality of treatment in the relationship between China and Belgium. It is political in character and no nation can consent to the basic principle of equality between states being made the subject of a judicial inquiry.'[53]

Despite Chinese opposition, on 3 January 1927 Belgium presented a memorial with thirty-five annexes to the International Court of Justice in the Hague in which it argued that the dispute arising from violation of the treaty's obligations was juridical in character and could be submitted to the Court. The Chinese argued in turn that it was instead a political matter, and accordingly it would refuse to recognise the Court's jurisdiction in the matter. Contrary to Belgium's hopes, the Court seemed to favour the modern Chinese courts over the continuation of Belgian consular jurisdiction. Hence, Belgium quickly returned to bilateral negotiations with China, declaring itself open to the possibility of suspending the extraterritorial Court's jurisdiction. By this point, China had already won half its political battle for existential equality. In this regard, the words of King of the Belgians Albert I in a note to Emile Vandervelde, Belgian Minister of Foreign Affairs, dated 25 November 1926, are revealing: 'It is difficult to predict the future, but one thing is certain: the unilateral treaties have had their day. The Orientals no longer accept

---

[52] Ibid., pp. 49–50.   [53] Ibid., p. 78.

them. Since the war of 1914–1918, they no longer believe in the superiority of our civilization over theirs.'[54]

In 1928, the negotiations between China and Belgium were further
complicated by internal turmoil in China and the coming to power of the
Kuomintang. The Nationalist government, led by Chiang Kai-shek, very
quickly demonstrated its resolution concerning treaty revision and continued with a non-compromising policy towards Belgium. As Nationalist
general Feng Yuxiang (1882–1948) remarked: 'If a small country like
Belgium refuses to conclude a treaty of equality with China, you can
imagine the obstinacy of the great powers to change in the present
situation.'[55] It thus seemed crucial not to compromise with Belgium,
but rather to conclude a new agreement based on equality and reciprocity
that could become a model for treaty revisions with other countries. After
recognising the new Nationalist government, Belgium decided to speed
up the treaty negotiations interrupted in the summer of 1928, and the
first draft of a provisional treaty based on the principles of equality and
reciprocity was ready for discussion later the same year. Article 2 of the
provisional treaty provided for the elimination of Belgian consular jurisdiction: 'The nationals of each of the two High Contracting Parties shall
be subject, in the territory of the other Party, to the laws and the
jurisdiction of the law courts of the Party.'[56] For Wang Qingji, the
then-Minister of China in Bruxelles, 'China attaches a very special
importance to Article 2 of the draft ... by accepting it, Belgium would
place itself in the front ranks of the friendly powers, which have indicated
their intention to contribute to the realization of the legitimate aspirations of the new China'.[57] Eventually, the draft was modified in accordance with Belgian requests, and article 2 become operative only in
1930 once the Chinese legal system had undergone further reforms.
The provisional treaty was signed on 22 November 1928, and Belgium,
while withdrawing the case at the Hague, speeded up the ratification
process, which took place in February 1929. Belgian Minister of
Foreign Affairs Baron J. Guillaume and Chinese Minister of Foreign
Affairs Wang Zhengting signed the final version of the provisional treaty,

---

[54] Albert I, King of the Belgians, to Belgian Minister of Foreign Affairs Emile Vandervelde,
25 November 1926; quoted in Martin, *Politics of Delay*, p. 102.

[55] Ibid., pp. 160–161.

[56] Appendix 2, Preliminary Treaty of Amity and Commerce between the Economic Union
of Belgium and Luxemburg and the Republic of China, with Exchange of Notes and
Declarations Relating thereto, Signed at Nanking, 22 November 1928; see Ibid., p. 221.

[57] Note written by Wang Jingqi in Geneva on 25 August 1928; quoted in ibid., p. 176

which granted China tariff autonomy and eliminated extraterritoriality. The provisional treaty was eventually replaced in 1943 by a new treaty based on the principle of equality and reciprocity, which was negotiated and signed by Guillaume and then-Chinese Minister of Foreign Affairs Song Ziwen.[58]

China's unilateral abrogation in 1926 of the Sino-Belgian Treaty of 1865 was fruitful. Not only did it mobilise the International Court of Justice to come up with a possible solution to the legality of the unilateral denunciation of a treaty in the light of the general principles of the laws of nations, but it also engendered lively academic debate in the years immediately after, creating a new sensitivity among scholars of international law towards the gap between formal equality and hierarchies.[59] American Political Science Professor J. W. Garner, reasoning in terms similar to those of the Chinese, supported China's denunciation of the treaty with Belgium: because of China's internal reforms the situation had substantially changed, he argued, allowing China to become a member of international society. Hence, the equality granted to China should become a matter of substance, or existential equality, not mere words:

> To deny the right of a state to denounce and terminate such a treaty in these circumstances would be to deny it the right to ... rid itself of an incubus upon its independence and sovereignty to which it never consented and which the other party never meant to impose upon [it]. If the treaty was never voluntary[il]y entered into by the dissatisfied state, but was extorted from it under pressure, as some of the Chinese treaties were,

---

[58] Treaty between Republic of China and Belgo–Luxemburg Economic Union concerning the abolition of extra-territorial rights in China and the settlement of questions relating relating thereto, signed at Chungking, 20 October 1943. Came into force on 1 June 1945, in Yin Ching Chen, *Treaties and Agreements between the Republic of China and Other Powers, 1929–1954* (Washington, DC: Sino–American Publishing Service, 1957), pp. 160–164.

[59] Lester H. Woolsey noted that the Court was formed by judges from countries with similar interests in China to the Belgium government; thus, the judgment itself was based on inequality. See Lester H. Woolsey, 'China's termination of unequal treaties' (1927) 21(2) *American Journal of International Law*, 289–294, at 294; Garner, 'The doctrine of *rebus sic stantibus*,' 509–516; John P. Bullington, 'International treaties and the clause "rebus sic stantibus"' (1927) 76(2) *University of Pennsylvania Law Review and American Law Register*, 153–177; Wesley R. Fishel, *The End of Extra-Territoriality in China* (Berkeley: University of California Press, 1952); Tseng Yu-hao, *The Termination of Unequal Treaties in International Law, Studies in Comparative Jurisprudence and Conventional Law of Nations* (Shanghai: Commercial Press, 1931); George W. Keeton, 'The revision clause in certain Chinese treaties', in *British Yearbook of International Law 1929* (London: Oxford University Press, 1930).

and if it is based upon inequality which was never the result of a change of
conditions but was deliberately established by the terms of the treaty itself,
and especially if it is an inequality which derogates from the sovereignty
of the dissatisfied state, its right to terminate the treaty when the other
party refuses to consent to its modification, abrogation or replacement by
another one would seem to be incontrovertible[;] otherwise the postulate
that international law rests upon the principle of equality and sovereignty
of states has no meaning in practice.[60]

Most importantly, the unilateral abrogation was useful for renegotiation
of a Sino–Belgian treaty on the basis of equality and reciprocity, as well
as, more broadly, renegotiation of the meaning of juridical sovereignty to
include the existential equality of China, transforming the international
system into a more pluralistic one

6   Conclusion

The unilateral denunciation of the Sino–Belgian treaty by Republican
China, as part of an even larger project of treaty revision diplomacy,
which was initiated by the Beiyang government and continued by the
Kuomintang, was a crucial step towards China's recognition as an equal
sovereign nation and towards the abolition of extraterritoriality and
foreign control. After the Beijing Tariff Conference (October 1926–April
1927), the United States signed a treaty with Nanjing in July 1929 that
granted China tariff autonomy, and the same then occurred with Great
Britain, Germany, Norway, Belgium, Italy, Denmark, the Netherlands,
Portugal, Sweden, France, Spain and, in 1930, with Japan. With regard to
extraterritoriality, in 1929 the Nanjing government issued an order
according to which foreigners should abide by Chinese law. Two years
later, it issued another strong statement: 'All unequal treaties previously
imposed upon China by various countries would not be recognized by
the Chinese Nationalists.'[61] However, the Manchurian Crisis of
1931 meant that this provision had to be postponed. And it was only
on 11 January 1943, later known as 'justice day', that the Nationalist
government signed the Treaty of Relinquishment of Extraterritorial
Rights in China and the Regulation of Related Matters with Great Britain
and the United States. The same occurred in relation to nine other

[60] Garner, 'The doctrine of *rebus sic stantibus*', 516.
[61] Wang Tieya, 'International law in China: historical and contemporary perspectives'
(1990) 2 *Recueil des Cours*, 195–370, at 261.

powers, which signed new treaties with China based on equality and reciprocity with China: initially Japan, Belgium and Norway, and then, in the following years, with France, Portugal, Italy, the Netherlands, Denmark and Sweden.[62]

By ridding itself of extraterritoriality and foreign control over tariffs, China managed to affirm its existential equality, challenging the main doctrine of juridical sovereignty that relegated it to an inferior position in international society. As the unilateral abrogation of the Sino–Belgian treaty of 1865 demonstrates, the transplantation of international law to China was on the one hand deviant: Chinese diplomats asserted a different vision of juridical sovereignty in which the idea of existential equality overcame the anti-pluralistic mentality that characterised Western doctrine and the practice of international law.

On the other hand, it also contributed to redefine international law and international society in a more pluralistic and inclusive way. The promotion of 'extreme' sovereign equality by China and other newcomers to the international stage influenced the global understanding of juridical sovereignty, creating, for instance, a new sensitivity among scholars of international law in relation to the gap between formal equality and hierarchies. Furthermore, it exerted a concrete impact on the composition of international society, which after the Second World War became more pluralistic and universal. By promoting its vision of juridical sovereignty, China went from being considered an inferior semi-civilised country to being a country whose right to equal existence was formally recognised to the point of becoming one of the five permanent members of the United Nations Security Council after the Second World War.

---

[62] Turan Kayaoglu, *Legal Imperialism: Sovereignty and Extraterritoriality in Japan, the Ottoman Empire, and China* (Cambridge: Cambridge University Press, 2010), p. 151.

14

Consequential Court and Judicial Leadership

The Unwritten Republican Judicial Tradition in China

ZHAOXIN JIANG

My research has two major goals: to outline a new theory concerning what Chinese legal reformists can learn from the Euro–American judicial experience and to integrate the narrative of China's century-long history of judicial reform into the global discourse on the courts, 'consequential court' theory[1] in particular, to reinstate the Chinese judicial tradition in the study of comparative law. At the same time, it is my hope that this study will also provide substantive insights to inform China's current judicial reforms.

Although 'judicial leadership'[2] has been increasingly emphasised as a concept in the past decade, it remains relatively under-researched.[3]

---

[1] This theory is the product of a collective effort by leading scholars in the sphere of judicial studies. In addition to the common questions that the 'judicialisation of politics' scholarship generally asks, this new theory directs attention to 'the functional, substantive roles that judges and courts play in government, politics and policy' and to the courts as 'politically consequential actors in the life of a nation'. See Diana Kapiszewski, Gordon Silverstein and Robert A. Kagan, *Consequential Courts: Judicial Roles in Global Perspective* (Cambridge: Cambridge University Press, 2013), p. 2. For examples of judicialisation of politics scholarship, see Torbjörn Vallinder, 'The judicialization of politics: a world-wide phenomenon: introduction' (1994) 15 *International Political Science Review*, 91–99; Martin Shapiro, 'Juridicalization of politics in the United States' (1994) 15 *International Political Science Review*, 101–112; Ran Hirschl, *Towards Juristocracy: The Origins and Consequences of the New Constitutionalism* (Cambridge, MA: Harvard University Press, 2004); Javier Couso, Alexandra Huneeus and Rachel Sieder (eds.), *Cultures of Legality: Judicialization and Political Activism in Latin America* (New York: Cambridge University Press, 2010); Bjorn Dressel (ed.), *The Judicialization of Politics in Asia* (Abingdon: Routledge, 2012); Jiunn-rong Yeh and Wen-Chen Chang, *Asian Courts in Context* (Cambridge: Cambridge University Press, 2014).

[2] See Kapiszewski, Silverstein and Kagan, *Consequential Courts*; Martin Shapiro and Alec Stone Sweet, *On Law, Politics and Judicialization* (Oxford: Oxford University Press, 2002).

[3] Haig Patapan, 'Leadership, law and legitimacy: reflections on the changing nature of judicial politics in Asia', in Dressel, *The Judicialization of Politics*, pp. 219–233.

I tentatively define judicial leadership as a 'super chief'[4] project in which judges, as 'masters of comparative law',[5] network among themselves through their own knowledge and practice to sustain the overall 'effect of effectiveness'[6] of the courts in the national, supranational and international contexts. Every court system boasts its own super chief story. In studying judicial leadership, we can subject three types of courts to comparison: (1) judicial review constitutional courts; (2) fundamental rights-orientated 'courts (and court-like institutions) that have little or nothing to do with "judicial review"'[7] and (3) courts progressing towards judicial review and fundamental rights[8] (I see China's courts as falling into this third category). I argue in this chapter that a theory of judicial leadership is essential for bridging the comparative law gap between judicialisation-centred academic discourses on Euro–American courts and discourses on Chinese courts.

I argue broadly for the thesis that a theory of judicial leadership is constructive for a rethink of more fundamental theories concerning the rule of law, separation of powers and political governance. My more concrete thesis is that judicial powers in the ongoing process of 'global expansion'[9] have co-authored a super chief model of legal and political developments worldwide. Although a consequential court may not necessarily entail a super chief, a globally networking judicial leadership will

[4] This phrase was originally hammered out to glorify US Chief Justice Earl Warren, who 'provided leadership in a Supreme Court that has brought on a revolution in the field of human rights'. See John D. Weaver, *Warren, the Man, the Court, the Era* (Boston: Little, Brown, 1967), p. 5. Justice Brennan used to refer to Warren as the 'super chief'. See Bernard Schwartz, *Super Chief, Earl Warren and His Supreme Court: A Judicial Biography* (New York: New York University Press, 1983), p. 771. According to Weaver (*Warren,* p. 5), the *Washington Post* wrote: 'His robust, healthy good humor, goodwill and good sense did much to unify the Court in the spirit if not in opinion and to give it a sense of direction and force in meeting emergent social issues made dangerous by a failure of executive and legislative leadership.'

[5] Annelise Riles, *Rethinking the Masters of Comparative Law* (Oxford: Hart Publishing, 2001).

[6] Annelise Riles, *The Network Inside Out* (Ann Arbor, MI: University of Michigan Press, 2000).

[7] See Mitchel Lasser, 'The judicial dynamics of the French and European fundamental rights revolution', in Kapishewski, Silverstein and Kagan, *Consequential Courts,* pp. 289–310.

[8] See Xingzhong Yu, 'Judicial professionalism in China: from discourse to reality', in William P. Alford, Kenneth Winston and William C. Kirby (eds.), *Prospects for Professionalism in China: Essays on Civic Vocations* (Abingdon: Routledge, 2010), pp. 78–108.

[9] Neal C. Tate and Torbjörn Vallinder (eds.), *The Global Expansion of Judicial Power* (New York: New York University Press, 1995).

result in a consequential court. Hence, the future of China's judicial reforms ultimately hinges on judicial leadership within that network.

It is from this theoretical perspective that I examine China's early Republican judicial tradition and its legacy in this chapter, which comprises the four following sections. Section 1 briefly reviews the literature and explains my choice of consequential court theory to interpret Chinese Republican judicial history. In Section 2, I deal with the conceptualisation of judicial leadership based on my reading of US judicial history. In Section 3, I explain at length why Chinese Republican judicial history needs to be written and interpreted on its own terms. Finally, Section 4 concludes the chapter with a few additional thoughts.

1   Consequential Courts: A Theoretical Perspective

In an era of the 'globalised judiciary',[10] 'global constitutionalism'[11] and 'cosmopolitan constitutionalism',[12] spurred by the 'craze for constitutionalisation and judicial review',[13] it seems tautological to argue for the power of judges. For example, constitutional courts are seen as simply playing the role of 'positive legislators'[14] or as part of a move 'from democracy to juristocracy'.[15] The shift in judicial roles continues regardless of the wider debate on democracy and judicial review[16] or the

---

[10] Ken I. Kersch, 'The "globalized judiciary" and the rule of law' (2004) 13 *Good Society*, 17–23.

[11] Aoife O'Donoghue, *Constitutionalism in Global Constitutionalism* (Cambridge: Cambridge University Press, 2014).

[12] Sujit Choudhry, *The Migration of Constitutional Ideas* (Cambridge: Cambridge University Press, 2006); Jeffery Goldsworthy, *Interpreting Constitutions: A Comparative Study* (Oxford: Oxford University Press, 2006); Gabor Halmai, *Perspectives on Global Constitutionalism: The Use of Foreign and International Law* (The Hague: Eleven International Publishing, 2014).

[13] Hirschl, *Towards Juristocracy*, p. 220.

[14] Allan R. Brewer-Carias, *Constitutional Courts as Positive Legislators: A Comparative Law Study* (Cambridge: Cambridge University Press, 2011).

[15] Carlo Guarneri and Patrizia Pederzoli, *The Power of Judges* (Oxford: Oxford University Press, 2002).

[16] For a quick look at recent critiques of judicial review, see Scott Douglas Gerber, 'Popular constitutionalism: the contemporary assault on judicial review', in Scott Douglas Gerber, *A Distinct Judicial Power: The Origins of an Independent Judiciary, 1606–1787* (Oxford: Oxford University Press, 2011), pp. 345–361. For earlier critiques based on democratic and conservative–populist grounds, refer to Hirschl, *Towards Juristocracy*, introduction, footnote 4. Also see Mark Tushnet, *Taking the Constitution Away from the Courts* (Princeton, NJ: Princeton University Press, 1999); Lawrence G. Sager, *Justice in Plainclothes: A Theory of American Constitutional Practice* (New Haven, CT: Yale University,

defence of 'democracy against judicial review'.[17] New rhetoric or theories about these changing dynamics have been formulated by constitutional scholars and political scientists alike. To name but a few, such theories include 'courtocracy/courtism',[18] 'juristocracy',[19] 'positive legislators'[20] and, most recently, 'consequential courts'.[21] Within the literature, one trend in particular regarding the role of judges stands out: that is, judicial review has not merely turned judges into judicial politicians, but has also rendered them political leaders in a real sense, going beyond 'judicial supremacy'[22] to give judges something akin to a 'governing' role.[23] This phenomenon, however, has caused scholars of law and politics alike some difficulties in formulating a universally accepted theory. In fact, despite the ongoing debate, it seems to me that theorisation and interpretation in this area have to some extent stopped, either because of the difficulty of rendering the conversation less polarised and more reasonable or simply because of a lack of intellectual interest.

Consequential court theory, recently proposed by a leading group of experts in Euro–American and Latin American judicial studies, in my view constitutes a successful new start in this theoretical endeavour. The theory expressly aims 'to begin a new conversation in the field of

---

2004); Larry D. Kramer, *The People Themselves: Popular Constitutionalism and Judicial Review* (Oxford: Oxford University Press, 2004); Victor Ferreres Comella, *Constitutional Courts and Democratic Values: A European Perspective* (New Haven, CT: Yale University Press, 2009).

[17] Richard Bellamy, *Political Constitutionalism: A Republican Defence of the Constitutionality of Democracy* (Cambridge: Cambridge University Press, 2007), p. 260. In his preface to the book, Professor Bellamy harshly critiques judicial review–centred legal constitutionalism: 'Far from guarding against a largely mythical tyranny of majority, the checks imposed by judicial review on majoritarian decision-making risk undermining political equality, distorting the agenda away from the public interest, and entrenching the privileges of dominant minorities and the domination of unprivileged ones' (Bellamy, *Political Constitutionalism*, p. viii).

[18] Kim Lane Scheppele, 'Democracy by judiciary (or why courts can sometimes be more democratic than parliaments)', paper prepared for Conference on Constitutional Courts, Washington University, St Louis, MO, 1–3 November 2001 (available at http://law.wustl.edu/harris/conferences/constitutionalconf/ScheppelePaper.pdf),16.

[19] Hirschl, *Towards Juristocracy*. [20] Brewer-Carias, *Constitutional Courts*.

[21] Kapiszewski, Silverstein and Kagan, *Consequential Courts*.

[22] Keith E. Whittington, *Political Foundations of Judicial Supremacy: The Presidency, the Supreme Court, and Constitutional Leadership in the United States* (Princeton, NJ: Princeton University Press, 2007).

[23] Sweet, *Governing with Judges*; Richard Neely, *How Courts Govern America* (New Haven, CT: Yale University Press, 1981).

comparative judicial politics'.[24] Consequential court theory also strikes me as a useful summary of decades-long scholarship in this area. Generally speaking, the theory reasserts the expanded role of the judiciary in governance, albeit with the sober admission that 'courts are often most consequential when they exercise power in concert with, rather than in opposition to, other important actors'.[25] In addition to the implied defence of 'judicialisation of politics' arguments, this new theory shifts the emphasis towards 'the functional, substantive roles that judges and courts play in government, politics and policy' and towards the courts as 'politically consequential actors in the life of a nation'.[26]

Despite Martin Shapiro's caveat that 'the mighty problem continues',[27] the theory's collective authors (or 'provocateurs theoretiques', as they dub themselves[28]) believe that the 'courts – at various judicial levels, in every world region, in countries with varying legal traditions and histories of judicial independence – rule on important disputes in multiple arenas of political conflict and play consequential roles in governance'.[29] Here then arises a group of questions regarding 'when, where, and why'[30] or 'under-what-conditions'[31] courts are consequential.

I would say in fact that it is leadership upon which the solution to the 'mightiest' question rests. Or rather, it is at least true to say that it is through the chief's leadership that the court becomes 'an independent partner, not merely an agent', rendering the court 'itself a consequential participant in legal change and national governance'.[32] Therefore, regardless of the methodological and epistemological debates on the 'judicialisation of politics' or provocative claims about 'decentering courts in the analysis',[33] I believe this sense of judicial leadership per se, i.e. of courts being a partner and consequential participant in

---

[24] Kapiszewski, Silverstein and Kagan, *Consequential Courts*, p. 37.   [25] Ibid., p. 36.
[26] Ibid.,p. 2.
[27] See chapter by Martin Shapiro, 'The mighty problem continues', in Kapiszewski, Silverstein and Kagan, *Consequential Courts*, pp. 380–397.
[28] Kapiszewski, Silverstein and Kagan, *Consequential Courts*, p. 37.   [29] Ibid., p. 399.
[30] See Shapiro's chapter in Kapiszewski, Silverstein and Kagan, *Consequential Courts*, p. 380.
[31] See concluding chapter in Kapiszewski, Silverstein and Kagan, *Consequential Courts*, p. 399.
[32] Robert Kagan, 'A consequential court: The U.S. Supreme Court in the twentieth century', in Kapiszewski, Silverstein and Kagan, *Consequential Courts*, pp. 226–227.
[33] Michael W. McCann, 'Interests, ideas, and institutions in comparative analysis of judicial power' (2009) 62 *Political Research Quarterly*, 834–839.

national and international politics, has become a legitimate research topic. Patapan's comments on judicial leadership are apt in this regard:

> It is in crucial junctures of political and legal revolution, such as consti-
> tutional foundings when courts have just been created, or in periods of
> major constitutional change, that judicial leadership assumes particular
> significance.[34]

For a concrete example of such leadership, consider US Chief Justice Warren E. Burger's view that for his early forebear, Chief Justice John Marshall, 'Marbury v. Madison was an accident. But it was an accident which the solid, steady, and resourceful Marshall exploited to the fullest. The accident of fortuitous combination was the coincidence of a need, an opportunity, and a man – a man with the foresight, the wit, and the courage to make the most his chance.'[35] Another apt example is Earl Warren, who 'provided leadership in a Supreme Court that has brought on a revolution in the field of human rights'.[36]

To make the consequential court concept function realistically, we need to analyse how judicial leadership or a master plan would be available and workable in the first place. Along this line of thinking, I would suggest a general theory of judicial leadership is both necessary and worthy of exploration.

As a legal historian, I am pursuing a research project for understand-ing how China can successfully accomplish judicial reform through study of Republican era judges (1912–1948 in Mainland China and 1949–2007 in Taiwan). In the context of modern China, we are faced with a 'from discourse to reality'[37] difficulty regarding judicial professionalism and the judicial reform project. At present, Mainland China has approximately 200,000 professional judges, who are unevenly distributed across about 3,600 courts nationwide. Accordingly, the topic of judicial leadership not only has general theoretical value, but also practical significance in particular for judicial reform in China. However, a number of questions arise, the most basic of which are the following. Now that China is initiating an ambitious judicial reform project, implicitly aimed at

---

[34] Patapan, 'Leadership, law, and legitimacy', 221.
[35] David M. O'Brien (ed.), Judges on Judging: Views from the Bench (Washington, DC: CQ Press, 2013), p. 26.
[36] Weaver, Warren, p. 5.
[37] Xingzhong Yu, 'Judicial professionalism in China: from discourse to reality', in William P. Alford, Kenneth Winston and William C. Kirby (eds.), Prospects for Professionalism in China: Essays on Civic Vocations (Abingdon: Routledge, 2010).

'creative judicial activism',[38] does judicial leadership theory matter? What do Republican China's experience and experiments with the courts contribute to consequential court theory? The remainder of the chapter concerns itself with these questions.

2   Brinkmanship: Judicial Leadership Models

In this section, I take advantage of the observations of Bruce Ackerman in *The Failure of the Founding Fathers*[39] to tease out a conception of judicial leadership. Of particular interest is Ackerman's tackling of the authorship issue concerning a polemical newspaper article that was arguably written by Chief Justice John Marshall and is allegedly representative of politicians' 'constitutional brinksmanship'[40] in the founding era of the United States, which I take as a starting point for analysing judicial leadership. At the time Marshall's judicial leadership was being showcased on the political stage, he had three identities: as the polemical author Horatius, as a 'midnight judge' and as Secretary of State turned Chief Justice. I argue that this leadership structure is both profoundly constructive and destructive for his twentieth-century Chinese followers. A judicial leader very often turns out to be a Horatius, which has profound implications for his or her leadership.

Alongside the Marshallian/Horatian model of leadership, we have the 'Warrenian' model based on the example of Chief Justice Earl Warren. A simple comparison of the two, based on my reading and understanding, is presented in Table 14.1.[41]

[38] Alpheus Thomas Mason, 'Judicial activism: old and new', *Virginia Law Review*, Vol. 55, No. 3 (April 1969), p. 421.

[39] Bruce Ackerman, *The Failure of the Founding Fathers: Jefferson, Marshall, and the Rise of Presidential Democracy* (Cambridge, MA: The Belknap Press of Harvard University Press, 2005), pp. 111–141, 245–266.

[40] Ibid., 111.

[41] Sources include Shapiro and Stone Sweet, *On Law, Politics and Judicialization*; O'Brien (ed.). *Judges on Judging*, p. 26; Kapiszewski, Silverstein, and Kagan, *Consequential Courts*; Ackerman, *The Failure of the Founding*; Schwartz, *Super Chief, Earl Warren and His Supreme Court* G. Edward White, *The American Judicial Tradition: Profiles of Leading American Judges* (New York: Oxford University Press, 1976); John P. Dawson, *The Oracles of the Law* (Getzville, NY: William S. Hein & Co., 1986); Mason, 'Judicial activism: old and new' Brewer-Carias, *Constitutional Courts as Positive Legislators*; Alexander M. Bickel, *The Least Dangerous Branch: The Supreme Court at the Bar of Politics* (New Haven and London: Yale University Press, 1986); Chris Berry, Ethan Bueno de Mesquita, Jacob Gersen, *Pro-Majoritarian Courts*. Available at: http://cniss.wustl.edu/files/cniss/imce/revised_major itarian_courts-2011-08-09.pdf (Accessed on 17 March 2014).

Table 14.1 *Marshallian vs. Warrenian leadership models*

Marshallian Model		Warrenian Model	
Characterisation	Consequence	Characterisation	Consequence
Willing to lead in national politics	Judicialisation of politics	Willing to lead in national politics	Judicialisation of politics
Fortuitous combination	Accidental but successful	Fortuitous combination	Accidental but successful
Consequential court	Creative but weak	Consequential court	Creative and strong
Counter-majoritarian	Nationalism; Federal versus state	Pro-majoritarian	Rights; Federal versus state
Judicialisation of politics	Midnight judges; Federalists' counter-attack	Politicisation of judiciary	Taking the lead in civil rights movements
Strong leadership	Oracle of law	Strong leadership	Legislator
Passive judicial review	Review	Active judicial review	Active legislation
Politician turned Chief Justice	Political court	Politician turned Chief Justice	Political court
At odds with the president	Horizontal review	Beyond president's expectation	Vertical review
Judge in the best sense	Ideal type	Judge in the best sense	Ideal type
Brinkmanship	Landmark cases	Brinkmanship	Landmark cases
Jurisprudential activism		Remedial activism	

Source: This table is based on my reading of historical, legal and political writings on these two 'super chiefs' and their courts. Xie Guansheng, *Zhanshi Sifa Jiyao (A Summary of War-Time Judicial Development)* (Nanjing: Ministry of Justice, 1948), pp. 3–5 and Zhaoxin Jiang, *China Law 'Cannot See China'* (Beijing: Qinghua University Press, 2010), pp. 17–33.

However, my main interest is in how later chief justices compared themselves and their own court leadership with their two American counterparts. Through a distinct type of networking, they can either rebuild or enhance their own leadership based on the Euro–American model as a whole or the Marshallian or Warrenian model in particular. I tend to view judicial leadership through the lens of 'a world-wide phenomenon',[42] i.e. the 'judicialisation of politics', and also take advantage of consequential court theory.[43] My reading of the judicialisation of politics literature suggests that after decades of growth and networking, judicial leadership the world over has achieved a super chief consensus, that is, willing to lead, practise brinkmanship and sustain consequential courts. Although comparison of consequential courts worldwide demonstrates the spread of the Euro–America battleground to the courts of other countries, most notably South Africa, Israel, Hungary,[44] South Korea and Taiwan, this expansion of judicial leadership has only enhanced the super chief consensus. It has not shaken its foundations, regardless of the differences in South African, Israeli and previous Hungarian courts' bolder enterprise of moving towards what I would call 'polarised judicial review' and Asian courts' relatively cautious stance towards judicial leadership.

My observations suggest the following rough constituents of judicial leadership: (1) networking through authorship or sole monopoly of comparative law knowledge (based on paramount linguistic command of legal knowledge); (2) brinkmanship and winning social/political status; (3) powerful personal connections with political leaders; (4) willingness/desire to lead; (5) adjudication being just a small part of leadership and (6) even when the courts themselves are largely invisible and inconsequential, judicial leadership may still play a powerful role in national politics. The question now is where the Chinese Republican judicial tradition should be placed within consequential court theory in general and judicial leadership theory in particular.

---

[42] Vallinder, 'Judicialization of politics'; Tate and Vallinder, *Global Expansion of Judicial Power*.

[43] Kapiszewski, Silverstein and Kagan, *Consequential Courts*; Brewer-Carias, *Constitutional Courts*.

[44] For the most recent work on the Hungarian courts and constitutionalism, see Halmai, *Perspectives on Global Constitutionalism*.

3 The Republican Judicial Tradition: An Unwritten History of Consequential Court

Consider the 2013 show trial of Bo Xilai.[45] The mass media and academe alike have produced an enormous body of discourse on the political nature of Bo's trial, but few have asked who the presiding judges were, and fewer still have commented on them. In light of China's politicisation of the judiciary, academics regularly discuss the politics of the courts, even the politics within courtrooms, and possibly even constitutionalism, without ever mentioning the functioning role of judges. The predominant popular image is of weak Chinese judges with no independent political agency. However, China currently has about 200,000 judges. Is it true that all of these judges are helpless, weak and submissive to political power to the extent that nowhere in the country do consequential courts, let alone judicial leadership, exist?

With this question in mind, one major goal of this chapter is to decipher the process of judicial politicisation from a historical perspective, starting with the beginning of the Republican era. In contrast to the common understanding of the judiciary in that era, my argument is as follows. There was an era of independent courts (1912–1921) that began with a judicial revolution and ended with a judges' strike. The end of the independent court era marks the beginning of the politicisation of the judiciary and the eclipse of judges' role. In the wake of such politicisation, however, the first generation of judges left a legacy of sensitivity to change, independence, professionalism, political initiative and accountability. Moreover, that legacy persists to the current day, which potentially renders the prospects of judicial reform in China promising.

3.1 Basic Facts

Before we can understand the Republican era, a few basic facts are necessary. First, in terms of numbers, the Republican era judiciary does not look good at all (see Tables 14.2 and 14.3), which should disabuse

---

[45] Bo Xilai was a powerful and ambitious politician in China before the trial. On his political resume is a long list of prominent governmental positions including provincial governor, Minister of Commerce, member of the Central Politburo, that proves Bo's privilege as a politician in China. For reasons publicly known and unknown, he ended his career in a criminal trial. In September 2013, Bo was found guilty of accepting bribes and abuses of power, and sentenced to life imprisonment.

Table 14.2 *Annual number of courts nationwide from 1912 to 1947*

Year	Total Number of Courts
1912	327
1925	260
1926	139
1928	221
1929	302
1930	320
1931	342
1932	309
1933	336
1934	301
1935	382
1936	398
1937	1290
1938	1300
1939	1335
1940	1388
1941	1453
1942	1480
1943	1516
1944	1585
1945	1858
1946	2138
1947	2223

Source: Xie Guansheng, *Zhanshi Sifa Jiyao* (A Summary of War-Time Judicial Development) (Nanjing: Ministry of Justice, 1948), pp. 3–5, and Zhaoxin Jiang, *China Law 'Cannot See China'* (Beijing: Qinghua University Press, 2010), pp. 17–33.

us of any wishful thinking concerning a good judicial system in the Republican era. Second, in the inchoate Republic, ideological upheaval was the most striking feature of the newly created judiciary. Third, in the eyes of the government, a politically mobilised court posed a danger, which gave subsequent judicial developments an ominous start. When

Table 14.3 *Annual increase in overall number of judges from 1913*

Year	Increase in Number of Judges
1913	171
1916	38
1918	143
1919	189
1921	102
	11
1926	135
	50
1927	27
1929	172
1930	142
1932	125
1933	32
1935	60
	18
	126
1936	33
1938	130
1939–1941	92
1941	205
1942–1943	60
1944	20
1945	17
	70
1946	356
1947	255
1946–48	>361
	3000 more or less in total

Source: Xie Guansheng, *Zhanshi Sifa Jiyao*
(A Summary of War-Time Judicial Development)
(Nanjing: Ministry of Justice, 1948), pp. 3–5, and
Zhaoxin Jiang, *China Law 'Cannot See China'*
(Beijing: Qinghua University Press, 2010), pp. 17–33.

the Republic was born in 1912, China had twenty-two provinces and more than 400 million people, and covered a much larger area than its current 9.6 million square kilometres, which rendered overall judicial reform a very difficult task, as is vividly reflected in the numbers of courts and judges throughout the Republican era.

If we consider the judiciary in terms of institutional change, the numbers paint a picture of failed early Republican judicial reforms. The number itself ruled out the popular confidence on the court, regardless of the three-tiered procedural safeguards. It is in this institutional context that we can begin to understand the politicisation story. We first consider the first generation of judges, that is, those practising in the first ten years of Republican China.

3.2   How the Brinkmanship Plays

My story begins with the deaths of three prominent judicial officials of the final imperial generation. One committed suicide[46] in the midst of the Boxer Rebellion, and the other two (the president and vice president of the Board of Punishments) received the death penalty, in accordance with the Xinchou Treaty signed between China and the major foreign powers, which forced China to carry out judicial reforms. Article 2 of the treaty refers to 'punishments on the principal authors of the attempts and of the crimes committed against the foreign Governments and their nationals: ... Zhao Shuqiao, President of the Board of Punishments, [was]condemned to commit suicide ... and Xu Chengyu, formerly Senior Vice President of the Board of Punishments, [was] condemned to death'.[47] This episodes parked immediate ideological upheaval among judicial officials, and provoked a strong sense of nationalism and pragmatism. One result was that the judiciary was psychologically ready for radical reform. Ideological change occurred immediately before actual judicial reforms, which rendered the initial

---

[46] After the breakout of the rebellion, Judge Han Shaohui hanged himself in his office in the Board of Punishment. See Kang Dong, 'Memories of Two Decades' experience as a Judge' (1943) 6 *Guoli Huabei Bianyiguan Guankan*, 5.

[47] See *Peace Agreement between the Great Powers and China* (Xinchou Treaty, 1901).

era of such reforms relatively easy and smooth, subsequently galvan-ising judges' bolder ambitions.[48]

Xinchou and other treaties not only lent momentum to China's judi-cial reforms, but also deeply embedded a sense of judicial nationalism in judges. They also helped to legitimise the early process of professionalising judges. The first generation of judges emerged on the historical stage as a members of an ideology-laden profession. They cherished their role in collective efforts to redeem and consolidate China's sovereign rights, and undeniably enjoyed political power. As the Republican era progressed, judges became more active politically. In Sun Yat-sen's words, judges launched a 'judicial revolution'[49] in 1912.

From the outset, the judges of the new republic formed themselves into a political party, the Co-Progressive Association (founded in February 1912), and, in showy fashion, became partisans. Membership of the new party included such active judicial luminaries as Wu Tingfang, a minister in the provisional government's Ministry of Justice (MOJ);Wang Chon-ghui, a minister in the first Republican MOJ; Xu Shiyin, the president of the first republican Supreme Court and later Minster of Justice; and Xu Qian, Vice Minister of the first MOJ. Later in 1912, the party merged with two other parties to become the unified Kuomintang Party, which won the national election and constituted a congressional majority.[50]

In 1912, under the leadership of this judge-led party, members of the Chinese judiciary launched a 'revolution'. For the first time in Chinese history, Wang Chonghui referred to 'human rights' protection as a political agenda in his inaugural address. A judicial reform plan pub-lished in Xu Shiying's name sets out an ambitious five-year plan (1914–1917) that served as a centralised model for the planned develop-ment of judicial reforms for later generations. In a nutshell, this first national judicial reform plan had two basic goals: (1) to build two

---

[48] See Guilian Li, *Shen Jiaben Nianpu Changbian* (Ji'nan: Shandong People's Publishing House, 2010).

[49] See Bodu Huang, *Xu Shiying Xiansheng Ji'nian Wenji* (Taipei: Wenhai Chubanshe, 1978), p. 1.

[50] Ironically, in the late 1920s, the core members of the same group, Xu Qian and Wang Chonghui, each took initiatives to relinquish his strong judiciary ideas – first Xu and then Wang. They helped to institutionalise a weak judiciary by undermining the courts' independent political agency and subjecting judges to dominant party ideologies. For more information, see Zhaoxin Jiang, *China Law 'Cannot See China': A Study on Juzheng Judicial Era (1932–1948)* (Beijing: Qinghua University Press, 2010), chapter 3.

Table 14.4 *Actual numbers of courts in 1912*

High Courts	Local Courts	Local Court Branches	County Courts	Supreme Court	Total
19	23	11	196	1	260

Source: *Sifa Gongbao*, No. 3 (1912), pp. 1–3.

thousand courts within five years (i.e., four hundred per year) and (2) to have forty thousand judges by 1917 (i.e., eight thousand annually).

Quick comparison between the numbers in the plan and those in reality reveals a huge gap (see Table 14.4). However, the judicial reformers' revolutionary passion and imagination were not thwarted, with the core such reformers sharing a sense of judicial activism. A widely shared belief was that 'judicial independence is [a] top priority [in] the new Republic's political agenda'.[51] The reformers assumed that other branches of government would respect this belief and respond with support. In other words, the judges and their partisan politics produced a powerful self-image on the political stage of the newly born republic. Unfortunately, that image was not well received by the executive branch. Instead, a suspicious executive power received only the threatening signal that the courts are dangerous. The historical archives show the political reactions of the executive. First, the administration wielded its financial sword and substantially reduced the courts' budget. Second, it acted to reduce the overall number of courts by simply removing all county-level courts. In many cases, it closed courts at various levels. All of this occurred in the two years immediately following the so-called 'judicial revolution' (1913–1914).

Many factors played a role in and changed the route of republican judicial development. In September 1913, for example, Xu Shiying was forced to step down as the Minister of MOJ, and was replaced by Liang Qichao, who placed emphasis on judicial restraint. For better or worse, this handover of judicial power marked the beginning of ideological change in the judiciary. At about this time, the Political Meeting was convened by the then-President Yuan Shikai in the capital. What was so political about this meeting, in my view, is that it targeted the judiciary as its No. 1 enemy. The meeting held the courts accountable for the government's political chaos and reaffirmed growing doubts over the

---

[51] See 'Yizhang Wang Fuwei Daci' in records of the First Meeting of Central Judiciaries of the Republic of China, in *Sifa Gongbao*, No.5 (1913).

functional role of the courts in society. Accordingly, the judicial budget was categorised as 'uneconomic' spending, and the meeting decided that three hundred courts for the whole of China was too many, resulting in a dramatic reduction in the number of courts nationwide. From 1914 onwards, the government further pared down the number by removing all county courts, reinstating the ancient magistrate system and significantly restricting financing for court building projects.

Court closures are just one part of the story. On 19 November 1921, judges, prosecutors, law clerks and other court employees in both the high and local courts (and procuratorates) of Beijing, acting in concert, requested 'indefinite leave'. The pretext they gave was that they had not received their salaries (in full or part) for years. However, in accordance with the rules regulating payments to the judiciary, judges in Beijing actually received much better salaries than their counterparts elsewhere. If they were not receiving their salaries, other judges were clearly even worse off. Therefore, it was assumed that a judicial strike in the capital would generate far-reaching effects. According to the diary of a leading judicial official, the strike began in early September and ended in December, and quickly captured the attention of people from all walks of life. It constituted reliable evidence, in many people's eyes, of the utter failure of government finances and of the government's political frailty.[52] In the wake of the strike, the government offered its solution, to the dismay of judicial reformers: a further reduction in the number of judges and court staff, with many losing their posts.[53]

The judges' strike had profound implications for republican judicial reforms, with its backlash lingering for decades. For the first generation of judges, the strike heralded the failure of the judicial revolution and the end of an era of judicial activism. More importantly, the Beijing judges' strike, together with the conclusion of the Washington Naval Treaty (signed at about the same time as the strike's launch), announced the start of a new politicisation process for the judiciary that lasted from 1922 to 1931.

The treaties signed during the Washington Conference (1921–1922), particularly the Nine-Power Treaty on China, generated a new political movement. The conference's emphasis on China's integrity under a

[52] See Zhiyan Xu, *Minguo Shizhounian Jishi Benmo* (Shanghai: Minyou Publishing House, 1922), pp. 22–28.
[53] See Shaosong Yu, *Yu Shaosong Riji*, Vol.2 (Beijing: Guojia Tushuguan Chubanshe, 2003), pp. 307–393.

unified central government changed the course of judicial development. The treaties signed in the early 1900s between China and the foreign powers without exception prioritised the need for China to overhaul its judicial system and the necessity for judicial reform. The new treaty, in jarring contrast, intentionally side-lined previous mandates on such reform. Politics at the conference prompted an immediate response from a sensitive judiciary. Judges came to understand that they had no choice but to abandon their cherished ideas, including the ideology of 'building a new state through the judiciary', and it did not take long for them to submit themselves to government (and later party) power. The Washington Conference thus altered the judicial history of the Republic of China.

A number of facts about the government at that time need to be borne in mind. In the early 1920s, China was in a state of chaos,[54] which only worsened the judiciary's overall situation. In 1926, members of the fledging republican judiciary again went on strike, this time staff of the MOJ. This must have been alarming at the time because it was the ministry that had helped the judiciary to survive the crisis caused by the earlier judges' strike. The second strike indeed proved catastrophic. At the time of the MOJ strike, China had 996 judicial officials nationwide, including both judges and prosecutors.[55] The strike left the judiciary vulnerable to potential harm of all sorts from all sides. By the time the *Report of the Commission on Extra-Territoriality in China*[56] was released, there were both widespread popular disappointment with the judiciary and a sense of desperation within the judiciary. It was in this context that politics started to dominate the fate of judicial progress completely. In 1926, Xu Qian called for all judges to join the Kuomintang Party. In 1928, in his capacity as president of the Judicial Yuan, Wang Chonghui officially urged judges to join the party in the national judicial reform policy. Up to the early 1930s, even the Supreme Court was turned into

---

[54] See Herbert A. Giles, *Chaos in China* (Cambridge: Cambridge University Press, 1924), pp. 33–35.

[55] Yao-tseng Chang, Chairman of the Commission on Extraterritoriality, wrote: 'Today throughout the whole of China, there exist a Supreme court, a Chief Procuratorate, 23 High Courts, and as many High Procuratorates, 26 Branch High Courts and an equal number of Branch High Procuratorates, 64 district Courts and as many procuratorates, 22 District Divisions, 9 Judicial Departments and one Judicial Preparatory Department – altogether 260 courts.' See Chang, 'The present conditions of the Chinese judiciary and its future', address delivered to the Chinese Social and Political Science Association, 8 December 1925.

[56] See *Report of the Commission on Extra-territoriality in China* (Shanghai: Commercial Press, Ltd., 1926).

local party headquarters.[57] The first generation of judges and their leadership ideology thus seemed a thing of the past. Brinkmanship seemed to have backfired. Judges began to take on their current appearance – politically submissive and conservative. However, history is not that simple.

3.3   Republican Judicial Leadership: A Broader Perspective

Historically speaking, Chinese judges as a modern profession emerged in an era of judicial colonialism and judicial nationalism. [58] They were trained both as comparative lawyers and constitutionalists. To a certain extent, judges themselves historically performed as 'oracles of law'[59] in creating a new judicial tradition. Against the historical backdrop of the late nineteenth century and entire twentieth century, we cannot understand modern Chinese legal systems and their general history without understanding the leadership of Chinese judges and the legal tradition they created through their wisdom, vision and courage. Unfortunately, the judges of Republican China are largely absent from the comparative law literature, at least from the English-language literature, despite renewed interest of late in 'Confucian constitutionalism',[60] 'East Asian constitutionalism'[61] and 'law with Chinese characteristics'.[62] In jarring contrast, the focus on judges[63] in US scholarship has, over time, assisted

---

[57] For further details, see Jiang, China Law 'Cannot See China', chapter 3.

[58] It should be noted that this section is limited to general observations. Although I understand that this limitation affects my overall argument, additional time and sources are required to support that argument further.

[59] See Dawson, The Oracles of the Law.

[60] Tom Ginsburg, 'Confucian constitutionalism?: the emergence of constitutional review in Korea and Taiwan' (2002) 27 Law & Social Inquiry, 763–799.

[61] Jiunn-rong Yeh and Wen-Chen Chang, 'The emergence of East Asian constitutionalism: features in comparison' (2011) 59 American Journal of Comparative Law, 805–839.

[62] David Kennedy and Joseph E. Stiglitz, Law and Economics with Chinese Characteristics: Institutions for Promoting Development in the Twenty-first Century (Oxford: Oxford University Press, 2013).

[63] It strikes me that US scholars and laypersons alike have a tradition of glorifying their great judges and presidents. The privileged status of judges in the United States has helped the judicial tradition to thrive. However, my impression is that much less ink has been invested in members of Congress. To an outsider, the US Congress is often invisible apart from occasions in which it garners attention by engaging in fights with the president or a given judge. The result has been the creation, whether intentional or inadvertent, of a glorious American judicial tradition and history. Such selective scholarship is similarly explanatory in considering why the Chinese judicial tradition is largely undervalued or even ignored.

in the creation of an 'American judicial tradition'[64] that, like it or not, is prominent and powerful. Therefore, I hope to afford a general readership with an understanding of the equally important role of Chinese judges and their wisdom and achievements. Republican judicial history needs to be understood from this broader perspective.

Here, I highlight three genres of judicial leadership practice in which are embedded a version of the consequential court concept in the Republican era and beyond: (1) Wang Chonghui's judicial nationalism (1912–1931, 1949–1958) and that of his follower Xie Guansheng (1958–1971); (2) Ju Zheng's Confucianism constitutionalism movement (1932–1948); and (3) Weng Yuesheng's judicial constitutionalism (1972–2007). The first two genres secured a reputation on the mainland, and the third in Taiwan. My argument for the purposes of this chapter is that regardless of their distinct style of leadership, all three genres were successful in rendering the courts consequential in Chinese politics and society. Expressly or otherwise, they drew on and breathed life into the legacy of the first generation of judges active in the early years of the republic.

In addition to his unparalleled academic achievements and contributions to Republican era judiciary-building, Wang Chonghui was politically active over a long period of time.[65] Prior to his death in Taipei in 1958, he held sixty-two more central government positions, most of them leading political or social positions (including prime minister and president of the Judicial Yuan).[66] In this sense, he was more politician than judge, or, more precisely, a political judge.

In terms of Confucian constitutionalism, which has been passionately discussed and promoted in East Asia,[67] Ju Zheng's judicial era actually constitutes the only time that Mainland China has experimented with it.

[64] Edward White, *The American Judicial Tradition*.
[65] Concerning Wang's legacy in the areas of law, politics and society, an extensive body of literature is available across the Straits. Although there is unabated interest in him in the Chinese mainland, academics and society at large in Taiwan have not afforded him the attention he deserves. I believe that Wang occupies an unrivalled and undisputed position in the development of the republican judicial tradition.
[66] Academia Historica in Taipei holds a copy of his resume produced by the Chiang Kai-shek government in its archives. His personal story offers a snapshot of China's republican political history, with its judicial history constituting just a small part. See archive No. 129000098244A.
[67] See Ginsburg, 'Confucian', 763–799. Tom Ginsburg, 'Constitutionalism: East Asian antecedents' (2012–2013) 88 (1) *Chicago-Kent Law Review*, pp. 11–33.

Ju was particularly interested in Roscoe Pound's ideas about comparative law. Pound lived in China from 1946–1948, serving as a Chinese government adviser. His comparative law concepts provided Ju with powerful justification for his experiments with Confucian constitutionalism.[68]

Finally, Weng Yuesheng was the first Taiwanese to receive a doctoral degree from a prestigious German law school and was the mastermind of the 'judicialisation of politics' in Taiwan. Weng began his judicial career in 1972 as a grand justice, and served as president of the Judicial Yuan of Taiwan in 1999–2007. He was also a two-time Chief Justice of the Council of Grand Justices, and is the only constitutional court judge in Taiwan to have served thirty-five years on the bench. The republican judicial tradition cannot be fully understood without taking Weng's judicial era in to consideration.[69] Although the political situations of Mainland China and Taiwan are sharply different, the consolidation of their judicial history is appropriate and necessary when considering the republican judicial tradition from the theoretical perspective of consequential courts, particularly if we are to appreciate properly the first generation of judges.

In a nutshell, my main point is that the politicisation process did not nip the consequential courts of Republican China in the bud, but rather provoked an epic of sustainable judicial development, which I see as the true legacy of the republican judicial tradition. This legacy has helped embed a living judicial tradition in Taiwan, but also remains deeply rooted in the mainland judiciary despite numerous twists and turns over time. Compared with its republican forebear, today's judiciary in Mainland China has in my view little reason to fail in its efforts of reform.

4   Some Additional Thoughts

There are numerous theories concerning judicial power, with large amounts of ink spilt on successful narratives of judicial review or judicial constitutionalism or the wise decisions of constitutional and supreme courts. However, it seems to me that such accounts do not clearly define consequential courts in the political context. Is there any room for a weak court without judicial review power to be a consequential actor in

[68] For further details, see Jiang, *China Law 'Can't See China'*, chapter 4.
[69] To date, I have interviewed President Weng about a dozen times. My new book project focuses on the Weng judicial era and its legacy.

national political life? To what degree can a judicial system characterised by a rigid bureaucratic hierarchy and a political adjudication process be politically consequential? If a weak court cannot safeguard even such basic judicial values as independence, fair process, public confidence and accessibility, or produce effective procedures, can it still be said to be a consequential court? Study of Republican era judicial history has convinced me that consequential courts were embedded into the political system of Republican China, with judicial nationalism and judicial Confucianism being just two examples. Judgments of whether a court is consequential need not be contingent upon the extent of judicial review power, but rather hinge upon judicial leadership.

By focusing on judicial leadership and the judges themselves, this chapter also invites the readers to rethink the modern China-made judicial tradition and historicize the thinking of the problems with Chinese judicial reforms. Can the current courts of China become value-orientated, effective and consequential? My answer is yes. Such an endeavour should not be difficult for China, as the country need only look to the example of the first generation of judges and to the republican judicial tradition. At the beginning of the Republican era, the concept of a strong court was well received by people of all walks of life. That popular conceptualisation, however, was not the result of the constitutive power of the judicial branch, but rather a treaty requirement. At the era's outset, a weak but politically mobilised court was expected to function as if it had the utmost judicial power. Nonetheless, the first generation of judges successfully launched a judicial revolution and embedded the concept of consequential courts into the judicial system. Regardless of so many ups and downs from time to time, Chinese judges were politically powerful and capable, judging from a historical perspective. The Republican era judicial tradition and the judicial leadership thereof had safeguarded a strong version of consequential court history, not vice versa. This is the point this chapter ends with. It is my hope that what the Chinese Republican era judges did their contemporary counterparts can do as well or much better.

INDEX

Ackerman, Bruce, 284–286
adaptive flexibility, of international law, 11
administrative judgments, specifications of, 70
administrative law judges (ALJs), 96–97
Administrative Procedure Act (APA), 96
Administrative Procedure Law (APL), 67–68
Administrative Sanction Commission (ASC), 5, 99–102
Administrative Sanction Law, 97
ADR. *See* alternative dispute resolution
African Union (AU) Agenda, 117–118
Agreement on Trade in Service, 114
Alcock, Rutherford, 195
ALJs. *See* administrative law judges
alternative dispute resolution (ADR), 10, 241–244. *See also* commercial dispute resolution
in Shanghai book industry in, 244–255
alternative punishments
for drug dependency, 21–23
for sex crimes, 21–23
under PSAPL, 21–22
American Society for International Law, 270
Ancient Law (Maine), 203
APA. *See* Administrative Procedure Act
APL. *See* Administrative Procedure Law
arbitration. *See* alternative dispute resolution; commercial dispute resolution
arbitration transplantation, 241–244
in Japan, 254–255
Western models of, 244

ASC. *See* Administrative Sanction Commission
AU Agenda. *See* African Union Agenda
authoritarian states, human rights in, 64–65

'backward rest,' 224–227
Ball, James Dyer, 230–231
Beccaria, Cesare, 193
Beijing Consensus, 115–124
AU Agenda and, 117–118
elements of, 116
FDI in China and, 116–117
global economic convergence influenced by, 123–124
global economic divergence influenced by, 123–124
legitimacy of, 119–123
selective adaptation under, 119–123
self-determination as foundation of, 118–119
Washington Consensus compared to, 105–107, 115–119
Belgium, 272–275. *See also* Sino-Belgian Treaty
Bentham, Jeremy, 193
Bernhardt, Kathryn, 216–219, 228
bigamy
CFA on, 215–219
as Chinese cultural practice, exceptional circumstances for, 217
concubinage differentiated from, 216–219
under Provisional Criminal Code, 216–218
Bo Xilai, 287

299